VIKTOR LOWENFELD
W. LAMBERT BRITTAIN

Creative and Mental Growth

EIGHTH EDITION

PRENTICE HALL
Upper Saddle River, New Jersey 07458

LIBRARY OF CONGRESS CATALOGING-IN-PUBLICATION DATA
Lowenfeld, Viktor.
  Creative and mental growth.
  Bibliography: p.
  Includes index.
  1. Art—Study and teaching. 2. Creation (Literary,
artistic, etc.) 3. Children as artists. 4. Artists—
Psychology. 1. Brittain, W. Lambert. II. Title.
[DNLM:1. Art.) 2. Child Development. 3. Creativeness—
in infancy and childhood. N 85 L917c]
N350.L62   1987   707   86-8529
ISBN 0-02-372110-3

©1987 by Prentice-Hall, Inc.
A Simon & Schuster Company
Upper Saddle River, New Jersey 07458

Earlier editions by Viktor Lowenfeld, copyright © 1947 and © 1952
and 1957 by Macmillan Publishing Company. Earlier editions by
Viktor Lowenfeld and W. Lambert Brittain, copyright © 1964 and
©1970 and © 1975 and © 1982 by Macmillan Publishing Company.

Printed in the United States of America
20 19 18 17 16 15 14 13 12 11

ISBN 0-02372110-3

Prentice-Hall International (UK) Limited, *London*
Prentice-Hall of Australia Pty. Limited, *Sydney*
Prentice-Hall Canada Inc., *Toronto*
Prentice-Hall Hispanoamericana, S.A., *Mexico*
Prentice-Hall of India Private Limited, *New Delhi*
Prentice-Hall of Japan, Inc., *Tokyo*
Prentice-Hall of Southeast Asia Pte. Ltd., *Singapore*
Editora Prentice-Hall do Brasil, Ltda., *Rio de Janeiro*

Preface

It comes somewhat as a surprise to me to find that this is the eighth edition of *Creative and Mental Growth*. Each new edition has been both a challenge and a source of satisfaction. This latest edition incorporates much new material drawn from many sources. Research reports, publications from foreign countries, and the comments of many of my colleagues have been a source of inspiration.

For those who are reading this book in this edition for the first time, it is important to realize that the content is aimed at an understanding and appreciation of children and their art products. It is not a book that will provide answers to all questions; it is not designed to provide nice projects for teachers or parents to do with children. Rather, it is aimed at an understanding of how cognitive development relates to creative and artistic expression. It is not the making of products that is the concern of this book, but rather it is the process of art and the value of these experiences to children's learning that is crucial. It is fascinating to realize that as children grow and experience the world in both physical and psychological settings, their physical, mental, and creative growth also change.

The reader who has seen previous editions will find some sections that are new to this edition, and some sections that have been rewritten entirely to clarify concepts and to take into account recent research on children's behavior. There are entirely new sections dealing with the computer and art, graffiti, and copying abilities. There is additional information dealing with the left brain–right brain investigations, an expanded section on the history of art education, and one part dealing in depth with the importance of metaphor. Over one hundred new references, most of these from empirical research reports, have been woven into the text where it seemed most appropriate.

This book is not fiction. The reader can start anywhere and return to missed sections at will. Although I have tried to have some logic in the arrangement of the text, an overview can be obtained just by thumbing through the pages and seeing the tremendous variations in children and in what they produce. The first two chapters attempt to give support for the area of learning in art as an essential ingredient in children's development. The two chapters that follow, Creativity and Aesthetics, deal with considerations particularly important today in our society. Chapter 5 acknowledges some of the problems and satisfactions of teaching art in the elementary school. The following chapters, 6, 7, 8, 9, deal with the developmental differences in children as they grow from making scribbles, to the young adolescent of 12 whose artistic development is complete unless further training and education is undertaken. Chapter 10 gives an overview of art for older children, and Chapters 11 and 12 deal with the meaningfulness of art expression for both younger and older adolescents. Also included is a chapter which tries to summarize the essential differences and the developmental changes in children as seen through their art.

Although this book focuses primarily upon developmental changes in how children draw and paint, it should be emphasized that this book is for teachers and parents. It is only through children's interaction with adults that positive values are established and reactions to the environment are encouraged. It is this interaction that is crucial in learning; this is particularly true in the area of art expression. It is not the development of transitory skills that is important, but rather the development of a sensitive, creative, involved, and aware child that is the goal of this book.

Viktor Lowenfeld died in 1960. His dynamism and sincerity in convincing others of the importance of understanding the mental and emotional development of children, and how this influences their art products, are still being felt today. His writings and tapes of his speeches are as vibrant and meaningful as they were 30 years ago. I have been fortunate in having support from Mrs. Viktor Lowenfeld and Dr. John Lowenfeld in continuing to strive toward the goal of making children's lives more rich and meaningful, through the process of art expression.

To the many people who have helped to make this new edition possible, I express my thanks. It is to the children who served as willing subjects for experiments and who provided many illustrations that I owe the most gratitude. It is they who have taught me the importance of creativity. My graduate students and undergraduate classes have freely commented on sections of the previous edition. I have taken their suggestions seriously, and this new edition reflects some of their input.

I am grateful to Veronica Terrillion for allowing me to photograph her sculpture which is seen in Figure 8. Also, Jason Seley was kind enough to share with me his bumper sculpture in Figure 61. I have had pleasant discussions with Peter Wilson regarding the relationship between map reading and drawing ability; I am indebted to him for Figures 43 and 136.

Many teachers have shared with me the drawings and paintings that they have collected from their classes. This book could easily double in size if I allowed myself to yield to the temptation to include a larger fraction of the art products available. I do owe special thanks to Irene Russell for Figure 77, to Yu-Chin Chien and Anne Liebermann-Lloyd for Figure 87, and to Marjorie Martin for Figure 133. Pat Bechtold was a valuable source, providing Figures 67, 218, 227, 229, 231, and 234, as well as Plates 34 and 35.

Jane Hooper helped gather a large number of drawings on the topics "Eating" and "Rain." This includes Figures 30, 139, 140, 159, 191, 202, 203, 209, 210, and 220. Also I wish to thank Brian Dean for Plate 8; Jean Holland for Plates 10 and 26; Bernard Young for Figures 121 and 224; Julie Memis for Figure 160; the New York State College of Human Ecology, Cornell University for Figure 56; and Erik Strommen for Figure 103, which is adapted from his work.

In addition, I have had the help of fellow photographers; I wish to thank Barrett Gallagher for Figures 57, 84, 91, and 222; Jack Grant for Figures 78 and 190; Lynn Haussler for Figures 83a, b, and c; Jean Warren for Figure 119; the Photo Science Studios at Cornell University for Figure 74; Rebecca Reiss for Figure 213; and Constance Bouchard for Figures 47 and 52.

Several research projects have provided information for parts of the present volume. The Cornell research project in early childhood education was responsible for Figure 4, and the Cooperative Research Project #6-8416, U.S. Office of Education, was responsible for Figure 55. Also, many museums and art collections helped with illustrative material. I wish to thank them for their help and cooperation, particularly Roger Hardley, Curator of Australian Ethnography, Queensland Museum, for Figure 50; the Herbert F. Johnson Museum of Art, at Cornell University, for Figures 45, and 49; the Ithaca College Collection for Figure 59; the Australian National Museum for Figure 198; and the Indiana University of Pennsylvania for Plate 21.

Additional thanks are due to the designer of this book, Robert Freese, and to its tolerant and patient production supervisor, John Travis.

Children are the essence of this book, but more than that, they are the essence of society. How children are cared for, nourished both physically and psychologically, gives an indication of the value society puts upon itself and its future. Creative and intellectual growth are the basis of any educational system, and it is the hope that this book can contribute to an understanding of the importance of this area so as to make the education of children a joyful and meaningful experience.

W. LAMBERT BRITTAIN

*Department of Human Development
    and Family Studies*
Cornell University
Ithaca, New York 14853

PREFACE

Contents

3

The Development of Creativity   73

4

The Development of Aesthetic Awareness   101

5

Art in the Elementary School

6

The Beginnings of Self-expression
The Scribbling Stage, Two–Four Years

7

First Representational Attempts

The Preschematic Stage, Four–Seven Years   219

8

The Achievement of a Form Concept

The Schematic Stage, Seven–Nine Years   257

9

The Dawning Realism

The Gang Age, Nine–Twelve Years   305

10

Art in the Secondary School   345

11

The Age of Reasoning

The Pseudo-naturalistic Stage, Twelve–Fourteen Years   391

12

The Period of Decision

Adolescent Art in the High School, Fourteen–Seventeen Years   433

13
Summary   /   469

Bibliography   481

Index   501

Color Plates

Creative and
Mental Growth

The Importance of Art for Education

1

The Meaning of Art Activities

Art is a fundamental human process. Every society, from the most primitive to the most sophisticated, has expressed itself through art. But more important, every person has put thoughts and emotions into an art form. Art is a personal and satisfying activity at any age, for although the arts are responsible for a greater awareness of the external world, it is also the arts that give vent to the emotions, the joys and fears of life. Young children use art as a means of learning, through the development of concepts which take visible form, through the making of symbols which capture and are an abstraction of the environment, and through the organization and positioning of these symbols together in one configuration.

Art is a dynamic and unifying activity, with great potential for the education of our children. The process of drawing, painting, or constructing is a complex one in which children bring together diverse elements of their experience to make a new and meaningful whole. In the process of selecting, interpreting, and reforming these elements, children have given us more than a picture or a sculpture; they have given us a part of themselves: how they think, feel, and see.

Formal education is tremendously important when we realize that our children—from the age of five or six to sixteen, eighteen, or beyond—are forced by law and job requirements to spend ten, twelve, sixteen, or even twenty years behind school doors. That is a severe sentence just for being born a child. The serving of this sentence is supposed to qualify a youngster to take his place as a contributing and well-adjusted member of society. Yet there is alienation when clients can't escape, as in schools and prisons (Newman, 1981). From some points of view education has done its task; looking around us today, we can see great material gains. But serious questions can be raised about how much we have been able to educate beyond the making and consuming of objects. Have we in our educational system really put emphasis upon human values? Or have we been so blinded by material rewards that we have failed to recognize that the real values of a democracy lie in its most precious asset, the individual?

In our present educational system most emphasis has been put upon the learning of factual information. To a great extent the passing or failing of an examination or of a course, or the passing on to the next grade, or even the re-

THE IMPORTANCE OF ART EDUCATION

maining in school depends upon the mastery or memorization of certain bits of information that are already known to the instructor. The function of the school system, then, would seem to be that of producing people who can file away bits of information and can then repeat these at a given signal. Once the student has achieved a certain competency at producing the proper bits of information at the correct time, he is considered ripe for graduating from school. What is most disturbing is that the skill in repeating bits of information may have very little relationship to the "contributing, well-adjusted member of society" we thought we were producing. A sociobiologist has remarked that we operate under the assumption that "a culture can first be designed by the wisest members of society, and then children fitted painlessly to it" (Wilson, 1978, p. 64).

Mankind will not be saved by merely developing a good creative art program in public schools; but the values that are meaningful in an art program are those which may be basic to the development of a new image, a new philosophy, even a totally new structure for our educational system. More and more people are recognizing that the ability to learn differs from age to age and from individual to individual and that this ability to learn involves not only intellectual capacity but also social, emotional, perceptual, physical, and psychological factors. The process of learning is very complex and there may, therefore, be no single best teaching method. Our tendency to concentrate on developing the capacity to regurgitate bits of information may be putting undue emphasis on only one factor in human development, the one that is measured by intelligence tests. Intelligence as now tested does not encompass the wide range of thinking abilities that are necessary for the survival of mankind. The abilities to question, to seek answers, to find form and order, to rethink and restructure and find new relationships, are qualities that are not generally taught; in fact, they seem to be frowned upon in our present educational system.

Some time ago Combs (1962), in a report for the Association for Supervision and Curriculum Development, decried the schools' emphasis on facts, pointing out that they have no value in themselves, but are useful only as they are organized into convictions, beliefs, frames of reference, and attitudes that result in intelligent behavior. Two decades later, Boyer (1983), in a report for the Carnegie Foundation, emphasized that it is not the facts which are important, but that students must develop the capacity to think critically and communicate effectively. In the intervening years, there seems to have been little change in school practice.

It may be that one of the basic abilities that should be encouraged in our public schools is the ability to discover and to search for answers, instead of

FIGURE 2.
For children, art is an engrossing activity
which utilizes their knowledge, observations, and experiences.

passively waiting for answers and directions from the teacher. The experiences
central to an art activity require self-direction. This is equally true of a nursery
school child experimenting at the easel and of a college student painting a picture that necessitates mixing colors and inventing new forms. One of the basic
ingredients of a creative art experience is the relationship between the artist and
the environment. Painting, drawing, or constructing is a constant process of assimilation and projection: taking in through the senses a vast amount of information, mixing it up with the psychological self, and putting into a new form
the elements that seem to suit the aesthetic needs of the artist at the time.

We learn through our senses. The ability to see, feel, hear, smell, and taste

THE IMPORTANCE OF ART EDUCATION

provides the contact between us and our environment. But the process of educating children can sometimes be confused with teaching certain limited, predetermined responses, and the curriculum in public schools tends to be little concerned with the simple fact that man, and the child too, learns through these five senses. The development of perceptual sensitivity, then, should become a most important part of the educative process. Yet in most areas other than the arts, the senses are apt to be ignored. The greater the opportunity to develop an increased sensitivity and the greater the awareness of all the senses, the greater will be the opportunity for learning; more on this later.

If we look at formal education, we realize that the transmission of knowledge rests upon 26 letters and 10 numerals. These are merely tools to use in the pursuit of knowledge and are not in themselves learning. These 36 abstract figures are manipulated and reshuffled from kindergarten through college. The development of mental growth, then, tends to become an abstract function as these figures take on different and more complicated meanings. However, it is

FIGURE 3.
The interaction of children with their environment provides the means for the development of thinking. These children are learning by firsthand experience in the sandbox about volume and texture.

not the knowledge of these figures or the ability to rearrange them that makes for mental growth, but rather understanding what these figures mean. Being able to assemble letters in proper sequence to spell *rabbit* does not constitute an understanding of a rabbit. To really know a rabbit a child must actually touch it, feel its fur, watch its nose twitch, feed it, and learn its habits. It is the interaction between the symbols, the self, and the environment that provides the material for abstract intellectual processes. Therefore, mental growth depends upon a rich and varied relationship between a child and his environment; such a relationship is a basic ingredient of a creative art experience.

Factual learning and retention, unless exercised by a free and flexible mind, will benefit neither the individual nor society. Education has often neglected those attributes of growth that are responsible for the development of the individual's sensibilities, for his spiritual well-being, as well as for his ability to live cooperatively in a society. The growing number of emotional and mental illnesses in this nation, coupled with our frightening hesitation to accept human beings as human beings regardless of nationality, religion, race, creed, sex, or color, are vivid reminders that education so far has failed in one of its most significant aims. While our high achievements in specialized fields, particularly in the sciences, have improved our material standards of living, they have diverted us from our emotional and spiritual values. They have introduced a false set of values, which neglect the innermost needs of an individual. Art education, as an essential part of the educative process, may well mean the difference between a flexible, creative human being and one who will not be able to apply his learning, who will lack inner resources, and who will have difficulty relating to his environment. In a well-balanced educational system, the total being is stressed, so that potential creative abilities can unfold.

The Meaning of Art for Children

Art is not the same for a child as it is for an adult. Although it may be difficult to say just what art means for any particular adult, usually the term "art" has very definite connotations. Among them are museums, pictures hanging on walls, disheveled painters, full-color reproductions, attics with northern exposure, models posing in the nude, a cultural elite, and generally a feeling of an activity that is removed from the real world of making a living and bringing up a family. Somehow art is supposed to be "a good thing," and art books on the coffee table or "good" pictures for the walls of one's home ought to bring some kind of elevating spirit into life. But for the common man art may be like taking a dose of medicine. Art for the adult, at any rate, is usually concerned with the area of aesthetics or external beauty.

Art for the child is something quite different. For a child, art is primarily a means of expression. No two children are alike, and, in fact, a child is not static, but is constantly growing and changing, with increasing perception, understanding, and interpretation of the environment. A child is a dynamic being; art becomes a language of thought, so that art expression changes as the child grows.

Sometimes teachers, intrigued by the beauty of children's drawings and paintings, will save these paintings and admire them as examples of true spontaneous art. Occasionally teachers may go a step further and suggest the proper colors or correct forms. While professing enthusiasm for the freshness and directness of children's paintings, they impose their own color schemes, proportions, and manner of painting upon children. Some adults wish to hasten academic achievement and may try to push children beyond their developmental level, although there is evidence of problems with such pushing, including greater stress, the need for more remedial services, and more children having to repeat grades (Bjorklund and Krebs, 1985).

If it were possible for children to develop without any interference from the outside world, no special stimulation for their creative work would be necessary. All children would use their deeply rooted creative impulses without inhibition, confident in their own means of expression. When children lose self-confidence in their own means of creative expression to the extent that they say "I can't draw," some interference in their lives has caused this inhibition and withdrawal into the self. Often the mistake is made of evaluating children's creative work by how the product looks, its colors and shapes, its design qualities, and so forth. This is unjust, not only to the product but even more to the child. Growth cannot be measured by the tastes or standards of beauty that may be important to an adult. However, art has been traditionally interpreted as relating mainly to formal aesthetics, and this concept has in some cases limited the opportunity for art to be used in its fullest sense. In art education the aesthetic quality of the final product is subordinated to the creative process. It is the child's process—including thinking, feeling, perceiving, and reactions to the environment—that is important.

Expression grows out of, and is a reflection of, the total individual child, whatever the level of development. A child expresses thoughts, feelings, interests, and knowledge of the environment in creative expressions. A ten year old who is concerned with the mechanical operation of parts, gears, levers, and

A

B

FIGURE 4.

These are four drawings of a man done by Rachel, a kindergarten child, over a short period of time. Part A shows a five year old's concept of a man. Note the lack of arms; but Rachel does include a head, body, and legs with toes. In B Rachel has drawn much more, and her concept of a man now includes arms with hands and fingers. The toes are now attached to a foot and buttons have appeared. In C the single line previously used for legs and arms is now double, as if the limbs had volume. Note the hat that does not rest on the head but floats above it. The final drawing D shows a rather complex and complete drawing, much more typical of a six year old.

8

THE IMPORTANCE OF ART EDUCATION

C   D

pulleys will work through these relationships in his drawings. Note the intense concentration shown in Figure 5. Much thought and planning have gone into the details of the operation of the airplane that the boy is drawing. In Figure 6 the wings and the joining of the various struts have been thought through in detail. Notice the mechanism for adjusting the rudder. It is irrelevant that this looks little like an adult concept of a plane. The child's interests, capabilities, and involvement are revealed in art, although these may in some cases bear little relationship to "beauty."

Occasionally we hear of a child who is outstanding in art. This may be a child who performs in ways that are neat and proper, who satisfies the artistic

THE MEANING OF ART FOR CHILDREN   9

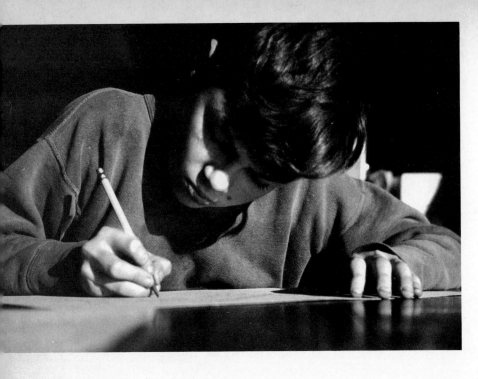

FIGURE 5.
The concentration of this ten year old boy is typical of a child who is confident of his own creative ability.

FIGURE 6.
This plan for a working model of an airplane, drawn by a ten year old boy, shows his thinking through of the functions of the various parts and an inventive awareness of mechanical details.

likes of the teacher. Sometimes a child who is frustrated in school subjects such as reading, writing, or arithmetic may turn to art for a release from frustrations, because in art there is no right or wrong answer. Both of these children may get a great deal of satisfaction from drawing, and if they are rewarded for their efforts, they will certainly continue to try to gain recognition. However, it may be a youngster who is silent and withdrawn who most needs the opportunity for art expression. A teacher who has certain tastes and artistic standards may find it difficult to understand that these standards are irrelevant for the self-expression of youngsters and must be subordinated to the needs of children.

It is through the process of art that art itself unfolds. To focus on the art product is to be concerned primarily with the making of beautiful objects rather than with the effects that making has upon children. Art education, therefore, is primarily concerned with the effect that the *process* has on the individual, whereas the so-called fine arts are more concerned with the resulting *product*. Yet paintings and drawings by children can have great beauty.

Every school, not only in kindergarten and elementary classrooms but also in the secondary school, should try to encourage all youngsters to identify with their own experiences and help them to go as far as they can in developing concepts that express their feelings and emotions, and their own aesthetic sensitivities. The stereotyped response or the unfeeling or automatic drawing indicate that children are insensitive to their own feelings and experiences. The essential ingredient is the child, a child who has feelings, emotions, love, and hate, and who has no need for the stick figure that may be taught in first grade or the abstract design that is taught in junior high school. Individual expression is just as important to a child as the artist's creation is to the adult. The teacher should recognize that his or her own learning experiences will avail children nothing, for it is the children's learning that is important in the educational process. It is not the adult's answer but the child's striving toward an answer that is crucial.

The Senses As Basic to Learning

It is only through the senses that learning can take place. This may sound like an obvious statement; however, its implications seem to be lost in our educational system. It may be that education merely reflects the changes in our society, for people seem to be relying less and less on actual sensory contact with their environment. They are becoming passive viewers of their culture rather than active makers of it. Football and hockey games are watched, not played. Music has become a soothing background syrup in public places, or else a distracting noise from a neighbor's apartment, rather than an opportunity for actual participation. The television has become a mass means of distraction in which the viewer's only involvement is that of turning the *on* or *off* switch. Most groceries come packed in their own sterile plastic containers, removed from touch and smell, although the increased availability of bulk foods and the rise of farmers' markets are encouraging developments.

Schools have done little to educate these senses that are our only avenue to learning. Although a number of activities are included at the nursery school level that involve manipulation and movement, most of these activities are taught as ends in themselves. The purpose seems to be to develop particular skills so that these can be checked off as having been taught, rather than utilizing them as a means to expression. The first grade teacher is satisfied when children learn how to manipulate scissors, but the possibilities of using scissors

FIGURE 7.
Blackeyed peas in an open container create an interesting pattern. Prepackaged merchandise, each item in its own sterile plastic pack, has removed the senses of touch and smell from many of the goods we buy.

creatively are limited. The farther up the educational ladder we go, the farther removed children become from relying on their own senses, until a good deal of learning becomes not only vicarious, but also abstract in nature.

Our forefathers were in daily contact with their environment. Not only did they build their own homes and grow their own food, but they also made their own music and art and entertainment. Even in the last fifty years there have been dramatic changes. The local hardware store has lost its bin of nails, sacks of grain and seed are no longer available to run one's fingers through, and the grocery store no longer smells of freshly ground coffee or oranges that have gotten a little too old. The smell of freshly baked bread or the taste of one's own homemade root beer are sensory experiences that have almost disappeared. It is encouraging to observe an increased awareness of nature, particularly among our young people. Our national parks attract increasing numbers of visitors. Possibly the greater interest in camping, hiking, and skiing is a result of the urge to experience the senses more fully.

There is little opportunity today for youngsters to dam up a stream, dig a tunnel to China, or build a tree house. The complete involvement of oneself in a project of a purely physical, sensory nature is rapidly disappearing. Paint-by-the-number kits and preplanned, precut projects have made art sterile. A family may now be more concerned about selecting the current fad in furniture styles for their living room than with expressing their own likes and dislikes or personal interests.

Touching, seeing, hearing, smelling, and tasting involve the active participation of the individual. There is evidence that even the young child needs to be truly encouraged to see, touch, or become involved in the environment. In a case of sensory deprivation, a youngster may be isolated from external stimulation. It is not just a question of the presence of sounds or of having things available to touch and see; it is the stimulation of the interaction between the youngster and the environment through the senses that makes the difference between the child who is eager to explore and investigate that environment and one who retreats from it. Obviously, youngsters deprived in this manner can come from what might be called affluent surroundings. Even if a child's basic physical needs are met, he may nevertheless be seriously deprived in other areas of development. For example, in families where constant status seeking is a consideration, children may be ignored or considered merely as objects to be displayed at appropriate times. Apparently this type of behavior is also seen in the animal kingdom, for it has been observed that, when animal parents are occupied with status-seeking pursuits, they neglect their offspring (Morris, 1969).

One observational study of young deprived children reported that these youngsters were not alert to, or even responsive to, the teacher's spoken directions or to a display of colored paper, scissors, and paste set out for them. Although the children were constantly scanning the environment, these objects failed to attract their attention (Malone, 1967). It is obvious that for young children the senses are extremely important, but in later years too the development of refined sensory experiences should be a continuing process. Art education is the only subject matter area that truly concentrates on developing the sensory experiences. Art is filled with the richness of textures, the excitement of shapes and forms, the wealth of color, and youngster and adult alike should be able to receive pleasure and joy from these experiences.

Auditory sensitivity means detailed listening, not just hearing; visual sensitivity means an awareness of differences and details, not just recognition; experiencing texture is not just touching an object. We are living in a time in which mass production, mass education, and mass seeing and experiencing have suppressed the sensitive relationships of the individual. Art education has the special mission of developing within the individual those creative sensitivities that make life satisfying and meaningful.

Self-identification and Self-expression

People today have to a great extent lost their ability to identify with what they do. Few of us can point to our own contribution to society. Technology has made man little more than a machine. The worker often is not a part of the planning or design of the product; the job no longer requires a skilled or able workman, but a reliable employee. In some instances, mechanization of production has reached the point where the operators may neither see the product nor work on it directly. A study of the organization of the factory—an organization that made workers feel isolated, dominated, detached, and discontent— was made by Blauner (1964). His data show that this is not necessarily true of all occupations; those that entail a good deal of craftsmanship and personal involvement have more satisfactions to offer to workers than mere money. This dehumanization of the worker is of great concern to many, and there is a call for a new basis for the organization of the workplace which would allow for an

THE IMPORTANCE OF ART EDUCATION

PLATE 1.

"Man," painted by a five year old boy. A painting by a young child is usually direct and uninhibited. Here red, blue, yellow, and green are boldly used for the figure with no attempt at naturalism.

PLATE 2.

"I Am Putting on My Sweater," drawn by a seven year old boy. This picture might mistakenly be considered that of a child who has problems, because he has apparently scribbled over his own face and body with a green crayon. However, it actually is a drawing of getting dressed and putting a sweater on over his head.

PLATE 3.

"I Have a Loose Tooth," drawn by a six and a half year old girl. Here a girl shows that she has a loose tooth. The exaggerated size of the mouth and great number of teeth show how important this experience was.

increase in the quality of life for the worker (Heisler, 1977; Trist, 1978; Wilson, 1978). Psychological problems, social concerns, and vexations such as indoor pollution and windows that don't open are more difficult to solve than technological problems (MacDonald, 1985). With the spread of personal computers, more small businesses tend to be operated from the home, possibly to avoid such office-related difficulties (Lublin, 1984). Sometimes the demands of a job and what the worker expects may lead to serious conflict, and the results reduce the worker's self-initiative (Gowler and Legge, 1978). But satisfaction and involvement in a job are apparently directly related to the perceived value of a worker's skills, the variation in tasks, and how much can be learned on the job (Rousseau, 1977). Many retired workers return to the workforce, especially those in top jobs in big companies, where the rewards and satisfactions are presumably greater (Trost, 1984).

When work is only a means of survival, the rewards and satisfactions of life are sought in entertainment or diversions. The questions "Who am I? Where am I going? What do I stand for?" reveal a serious dilemma. It is not only youth who are searching for identity. Although no one is happy to become a number, we are all rapidly becoming merely a series of numbers for the purposes of tax deductions, bank collections, vehicle identifications, insurance payments, mail delivery, licensing skills, and even hospitalization. It may not even be possible to build one's own woodshed or porch without approval from the local zoning

FIGURE 8.
Few people have the freedom to build statues on their front lawns. In this life-size, painted concrete equestrian statue, an elderly woman's artistic expression is reflected through her creative manipulation of the material.

board. Restrictions on one's creative productions are legalized pressures for conformity; no innovations are allowed; different is wrong. In spite of restrictions, a few people have been able to assert their own individuality and build some remarkably ingenious structures (Boericke and Shapiro, 1973; Moholy–Nagy, 1976; Wampler, 1977). These houses have often required great effort and sacrifice, but they show that man is capable of creative effort in spite of restrictions and pressure to conform. In a democratic society it is essential that the individual be able to have and express an opinion and to help remake the world.

Our educational system has done little to change the increasing loss of identity with oneself. Rewards are given for neat papers, for correct answers, for recalling the proper information. Little is done to stimulate children to find the rewards from within the learning process: to find satisfaction in solving their own problems, to take pleasure in developing greater knowledge and understanding for its own sake, or to measure success or failure in areas they feel are important.

Learning does not merely mean the accumulation of knowledge; it also implies an understanding of how this knowledge can be utilized. We must be able to use our senses freely and creatively and develop positive attitudes toward ourselves and our neighbors for this learning to become effective. Children rarely have the opportunity to share ideas and develop attitudes about themselves and others. Although from the outside the school may look like a center of learning, this learning takes place in isolated cells, with fifth graders rarely seeing a kindergarten child except when passing in the halls. Adults are excluded and, except for the teachers, many children see no adults for hours at a time. For a fifth grader, the world is largely made up of other fifth graders. Bronfenbrenner (1970) has warned that, when children have contact only with their age-mates, they have no opportunity to learn culturally established patterns of cooperation and mutual concern. He sees the likelihood of a very unfortunate outcome: increased alienation, indifference, antagonism, and violence.

No art expression is possible without self-identification with the experience expressed as well as with the art material by which it is expressed. This is one of the basic factors of any creative expression: it is the expression of the self. This is as true at a very young age as it is for adult artists. It is individuals who use their art materials and their form of expression according to their own personal experiences. Because these experiences change with growth, self-identification embraces the social, intellectual, emotional, and psychological changes within the child.

There is also a need for the ability to identify with others. In a peaceful society that combines humans of different heritages, it is essential to be able to

FIGURE 9.
The opportunity for young children to draw or paint provides a basis for developing a self-concept.

identify with those we fear, those we do not understand, or those who appear strange to us. Scientifically we have made great gains, but socially we no longer know our immediate neighbors and are unable to communicate with them peacefully. It is only through self-identification that we can begin to identify with others. As a child identifies with his own work, as he learns to appreciate and understand his environment by becoming involved in it, he develops the attitude that helps him understand the needs of others. The process of creation involves incorporating the self into the activity; the very act of creation provides understanding of the process that others go through in facing their own experiences. To live cooperatively as well-adjusted human beings and to contribute creatively to such a society become most important objectives for education. This ideal is widely shared; Novlianskaia and Melik–Pashaev (1979–1980) emphasized that contact with the aesthetic brings profound positive changes and a harmoniously developed human personality, which they feel is the goal of Soviet education.

The term "self-expression" has often been misunderstood. Self-expression is giving vent in constructive forms to feelings, emotions, and thoughts at one's own level of development. Technical perfection bears little relationship to self-expression; the production of technically excellent art products may be far removed from the real expressive needs of the producer.

There is great satisfaction in expressing one's own feelings and emotions in art. Even the very young child who knows nothing about the technical difficulties in pencil rendering, or the various gradations of graphite hardness, can get great satisfaction from making a scribble with a soft pencil. The child expresses self-importance through scribbling, and the satisfaction derived from this achievement is self-evident. The self-confidence that can develop from this type of expression provides the basis for more advanced levels of art.

This area of discussion is closely related to the development of self-concept. It has been recognized that young children need to see themselves as being worthy to deal with the complex environment in which they find themselves. In a longitudinal study of sixth graders in Australia (Williams, Poole, and Lett, 1977), those children who were in the top 5 percent on a creativity test were higher in self-esteem than less creative children.

The self-concept of ability and attitudes toward achievement are much harder to change as the child grows older. One study attempted to change the self-concept of a group of ninth-grade low achievers. Their parents were involved in helping to change that image; as the self-concept of the ninth graders improved, their academic achievement improved (Brookover, 1967). The relationship between creativity and ego development in college populations has

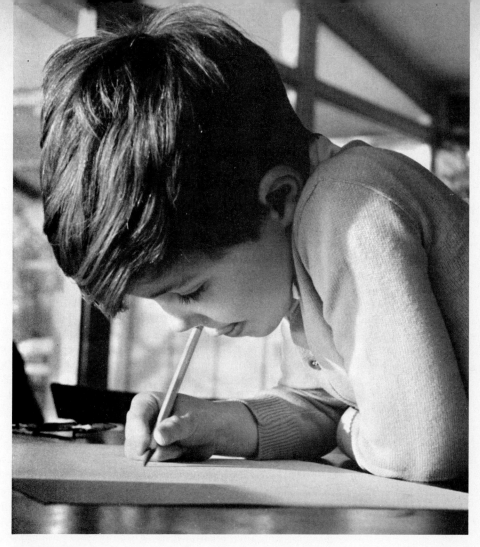

FIGURE 10.

A young boy derives great satisfaction from his creative expression. He is not inhibited in the use of his tools because of a lack of technical training.

been studied by Phillips (1973) and by Workman and Stillion (1974); both studies found a significant correlation between creativity and a positive self-perception. A basic goal of art education is to develop in the child the ability to create a product using whatever skills one has, without having to follow a pattern or methods prescribed by others and without having to rely on external rewards for satisfaction. Getting satisfaction from one's own expression is a step toward a positive self-concept.

The Meaning of Art for Society

Art is often considered the highest form of human expression. It is certainly true that art is something that is cherished, is sometimes valuable for the collector, and can even be stolen for ransom. Art is also a reflection of the society that creates it. The art of ancient Greece or Egypt tells us a great deal about the society in which it was produced. It is a little difficult to evaluate the present forms of art within our own society; although art critics enjoy tackling this task, the artists themselves seem to be less interested in the meaning of the art they produce.

For some people the field of contemporary art is a mystery. Having broken away from past traditions, to some extent it seems more closely related to smashed automobiles or the stacked soup cans on the grocer's shelf. At times it may resemble some of the bad dreams one does not speak about or the nonsensical play of lights and forms. Some contemporary art is almost accidental, with no creative organization involved; much is high in impact but transient. For many people, today's art is distant from their interests and far removed from the refined cultural taste supposedly associated with "art." It may seem especially unrelated to the scientific world in which we live.

Snow (1961) has written about these two extremes within our society: the artistic, literary pull on one side as against the scientific on the other. The dissolving of space in science has been matched by the dissolving of space in paintings. Einstein's theory of relativity and the nonobjective movement in art developed about the same time. Although few people today claim to be scientific experts, many believe in the value of advanced scientific experimentation. There is growing concern over the sources of energy and the preservation of natural resources. Most scientific reference books have been overtaken by new and pertinent data (Mitton, 1977). At the same time, most people claim to know what they like in art and doubt the value of new experimental art forms. It seems strange to realize that one segment of our society is given approval, but another segment is condemned for its investigations. The physical scientist has gained control over parts of the environment through experimentation and manipulation of symbols. The artist also must come to grips with mass, energy, and motion, but attitudes and values also play a part. Both scientist and artist continually try to fathom the unknown in their search for truth; they have a common quest to understand reality.

Art can have meanings within our society other than as the highest form of expression. It can be used in the most crassly commercial fashion to advertise, promote, and sell a variety of products, candidates, and ventures. Many would object to calling this art, but its use of color and form and its concern about audience impact makes it a very evident part of our culture. It may be that this type of art is more truly representative of our culture than the art that is being produced for the connoisseur. It could be interesting to look at our society from the point of view of an archaeologist a few thousand years from now and guess at the kind of society that might be pieced together from the variety of art forms found in the drugstore, automobile showroom, or airport novelty shop.

Somebody has to worry about the future of our country. With poorly designed "builder" houses, big billboards proclaiming the virtues of particular brands of beer, the ruinous effects of acid rain, local streams used as garbage dumps, and hazardous waste carelessly discarded, the prospects for the future beauty and health of the earth look very dim. Most schools do nothing about the problem of deciding what the world that we and our children are going to live in will look like. The art teacher, the biology teacher, and a few concerned individuals may be able to enlist the aid of the young people who look with anger at the degradation of our common inheritance. Politicians can no longer afford to ignore group protests that call attention to loss, blight, and waste. There are increasing numbers who would like to preserve and protect our environment. Examining our surroundings in detail, seeing beauty not only in the spectacular but also in the smallest growing things, is not limited to any one field. But the heightened sensitivity of an art experience can bring new realizations of this environment, evaluations based on reasons other than economic. The conservation of our resources depends in part on the sympathetic preservation of that which is beautiful, that which has intrinsic value, and that which is reusable in other forms.

Art ability has often been considered something one is born with, something that comes intuitively to a sensitive individual. There has been serious questioning whether art can really be taught. But there are also people who feel that art is so vital to our society that we must begin early in our educational system to teach good taste and to develop habits of care in selecting objects from the environment. Both of these views seem too extreme. On the one hand is the opinion that nothing can be done to encourage or stimulate youngsters in their art experiences; it is almost as if a magic spark from heaven somehow alights on the chosen few. The other extreme tries desperately hard to develop a curriculum that, through proper rewards and appropriate disciplinary action, makes youngsters conform to the standards of the teacher. Somehow excluded from both

FIGURE 11.
The teacher can do much to
encourage children's sensitivity
to the beauty in our environment. Noticing the detail and
intricate arrangement of seeds
in this milkweed can be an
exciting discovery.

views is the individual who should be free to reject or accept, to formulate considered opinions, and to evolve new directions, but who should *not* be free to be
a passive bystander in our society.

Art should play a meaningful role in the development of children. The focus
of teaching is the developing, changing, and dynamic child. Art education can
provide the opportunity for increasing the capacity for action, experience,
redefinition, and stability needed in a society filled with changes, tensions, and
uncertainties.

The Meaning of the Art Product

There are many ways of looking at children's drawings. Probably most adults see children's art as being interesting, exciting, and colorful examples of self-expression. Often the product has appeal because it exhibits a certain magnetism, possibly reflecting one's own childhood, or possibly inducing a certain amount of envy of the freedom and spontaneity that are apparent in the product. This is particularly true of the work of young children. Older children may develop a technical skill and begin to develop a naturalistic representation which is admired for the interesting solution to a visual problem or for the skill in mastering a particular procedure.

Professionals in the field of art and psychology often look at art from different points of view. Sometimes the art product is seen as a reflection of the inner personality of the child, as an indication of the child's development, or possibly as a reflection of the achievement of the student toward the goals set by the teacher. In any case, here the end product is considered important. Probably most important is the frame of reference that the examiner brings to this task. A clinical psychologist, a parent, and a teacher will all see different things in the same representation—this can sometimes be confusing. What may seem a wonderful picture to one may seem merely a symptom of behavior to another or may seem a failure to the third. Maybe we should be more specific.

1. One method of looking at children's drawings and paintings is called the psychoanalytic approach; here the viewer is usually one with some background in clinical psychology. A drawing or painting is used as a projective technique in which the child paints or draws what is important to him, and each line or space is looked at in terms of its relationship to the whole painting. Particularly interesting to this type of viewer is the drawing of the human figure. How the arms are drawn, the size of the body in comparison to the rest of the figure, and the number of buttons on the shirt or dress is sometimes felt to be important. The central concern of the clinical psychologist is to develop a healthy person. The art, then, is a means of discovering the internal conflicts and disturbing experiences that influence the child's development. It is assumed that there is constantly conflict between the self and the environment and that the ways in which these conflicts are resolved determine a child's personality.

The drawing or painting activity is also considered therapeutic. That is, the child usually paints freely the events and problems that have caused conflicts.

The ability to put these on paper and to see these things in context with other parts of the child's environment serves as a catharsis. The child is usually encouraged to act out or to paint those things that seem to be most important, and the verbalization of these activities is supposed to provide good therapy. The product then becomes important, not only as a record of the problems and conflicts the child is facing, but also as a record of progress toward the healthy personality.

There has been a great deal written on the use of art as a projective measure in helping to understand the problems faced by children and adults. However, there is much inconsistency in the method of interpreting drawings, even by those who are supposed to be expert in the field. There is no standard system of scoring drawings, and much of the interpretation is intuitive. In practice, drawings are often used as one part of a battery of information that helps the experienced clinician obtain a broader understanding of a client. But this is no area for the uninitiated to tread; it is thin ice for the best clinician, since it is difficult to distinguish between the drawings of emotionally disturbed children and normal children of a younger age (Blum, 1979).

Sometimes children's drawings are analyzed by individuals with little or no background in understanding children's art; the results would be quite funny if these people were not sometimes taken seriously. Often what happens is that the individual will see forms or shapes in children's drawings that have meaning to the person looking at the drawings, though not to the child who drew them. To some extent we get a better understanding of the person making these interpretations than we do of the child who made the picture.

2. Another and diametrically opposed view of children's art is exemplified by one who holds to a behavioral approach and who may see entirely different configurations. The behaviorist is more concerned with the activities of the child that reinforce and shape behavior and basically believes that the environment is primarily responsible for the making of the child. As we change or build the environment in different patterns, the child will change and will reflect these experiences. As the thinking process changes, so will a child's drawing. It would be necessary, then, to determine what would be important for the child to learn and then to set up the conditions for that learning to take place. The drawing becomes an indication of the child's understanding of the task at hand, though often this task may not be known to the child. The success or failure of the youngster's achievements is measured against a preestablished criterion, which may be called the development of perceptual skills, the realization of color harmony, the development of spatial relationships, the awareness of proportion, or some other name. In each case, the goal is quite clear to the adult, and the

FIGURE 12.

An adult might see this second grader's drawing as being full of aggression, with a large axe form, a hanging child, and a youngster shielding his eyes. Actually, it is a drawing of favorite activities, such as climbing a rope and riding a bicycle, with only the necessary parts of the tree shown. The child's regular schema for a person did not provide two hands for riding the bicycle, so one arm extends over the head to the other handlebar.

program toward its successful completion is laid out in advance. Usually the child has little voice in these goals.

If we look at the art product to determine how well a child has achieved some predetermined instructional objectives in art, we must make some sort of evaluation; the objectives must be measurable. Has the child achieved greater use of color in drawings? Has perspective been understood and used correctly? However, this way of examining the product means that the process of painting must be dissected into fragments, and the real meaning of expression becomes lost. Examining the art product for the acquisition of particular skills assumes that these skills are somehow necessary to further expression; it also assumes that the teacher knows what these skills are and how to put them into proper sequence so that the learner can develop competency. A kindergartener draws

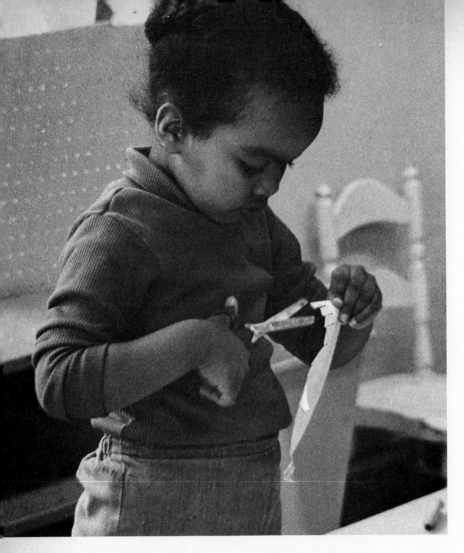

FIGURE 13.
The child has discovered how to manipulate scissors. The task she has set for herself requires concentration and the achievement is a source of satisfaction.

with freedom and spontaneity, with all the ability and skill needed; it is not until the child has been in the educational system for a number of years that this freedom is lost. It will not be the skills the youngster lacks, but the urge and desire to paint directly and freely, without fear of evaluation, and without being told to improve his or her color sense or to learn the rules of perspective.

The person who determines what another must learn and how this learning must take place looks at the art product primarily to see if these predetermined goals have been attained. The teacher is asking if there is evidence of successful teaching methods; the behavioral psychologist is looking for changes in attitude or behavior. This approach is certainly different from that of the clinical psychologist, but no more valid.

THE IMPORTANCE OF ART EDUCATION

3. A third way of looking at children's drawings is the developmental approach. Here the drawing or painting is examined from the point of view of seeing how the child measures up to what is expected of him at any particular age. It is assumed that the child is basically a changing, moving person who follows a predetermined growth pattern, although this pattern varies considerably. Each stage of development follows the preceding one in logical sequence and each stage is a springboard for the next. To some extent the developmental psychologist has very little influence over the way in which the child behaves artistically. The drawing or picture will reflect the particular stage of development that the child has reached; although the youngster can be encouraged to expand or enlarge the painting, the way in which it is painted or the concept that the child is trying to portray will not change. The feeling is that a child cannot change until he is ready, and this is predetermined by his developmental level. When he says his paintings do not look right or when he is dissatisfied with the method of representation, a child is at a transitional stage and is ready to be helped but cannot be pushed into the next stage of development.

A teacher who adheres to a strict developmental approach to viewing children's art may feel that the best thing to do is to stay out of the way. Besides providing materials and a place to work, there may be little left for this teacher, since the art product's appearance is essentially out of both the teacher's and the child's control. However, all children do not arrive at the same concept of their environment at the same time. If every child were preprogrammed to develop artistic concepts at a set rate, then environmental influences would seem to play but a minor role. However, such is not the case, and psychological literature is filled with evidence that changes in the environment can drastically affect the rate of growth but not its pattern. This theory needs further discussion, but not in relation to ways of understanding the art product.

4. A fourth approach to looking at children's art is assumed by one who is concerned about art as a discipline. Sadly enough, this approach has the least amount of excitement in it. Here the basic assumption is that children need to develop a vocabulary, both verbal and pictorial, upon which they can build their expression. The role of the art teacher seems to be that of providing the materials, developing tasks that will be executed by the child in mastering certain artistic skills, and motivating the child so that the drawing and painting activities continue. The art activities become sequential, building upon one another from the point of view of artistic achievement and not from the point of view of the child's development. Experts establish policy in order to ensure quality control and to maintain accountability. Teachers who favor the mastery

of skills before the development of expression feel that it is necessary to teach how to use a brush, to clean off the excess paint, and to control the quality of line before real expression can take place with that material. For older children, it apparently is necessary to teach linear perspective and a good pencil technique so that these may be used in case there is ever an expressive need. A progression of materials is presented to be mastered by children. For example, the nursery school teacher may feel it important that a child should be able to use tempera paint, some simple drawing instruments, and paste. The junior high student will have copper embossing, styrofoam carving, simple weaving techniques, the use of pen and ink, and possibly some design principles to master. The high school student will be concerned with etching, throwing clay on the wheel, using the air gun, producing computer art, and mastering acrylics or oils. The art product in these cases becomes a record of the youngster's preparation and success in achieving certain levels of proficiency within the realm of school art.

Which of the preceding methods of looking at children's art is correct is not the basic question. Although the differences between these four ways of looking at the art product have been artificially stressed, maybe unduly so, it is important to bear in mind that these ways of looking at children's products influence the way we treat the product and motivate the child. It certainly influences our favorable feedback. However, a person who works with children in the area of the arts will probably assume all of the preceding roles at various times. There are moments when a child is full of excitement about something that has recently happened or is anxious to express feelings about a scraped knee or is upset because of some felt injustice. Art is certainly therapeutic. But there are times when certain behaviors need to be encouraged, and the arts are a good way to attain some of these. For example, a mural may provide the opportunity for interaction between children; for the insecure child, being a part of a large group may be terribly important. And the teacher must be aware of the developmental level of the children. It is not possible for kindergarten children to grasp the concept of three-dimensionality in drawing, nor would we expect a fourteen year old boy to be naturally excited about drawing a vase of flowers. Also, there are some things in the area of art that can be brought to the attention of children if they are ready to understand the concepts involved and if this knowledge can further their interests and abilities. The area of adult art need not be hidden from children.

The parent or the teacher of art may have certain preferences for abstract art, superrealism, or whatever; but these preferences should not influence our

FIGURE 14.

A seven year old boy saw a traffic accident which distressed
him. This is one of several drawings he made in the days
that followed.

attitudes in working with children. Obviously the training and background of
adults will influence how they perceive the product that a child produces. However, it is important to realize that art is for children and not for providing an
ego trip for adults.

Summary

One important factor to be kept in mind is that creative work must be understood individually. We can only appreciate the significance of creative work by understanding the child and seeing his picture as part of his life. For example, it may happen that a child portrays an emotional event that has great personal significance, such as a fire that has burned down his house or an accident in which he was involved. To the adult these may be ordinary paintings; they may even be ugly from an aesthetic point of view. Yet the work produced may be an important resolution within the child's own life; to direct attention only to the painting and to be concerned only with technical abilities would be an injustice. It is also true that an insignificant and timidly executed work may provide insight for the teacher so that activities can be planned that will give the child the opportunity to develop confidence in his expression. Each art work must be considered on its own merits, and this is true for all levels of teaching.

Children's creative works differ from one individual to another. In one study (Hartley, Somerville, Jensen, and Eliefja, 1982) adults were shown five year olds' drawings; they were able to match subsequent drawings by these children to the appropriate child, even though some of the drawings were made nine months later. Great differences can be seen from one stage of development to another. An experience that is meaningful to a child of twelve may be meaningless to a child of seven. It is not the content that becomes the important consideration in children's drawings, but the way in which youngsters portray this content. A child will draw and paint from what he is. These feelings, desires, thoughts, and explorations with paint and subject matter will all appear in the painting. Particularly a young child, but to some degree everyone, paints in a direct manner with no thought of hiding or concealing true feelings.

For the child, the value of an art experience is in the process. In the discussion of the importance of the art product we have been concerned primarily with the adult, what the drawing, painting, or three-dimensional construction means for the viewer. To examine the picture without understanding what the child's intention was, to make assumptions about personality from one example of art work, or to assess competence in art on the basis of what is included or omitted from the product do both the product and the child an injustice. To say that this child has weaknesses or that that one has strengths, based upon one teacher's opinion, helps neither the child nor the teacher. If the purpose is to understand the child and to give support for his expression, to find out how we can involve him more fully in life, then it is a legitimate one for teachers. The preschool child may not recognize his own painting the next day. However, the high school student looks at his painting with a very critical eye; his purpose is quite different. But for both, the excitement of painting is in the subjective reaction to the world, in displaying on the painting surface the thoughts and sensitivities that are part of creative and intellectual growth.

SUMMARY

2

Understanding Growth and Development

Art as a Reflection of Development

The study of children's art can be fascinating. Through an understanding of the way youngsters draw and the methods they use to portray the environment, we can gain insight into their behavior and develop an appreciation of the complex and varied ways in which children grow and develop. Working with children in the area of art necessitates both an understanding of the various developmental stages and a thorough knowledge of the possibilities for growth. Such awareness is necessary for the teacher to determine to what extent youngsters can comprehend and benefit from the art experience.

The art products of children tell us a great deal. Children create directly and without fear. Art is more than a pastime; it is meaningful communication with the self, as children select and organize parts of the environment into a new whole. As well as being important in children's cognitive development, art also provides the stimulus for perceptual, emotional, social, and creative development. It is obvious that correcting drawings or imposing particular demands that children cannot understand serves no purpose and may instead establish a pattern of dependency upon the adult for direction and support.

Knowledge is usually thought of as flowing from the teacher to the students. The teacher has the responsibility for organizing a stimulating environment, providing the instructional materials, deciding upon the best method of conveying the appropriate information, and developing a curriculum that supposedly covers the syllabus materials. The children, on the other hand, are usually graded on acquisition of this knowledge and on ability to deal with the structure of the classroom in a socially acceptable way. The students' responses are judged as if they were signs of growth, although they may be primarily mimicking the teacher's own values.

Art can bring a new dimension into this organization, a dimension that is concerned with the psychological processes that are experienced and developed in the youngster while involved in learning. This may be a high-level intellectual process quite akin to the thinking carried on by adults at the frontiers of our knowledge. Art provides youngsters with a wide range of possibilities. Growth is not limited to the areas that have been predetermined by the educational system. The manner of seeking answers and finding solutions reflects children's growing ability to deal with a diverse range of possibilities constructively.

Subject Matter in Art

Art is not the same type of subject matter as arithmetic. In arithmetic, as in many other subject matters areas, the teacher plans gradations in the difficulty and amount of new material presented so that youngsters can properly grasp and deal with the content involved. In art, however, there is no external subject matter that needs to be presented in small doses. Subject matter in creative activities has a different meaning from that in other fields. The same content is used in art by very young children as is used in art by professional artists. A person can be drawn by a five year old or by a sixteen year old. The child will draw a head and legs, and this will be satisfying; the sixteen year old will represent a person with a conscious consideration of size and proportion and will include all of the visible body parts. The difference between the two drawings is not in the subject matter but rather in the manner in which it is represented. What changes is the subjective relationship between the creator and the environment. It is this subjective relationship that is important and not the drawing itself.

The content, such as trees, houses, plants, flowers, and people, will vary depending upon who is doing the drawing. For the five year old a tree has a trunk and something indefinite on top; a ten year old would draw the tree with branches to climb on; the sixteen year old would draw the tree as part of the environment, with concern for proper proportions. It is the same tree, but what has changed is the subjective relationship of the people to the tree. The tree, as in the example of a person, is understood in different ways and therefore will be drawn in quite different ways. It would be beyond the comprehension of the five year old to draw a tree in all its details as part of the environment. To say which tree is better would be ridiculous. Each tree is symbolic of the youngster's relationship to the subject matter. For the sixteen year old to draw like the five year old would be as unnatural as it would be for the five year old to draw like the sixteen year old. In a sense there is no subject matter in art, only different ways of portraying the artist's relationship to objects, people, feelings, and emotions about the world.

The drawing by a five year old boy does not really represent his knowledge of a person. Every five year old knows that we have fingernails if attention is directed toward them, but no average child of this age ever draws fingernails.

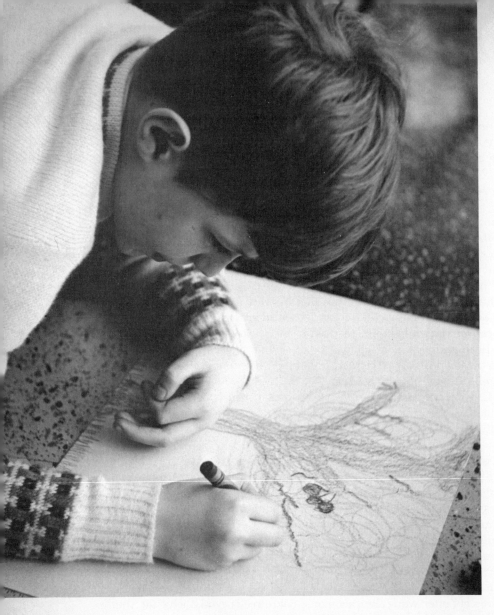

FIGURE 16.
This eight year old boy draws a tree as he understands it, complete with large apples.

The child draws only what is actively in his mind. Therefore the drawing provides an excellent record of the things that are of importance to the child during the drawing process. A child knows a great deal more in a passive way than is included in the drawing. Part of a teacher's responsibility is to make this passive knowledge more active.

Each child draws the environment differently from any other child. A sixteen year old boy, for example, may be concerned about distances and sizes and his role in society; his mental and emotional growth are reflected in the way he

UNDERSTANDING GROWTH AND DEVELOPMENT

portrays these differences. A five year old, however, experiences everything through himself; his spatial relations are limited to his own immediate surroundings, which he can touch, feel, or experience kinesthetically. It is not the subject matter itself, but how that subject matter is portrayed, that is important. Knowledge of the changes in drawings that appear at various developmental levels and of the subjective relationship between the child and his environment are necessary to an understanding of the growth of creative activities.

Developmental Stages in Art

As children change, so does their art. Children draw in predictable ways, going through fairly definite stages, starting with the first marks on paper and progressing through adolescence. DiVesta (1974) has said, "The changes in the way the child perceives, represents, and operates on the world appear to emerge in very regular and systematic ways analogous to the regularity of biological and language-structure development" (p. 38). It is sometimes difficult to tell where one stage of development stops and another begins. That is, growth in art is continuous, and stages are typical midpoints in the course of development. Not all children move from one stage to another at exactly the same time; except for the abnormal or exceptional child, these stages follow one another, however, and a description of each is valuable in understanding the general characteristics of children and their art at any particular time.

Very young children begin drawing by making random marks on paper. This stage is usually referred to as the *Scribbling Stage.* These random marks become much more organized and controlled, but it is not until about the age of four that youngsters make any recognizable objects in their drawings. Therefore, we can say that the scribbling stage usually lasts from two to four years of age. Even scribbles go through various stages of development, from random marks to controlled scribbles. Sometimes parents try to teach youngsters at this stage of development how to draw something like an apple. It is a mystery to the child that these marks drawn by the well-meaning parent can have any relationship to a real apple. This can be a frustrating experience for both parent and child, whereas the scribbling activity in itself is usually pleasurable; having an adult interested usually makes it even more interesting to the scribbling child. Apparently, paying attention to scribbling, and providing opportunities to draw and encouragement in using materials, can speed up development, but not very much. At any rate, children tend to scribble until about four, and they seem to have a good time doing it.

FIGURE 17.
For young children, scribbling is a purposeful activity. Painting provides
the ideal opportunity for the manipulation and enjoyment of color.

The next stage is usually referred to as the *Preschematic Stage*, where children make their first representational attempts. This stage usually starts at about four years of age and lasts until around seven. Here children draw the typical head–feet representation of a person and begin to draw a number of other objects in their environment with which they have had contact. These figures or objects appear somewhat randomly placed on paper and can vary considerably in size. These first representational attempts provide an opportunity for adults to converse with children about their drawings, and usually children of this age are eager to explain and show what they have done without self-consciousness.

The next stage is the *Schematic Stage*, which starts somewhere around seven and lasts until about nine years of age. Here children develop a definite form concept. Their drawings symbolize parts of the environment in a descriptive way; children usually repeat with some variation the schema that they have developed for a person again and again. It is at this time that one interesting characteristic of children's drawings appears: children arrange the objects they are portraying in a straight line across the bottom of the page. The house is followed by the tree is followed by the flower which is next to the person who may be next to a dog which is the end of this picture. These works of art look quite decorative.

It is usually the first three stages of development that attract the enthusiasm of adults, who admire the freshness and the spontaneity of children's drawings. However, this spontaneous and fresh method of painting comes naturally to children; possibly adults wish that they too could enjoy the freedom of childhood, forgetting that growing is not always full of joy and happiness.

By the time children reach the age of nine they are entering the *Stage of Dawning Realism*, which lasts from nine to twelve years. Peers become so important that this is sometimes referred to as the *Gang Age*. The drawings by children of this age still symbolize rather than represent objects. Youngsters are much more aware of themselves, and this awareness shows in their drawings. Objects are no longer placed in neat rows across the bottom of the page. Children are becoming interested in detail and no longer make the large, free drawings that they made at a younger age. They are no longer eager to show their drawings and explain them, but hide them from adult observation. Their art work reflects their greater consciousness of themselves as part of society.

Somewhere around the age of eleven or twelve youngsters become increasingly aware of natural surroundings and worry about such things as proportion and depth in drawings. This stage is referred to as the *Pseudo-Naturalistic Stage*, the stage of reasoning. There is a great deal of self-criticism, and drawings are now hidden in notebooks or are attempts at cartoons. The drawing of

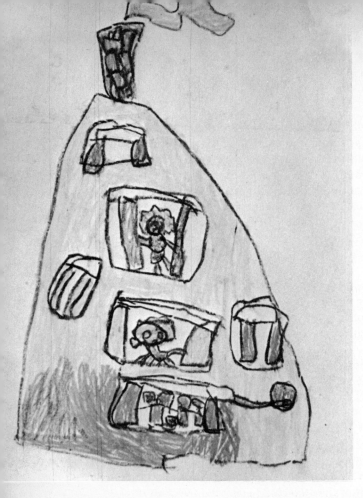

A

FIGURE 18.

A. This house, drawn by a five year old girl, shows an awareness that the house encloses space, with people indoors, drapes at randomly placed windows, and a chimney on top. B. Here a fourth grader has drawn herself jumping rope in the yard of her house. Everything is lined up along the bottom of the paper: the tree with its round top which is symbolic of leaves, the girl rigidly looking straight forward, and the house with the important details of chimney, front door, garage door, and, of course, the TV antenna. C. A ninth grade boy has included a great deal of detail in his drawing of a downtown brick building. His observations of his neighborhood are combined with an active imagination and a sense of humor to produce a visually pleasing picture.

B

C

the human figure shows a great deal of detail and, as might be expected, an increase in the awareness of sexual characteristics. There is also a greater awareness of differences and gradations in color, although some youngsters are not able to develop this visual awareness. For some, this stage marks the end of their artistic development. Often adults, when asked to draw something, will make a drawing that is typical of a twelve year old.

At about the age of fourteen or later, youngsters are at the age of development where a real interest in visual art can take place. They develop a conscious awareness of art and are often eager to develop artistic skills. Some high school students gain great competency in mimicking art forms or styles that

ART AS A REFLECTION OF DEVELOPMENT

may be currently in vogue, and some youngsters develop what might be thought of as a talent for portraying their visual environment. This age may be somewhat shallow in its artistic form, particularly if the perfected style or technique has been laboriously copied from elsewhere. To some extent, the natural development of a youngster does not extend beyond this stage, but it is possible now to develop artistic skills consciously.

Apparently, these developmental stages are fairly consistent with all children, wherever they happen to be. This is especially true of the beginning stages of representation before the culture influences children in their artistic development. What they draw will differ, depending upon the environment in which they live and the drawing instrument that is used, but all children scribble until about the age of four; the period of first representational attempts will continue until about six or seven regardless of where children live.

It also appears that instruction in drawing does not have much influence upon these stages. This is particularly true of young children, but by the time youngsters are eleven or twelve, some effects of training can be seen in the quality of their work. In encouraging children to look for information about contours of objects or patterns such as angles and curves, Salome (1965) found that this training had no influence over the drawings of fourth-grade youngsters but apparently made some improvement in the drawings of fifth graders. However, in an experiment with fifth graders, Neperud (1966) found that only girls of high intelligence were able to profit from instruction that emphasized visual elements.

A number of studies have attempted to document the various developmental stages in children's growth. These sometimes give different names to the stages, such as calling the scribbling stage a stage of manipulation, and so forth, but there is general agreement as to the stages themselves. Using a statistical analysis of some 38 features of 107 children's drawings, Leeds, Dirlam, and Brannigan (1983) found similar developmental stages. Lark–Horovitz and Norton (1959) found that these drawing characteristics varied more as children grew older and that it was sometimes difficult to tell where one stage of development started and another stopped. Applegate (1967) found that those children who were higher in the stage of development than their chronological age would indicate were generally higher in mental age, whereas children lower in intelligence drew according to their mental age rather than chronological age. It is understood, therefore, that the developmental stages as listed here are primarily for normal children.

UNDERSTANDING GROWTH AND DEVELOPMENT

Significance of the Developmental Stages

Before examining the various developmental stages in more detail, it is probably important to emphasize the significance of these stages and to give some rationale for their importance in the whole educative process. Although separate stages can be identified, actually the stages fuse into one another, as children reorganize their thinking abilities and begin to form new relationships with their environment. The concept of stages, according to Flavell, "refers to an extended process of concurrent, interdependent developmental changes" (1985, p. 293).

It is easier to see the changes in children's drawings as they grow than it is to explain why these changes occur. Children do not attempt to copy nature as adults know it. There is no straight-line progression from a very poor drawing or the scribble that a young child makes of an object to an advanced likeness such as an adolescent youngster might draw. Lewis (1963) gathered drawings from children from kindergarten through eighth grade in which they represented, among other things, a house. She found that kindergarten children actually drew a house that was more naturalistically correct than did children in older grades up through fourth. Children in the first, second, and third grades were concerned about drawing several sides of the house, which it would be impossible to view naturally. Obviously youngsters are not trying to portray their environment in a natural way. It is not that they are unable to do this because they lack the competency or coordination, but apparently that they are satisfied with their own means of representation.

FIGURE 19.

A first grade boy has drawn himself playing soccer outside his house. Notice how he has attempted to show what he knows about the house and its roof, with a peak at each end.

We may well have been led down the wrong road by comparing children's drawings to nature. Drawing is a process that children use to signify and reconstruct their environment; the process of making a drawing is much more involved than a mere attempt at visual representation. That is, children may be acting out or moving part of their environment around, and the parts are merely symbolized by whatever happens to be satisfying enough to connote the image or object. Looking at children's drawings from this point of view, it becomes apparent that youngsters themselves are actually involved in every drawing, as spectators and actors at the same time.

For example, drawings by five year old children have no space relationship except from the self. The five year old draws those things in the surrounding space that are important, and the finished picture looks as if the youngster had placed objects randomly around the page. By the age of seven the child begins to place objects in a line, but each of these objects is drawn facing the child as if they were lined up to be seen. These objects do not relate to each other but rather to the child artist. It is not until about the age of nine that objects in drawings relate to each other rather than to the viewer. About the age of twelve or so, pictures start to become representations of space and objects within that space. Drawings give a good indication of the child's growth, moving from an egocentric point of view to a gradual awareness of the self as part of a larger environment.

Piaget (1959), in studying children's thinking, discovered that there were stages in development that closely parallel the stages of development just mentioned. The first stage, which lasts until about the age of two, he calls the *Sensory–motor Period,* and this is followed by a *Preoperational Period,* which lasts until about the age of seven, followed by a stage of *Concrete Operations,* which lasts from about seven to age eleven. Another stage begins at age eleven or twelve and is usually called *Formal Operations.* Piaget, with his collaborators, has produced a tremendous amount of material that supports the proposition that the child thinks in quite different ways from an adult. It is not necessarily poorer reasoning or lack of education that makes the child a child. According to Piaget, these stages are indications of ways in which children typically deal with information, and these modes of thinking actually prevent certain kinds of learning. A well-known example of this is the experiment in which a child views water being poured from a squat beaker into a tall one and believes that the water increases in quantity through some trick; and when it is poured back, the child believes the quantity has suddenly diminished. It is not until after the age of six or seven that a child will realize that the volume of water does not change. A study of this conservation-of-volume experiment was made by Green-

FIGURE 20.
Painting the water level in a vertical bottle is not much of a problem, but it is much more difficult to comprehend what happens to the water level when the bottle is tipped.

field (1966) with Wolof children in Senegal. At first children thought the volume changed through the experimenter's magic. When the six and seven year old unschooled children poured the water themselves, their correct responses increased from one quarter to two thirds.

Although Piaget's stages are for intellectual development, it is not surprising to find the same stages in art. When asked to draw the level of water in a container that was tipped at different angles, children from four to seven represented the water as parallel to the base of the container, whatever its position. Only after the age of eight did children begin to represent the water level as being constantly horizontal (Piaget and Inhelder, 1967). This experiment was duplicated (Maxwell et al., 1975) to try to teach this concept to eight to ten year olds, but the children's drawings improved only minimally.

Several studies have given support to the theory that young children cannot visualize a scene from a vantage point other than their own. One experiment (Coie et al., 1973) had children look at a model of several small houses. Then a doll was moved to a location away from the children, who were asked to pick out from a series of photographs what they thought the doll would see. This task was almost impossible for five year olds to accomplish. Usually the children selected photographs that looked like what they themselves saw. However, the responses improved up to the age of eleven, which was the oldest group tested. But even here there were errors. The same stages of development can be seen in children's drawings. Young children draw everything positioned in relation to themselves. It would almost appear that they have no concept of space removed from themselves; that is, they are egocentric and are not able to take another's point of view, although photographs and three-dimensional drawings utilizing perspective have certainly been a part of their environment. It is not until the Gang Age, about nine years, that we find drawings beginning to have a life in themselves; that is, action can take place within the drawing and people can begin to look at each other or go into the house or observe the scenery without having to stand at attention for the observer.

Drawings may reflect the ability of children to deal with parts of their environment in a very practical way. The teaching of particular skills becomes meaningful only when children can use this information. For example, five year olds do not put shadows in drawings. To try to demonstrate that shadows exist, to teach methods of shading and how a shadow is cast, would be meaningless. Lee (1968) asked youngsters of a variety of ages to make an actual shadow using rings of various sizes placed in front of a light. Younger children were unable to deal with the problem and believed that the bigger the ring the bigger the shadow, regardless of where this ring was placed. It was not until the age of eight that the youngsters began considering distance from the light as influencing the size of the shadow. At the age of thirteen both the dimension and distance factors were considered, but it was not until the age of seventeen that even half of the youngsters could verbalize the operating principles involved.

Drawing and other art activities obviously are not merely the results of manipulative skills. The ability to do certain tasks that require manual dexterity can often be accomplished fairly early in life, but the concepts that children draw do not reflect the eye–hand coordination that one might expect. The young child who threads the needle for grandmother may have a great deal of coordination; however, a drawing by this child will clearly reflect the stage of cognitive development and can easily be distinguished as the work of a child. For teachers to be concerned with manipulative skills, symbol development, or mastery of various art materials puts the emphasis on the products of learning

PLATE 4.

"Mother Is Picking Tulips," drawn by a seven year old child. At this age objects are placed on a base line across the bottom of the page. Notice how the flowers remaining to be picked are large and stereotyped in form, whereas the picked ones are much smaller.

PLATES 5.

"We Are Playing on the Playground," drawn by an eight year old girl. This picture is unusual because it departs from the base line concept. The children standing in a circle are represented according to the child's experience of a circle, rather than perceived visually. There is a schema for running and a separate one for standing.

PLATE 6.

"I Caught a Fish," drawn by a five and a half year old girl. The five year old child has an interesting space concept. Here a girl stands on a dock symbolized by the line encircling the figure, the steps behind her are in the upper corner, and the fish are shown swimming around in a mass of water at the bottom of the page.

FIGURE 21.
Art is a way of learning, as relationships are figured out during the act of drawing. A challenging activity, it must be meaningful for the youngster.

rather than on the process. For children, art is a way of learning and not something to be learned.

It seems that some things cannot be taught until a child is cognitively able to grasp the concepts. Brittain (1969) attempted to teach preschool children the simple task of copying a square. Although he tried to do this with a variety of means, thoroughly saturating nursery school children with the square concept, he was not able to improve their square-making ability. However, at the age of four, children that he worked with did accomplish the task of copying a square successfully. But those children who were not so lucky as to be taught square-making abilities also accomplished the task successfully at the age of four. The ability of children from five to eleven years to perform visual, haptic, and kinesthetic tasks was tested and reported by Birch and Lefford (1967). Intersensory organization was explored, as well as controlled motor performance, spatial orientation, and discrimination of form. As much growth in the ability to perform tasks with geometric shapes occurred between ages five and six as between six and eleven.

It is possible to look at children's growth in art as being a process of organizing thoughts and representing environment in such a way as to give us an understanding of the development of thinking. It seems clear then that these developmental stages are not merely developmental stages in art, but are developmental stages in the whole growth pattern and that the art product is merely an indication of this total growth. Actually, the art activity may *be* growth in itself.

The Importance of the Art Experience

Although the developmental stages are always found in the same sequence, the inference should not be made that this sequence cannot be accelerated or retarded. Heredity undoubtedly plays a part in this, but the environmental influences are those that can be altered and enriched, and it is this aspect that is of crucial importance to the teacher and parent.

Unusual children require unusual amounts of time to follow the sequence. Some may seem stalled on one stage for an indefinite length of time, as is often the case with retarded children. Gifted children may go more quickly through these stages. Just why this is so is apparently tied up with the whole process of cognitive development: progression through the sequence follows intellectual growth.

Sometimes children are taught by teachers or parents to draw particular symbols that are more typical of later developmental stages. A frequent symbol is the stick figure, though sometimes an outline form or even a method of drawing a house or cat is shown to and mastered by a child at an early age. Occasionally the seven or eight year old can even master a system of representing a box in perspective, but in all these cases, the symbol is drawn automatically without a real understanding of the reasoning involved.

It should be emphasized that learning takes place in the context of that which is known. The brain assimilates new information that is only understood in relation to information it has already processed. When new learning is insufficiently anchored in an existing structure of knowledge, the details become obliterated by generalities and are soon forgotten (DiVesta, 1974). An eight year old child who is drawing a baseline can not be suddenly shown the theory behind three-point perspective and be expected to gain any understanding of the concepts involved. A nursery school child who is drawing a head–feet representation of a person will not understand the rationale behind the dictum that a person should be seven heads tall. Even showing illustrations, measuring an adult head and showing that it will go into the length of the body seven times, would have no effect upon the nursery child's drawing. In these examples, the adult does not take into consideration the inability of the child to understand the concepts involved.

Some biologists have established basic nutritional needs for the physical development of children. Psychologists have also established certain needs for the proper psychological development of children. In these lists there does not appear the need to draw and paint. Apparently somebody overlooked the impor-

FIGURE 22.
The teacher needs to support the students, who work toward their own goals in planning and carrying out their own projects.

tance of this area. Drawing and painting are enjoyable activities for children. No motivation is necessary for young children; it seems to be a natural form of learning. The activity varies in length and in intensity, depending upon the child and the particular time of day and other circumstances. But there seems to be a need to draw: a need to represent parts of the environment with which the child has come into contact, a need to put down thoughts, a need to clarify the relationship between objects and people, a need for tangible expression. The role of a teacher of art is more than to make it possible for this to happen; rather, it is the teacher's role to provide the circumstances, the motivation, the materials in such a way that the experience has to happen.

ART AS A REFLECTION OF DEVELOPMENT

It is important to start where the child is and to broaden the child's store of experiences. Except in special cases, there is no reason for praise since the experience itself is rewarding. The scribbling child should have the attention of an adult and the necessary paper and drawing tools; the older child should have the opportunity to talk with a sympathetic listener. The teenager who is having a problem with a wood project ought to have someone to ask if there might be other ways of accomplishing the task; the young adult who is developing artistic skills should have a teacher to help when needed.

The developmental stages, then, take on a great deal of meaning when we realize that the educative process goes on in the child's thinking and not in a teacher's list of potential artistic accomplishments, regardless of how enthusiastic a teacher may be about these goals.

Art as a Basic Means of Learning

Usually when one talks of the basics in learning, what comes to mind is reading, writing, and arithmetic. In fact, the three areas have sometimes become so important in the thinking of non-educators that the mastery of these areas by children is confused with learning. Reading, writing, and arithmetic are merely tools to use in the learning process. Children need to be curious; children need to seek answers and to pursue the acquisition of information at their own level of understanding. Seeking help in the written word can sometimes be of value in this search for knowledge; sometimes the use of numbers can supply answers; the communication of thoughts, feelings, and emotions can sometimes be put into words. However, unless reading, writing, and arithmetic are important and useful to children, they are but meaningless symbols to be manipulated and remain within the confines of the classroom.

Actually, there is very little known about how children learn to read. Most of the reading methods presently available are those devised and supported by publishing houses. In fact, there is even some problem in defining what reading is. Too often we look upon the mere recognition of letters or words, or the verbalization of these symbols, as being reading. However, reading implies much more than recognition and even more than understanding the particular meaning of each word. Reading should be able to evoke thoughts, to raise questions, and to be open to interpretations. What is read needs to be assimilated and should be related directly to the experience of the child so the meaning can be evaluated in terms of his or her own experiences. Reading is much more than a recognition game. Merely translating the observed symbol into sound is not a sign of literacy.

Learning to write can sometimes become a meaningless activity for children. The physical problems of trying to copy or trace the written word are tremendous. This is particularly true of the young child who is beginning to write his name. An examination of any college graduate's handwriting will quickly reveal that skills learned in the elementary grades relative to making letters with a nice, round hand have been forgotten. It seems almost as if there is an inverse relationship between education and the ability to write legibly. This is not to suggest that the time spent teaching young children how to write is wasted; rather, the time is an imposition on both teachers and children, and for the less coordinated may cause anxiety and negative feelings about school. Even in the

FIGURE 23.
This nursery school boy is working diligently, making his own symbols for letters, a first step in learning how to write. He already has a rough notion of the letter E, but with numerous horizontal lines.

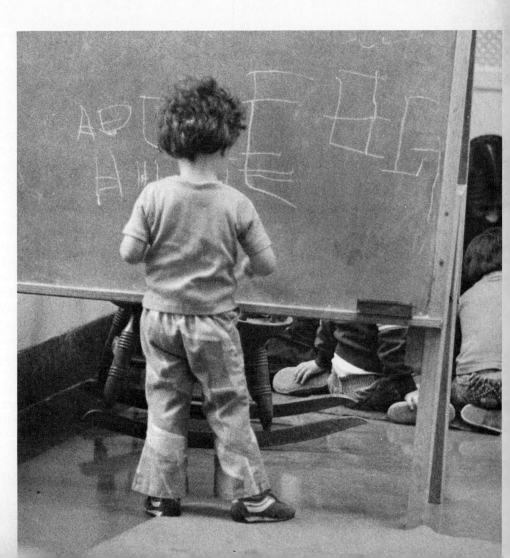

upper grades where children are writing compositions, too often the grammar and proper spelling are checked but the content ignored. The ability to communicate with others, the ability to confront oneself with one's own thoughts and to organize and put these on paper in a logical manner are all important parts of the educational process. Somehow the usual writing skills do not seem to incorporate these factors.

Arithmetic fares no better. The young child can recognize the numeral 5, but the parent or teacher does not know what meaning this has for the child. For example, a 5 can be an interesting shape, somewhat like a curled-up snake, and one must be careful not to confuse it with another curly one, the 2. On the other hand, the 5 may be part of a series falling between 4 and 6. There seems to be some order in numbers, and the 5 is sort of the middle one. Possibly the child sees 5 as a quantity. It is about as many marbles as can be held at one time or as many peas as will fit on a spoon. Possibly 5 is merely a symbol that indicates the location on the dial for a favorite TV program or the number over the classroom door.

Meaningless drills often are part of the method of trying to teach these skills. Prepositions may be memorized, poems may be recited, or arithmetic tables may be learned by rote. Except for escaping the wrath of the schoolteacher, these seem to be of little value outside of school. Few of us can remember how to divide by fractions, and fewer of us ever use that skill in our daily activities. To think that reading, writing, and arithmetic have become so important in the learning process is to confuse the tools with the objectives.

Some school systems have a yearly reading ability test. On the basis of this test, children are called overachievers or underachievers or are earmarked as reading at grade level. Teachers whose classes fall below the norm are sometimes admonished to spend more time on the reading program. What is ironical about all of this is that there is serious question whether reading tests actually test reading skills (Livingston, 1972). Different reading tests will give different answers, and there is little experimental information to show that these tests are valid. In other words, they may not be measuring what they claim to measure, and the youngster who does poorly on one of these tests may be subjected to a remedial program based upon the notion that there are certain elements of language behavior that can be identified and corrected. But the success of any remedial program can be seriously questioned (Hammill and Larsen, 1974).

Most parents and many teachers do not view art as a subject matter to be mastered. Occasionally there is a school administrator who feels that art needs to be as rigorous a course of study as reading, writing, or arithmetic. The

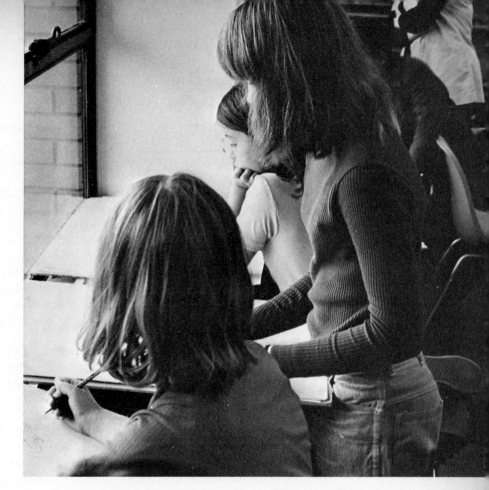

FIGURE 24.
A vital learning environment, with flexible use of space, stimulates the thought processes of inquiring minds. The continuous process of problem solving in art requires intellectual activity.

thought is that there are certain fundamentals that need to be learned, such as working with particular materials, learning the principles of design, memorizing the names of great artists, mastering complex procedures, and following a prescribed sequence of activities. The mastery of these artistic gimmicks is of no more value to a child than is the time spent on learning to divide by fractions: interesting information for the moment, but quickly forgotten once the youngster closes the classroom door.

If we really expect to develop an inquiring mind in a child, one that is eager to tackle the problems of today, a mind that is flexible, inquisitive, and seeks for solutions in unusual ways, then the attention that we have paid to the so-called basic learning areas may be ill-placed. The arts can play a tremendous role in learning and may be more basic to the thinking processes than the more traditional school subjects. Every drawing, whether by a scribbling child or a high school student at the peak of learning efficiency, demands a great deal of intellectual involvement.

When moving from the scribbling stage, about the age of four, to the stage of making first representations, the young child develops a symbol or symbols for parts of the environment. For example, the head–feet symbol stands for a man. In attempting to represent what has been seen and experienced, the child produces an image that is more faithful to thinking than to perception. This image is remembered and reproduced as a symbol in context with other symbols. And it is the child's own personal form of categorizing, cataloging, and organizing the objects and things that are of importance.

Not until the stage of making and reproducing symbols at will can the child begin to understand that other people have also made symbols. A three-humped line followed by a circle with a tail and a two-humped line also can stand for a man. The ability to understand these more complex symbols as part of reading comprehension must follow the development of the child's own symbolic discoveries.

Dodge (1984) compared a number of eye–hand coordination and visual discrimination tasks with drawing and handwriting exercises of forty-five preschool children. She found that there were correlations between some of these tasks but that those children who did well on drawing also did well on handwriting and copying geometric forms. It was suggested that the ability to recognize and make symbols was a more important factor in learning how to write than perceptual–motor abilities.

Although the early symbols by children tend to be isolated and somewhat randomly distributed on the drawing surface, within a year's time the symbols begin to relate one to another and are usually drawn in reference to a continuous baseline. This organizational ability is one that is continuous and evolves from a mere placing of one object next to another as in a series to a much more complex relationship where objects overlap and begin to have depth at about the age of eleven or twelve. This manipulation of symbols that still retain their meaning although they are moved up or down, left or right requires a method of thinking that is akin to algebraic reasoning. This type of thought process cannot be imposed from without, but develops through the child's manipulation of mental images. It is becoming more and more evident that the manipulation of forms and shapes relevant to the child's own experiences is a necessary prerequisite for the utilization of words and numbers. It is amazing that anyone would consider art an educational frill; it is a fundamental catalyst in the thinking process and development of cognitive ability in children.

Historical Trends in Art Education

Over the past century there have been various emphases placed on art in the schools. Sometimes the rationale sounds a little strange to us now, but the history of art in the schools is a fascinating subject. Others have studied this subject in depth, but it is worth mentioning a few interesting highlights.

There seem to have been two movements in the push for art programs in the schools during the late 1800s. One was the necessity for developing skilled workmen who could draw with some precision for the area of architecture, mechanical drawing, landscape planning, and so forth. The other direction seemed to be the concern on the part of educators that the United States was devoid of real culture, so it was necessary to introduce art into the schools, particularly the art of Europe and especially from France, to elevate the appreciation and tastes of the school children.

Walter Smith (1872) made a strong plea for including: "Instruction in such branches of drawing as will make all those engaged in industrial occupations better workmen, through the improvement of their knowledge, and elevation of their taste. . . " He envisioned skillful draftsmen coming from the schools and therefore a great improvement for industry: " . . . in every workshop or factory where no knowledge of drawing is possessed by the workmen, there is a waste of material, a waste of time, and an inferior article produced in the end." One still sees remnants of this point of view today, although the rationale may have changed; there is even the notion that self-expression and fantasy of children would have more substance if we first trained children in the formal visual skills of drawing (Duncum, 1985). It is easy to see that many adults forget that children do not have the same goals as adults and that drawing and painting have different purposes than that assumed by teachers.

Also at the turn of the century there was a flurry of books dealing with art appreciation and art history for children. Emery (1898) felt that in studying reproductions of great paintings: "We come in touch not simply with the reflected images of real things such as we see in the world about us, but with the thoughts and feelings, the joys, hopes, and aspirations, of some of the great men who have looked at the world and lived in it." Wilson (1899) authored a manual of picture study including the reproductions of "famous" artists and the criticisms by famous men who have studied these artists. The examples that Wilson shows of modern masters include paintings by Bashkirtseff, Israels,

WALTZ TIME 1-2-3

MARCH TIME 1-2-3-4

STATIC RHYTHM

RHYTHMIC MOVEMENT

FIGURE 25.
This exercise in rhythmic movement was supposed to develop an art sense in girls in sewing classes, for greater efficiency in the home, and to perfect the joy of living (Morgan, 1928).

Richter, and others. Obviously, a number of these painters would not be recognized today, probably even by the children who studied them back in the early 1900s. However, there are still people today, particularly those who have themselves studied art history or art criticism, who believe that children should be taught to recognize great art, not realizing that great art changes from one generation to the next and that children do not have the same frame of reference that adults do in viewing pictures.

It was not until nearly 1940 that the art of children was generally looked upon as being interesting in itself. A number of books dealing with art for children were published at this time. For some the focus was that children can by themselves be expressive and that what adults need to do is basically provide the materials, and the creative spirit of childhood will automatically be released. Children were sometimes told: "Instead of worrying and trying to think things beautiful, you just feel them inside and they come out that way" (Cole, 1940, p.45). It made a good deal of sense at the time. On the one hand the child had been told to improve drawing skills by exercises provided by a teacher and at the same time had been confronted by the art of so-called masters. The youngsters' own expression was finally recognized, and for some teachers this became the goal of art: to release the natural expressiveness of young children.

Needless to say, the society and cultural background of any period helps to dictate what art is taught to children. When industry needs support, then is the time to teach accurate drawing skills; when our culture is lacking, then is the time to bring in the Frenchmen with their paintings; when society shows concern for children, then is the time to praise the self-expression of young children. However, as we get closer to the present, these trends continue. When the need for scientific discovery is paramount and we need to catch up with the Soviets, art is the area that is turned to, to develop creative thinkers. When society feels we need to get back to the basics, art then becomes the teaching of skills to improve the perceptual awareness of children and to develop eye–hand coordination. More recently there has been some indication that there is a push back toward teaching children art history, art criticism, and aesthetics (Greer, 1984). It has been pointed out (Hamblen, 1985) that the teaching of art has been given justification on the basis of fostering world peace, perceptual literacy, the development of consumer awareness, or even an improvement in math skills.

It is probably most important to look at the purposes and goals for including art in any program for children. No doubt each of the previous directions that art has taken provides some rationale for art programs. Children do need to have the opportunity to be expressive, we do need to pass on some heritage in the area of the arts, children have an inborn drive to be creative and to assemble and represent their environment, and there are some technical skills that can be taught, particularly at the high school level, that may indeed, as Smith (1872) has said, make better workmen and provide for an elevation of their taste. However, there are many other factors involved in the teaching of art that cannot be learned purely from an investigation of where the teaching of art has been. This includes the involvement of the child in a meaningful experience in artistic development.

FIGURE 26.
Children who feel secure are not easily distracted by their surroundings and are confident in their artistic expression.

Art as a Means of Understanding Growth

The picture that a youngster draws or paints is much more than markings on paper. It is an expression of the total child at the time of painting. Sometimes children can become very engrossed in art, and the product may have a real depth of feeling and completeness; at other times the activity may be merely an exploration of a new material, but even in this case the picture shows the youngster's eagerness or hesitation in attempting a new task. Although it is stating the obvious to say that no two children are alike, it is also true that of thousands of drawings by children, no two are ever alike. Each drawing reflects the feelings, the intellectual capacities, the physical development, the perceptual awareness, the creative involvement, the aesthetic consciousness, and even the social development of the individual child. Not only is each of these areas reflected in the drawing that a youngster does, the changes as the child grows and develops are also clearly seen. In order to better understand and evaluate the importance of these changes, the significance of the different components of growth should be understood.

Emotional Growth

A drawing can provide the opportunity for emotional growth, and the extent to which this is accomplished is in direct relation to the intensity with which the creator identifies with the work. Although this is not easily measured, the degrees of self-identification range from a low level of involvement with stereotyped repetitions to a high level where the creator is truly involved in portraying meaningful and personally important things; young children themselves appear in their pictures. It is here that there is the best opportunity for personal identification.

Frequent stereotyped repetitions are apparently seen only in drawings by children who have developed rigid patterns in their thinking. In a case study, Lowenfeld (1957) drew some conclusions about a girl with whom he had extensive contact. He felt that every adjustment to a new situation implies flexibility—flexibility in thinking, flexibility in imagination, and flexibility in action. In this severe case of emotional maladjustment there was real difficulty in adjusting to new situations. In her drawings she felt most secure by repeating the same meaningless, stereotyped schema of a figure. Such stereotyped, rigid repetition indicates a lack of emotional involvement.

At certain stages of development a youngster may spontaneously repeat forms to insure mastery over these forms. The flexible use of a symbol can be readily seen by changes and modifications. A youngster drawing a flower garden will include flowers in a variety of positions, some tall, some short, some bent over, and maybe one that has been broken or stepped on. However, if a stereotyped flower is repeated in a meaningless way, without any involvement or new experience shown on the part of the youngster, this may be an escape from facing a world of experiences, although it may in fact be satisfying to the individual who made it.

An emotionally unresponsive child may express detached feelings by not including anything personal. "There is a tree, there is a house." Nothing is included that will indicate a relationship to these objects; such a child is merely passively representing objects. This detached art expression shows neither action nor variety, but rather indicates only enough to signify an object. Figures usually are not included, but if they are, they show no action. The experienced artist may also show this lack of involvement by repeating a technically proficient piece of art or a certain mannerism without any changes or involvement of the self.

When involved, the child actually participates in the drawing, appearing directly in the creative work. The tree drawn is a particular tree; the house is no longer any house but has certain characteristics that are important in the act of drawing. The child feels free to explore and experiment with a variety of materials without fear of making mistakes or worrying about a grade on this particular project. The intensity of involvement provides for emotional growth.

Intellectual Growth

The intellectual development of children can be readily seen in their drawings. How aware children are of their surroundings, the amount of knowledge that is actively used, and their ability to portray a relationship to the environment are all indicators of intellectual development. The use of details and awareness of the environment both change with age. A child who lags behind in developing concepts and awareness of the environment may show a lack of intellectual growth. For example, a child who at the age of seven draws like a five year old may in fact have the intellectual abilities of a five year old. But there may be

FIGURE 27.
There is a wide range of differences in active knowledge, as indicated in these drawings of a man by two five year old children.

other factors involved. Sometimes it may be merely a lack of involvement in a particular drawing. Or there may be emotional restrictions that block the child's expression. However, usually a drawing full of details, reflecting a child's awareness of the world, indicates a child of high intellectual ability.

Intelligence is usually defined as the ability to think in rational ways, to deal effectively with one's environment, and to learn the kinds of things expected in school. Most children, before they are finished with the public schools, will have taken several group-administered and at least one individually administered intelligence test. These tests basically assess the way in which children respond to particular verbal, spatial, memory, and problem-solving tasks as compared to other children the same age. So a normal IQ score of 100 indicates that a child responds to these questions in about the same way as an average child of the same age. If a child has difficulty communicating to an adult, because of language differences or because of some verbal handicap, a drawing test is often used. The best known measure of mental maturity is the Draw-A-Man Test (Harris, 1963). There is substantial documentation for the validity of this test.

Children are provided a pencil and a sheet of white paper and told to make a picture of a man, to make the very best picture that they can, and to make the whole man, not just his head and shoulders. Most test givers today modify the instructions, asking the child to draw a person. The finished drawing is scored basically on the number of details included and is compared with the typical drawing for any particular age.

The relationships between intelligence tests are reasonably high. Apparently, the development of artistic ability closely parallels a child's intellectual growth up to the age of ten years (Burkhart, 1967). The importance that parents and sometimes teachers place upon intelligence tests is often not warranted. Environmental conditions, social factors, and emotional and psychological variables can all affect a child's intellectual functioning. For most children, however, intellectual ability remains fairly stable. But sometimes a child may seem to have special talent in art and not score very highly on the standard intelligence tests. In this case, the drawing itself should be looked upon as the valid measure of a child's functioning. Sometimes certain personality or behavioral traits will have negative influence or depress children's scores in the usual testing situation. How children react to adults, their feelings about themselves, or their nervousness in a test-taking setting all can be negative factors. A study that compared scores on individually administered intelligence tests with a drawing test (Lewis and Livson, 1980) found that eight year old children who did better on the Draw-A-Man Test than on the other test measures tended to be more withdrawn, shy, and unsure. Those children who did better on a more conventional test were more open, verbal, and socially alert. The quiet child who has artistic talent is demonstrating intelligence clearly. This is not to suggest that anyone, merely by looking at drawings, can estimate a child's abilities. However, a sensitive teacher can gain insight and an understanding of some of the problems a child may not be able to deal with by realizing that drawings and paintings reflect the child's thinking process.

Although drawings can reflect a child's intellectual growth, drawings can also stimulate and encourage that growth. Matoba (1985) has called art a tool for critical thinking, a basic skill for children's reasoning. Everyone functions with a storehouse of passive knowledge, the knowledge that we use to move from place to place, to recognize objects and people, and to provide us with the necessities of life. However, few of us take active notice of a particular tree, the arrangement of food on our plates, the shape of the crack in the sidewalk in front of us, or even the number of buttons on the coat that we may put on daily. When a child draws a picture and is actively aware of the environment, these details become important; the tree becomes a particular tree in front of a certain house, and the correct number of buttons on a shirt is important. Art can contribute a great deal to intellectual growth.

Physical Growth

Physical growth is seen in children's visual and motor coordination, in the way they control their bodies, guide their lines, and perform skills. The changing physical growth can be easily observed in children at the scribbling stage, when the marks on the paper change from a few random marks to a controlled scribbling within a relatively short period of time. Also, the desire to make more refined and minute changes in sculptural form can develop motor skills very rapidly in adolescence.

Not only the physical involvement in creative activities, but also the conscious and unconscious projection of the body indicate physical growth. This projection of the self into the picture is usually referred to as body imagery. Essentially, the physically active child will portray active physical motions and will develop a greater sensitivity to physical achievements. Often the unconscious presence of muscular tensions or body feelings will also be portrayed. Sometimes children with impairments will project these into their creative work. The ear that aches or the knee that has been scraped will be given emphasis. Continued overemphasis or omissions of body parts may reflect a physical condition.

Perceptual Growth

The cultivation and growth of the senses are important parts of an art experience. This is of vital importance, for the enjoyment of life and the ability to learn may depend upon the meaning and quality of sensory experiences. In creative activity, increased perceptual growth can be seen in children's increasing awareness and use of a variety of perceptual experiences. Visual observation is usually the most emphasized in an art experience, with a developing sensitivity toward color, form, and space. Young children's paintings indicate enjoyment and recognition of color, whereas on the advanced level the ever-changing relationships of color in different lights and atmospheric conditions can be stimulating. Perceptual growth is a growing sensitivity to tactile and pressure sensations, from the mere kneading of clay and touching of textures to sensitive reactions to clay modeling in sculpture and the enjoyment of different surface and textural qualities in a variety of art forms.

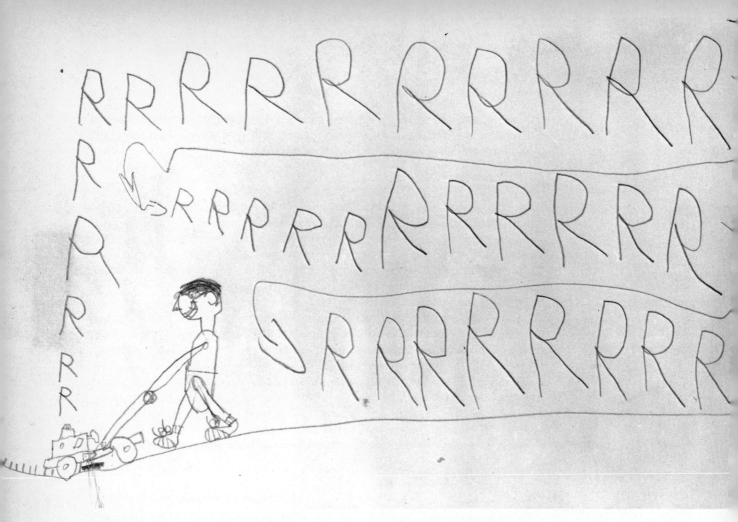

FIGURE 28.

This is a pencil drawing by a six year old boy who has watched his father mow the
lawn. Notice how very much aware he is of the sound, of the grass ahead of the mower
that still needs to be cut, and of the mechanical features of the mower. See too that the
boy identifies so closely with his father that he puts his own sneakers on him, with the
important laces he has just learned to tie.

Perceptual growth also includes the complex area of space perception. A
young child knows and understands the immediate area, which has personal
significance. As the child grows the surrounding space also grows, and the way
it is perceived will change. Auditory experiences are often included in art
expression, ranging from mere awareness of sounds to sensitive reactions to

musical experiences. Kinesthetic experiences that range from simple, uncontrolled body movements to highly developed coordination can also be seen as the basis for a variety of art forms. Space, shape, colors, textures, kinesthetic sensations, and visual experiences include a great variety of stimuli for expression. Children who are rarely affected by perceptual experiences show little ability to observe and little awareness of differences in objects. Awareness of variations in color, differences in shapes and forms, smoothness and roughness, sensitivity to light and dark are all part of the creative experience. Inability to utilize perceptual experiences may indicate a lack of growth in other areas. The teacher must play an important part in developing in youngsters the eagerness to see and feel and touch their surroundings and in providing a wide range of experiences in which the senses play an important part.

Social Growth

The social growth of youngsters can readily be seen in their creative work. Drawings and paintings reflect the degree of identification they have with their own experiences and the experiences of others. Usually, the first recognizable object drawn by a child is a person. Child art reflects a growing awareness of people, as shown by the large percentage of subject matter devoted to social activities.

The art process itself provides a means of social growth. Expressing the self on a sheet of paper also means viewing that expression. This viewing and looking at one's own work and one's own ideas is a first step in communicating these thoughts and ideas to others. Art has often been thought of primarily as a means of communication, and as such it becomes a social rather than a personal expression. The drawing can then become an extension of the self out into the world of reality as it begins to encompass others in the viewing of the subject matter. This feeling of social consciousness is the beginning of an understanding of the larger world of which the child is a part.

The development of social awareness goes on also in the portrayal of parts of our society with which the child can identify. This includes those forces that are established to preserve society itself. Drawing the fireman, the road crew repairing a hole, the nurse helping people in the hospital, or the policeman giving directions all provide stimuli to develop this social awareness. The arts can also contribute, through cooperative work, to a greater awareness of each individual's contribution to a large project. This is particularly effective when the opinions of peers are sought and when the need is developed for social interdependence.

FIGURE 29.

Art may provide the opportunity for social interaction with peers. Developing an awareness of others and their creative efforts can be an important part of an art experience.

It is important to stress the significance of the individual's ability to live cooperatively in society. Children need to have the opportunity to assume responsibility for their own actions. A drawing of some cooperative activity or group game enables a youngster to see the part each person plays and to identify with other's actions. Creative activities provide an excellent means for taking this important step.

For older children, the art of other cultures provides a means by which a

UNDERSTANDING GROWTH AND DEVELOPMENT

society or a people can be felt and understood; the values of one generation can have some influence on the next, as when watching Grandfather work at wood-carving or a neighbor doing intricate needlework, preserving the traditions of her native country. Studying the variety of contemporary art from today's cultures can give indications of the attitudes and feelings of these artists. One investigation, examining the drawings by children from a variety of societies, indicated that group values can readily be seen in children's drawings of men (Dennis, 1966).

Aesthetic Growth

Aesthetic growth is often considered the basic ingredient of any art experience. Aesthetics can be defined as the means of organizing thinking, feeling, and perceiving into an expression that communicates these thoughts and feelings to someone else. The organization of words we call prose or poetry; the organization of tones we call music; the organization of body movements is usually referred to as dance; and the organization of lines, shapes, color, and form make up art. There are no set standards for aesthetics; rather, the aesthetic criteria are based on the individual, the particular work of art, the culture in which it is made, and the intent or purpose behind the art form. There is a tremendous variety of organization in art. Aesthetic form is not created by the imposition of any external rule, but rather a creative work grows by its own principles. There is a branch of philosophy which is concerned with aesthetics; however, our concern here is not a formal study of the abstract principles of art, but rather a study of the manner in which children develop a cohesive framework in their art.

In the creative products of children, aesthetic growth develops naturally and is shown by a sensitive ability to integrate experiences into a cohesive whole. This integration can be seen in the harmonious organization and expression of thoughts and feelings through the lines, textures, and colors that are used. Young children organize intuitively, whereas those in the secondary school can find pleasure in the conscious manipulation and organization of spatial relationships in paintings. Each art material has different demands in terms of its aesthetic use; sculpture, for instance, presents an entirely different concept of organization from a fine line drawing.

Aesthetics is also intimately tied to personality. Painters are recognized by their organization of colors and forms; a Van Gogh can be picked out anywhere by one who is familiar with his style of organization. The organizational framework used to portray experiences in art can often give an indication of some of

FIGURE 30.

'It's Beginning to Snow," shows a simple, direct organization of space, resulting in a satisfying representation which conveys a child's feelings about the holiday season.

the unconscious ordering that is unique for each person. Lack of organization or the disassociation of parts within a drawing may often be an indication of a lack of integration within the individual. One of the methods sometimes used to assess the value of therapy with psychotic patients is a study of the cohesiveness of organization in the drawings they produce.

Education has been thought of as the cultivation of expression in an organized manner. That is, it is the organization of words to make verbal communication, the organization of numbers or symbols to develop mathematical thinking, and the organization of images to make the arts. Education can therefore be looked upon as the development of aesthetic behavior. The thesis that art should be the basis of education has been pursued in depth by Herber Read (1958). Some balance and organization must be built into the educational system through the development of courses in the humanities, such as those that are offered in several school systems. Aesthetic development is certainly an integral part of education.

Creative Growth

Creative growth shows as soon as the child begins to make marks, inventing forms and putting down something personal in a way that is unique. From this simple documentation of oneself to the most complex form of creative production there are many intermediary steps. Within the drawings and paintings of children, creative growth can readily be seen in an independent and imaginative approach to the work of art. Children do not have to be skillful in order to be creative, but in any form of creation there are degrees of emotional freedom: freedom to explore and experiment and freedom to become involved. This is true both in the use of subject matter and in the use of art materials.

The literature on creativity has grown tremendously in the last few years. This area is becoming of increasing concern, both to educators and to researchers. Art experiences have always been considered the basis of creative activity within the schools. However, an awareness of this literature avails us nothing unless we can relate it directly to the individual child. We will go into detail later about the importance of creativity for art. For now it is sufficient to say that every art product, if it is truly the work of the youngster, is a creative experience in itself.

Those children who have been inhibited in their creativity by rules or forces unrelated to themselves may retreat or resort to copying or tracing. They may quickly adopt styles from others, constantly ask for help, or follow examples of work that has been produced by their peers. Needless to say, the mere command to stop copying and become creative accomplishes nothing. Creativity cannot be imposed but must come from the child. This is not always an easy process, but the development of creative abilities is essential in our society. Both the process and the product reflect the youngster's creative growth.

Summary

Although the art of children has been considered free and spontaneous, it is in reality a serious attempt by children to organize their environment and display it in a meaningful way. Children think in different ways than adults, and this accounts for the fact that efforts to change or modify the way children draw and paint have had little success. Apparently, it is much more important to provide the tools, the atmosphere, and the support for expression than it is to worry about what is actually drawn. When symbols appear, and are repeated again and again for the same object, it is clear that children are understanding symbols in the same way that adults look at the printed word and recognize symbols. The arts are more than a reflection of children's growth; they are a way that children learn.

The art of children provides us the opportunity to understand youngsters' emotional growth, is an excellent measure of their intellectual abilities, gives us some clues as to their social development, indicates their aesthetic awareness, and also provides a means for understanding their creative growth. The art of children documents clearly the interaction a child has with the physical and psychological environment. The drawings and paintings by children are fresh and spontaneous; they are that way because children are eager to explore and eager to paint. We as adults have a lot to learn from them.

Related Activities

1. Observe the changes that take place in art expression by collecting drawings from children from kindergarten through high school age. Trace the development of the representation of a single object, such as a tree. Notice how the subject matter does not change, but the *manner* of representation changes as the child changes.

2. Observe a class of fifth grade children as they draw. Notice which ones are restless, easily distracted, uncertain, or asking adults for approval. Compare the art products of these children with those of the youngsters who appear to be very involved in their work and self-sufficient. Look for stereotypes, inclusion of the self, simple objective reports, rich detail, action of the figures, and aesthetic quality. What conclusions can you make?

3. Work with a class of third grade youngsters. Plan one lesson emphasizing environment: trees, homes, school, and so forth. Plan a second lesson that emphasizes the imaginative: dreams, make-believe animals, strange creatures. Do the same children seem to enjoy both lessons?

4. Plan a lesson that includes drawing people; carry it out with kindergarten, second grade, and fourth grade children. Use the same materials and paper size for all classes. Compare the finished products and note the differences in developmental levels.

5. Collect drawings from a kindergarten class and list the various methods of portrayal of sensory experiences. Check especially for symbols for sounds and movements.

6. In second and sixth grade classes, pour colored water into a large jar while children watch. Give each child a sheet of paper on which are drawn two outlines of your empty demonstration jar, one vertical and one tipped at about a 45-degree angle. Ask the children to draw the water level in the vertical jar, and then as it would appear if the jar were tipped. How many children in each grade showed the water level horizontal in both jars? Do not try to correct the drawings.

3

The
Development
of Creativity

The Importance of Creativity

The development of creative thinking has tremendous importance for us, both as individuals and as a society. It offers a change from what is and has been to what might be or what is yet to be discovered. The term *creativity* may have become too popular, for it is applied like sparkling paint to book titles, do-it-yourself projects, or performance groups. The definition of creativity depends upon who is doing the defining. Often researchers are rather narrow in their definition, stating that creativity means flexibility of thinking or fluency of ideas, or it may be the ability to come up with new and novel ideas or to see things in new relationships or to think in ways that are different from other people. Usually creativity is thought of as being constructive, productive behavior that can be seen in action or accomplishment. It does not have to be a phenomenon unique in the world, but it does have to be a contribution from the individual.

Creativity has been considered the opposite of conformity, but this may not always be true. We have to conform a great deal in our society to rules and regulations that provide safety for ourselves and others. This kind of conformity, conformity to rules of physical behavior, is basic to society so long as these rules are able to be changed by those affected. There is another whole area of conformity, that of mental conformity, that may be of danger to our society. We need to differentiate between these two. This may be a difficult thing for young children to do, but adults must be sure that the pressures of conformity are limited to those areas that are necessary for the sake of society. One of the difficult tasks of a teacher of young children is to provide socially acceptable ways in which children can use and be encouraged to use their creative abilities while keeping to a minimum the areas in which they will have to conform.

Probably the most crucial time in the encouragement of creative thinking is when the child is beginning formal schooling. It is here that initial attitudes are established, all too seldom with the realization that school can be a fun place where the individual's contribution is welcome and where changes can be sought and made. Very young children have a freedom to act without regard for the amount of knowledge mankind has already amassed about such an action. Children learn to walk without an intellectual understanding of the motor control involved. What a person knows or does not know may bear no relationship to creative action. Children create with the aid of whatever knowledge they

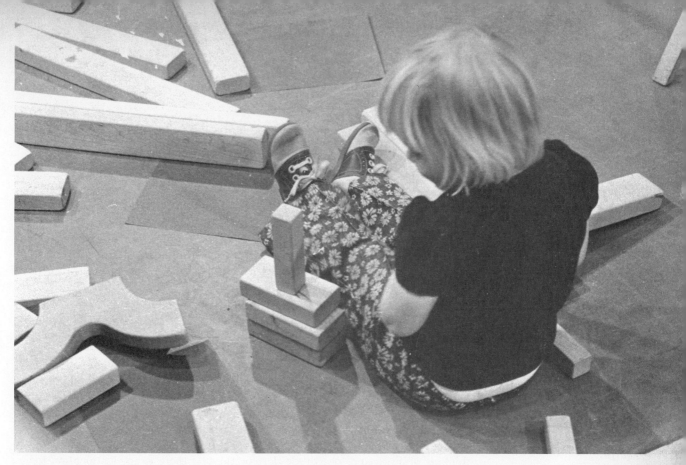

FIGURE 32.

Construction with large blocks in nursery school can develop in unexpected ways. Active participation in such activity is a form of creative problem solving.

happen to have at the time. The very act of creating can provide new insights and new knowledge for further action. Probably the best preparation for creating is the act of creation itself. Stopping children from creating until they know enough about the subject to act intelligently may inhibit action rather than promote it. Giving children opportunities to create constantly with current knowledge is the best preparation for future creative action and thinking.

A second crucial period is in early adolescence, when attitudes are formed that remain into adult life: feelings of personal worth and assessments of one's place in the larger world. It is important for these young people to know that they can have an effect upon their environment and that their ideas and thoughts are valued. The pressures for conformity are severe; the slightest deviation from the norm may be ridiculed. Creativity at this age needs to be supported; the youngster who enjoys the arts or sees the world in a different way may need the encouragement and reassurance of an adult.

Creativity does not just happen. It is an essential part of the learning process, but there are many elements to consider in planning class activities. These include the environmental factors over which the teacher has direct control: the physical structure of the room, the materials, and also the psychological environment, which may be much more important. Other factors include the social values involved, for at certain ages the youngsters will become more dependent upon peers for direction and approval than upon the teacher. Of course, we must consider the personality of each child. In addition, there is the problem of developing a program or method by which creativity can become unleashed. It is this last aspect that is emphasized in most books and texts on creativity, but the development of skills and competencies in art will bear little relationship to the development of creativity unless all these factors are involved in the planning process.

At one time distinct stages were suggested for the development of creative thinking. These consisted of an initial stage called *preparation*, a thinking period called *incubation*, a stage of *illumination*, which was followed by *verification*. These stages were looked upon as sequential, and the school's role seemed limited to the initial stage of preparation only. Now it is outmoded to think of creativity in so limited a format. Rather, creativity is more closely related to thinking abilities and to attitude development. If there is any justification for saying that these four steps exist in the creative process, then they would have to be varied considerably to include both the many periods of illumination that a nursery school child goes through in building with blocks and the one sudden illumination that results in an invention by a research engineer. It is probably best to think of creativity as a continual process for which the best preparation is creativity itself. In fact, there is real joy in discovery—which not only is its own reward but provides the urge for continuing exploration and discovery.

Creative and Intellectual Behavior

Every child is born creative. The urge to explore, to investigate, to discover, is not limited to human behavior, but is experienced by the whole animal kingdom. There have been numerous studies of rats showing that, given a chance, a rat will investigate an unknown maze, explore a new box, or go down a pathway that has been altered in some way. Harlow (1965) has demonstrated that monkeys can and do learn to solve mechanical puzzles when no motivation is provided other than the presence of the puzzle; monkeys will look through a window, put sticks together, explore a new trinket, all motivated by curiosity alone. Harlow says the monkey is actually a very incurious, nonmanipulative animal as compared to man, and the only justification for using monkeys in these experiments is that we have more monkeys available for research than children.

We should not be troubled about motivating children for creative behavior; what we should be aware of are the psychological and physical restrictions that the environment places on children to inhibit their own natural curiosity and exploratory behavior. Preschool children are full of questions, and hardly a parent exists who has not become tired of the question "why?" Yet our school system is so organized that, just a few years later, children have little opportunity to ask questions; it is now the teacher who asks. "Did you finish your homework? What is the answer to the fourth problem on page 27? Who can list three causes for World War I? Why are you late for class?" And so on and so on. It is possible for art to fall into the same trap. "What are the principles of design? What are hue, intensity, and value? List three outstanding painters of Renaissance art. What is the solvent for oil paints?" And so on and so on. Picasso, Magellan, and dividing by fractions are all in the same boat. It is not surprising that under these conditions children need to be encouraged to be inquisitive, since this is a skill that has not customarily been developed. But the asking, curious, creative individual must be a goal of our educational system.

Sometimes intelligence and creativity are confused. The problem is compounded by the fact that creativity is usually considered an attribute that has positive value; because intelligence is also valued highly, these two are often put together. Generally speaking, creativity may have little to do with intellect. The intelligence test deals with the workings of only one small part of the total mind. In some cases, the individual who scores well on IQ tests may also do well on tasks of creativity; in other cases, there may be no relationship. Wallach and Kogan (1965) demonstrated that traditional measures of intelligence do not measure the same things as what they call associative creativity, the latter being measured in a game-like, nonevaluative manner. Although they studied fifth-grade children, other work (Wallach and Wing, 1969; Ward, 1969) has found generally the same distinction between creativity and intelligence in both younger and older children. McKinney and Forman (1977) found that even at second-grade level there is a clear distinction between creativity and intelligence. An extensive review of research articles related to intelligence and creativity

FIGURE 33.

Fluency of ideas can be seen in drawings, as in this one by a six year old girl. She has indicated the motion as she swings and has shown variety in the trees and flowers in her surroundings.

(Barron and Harrington, 1981) indicated the same general finding, that tests tend to show but little relationship between these areas.

Intelligence tests stress convergent thinking, where the correct response has already been determined. This is the ability that seems important for success in school. On the other hand, creativity tests attempt to measure divergent thinking, where there is no single correct answer. Divergent ability includes thinking of a great number of different answers, or thinking of different methods or approaches to problems, or thinking of the unusual or novel. Possibly we have given intelligence too narrow a definition, for both intelligence and creativity are part of the cognitive processes. There seems to be evidence that although creativity and intelligence can be tested separately, both are important. Intelligent children may be able to memorize factual information, deal with numerical problems, and quickly master written material, yet may have difficulty when asked to go beyond the known, to formulate questions, to find ways of seeking new knowledge. Creative children have to be smart enough to deal with their creativity in constructive ways. It has been estimated that the most productive people in our society are not necessarily the most intelligent.

THE DEVELOPMENT OF CREATIVITY

PLATE 7.

"Playing on the Sidewalk," drawn in crayon by an eight year old girl with a high degree of creative awareness. Young children do not copy that which is before them; rather, they reorganize meaningful parts and ignore the irrelevant, to portray a particular moment of importance.

PLATE 8.

"Swimming in the Pool," painted by a young Japanese child, who shows all the activity at the crowded pool. The creative urge to find significance in one's actions and to adjust, adapt, and organize these into a single framework is a cognitive process which is basic to learning.

PLATE 9.

"The Coming Storm." Moods, feelings, and affective reactions to the environment are essential for the production of art. These aspects of creating need to be encouraged and supported. Expressing the wildness of the wind and the turmoil of the waves makes the usual concern for proportion, balance, and technical skill less important.

One theory about the structure of people's intellectual functioning supposes that there are five different operations in the mental process: cognition, memory, convergent production, divergent production, and evaluation (Guilford, 1964). Creativity is considered a divergent production. The creative arts are extremely important in our educational system if only because they stress divergent thinking, and any number of possible solutions to problems or any number of outcomes in painting or drawing can be correct. An art teacher's open-ended questions to stimulate divergent thinking might be "Which colors make you feel sad? How would you feel if you were purple? Which color would you like to be?" The importance of teaching toward divergent thinking is stressed by Burkhart (1962, p. 27): "The value of the divergent question is that it requires the student to look at a content area from a variety of viewpoints and to participate in an imaginative way in answering the question." By way of direct contrast, in a lesson on color, children might be asked factual questions that demand specific convergent answers, such as "What are the primary colors? What are the secondary colors? Give an example of a split-complementary color scheme."

In some cases, curriculum planners may try to justify the importance of art by stressing its academic aspects (Duke, 1983). Although there are many areas in the school's program that attempt to stimulate children's intellectual development, a prime purpose of the arts is to develop the creative domain. It makes no difference whether this creativity will be used in the arts or sciences. The creative elements in cognitive development cannot be left to chance.

Schools and Creativity

Creative growth seems to operate on a different set of patterns than do other areas of behavior. We are all familiar with the healthy child of about four who has a vivid imagination and a great deal of curiosity about everything. Some researchers have found, however, that the child of eight or nine seems much less creative, and again in the seventh and eighth grades there is a dip in creative growth (Torrance, 1962; Kincaid, 1964). We have to be careful not to assume that children are creative in the same way that adults are, but even so, these leveling-off periods seem to exist. There is some evidence that these plateaus may be related to the plateaus between growth spurts of the brain. Certainly the demands of parents, teachers, and peers may put a high value on conforming behavior at these times. There is no doubt that parents considerably squelch what might be thought of as childish behavior and insist that their teenage son or daughter stop being "silly."

FIGURE 34.
Children develop imaginative ideas in an atmosphere that encourages creativity. The classroom situation must be flexible enough to allow youngsters the freedom to express their own ideas.

It is sometimes said that the public school discourages creative thinking, but the school has many tasks, and we might be better justified in saying that creative thinking is not very high on the list of most teachers' objectives. Some research indicates that teachers do not like the creative child (Getzels and Jackson, 1962). A study of second graders (Stone, 1980) found that although teachers felt that their creative children were somewhat more distractible, the second graders thought that their creative classmates were misbehaving. There is reason to believe that the sweet, conforming child is rewarded in the classroom to the disadvantage of the development of imagination and creative thinking; this can happen in art classes too. Society in the form of parents, teachers, or peers undoubtedly rewards certain types of behavior at certain ages, and maybe this is why creative behavior develops in such an uneven pattern.

THE DEVELOPMENT OF CREATIVITY

Creativity needs to be nurtured in a particular kind of environment. The "anything goes" atmosphere is apparently just as negative an influence as the authoritarian atmosphere where individuals are completely dominated. In reviewing research on differences in open and traditional classrooms, no remarkable increase in creative skills for children taught in open classroom settings is found. Although popular philosophy seems to expect that a lack of traditional structure might encourage greater flexibility of thinking, apparently it is not the classroom structure as much as the nature of the student–teacher interaction that is important. In a study of 13 urban Head Start classes (Huston–Stein, Friedrich–Cofer, and Susman, 1977), it was found that high levels of adult direction produced conformity when adults were present. In less structured classes, they found more pro-social behavior and more imaginative play, which they felt is a necessity for promoting the overall cognitive and emotional development of young children. A creativity enrichment program in the informal setting of a summer camp in Israel (Goor and Rapoport, 1977) measurably enhanced the creativity of young adolescents; four months later the improvement was still evident. Schools do not have to restrict the creative thinking of children; instead, the development of creative thinking can be a part of the goals of an educational program.

The Measurement of Creativity

Probably at one time or another every person has made a judgment about who is a creative individual. Almost any teacher can tell you who the creative person is in the class, but sometimes it may be difficult to distinguish whether the youngster who was identified as creative in one class would also be identified as the creative child in another. We may get some of the terms confused, particularly since creativity is usually seen in a positive light and therefore is sometimes associated with responsiveness, or just looking awake. The youngster who is bored, gazes out the window, is unruly, or just talks too much may be thought of as creative if the teacher in charge sees creativity in a negative light. At any rate, almost any teacher does measure creativity but usually by personal standards.

Relying on the advice of some 87 teachers and counselors, Torrance (1967) lists some specific kinds of behavior that he thinks are indicators of creative talent. He feels that such a student can occupy time without being stimulated, go beyond assigned tasks, ask questions beyond the single why or how, come up with different ways of doing things, is not afraid of trying something new, and enjoys drawing designs and pictures even while the teacher is giving a lecture or directions. Also, the creative youngster is observant, does not mind the consequences of appearing to be different, and enjoys experimenting with familiar objects rather than just letting things be.

If it is possible to think of some actions of children as being creative, and if we can describe them so that everyone understands what these actions are, then it would be logical that these attributes could be tested. This has been done, and there are several tests for creativity that have been used for a number of years. One of the reasons these tests have been developed is to encourage the creative individual to get the training and background needed to contribute to society. Sometimes the motivation is a little more shortsighted than this, because some companies want to know who among their personnel are creative people, so that these people can be freed of routine tasks and can utilize their creativity for the company's benefit. Also, if one wonders if creativity can be increased, it is nice to have some sort of measure available to check any increase; and for this, some sort of creativity test would be necessary.

One of the most commonly agreed upon components of creative thinking is the ability to produce a large number of ideas. This is usually referred to as a "fluency factor." A simple way to test for this is to ask "How many uses can you think of for a brick?" Some responses might be: use it as a paperweight on a desk, use it to hold down the lid of a garbage can, warm it and use it as a bedwarmer, use it to hold down newspapers in the wind. The more ideas one can put down on paper, apparently the more fluent one is, which may relate to one part of creative thinking.

Another factor usually considered is the ability to shift easily from one type of thinking to another or to be flexible in one's thinking patterns. If we look at the list given for the uses of a brick, it seems that three of the four suggested uses utilized the weight of the brick only. Possibly the person responding was just stuck in a rut. An additional factor often considered part of creative thinking is the ability to come up with unusual or remote ideas, which is often referred to as an originality factor. Looking back at our brick example, it seems like an unusual response to warm a brick and use it for taking the chill off sheets, but this might be a good use. If we had a lot of people responding to our question on uses for a brick, it would be fairly easy to find the unusual or infrequent responses and to select the person who seems to have greatest originality. A number of other factors are often looked for in a testing situation: one is seeing relationships where others might miss them, another is being able to elaborate on or embroider an idea, and a third is being sensitive to problems or seeing ways of improving or changing a situation or an object.

THE DEVELOPMENT OF CREATIVITY

FIGURE 35.

Creativity is reflected in what and how people draw. This creativity test, called a circles
test, can be scored for fluency, flexibility, and originality or elaboration.

Creativity tests do not have to be verbal. In fact, there is an advantage in having both verbal and nonverbal tests, and there is some information that there is a clear distinction between these attributes (Richardson, 1985). A nonverbal or figural test for fluency asks someone to see how many objects can be made using a circle. The test is a sheet of paper with a whole lot of circles on it; this is scored for fluency by the number of circles used, for flexibility by seeing how many different ways these circles have been utilized, and for originality by seeing who used the circles in the most original manner. Probably the most prolific designer of such tests has been Guilford (Guilford, 1968). Many of the tests for creativity have stemmed from research that was done with college and professional people. Others have contributed a great deal to the literature on measurement (Barron, 1963; Mednick, 1973; Torrance, 1962). In fact, the list of instruments useful in studying creative behavior is lengthy, including such diverse methods as self-description, personal opinions, making up problems, playing with toys, or drawing completion (Davis, 1971; Kaltsounis, 1971; Kaltsounis, 1972).

There has been some criticism about the use of creativity tests in the classroom. Some of it stems from a doubt that a child can be creative in a school environment using tools that are usually considered school tools. Another more serious consideration is whether we want to give a child another score to carry around. Schools may feel it wise to locate the most creative children and give them special treatment. There would be some advantages in finding out who the least creative child in a class is, so that we could devise methods to encourage this child to explore the environment, to think more flexibly, and to be more fluent. We will discuss methods that might be helpful shortly.

Other criteria of the creative behavior of children are less tangible and therefore a little more difficult to measure. One of these can be thought of as the openness of the individual toward the unknown or the new. This is more than just being curious, since it connotes a whole way of looking at the world, of being receptive to things outside the self, of being acutely aware of things and sensitive to change. Another area that is difficult to measure is that of psychological health; Maslow (1962) has termed this self-actualization. A self-actualized individual is secure, cares little about mundane things, is basically motivated, and feels confidently capable.

Some schools have attempted to include creativity as an area to be assessed along with intelligence, motor skills, sight, and hearing. A few colleges have tried using such tests as part of entrance requirements, particularly for people in the arts. But there are many problems. Hattie (1977) mentions some of them: that creativity is not unidimensional; age differences are important; scoring procedures differ; and effects of stress or other conditions have not been standardized. It seems that there is a long way to go before creativity testing is part of standard procedures.

It is just as well that testing for creativity is a complex matter. Otherwise, every report card would probably have a space to mark in a grade for "creativity," and each grade school teacher might be responsible for teaching this area along with reading, writing, and developing mathematical skills. Can you imagine a class with one youngster who could not go to recess until he has thought of twelve uses for a coat hanger? Or a class memorizing an assembled list of six fundamental principles in the creative process? Or a youngster failing an examination because she could not think of a word that relates *slugger* to *belfry* and *ball*? At the same time, this lack of ease in measurement may be one reason creativity has not been considered an essential part of the curriculum. But things are changing, and it is comforting to know that creativity is being considered as a necessary part of the development of thinking.

FIGURE 36.
Painting is in itself a creative learning process, in which each youngster develops unique methods of organization, elaborates on his own theme, and derives satisfaction in the process.

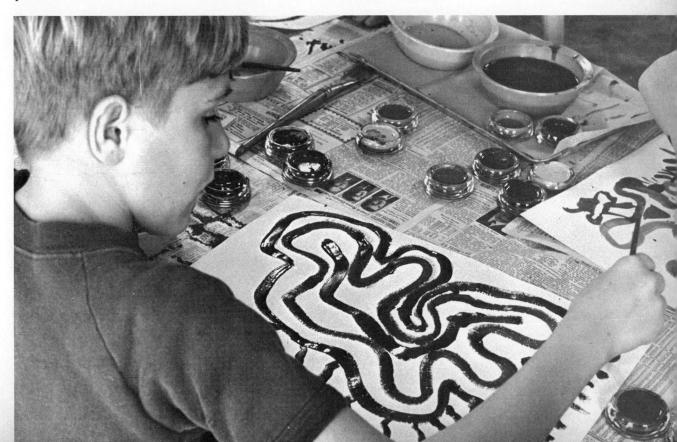

Methods of Developing
Creative Potential

There have been many attempts recently to develop programs designed to increase creative potential. There is evidence that these programs do increase the creative responses of individuals if they are tested on material similar to that on which they have been practicing. However, there seems to be less evidence that this increase lasts over a long period of time. Since most of these programs are a conscious effort at changing one's thinking patterns, it follows that one needs to be supported in this thinking. Sometimes in a school setting these kinds of supports might be rather hard to find.

There are some programs, designed primarily for the elementary school, that are supposed to increase the creative abilities of children. Although some of the theories behind these programs are similar to those for adult programs, the procedures are quite different. One rather elaborate program (Williams, 1972) consists of several books, tape cassettes, and posters for teachers to utilize. The program is divided into three groups, the first being designed for the college instructor who is preparing future teachers. The second group of materials is designed to be used by people in the training program, and the third group of materials is designed for use in the classroom with children. The program assumes that many innovative procedures have remained untried because teachers just do not understand how to use them. Certainly this criticism could not be leveled here. A broad approach to creativity is emphasized, with children carrying out many activities in many areas. Suggestions are offered for ways to plan a lesson that emphasizes eight traits: fluency in thinking, flexibility, originality, elaborative thinking, risk taking, complexity, curiosity, and imagination. Although the arts are utilized in this program, its objectives are to increase the creativity of individuals in the whole learning process. Obviously, with such a step-by-step procedure, not very much is left to the teacher's imagination.

Another program designed primarily for the upper elementary school leaves the teacher out entirely. This is a programmed learning series of fifteen lessons in cartoon form. The authors (Covington et al., 1972) have bypassed the teacher and designed comic books for children to read at their own pace. The youngsters follow the cartoon characters, Jim and Lila and their Uncle John, a high school teacher and detective, through a number of problem-solving processes in which the student is supposed to analyze the given information and to come up with possible solutions to some rather interesting little stories. As is customary, the publishers are very enthusiastic about selling these materials; at least this is one way of making creativity come to the attention of classroom teachers. However, there is little evidence that a packaged program can merely be inserted into the curriculum to make the children more creative, productive, original thinkers.

It might be helpful to examine a few programs that were designed for adults, with the idea that some of the suggested methods might be adapted for use with a secondary school population. These programs vary considerably, from those that operate with a group of people for reenforcement of ideas and support for members to programs designed to improve an individual's own creative power.

Probably the best known creativity workshop operates on a group basis with what is called a brainstorming method. Parnes (1967) lists several principles underlying his particular method. One principle is the development of many ideas and solutions to a given problem. This means thinking up a large number of possible alternatives with the rationale that the more solutions suggested, the greater the chances that one might be original. Parnes' second principle is deferred judgment; this suggests that, when one is working on a particular problem, judgment is withheld so that many ideas are generated without any immediate attempt at evaluation or at finding a quick solution to the problem. His third underlying principle is the formation of remote associations. Some things habitually go together, such as salt and pepper, snow and ice, and so forth. To help break down these patterns, unusual combinations of words are used to force workshop members to think of new verbal relationships; such words might be wind and book, water and dust, or tree and gas tank. In the evaluation process, judgment is also deferred until all of the criteria are established and a final solution can be arrived at.

Another approach to the development of creative thinking is called synectics (Gordon, 1961; Prince, 1970). This approach, differing considerably from the preceding one, emphasizes the use of metaphor or analogy. Speculation is encouraged and the emotional component is considered more important than the intellectual, with far-out, irrational thoughts encouraged and care taken in the group interaction that no thoughts are squelched or left unexamined. The synectics approach has been used primarily in solving some of the problems in industry, with some success. The role of the leader is important, since careful probing and constant encouragement seem crucial for uninhibited thinking. Apparently, both the synectics method and the brainstorming method produce

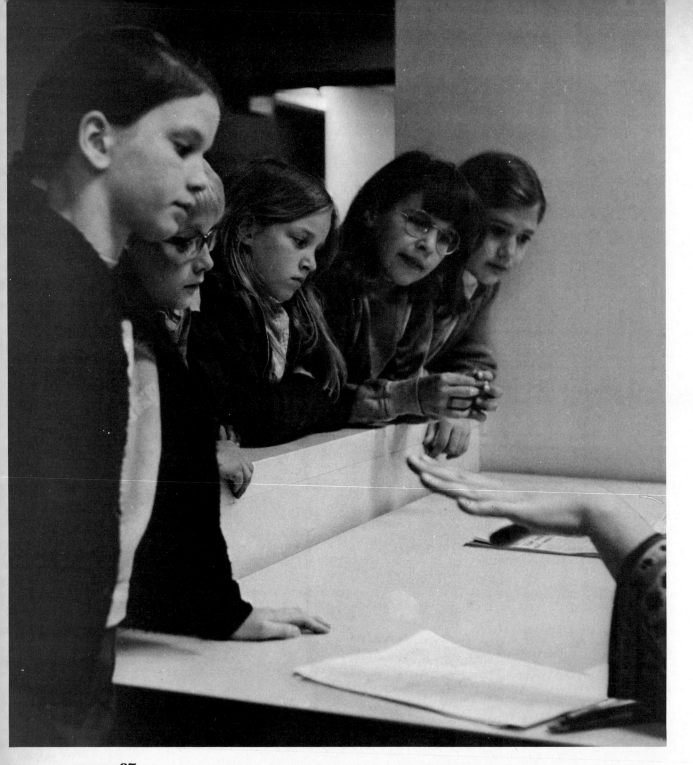

FIGURE 37.
These children are concentrating on the gestures of an adult and closely following the pantomime, which may be variously interpreted, depending upon the subtlety of motions and creativity of the beholder. Many common activities that take place daily can be the starting point for increasing children's creative thinking.

more original and creative ideas than if a group works without any specific technique (Necka, 1984).

Still another approach has been an individual one, with an emphasis on particular exercises and games (Kirst and Dickmeyer, 1973). The plan calls for spending a half hour each day doing a variety of interesting experiments and filling in exercises that, it is assumed, will develop flexibility, originality, inventiveness, and adaptability. An emphasis is put on fun and loosening up the thinking process.

There are other approaches to developing creative thinking, some of which are clearly designed to make money off the unsuspecting noncreative individual who has dreams of becoming an artist or plastic surgeon. But it would be entirely possible to develop a program for oneself or for a class utilizing some of the basic underlying principles. Each age has unique characteristics, and starting a conscious program to develop creative thinking could be a lot of fun and very rewarding. Obviously the leader, or teacher, is an extremely important part of the whole procedure. Important aspects of developing children's creative

FIGURE 38.
An imaginative child made this fierce creature from clay as a special fantasy pet to scare away intruders at night.

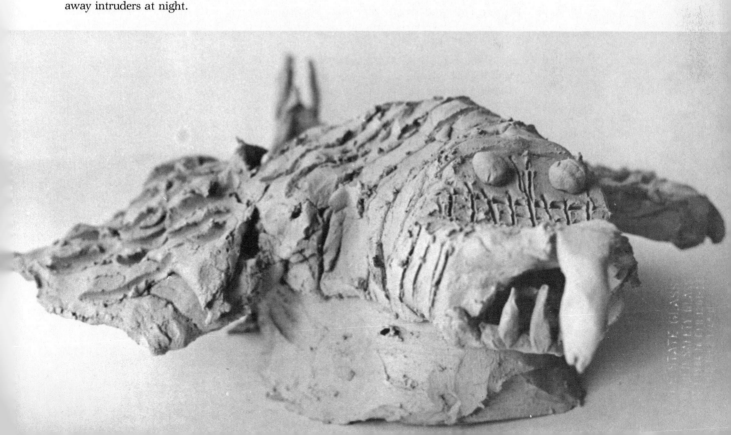

thinking are encouraging each member to participate, withholding judgment, stimulating and rewarding unusual thinking, and promoting the seeing of relationships between ideas as they grow into one another. Making pictures out of unusual words, in which the picture and the word must say the same thing, pasting together unusual captions on illustrations, putting together parts of animals to make the best animal in the world, or making a machine that does not do anything—such projects can develop a thinking process in which the unusual or original becomes acceptable. What would the world look like if you were a frog, or as big as an ant, or a tree in a windstorm? Suppose the world were turned inside out, or plants started to walk around, or you were really a red crayon. The list of interesting possibilities is endless, and students are usually eager to engage in fantasy, speculate on problems, and develop new ways of looking at the world.

One feature that pervades all of the commercial programs attempting to develop creative thinking is that the process is external; that is, problems are devised for adults to solve, children are seduced into learning through cartoon characters, exercises are figured out by someone else to be completed, and so forth. In art, however, the process is intrinsic; that is, the problem is not from outside, but originates within the youngster. Finding methods in three-dimensional materials to express an emotion, thinking of ways to make something look smooth and syrupy, finding a system of having something recede into the distance, or even struggling to make initial images are all problems that originate within the youngster. This is not to suggest that these programs have no value. Making creativity an essential part of the curriculum is important, and every teacher would probably be more successful if arithmetic, social studies, or writing could be seen as a creative activity.

It is even possible to improve one's own creativity on a self-instruction basis. At least one study (Huber, et al., 1979), using programmed instructional materials with fourth, fifth, and sixth grade students, found that verbal creativity scores improved as compared with a group that followed a regular school program. An experimental six-week program (Lowery, 1982) to develop creativity in elementary school children with IQs of at least 120 determined that verbal creativity is more easily developed than figural creativity in gifted children. A two-week creativity training study of 309 elementary school children was conducted by Furze, Tyler, and McReynolds (1984). Half of an obscure figures test was administered as a pretest, and the balance was used as a posttest. The scores of children who had received creativity training improved significantly, whereas the scores of children in the control group decreased. It apparently is possible to improve creative responses by merely telling children to be creative, something that may not be asked of students very often. Children at both the elementary and secondary level scored higher on an unusual uses test when it was labeled a creativity exercise than they did when the same test was labeled a word exercise (Speller and Schumacher, 1975). Evans and Forbach (1983) report that the quality of male college students' responses to a battery of creativity tests improved when the instructions to "be creative" included guidelines: an explanation that answers should be both unusual and worthwhile. Perhaps instilling a positive attitude results in a creative mode of thinking.

It is important to develop creativity at a young age. It may be that the attitude of being creative—finding the unknown challenging, coming up with many thoughts and ideas, looking for differences and similarities, having unique and original thoughts—is established early in life. At least it appears that these attitudes, once established, tend to be continuing. Some creativity measures were given to 75 four and five year old children; these same children were evaluated six and seven years later when the children were in sixth grade (Harrington, Block, and Block, 1983). There was a highly significant relationship between these early and late ratings, which might indicate that curiosity, self-confidence, and interest in new experiences are enduring traits. One research investigation (Kogan and Pankove, 1972) looked at the creativity of tenth grade students.

FIGURE 39.
An interested adult encourages inquiring minds by helping these nursery school children plant seeds. Curiosity is natural and should be supported at an early age.

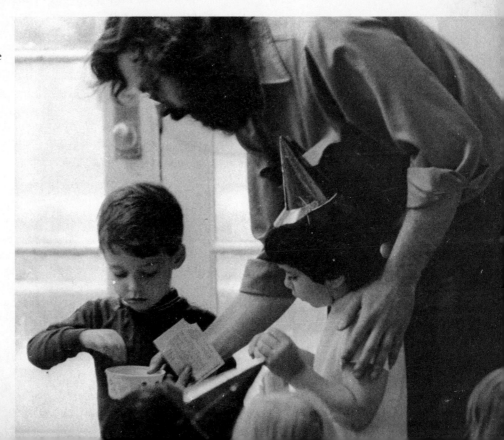

FIGURE 40.
The role of the teacher is not passive. Encouraging children's thinking, and not expecting a predetermined answer or solution, gives children the greatest opportunity to develop their creativity.

These tenth graders had been tested on some of the same measures five years earlier when they were in fifth grade. Although there was some variability in the individual scores, the report states that there was great stability in the level of productivity and uniqueness. Another study (Torrance, 1972) attempted to discover whether young people, identified as creative during their high school years, become productive, creative adults. Some 392 high school students had taken a battery of creativity tests; twelve years after graduation they were again contacted and asked what they were doing and where they had been. Their achievements were analyzed by judges on a ten-point scale. The young people who were identified as creative during their high school years had become productive, creative adults. In addition, Torrance found that these creative high school students tended to develop careers that involved detours for relevant reasons. Most of them included study or work in a foreign country; many chose unusual occupations compared to those who had scored low on the creative scale. If these studies are an indication, it will be interesting to see how those children who are identified today as creative will contribute to our society in another fifty years or so.

Another essential consideration is to provide a model for the youngster to emulate. By model, of course, we are referring to the teacher. Unfortunately, Torrance (1983) noted that only 9 percent of the young adults in his longitudinal study indicated that a teacher or school counselor had been a mentor. Although it is well accepted that art teachers value independence in thinking more than teachers in other fields (Davis and Torrance, 1965), there is pressure for teachers to conform to the school standards of behavior. Youngsters need an opportunity to see teachers who admit that they do not know, who are willing to accept the thoughts of others, who can enjoy life and like having others enjoy theirs, who have many ideas and the flexibility to allow children to have their own, and who accept every youngster as worthy. Such attributes make the art teacher an important person in the classroom, completely aside from teaching art.

Art and Creativity

As much as we might like to think of art and creativity as being the same, it seems that this connection cannot be left to chance. Sometimes the way art is taught may negate creativity, or possibly teaching for creativity might negate art. However, experiments have been done, focusing upon methods of teaching art, which may help insure that both creativity and art are fostered. Some art programs are designed to give students a great variety of experiences with many

materials, whereas others prefer to have students concentrate on a few materials that are explored more fully. Those who favor the "breadth" approach feel that the variety of materials accommodate the different interests of students and keep their attention; the "depth" approach advocates feel that concentration on a few materials leads to sequential learning.

A study of this problem of breadth versus depth was carried out with ninth graders over a period of a year (Beittel, Mattil et al., 1961). Three classes were given a battery of pretests; then for a year one class was taught art with only a breadth approach, one class was taught art with a depth approach, and one class was taught with what was their usual manner. Paintings were collected throughout the year and judged. Another battery of posttests was given to the ninth graders at the end of the year. The results favored the depth approach class, in both aesthetic sensitivity and spontaneity. The breadth approach is popularly supposed to encourage a spontaneous approach to art, but it actually lost ground. The control class was judged the poorest group of all. The report concludes that, in spite of some restless demand for variety from students, it seems wiser to begin early with a depth-oriented program.

A similar study was done with college students (Davis, 1969). Here a test on eight factors of creative thinking and some measures of art attitude and aesthetic quality were used before and after a semester of either a breadth or depth curriculum. The results were somewhat inconclusive, but the greatest amount of growth was in nonverbal originality in the depth group, with some other advantages comparable for both groups.

FIGURE 41.
In order to create with clay, a child needs a depth of experience during which he can develop a sensitivity to the material.

And a third study on this topic (MacGregor, 1967), using four classes in a high school, found advantages for the depth approach. One class was restricted in both subject matter and media, one was restricted in neither, and the other two classes were restricted in either subject matter or materials. Again, with judges and tests, the results showed the greatest gains in the group that was most restricted.

Although the depth approach to teaching art has support, the vast majority of programs, particularly in the elementary school, are basically breadth programs, with one project following another, week by week. Brittain (1969) even found the same pattern common at the nursery school level: clay work, followed by pasting, followed by string painting, and so on. The rationale usually given for such an approach is that students need to know how to use materials before they can create with them. The danger is that students may begin to feel that art is nothing more than a series of little projects or experimentations with materials, bearing little relationship to expression or creativity. Kern (1978) makes an appeal for shifting the emphasis in school art away from the cafeteria approach. He feels learning in the arts involves the mastery of complex skills. "None can be learned in an hour, a day, or a week and real mastery requires a lifetime."

The concern for externals, for the product, may be a factor if a teacher feels insecure in art. There are numerous articles and books showing step-by-step methods for doing innumerable projects. Certain teachers have an empty feeling, not knowing what to do for art this week. Other teachers are motivated by generosity, feeling that children must not be deprived of any opportunities to experience art materials—with the thought that "more must be better." The goal of art should not be the development of the teacher's creativity, but the youngsters'. Fluency of ideas, flexibility of approaches, originality of responses, and seeing new relationships are apparently not nurtured by a smorgasbord of art projects.

Sometimes the art product—the painting, sculpture, or whatever—is regarded as an isolated work of art to be examined, admired, or evaluated on its own merits. The artist is somehow forgotten except to receive the reflected glory or scorn. The creator's comments and thoughts, and even an explanation of the process that produced the product, are rarely sought. Is a creative painting produced by a creative artist? In our concern for the creative process and the emphasis on developing creative thinking, are we able to say that the art products produced by creative people will be judged better or more original? As part of a larger study (Csikszentmihalyi and Getzels, 1971), 31 college art students were observed during the process of producing a still life. The finished products were

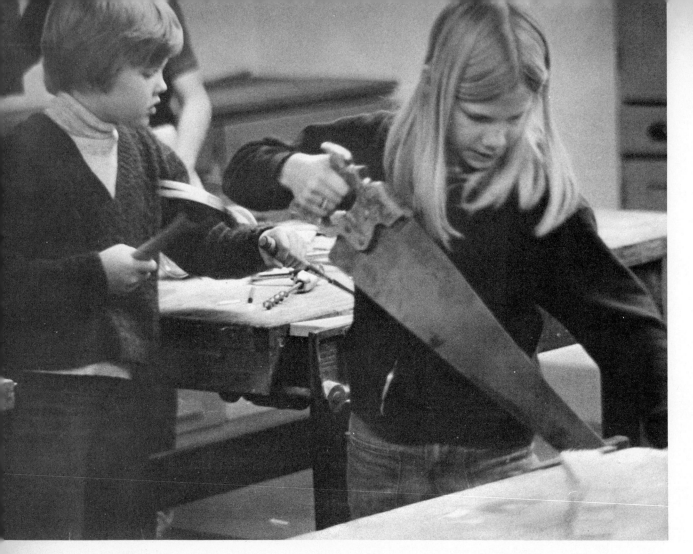

FIGURE 42.
Perseverance and determination seem important in carrying out plans in the wood shop.
Children learn much about the nature and special qualities of wood during the process
of creating three-dimensional forms.

judged by experts, and there was a close relationship between originality of
products and discovery-oriented behavior of the artist. But there was not the
same relationship of originality to craftsmanship.

In another study of art students in training (Barron, 1972), students were
interviewed, given a number of psychological tests, and their art work was ex-

THE DEVELOPMENT OF CREATIVITY

amined. The data indicated that art students as a group were higher in flexibility and were less well socialized, more impulsive, and more unconventional than the general population. Michael (1970) sent questionnaires to 350 recognized artists in several fields of art: painters, sculptors, weavers, jewelers, potters, and so forth. In analyzing their replies, Michael found that over 90 percent of the respondents felt that they are concerned with society and what goes on in the world, that the process by which they create is flexible and ideas are developed while working, that the product grows by constantly shifting and relating various elements, and that they do not try to identify with any particular art movement or approach.

It seems that to be a creative artist one must be a creative person. The students at art school and the professional artists have a behavioral approach to living that can only be termed creative. But all artists are not necessarily creative people. There are a lot of jobs that are certainly art-related that call for merely technical skill. And there are a lot of other fields of creative endeavor in the sciences, medicine, mathematics, and so forth that require creative thinking. Art experiences may be just as important for students going into these areas as into the arts.

FIGURE 43.
This drawing of playing tennis in the schoolyard illustrates a girl's creative solution to the problem of showing that the school surrounds the tennis court.

Summary

Art and creativity have always been closely entwined. For years the art program in the public schools has been the bastion of creativity, and often art experiences and creative activity have meant the same thing. However, with the great number of research studies in the area of creativity, it is becoming quite clear that it is possible to have an art program in the schools that is not automatically creative. Creativity is becoming of vital concern to many people. Stipp (1986) reported on a nationwide program to promote creative thinking in children from kindergarten to ninth grade. This program has generated much excitement; approximately 75,000 children are thought to have participated in a search for ideas for new inventions. We need to understand the process involved in developing the creative thinking abilities of children. There is no doubt that this area will be of concern in the future as society turns toward the unknown, and schools will of necessity have to teach not only what is known but also teach *toward* what we do not know. Art can play an important part in this field. In fact, it has been suggested (Gowan, 1981) that the arts are far more important than previously realized because they promote creative thinking, and the Carnegie Foundation for the Advancement of Teaching (Boyer, 1983) has emphasized that the arts are an essential part of the human experience and recommended that all students study the arts.

Creativity, and how best to promote it, is of interest to increasing numbers of people. Society values what Morris (1969, p. 37) has called ". . . man's insatiable curiosity, his inventiveness, his intellectual athleticism." According to Stenhouse (1967, p. 10), ". . . it is pre-eminently the task of education so to induct people into culture that their personal freedom and creativity are preserved and indeed enhanced."

Related Activities

1. Observe a nursery school child and a senior high school student in their drawing activity. Do their approaches to art indicate any differences in their apparent levels of creativity? Is one age more creative than the other?

THE DEVELOPMENT OF CREATIVITY

2. Observe several junior high school non-art classes. Notice differences in the ways the teachers accept creative behavior, such as when a student asks probing questions, wants to become involved in related or tangential activities, comes up with different ways of doing things, enjoys experimenting, is not satisfied with easy answers, and questions the text.

3. Observe an elementary school class. How much pressure for conformity is there, such as rote memorization and all children doing the same things at the same time, even trips to the drinking fountain? In rooms with pressure for conformity, are there also duplicated sheets for the children to color, or drawings that all appear very similar?

4. List some suggestions for encouraging creative thinking in a second grade class. Be specific in telling how this could be accomplished in reading, arithmetic, and art.

5. Have a college class select from their members the most creative individuals. Is there general agreement on who these creative persons are? What were the criteria on which selections were made?

6. Observe an elementary class for several sessions and list the number of opportunities for developing divergent thinking. Compare this with the number of times thinking is directed toward one "right" answer.

4

The Development of Aesthetic Awareness

The Meaning of Aesthetics

Aesthetic development cannot be separated from creative development. Both are bound up with the whole process of growing and are influenced by all of the variables from our environment that make us different personalities. In a broad sense, aesthetic education deals with a vast spectrum of experiences in art, including the production of art forms. Some definitions include the observation and understanding not only of art but also of nature, or at least those parts of nature that can be called beautiful. However, in a narrower sense, aesthetics refers only to the perception and appreciation of art. The development of aesthetic awareness is usually seen in a harmonious organization of parts, and this organization changes with age in the same way that other changes can be seen in growth. Aesthetics has little to do with sentimentality on the one hand or the accumulation of factual knowledge on the other. The gushy comment—"I just love modern art, don't you?"—probably shows as little aesthetic awareness as does the shrewd appraisal of the work of art from the point of view of its value on the market today. Aesthetics is an active perceptual process; it is the interaction between an individual and an object that provides a stimulating, harmonious experience.

Aesthetics may be thought of as the nonfactual, nonobjective reactions of a person to the environment. As such, aesthetics may be an attempt to discover the nature of self. Matters of belief and values take precedence over knowledge. The development of aesthetic awareness is a basic part of art education. Growth is on an ever-changing continuum, and this is very true in the area of aesthetics. The organization of our thinking abilities, the development of our perceptual abilities, and the close relationship to our emotional capabilities can be considered aesthetic growth. There is no formula for aesthetic growth. Aesthetic education does not take place simply by a teacher's criticism or guidance when an individual makes his art product. It is a much larger task and may bear little relationship to making a student aware of the principles or rules for organizing a work of art. Such matters are often regarded as part of the understanding that students should develop in relation to their own works of art and to the art work of others. However, there is no set of rules that can be readily applied to individuals, and aesthetic growth does not happen merely by applying external rules. Developing aesthetic awareness means educating sensitivity toward perceptual, intellectual, and emotional experiences so that these are deepened and integrated into a harmoniously organized whole.

THE DEVELOPMENT OF AESTHETIC AWARENESS

Any creative activity originates in a person utilizing a multitude of cognitive and sensory perceptions. In the process of creating a picture, for example, an artist paints from conscious awareness and unconscious or preconscious motivations, selecting the forms and colors that will make up the final painting. In the process, however, the artist may pause and say, "That is not right." Here the interaction between the painting and the artist takes on new meaning; the organization has been judged and found unsatisfactory. Therefore, it is easy to see that creative expression and aesthetic awareness are closely entwined.

It is possible to become overzealous about the importance of developing aesthetic awareness and a vocabulary of aesthetics. We must remember that this is something that cannot be imposed from without. Aesthetic education must not become indoctrination. The need for developing an understanding and an appreciation of those things around us must come from the individual. There is no evidence that aesthetics can be easily measured or that absorbing the vocabulary of aesthetics will refine one's tastes, make one a better person, or even help in the selection of a necktie. To quote Herbert Read (1966), "We have to live art if we would be affected by art. We have to paint rather than look at paintings, to play instruments rather than go to concerts, to dance and sing and act ourselves, engaging all our senses in the ritual and discipline of arts."

Art Appreciation

Closely related to our discussion is the role that art appreciation plays in the development of aesthetic awareness. Somehow the question of taste enters into the discussion, and it may be that taste is something that can be learned. As students develop the ability to make selections, based upon some criteria that have been established by art authorities, we assume that they are developing good taste; high school students are able, with enough encouragement, to be selective if they are properly rewarded. This may have very little to do with aesthetic awareness. Obviously, we all have different tastes, but there should be no justification for arranging these on a scale from good to bad. Good taste could probably be defined as what the art critic would select, so the uneducated individual would undoubtedly be thought to have little or no taste. But, of course, this is also tied up with culture, and it is quite obvious that we are not treasuring the same qualities in objects that our grandparents did. Each era has its own peculiarities, and these cultural differences play havoc with establishing rules for good taste. "A thing of beauty is a joy forever" is a saying rarely heard today in our rapidly changing culture.

FIGURE 45.

"Migration," by Rauschenberg. The artist in today's society has turned away from tradition. Although the artist is making a serious statement, many members of our society look upon such paintings as worthless. (Collection, Herbert F. Johnson Museum of Art, Cornell University.)

More important than these considerations is the fact that youngsters do not react to the environment in the way that adults do. Children's drawings differ considerably from one age to the next, and there is good reason to believe that the objects they appreciate also vary. A ten year old boy will have developed a natural appreciation for stones, frogs, rusty bolts, and other strange assortments of objects that probably mean a lot more to him than the painting that hangs in a museum.

Discussions of art appreciation are often concerned with the principles of design. These are not always given the same names, but they are essentially concerned with the surface pattern of a picture; such words as *harmony, balance, rhythm, unity, center of interest*, and so forth are often mentioned. There is often the notion that learning these particular words bears some relationship to developing an awareness of the good and bad qualities to look for in paintings and that therefore an appreciation of art will result.

Eisner (1966) gave a 60-item test dealing with information about art terms, art media, artists, and art history to secondary school students in several states and to some elementary education college students. He found that although there was some gain in knowledge with grade level, only about half the items were answered correctly in secondary school, with girls scoring somewhat better than boys. Eisner lamented the fact that 38 percent of his students thought that Picasso and Matisse worked in the seventeenth or eighteenth century; about a third knew what value or hue meant. Undoubtedly there is a need to understand terms if one is going to use them, and an exposure to art should increase a knowledge of such terms, but it would be a big mistake to confuse the learning of these terms with an appreciation of art.

Sometimes the history of art is considered an avenue to developing the aesthetic tastes. But art history cannot be taught by merely presenting a collection of facts. As Streb (1984) has pointed out, a student won't fully appreciate or understand the work of Praxiteles by knowing the kind of stone he used. There is no genuine history of art; rather, there are historians who have selected art objects from those that have remained from a society and collected these together in such a way that others look upon these examples as typical of a period in history. Which of these examples are shown depends to a great extent upon the art historian. Similarly, the history of the American Revolution can be seen quite differently by an historian who is writing a textbook for the American public schools than by an historian whose purpose is to show the influence of British naval power upon the development of Europe. Hieronymus Bosch is much more popular today than he was sixty years ago, and Rothko is no longer considered crude and inscrutable. And it is certainly the art historian who has rescued Van Gogh from obscurity. The anthropologist Harris points out: "In Western civilization a particular performance is deemed artistic or not by a distinct group of authorities who make or judge art and who control the museums, conservatories, critical journals, and other organizations and institutions devoted to art as a livelihood and style of life" (1980, p. 456). To some extent a study of the history of art can provide the opportunity to follow the development of art styles as seen by an authority, but it does not necessarily provide us with an appreciation of these styles, nor does it automatically develop an aesthetic awareness of objects outside the realm of art history.

Some art educators would no doubt argue that the art appreciation of individuals needs to be cultivated and taught by those who are somehow wise and educated. It is as if schools feel that we cannot trust the individual to come up with "right" answers. This goes against the basic assumption of democracy that every person, unless previously intimidated, is usually a strong defender of his own views and tastes. These views need to be expressed; the appreciation of art thrives on discussion and is not subject to the usual test of factual knowledge regarding style, period of history, or artist.

Culture and Aesthetic Awareness

It might be interesting to contemplate what a future archaeologist would think about our society if it were uncovered a thousand years from now. Art has been thought a good indicator of the values and attitudes of the society in which it was made. Today we cherish the remnants of past societies' art forms, and from these we draw conclusions about the particular society in which these forms were found. The Greek temple is very different from the Gothic cathedral, yet each of these forms expresses and represents its own culture.

Certainly the Gothic cathedral style would be uncovered a thousand years hence, housing our churches and some of our institutions of higher learning. These Gothic structures would, of course, be false façades, made of steel and covered over to look like Gothic cathedrals. There would be Greek temples, too, though somewhat altered, housing what might be government operations. Once again, however, these buildings would not be honest representations but rather duplicates from a past culture that considered these buildings an important part of their society. It may be somewhat symbolic to see governmental functions housed in buildings that are more representative of a bygone age.

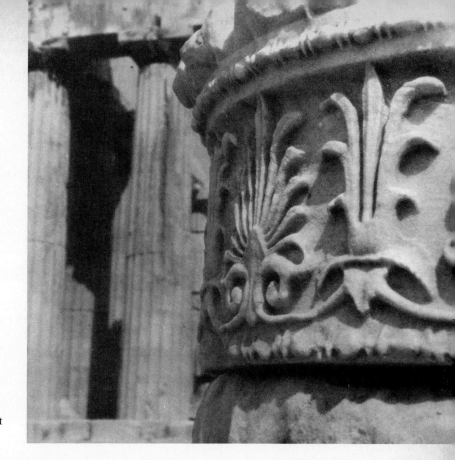

FIGURE 46.
A culture's values are reflected in the architecture of the period. The Parthenon's influence on subsequent periods is still felt today.

The archaeologist a thousand years from now would certainly be confused by finding homes that also had false façades. Some of them would be built in a style that was popular in the eighteenth century but for some reason were duplicated like stereotyped patterns for twentieth-century people, complete with big chimneys and small panes of glass. No, not big chimneys, but plywood cubes stuck on these houses to simulate chimneys, and not small panes, but plastic inserts that could be removed easily when the windows were to be washed. Inside, the homes would be even more confusing. The dining room might look surprisingly like a seventeenth century French room, with a chandelier and a table with built-in worm holes. But the chandelier would really be made for electricity and the furniture would have been mass-produced. The styles of the living room and the bedroom, too, would be from an earlier era, with even a television set hidden in a simulated wood colonial style cover. The kitchen and bathroom would have the most modern of appliances, although sometimes hidden under an "old" cooktop, or pseudo-Roman sculptured faucet handles. A computer would be displayed in naked modern plastic beside the digital clock masquerading as a Grandfather's clock.

FIGURE 47.
Fake half-timbers, fake shutters, fake chimney with stork, and fake thatched roof make a mockery of our architectural heritage. Styles from other ages and other places may be imitated and elaborated upon, without an understanding of the reasons why the structures were built as they were.

Undoubtedly our archaeologist would think that there was something wrong with a society where an individual could walk from one century to another by merely going from one room to the next. Apparently, the occupants of these homes had an unaware acceptance of these stereotyped patterns as symbols of a security that was not present in the culture itself. However, science was evidently an important element, since the range, refrigerator, and dishwasher were of the latest design. The occupants of these homes would seem to have been schizophrenic, escaping into a world of meaningless resurrected patterns.

There would be some contemporary buildings in existence, and the most forward-thinking architects would have been utilized for building airports, sports arenas, and factories. If these were representative of the civilization, the archaeologist would conclude that this strange culture had no confidence in its

108   **THE DEVELOPMENT OF AESTHETIC AWARENESS**

institutions, but a stronger belief in transportation, physical competition, and industrial power. Evidently, the individual was inclined to hide from the society and felt more comfortable in taking refuge in past periods. Even in the smaller examples of the art forms, the vase and bottle, the same discrepancy was seen. The most attractive plastic bottles were produced by industry and used for dispensing soap, shampoos, and lotions, whereas the vase selected by the homemaker was a piece of glass pseudo-styled as a sixteenth century hobnailed goblet in which flowers were displayed. Floor coverings, scientifically durable and easy to clean, simulated stone or wood, and the "solid" brick wall was made of plastic.

The archaeologist would probably be right in this opinion of our society. This is not just a question of aesthetics, because uncovering our art in museums would only support the idea that the artists of our time had turned their backs on the society in which they lived and were either poking fun at the society from which they had removed themselves or had become so self-centered and individualistic that they too had lost contact with their own society.

Changes in Aesthetic Taste

It is fairly obvious that standards of beauty are constantly changing. A car that is ten years old has no particular value, either for its aesthetic appeal or for its functional use. However, a thirty year old car takes on quite a different appeal and can suddenly be cherished. In the same way, the severity of architectural design that was popular a few years ago is becoming softened, and an interest in patterns and textural qualities is beginning to reappear. The taste and aesthetic standards of our time are undoubtedly influenced by many variables, and trying to put these into a context that can be explained to students in school presents a difficult problem.

It is revealing to look at the textbooks on art education that were published fifty years or more ago. Some of the problems seen at that time are still with us, but the examples of good art and the type of pictures that were supposed to interest children in grade school seem a little ridiculous to us today. However, art education was thought to be a means of elevating the thinking of every person, with the assumption that somehow an understanding of art would make people happier and better. As Nichols (1877, p. 153) put it, "Men are usually

FIGURE 48.

This candelabrum was admired a century ago. An art educator at the time remarked: "The flesh of the Indians, their costumes, the bark of the canoe are all truthfully rendered. One is also impressed by the classic character of this decoration." (Nichols, 1877, p. 160.)

selfish because they see so little. Teach them to observe, to compare, and they will discover the good and the beautiful rather than the bad and ugly; for there is nothing evil in itself, but only that which the mind conceives in its ignorance." In a *Manual of Drawing*, Thompson (1895) was quite certain how to produce the good and the beautiful. Beauty was considered as perfect form, with the principal sensuous elements being regularity, variety, and harmony. Thompson's examples of beauty seem a little strange in today's world. Wilson (1899) published a picture series for use in elementary schools that attempted to aid teachers in imparting to children a true appreciation and love for paintings by the world's great masters. In the preface to this series, James Hopkins, who was then director of drawing in the Boston Public Schools, said that picture study should be taken seriously: "The effort is not for amusement, entertainment, or decoration alone; it has an aim and a purpose larger, broader, and more dignified than any of these."

We can be amused at earlier attempts at developing aesthetic awareness in children by trying to establish methods for teaching the good, the true, and the beautiful; however, the uncomfortable thought creeps in that, maybe fifty or sixty years from now, our attempts to impress upon children the beauty of a Picasso, Chagall, or Klee will also be viewed as mildly amusing.

Changes constantly occur in the art field, and a sudden interest in assemblages gives way to an art that capitalizes on optical illusions. This may be followed by the enlarging or endless duplication of everyday items from the grocery store, which in turn is supplanted by other, newer interests, such as earth sculpture or a self-destroying art form, which is followed by kinetic art or light displays, in turn succeeded by multimedia shows, accidental art, soft sculpture, art deco, duplicator art, or computer-generated art, minimalist art or superrealism. This is not to say that these art forms are merely styles that change like the seasons, but rather that the teacher of art may be viewing art from the narrow perspective of personal background and training. The teacher's excitement about a new art form may not be shared by students, particularly when yet another direction in art is promoted by the popular magazines and the teacher's ideas suddenly become old-hat.

A development of self-awareness on the part of students, in fact, may be more important in the long run than the appreciation of any particular style of art. Honesty in design and excitement in art are important qualities, which can be felt only through the self. Art is a reflection of today's world that can provide a direction for the future; students need to be able to evaluate change and be curious about the unfamiliar. The prospect of teaching what is "good taste" in a society as confused as ours seems a little ridiculous.

FIGURE 49.

Educators seem to change in what they feel are appropriate pictures for young children to appreciate. "The Goose Girl," painted by Bouguereau, was typical of the pictures selected for study by children at the turn of the century. (Collection, Herbert F. Johnson Museum of Art, Cornell University.)

Aesthetics and Society's Values

Not too long ago the prospect of gracious living was an objective to strive for. Just what gracious living meant was apparently a stereotype in itself. Expensive accessories and pseudo-styled furniture were part of the scene; undoubtedly, shutters at the window and an antique knocker at the door were there too. Dinner would be by candlelight with soft music, with modern art looking down from the wall.

Young people today are certainly questioning this as an ideal, but a few educators still look upon the gracious-living model as the one they want to impose upon all children as a goal in life. This becomes particularly absurd when we realize that many parts of our society may have goals of their own, especially those persons who still retain some of their customs and traditions from Asia, Europe, Africa, or South America. Many children within our society come from environments that are both dreary and depressing, and the image of gracious living is unattainable and bears no relationship to their own existence.

Art was originally an integral part of society, and the aesthetic properties of an object were no more important than its function. The task of the artist was largely to decorate shrines, homes, and public buildings; to fashion utensils and ornaments; to record historic events; and the like (Dissanayake, 1980). However, a century ago aesthetic form began to be considered an element in art aside from its function. Quackenbos (1871) felt that the purpose of art was to excite the imagination with the novel, the wonderful, the picturesque, the sublime, and the beautiful. It becomes very apparent that we cannot teach aesthetic values unless we are aware of the individual's cultural environment. As a society we have inherited a good deal of our feelings about art from European traditions. Many art history books barely touch upon art outside that framework and then only as it influenced the European tradition. Yet art and aesthetics exist everywhere. The cultures of Africa, the societies of the Near East, the varied populations of the Far East, the Aboriginals in Australia, the native North and South Americans, have all developed aesthetic standards for art, value systems that are basically different from the one that is reflected in our teachings.

The society within which we live influences our tastes. And taste itself cannot be isolated from a lot of other variables that influence our thinking. Economics is an important part of our value system; the cost of items, the amount of money we have to pay for a variety of things, may help determine our likes

FIGURE 50.
This Australian Aboriginal wooden shield shows an aesthetic concern, completely apart from the formal teaching of design. The urge to decorate is universal.

and dislikes. So we may confuse cost with value. Children's aesthetic taste is not influenced by monetary value; for them plastic pop-it beads may be beautiful and better than a plain gold necklace. Diamonds are actually no prettier than glass; in fact, it may take a jeweler to tell the difference. But somehow the diamond is considered much better and is admired; if we find that it is merely glass that is the object of our admiration, we feel duped. It may not be the form but the cost of an item that makes it "beautiful."

Museums have proudly exhibited a painting by one of the old masters, only to discover later that the painting was actually a copy. *The Man with the Golden Helmet*, which ". . . modern critics have especially praised for the boldness of Rembrandt's technique . . ." (Rosenberg, 1980, p. 106), was one of the

THE DEVELOPMENT OF AESTHETIC AWARENESS

world's most celebrated paintings; however, experts have announced that the oil painting is in fact the work of an unknown artist (Scardino and Roberts, 1985). In such cases the paintings are quickly removed to the basement, and those who earlier praised the masterpiece feel cheated. Although the picture itself hasn't changed, it is now collecting dust, and another authentic masterpiece hangs in its place to be admired.

Taste may also be tied to fragility. Clothes that get dirty easily, or clothes that can't be used for work tasks, are saved for special occasions and are considered "beautiful." Dishes that are made of thin china, fancy white tablecloths, old chairs that can no longer support weight, or the high-heeled women's shoes that are uncomfortable and can't be run in, all of these things are frequently valued more highly than items of a more practical value.

Objects that take a good deal of time to make are also highly valued by adults in our society. Children, on the other hand, have no sense of the value of time, so an interesting stone is just as pretty to them as a delicately carved cameo. The early native American traded furs and even land for some of the trinkets and glass beads that the European exploiters used for barter. These beads were valuable to the native Americans because they could not be produced locally, but for the Europeans these things were of little value. It would seem then that what was held in high esteem, furs for the Europeans and glass beads for the American natives, were merely objects that were scarce in their respective societies. It may be that aesthetics and the monetary value we place upon objects are illustrations of the same principle.

Our perception of what is good or pretty is also related to what connotes leisure. These things tend to change as our culture changes too. For example, at one time a pale complexion on a woman was considered beautiful, in part because it indicated that she did not have to work in the fields. More recently, a suntan is considered beautiful (in spite of the danger of skin cancer) because it shows that she has the leisure time to sit in the sun. In somewhat the same way, a man's body may be considered attractive today if he has time to build muscles, now that most men have sedentary jobs. The muscles, though, must be built not by working in the fields, but by using muscle-building equipment in his apartment. Leisure as an important part of aesthetic taste is clearly seen in certain periods of history where intricate, lacy designs were considered attractive, possibly because they indicate that it takes a good deal of time to keep the object clean. "Gingerbread" on Victorian style houses—applied to the roof line, windows, and doors—was considered beautiful at the turn of the century, partially because it was expensive; it did nothing to make the house more livable or to ease maintenance.

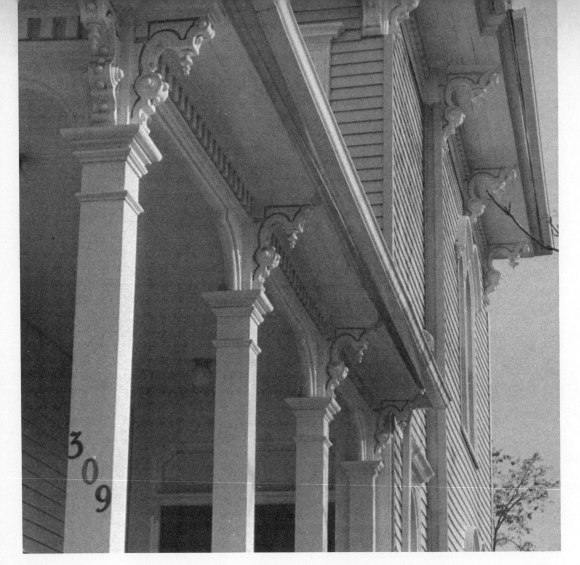

FIGURE 51.

The carved wooden details on this Victorian house required skill and time to produce.
Such detail was sometimes torn off in the 1930's, to make houses appear more modern
and in "good taste."

It is clear, therefore, that standards of taste, standards of beauty, and the
affective values that we place upon objects and our accumulated treasures are
dependent upon cultural values and are in a fluid, continually changing state,
influenced by changing technologies that determine the relative cost and availability of objects and activities.

THE DEVELOPMENT OF AESTHETIC AWARENESS

Preference and Personality

Aesthetic awareness is not an isolated variable in human behavior, because it relates to one's total personality. It may be possible to have high school students select the pictures that are judged "better," and even have them become quite proficient at selecting the ones that the teacher likes, but changing the patterns of likes and dislikes within the individual student is quite another matter. In a study of male graduate students, Barron (1963) found that there was a definite relationship between the paintings that these students preferred and their acceptance or rejection of tradition, religion, and authority. In general he found that those students who preferred portraits, landscapes, and traditional themes in paintings also preferred simple and predictable sketches; this was closely related to their personalities, which tended to be conservative, serious, deliberate, responsible, and so forth. Those students who preferred the experimental, sensual, and primitive paintings also preferred sketches that were complex and irregular; the personalities of this group of students tended to be more pessimistic, emotional, temperamental, and so forth.

Further work on the relationship between personality and art preferences has been done by a number of investigators (Knapp and Green, 1960; Roubertoux et al., 1971; Kloss and Dreger, 1971; Juhasz and Paxson, 1978). It is difficult to determine why this relationship exists, but it is well documented that people who have different personality characteristics do have different art preferences. A study by Barrett (1971) using college students concluded that "the aesthetic experience is apparently not closely related to objective visual skills such as color matching or form discrimination but may be based on individual personality factors instead." Bilotta and Lindauer (1980) concluded, on the basis of studies with 65 artists and nonartists, that responsiveness to the arts depends more on cognitive processes than on artistic training. This agrees with some extensive earlier work by Eysenck (1971) in the same area, in which Eysenck concluded that "Possibly we might here be dealing with some underlying aesthetic ability, or 'good taste,' demonstrated in all sorts of visual preference judgements and independent of intelligence, training and other external factors" (p. 163).

Judgments of art are usually justified by an individual by identifying certain qualities or preferences in the work. Yet these preferences elicited by the art tell us more about the viewer's disposition toward the work than about the work itself (Sharer, 1980). It is assumed that one's own interpretation of the characteristics of a work of art is embodied there for all to see. Aesthetic judgment is unconsciously filtered through an individual personality. But, in addition, that individual's personality is a result of social forces.

Possibly real changes in aesthetic preference cannot be made unless there is also a change in one's personality. Child (1983) presents evidence that trusting one's own judgment, having an ability to put up with uncertainty, and having a willingness to consider complex issues are closely related to the enjoyment of aesthetic experiences. Attempting to teach taste or standards in art to a senior high school art class may not produce a sensitive, alert, aware, and discriminating student unless changes in personality happen at the same time. Obviously this is a difficult task to accomplish, but the objective of education toward a more sensitive population—a population that is also willing to consider alternatives and to make changes—is certainly a goal worth striving for. However, achieving this goal is no easy task. A teacher in the usual high school is confronted with a group of students who may want to be somewhere else. Two thirds of the class is waiting for the time to be over, the day to be over, school to be over. Talk about art may seem to be of no value to their lives except to retain enough to pass the course, nor does it seem relevant for their future. To make aesthetic values meaningful presents a real challenge to educators.

Aesthetic Development

A fifth grade teacher was standing in the front of her room looking through a large stack of paintings that had just been picked up off the floor, where they had been drying. She was saying how much her children enjoyed their art experiences, that is, all but one child, "The one in the back row that needs the haircut," she said, nodding toward one boy who looked as if he could stand a bath. She began thumbing through the paintings. "Aren't some of these lovely?" Most of them looked tightly drawn and carefully colored. Suddenly she came upon one that was full of color, painted very directly, and apparently with a lot of feeling. It was a large head outlined in strong purple with a red background, looking somewhat like one of Rouault's paintings. She looked up and, shrugging her shoulders, said, "See, always this crude scribbling, no talent at all."

It was fairly obvious that this teacher had certain likes and dislikes in art, which she was using to evaluate the children's work. The fact that the boy needed a haircut and a bath may also have influenced her judgment. However, she was imposing her own tastes and aesthetic values upon these youngsters, and in so doing was undoubtedly having an impact upon their own values. Another teacher might not have been as outspoken or might have selected another

FIGURE 52.
This medieval stone capital is carved in a direct manner, with an intensity of feeling and almost childlike honesty of expression. Monsters seem ready to pounce upon the unholy in this 12th century capital, in the church at Yzeure, France.

picture to decry. There is no doubt that the aesthetic values of our society are transposed to youngsters, either directly or indirectly.

Probably our teacher would have been just as much at fault if she had selected the boldly painted head as an outstanding example of art and displayed this for the class to see. Our society has changing values in art; standards of goodness or badness may not be important, but what is most vital is the development of children's aesthetic awareness, based upon open, flexible minds rather than upon some changing aesthetic standard that may not be appropriate twenty years from now. We should be much more concerned with this fifth grader who might be the one to direct our society to a new and different form of beauty, breaking away from our own narrow definitions.

AESTHETIC DEVELOPMENT

The Preschool Child

During the first couple of years of life, children discover a great deal about the environment by examining everything within reach. Objects are explored not only by sight but are also handled and tasted. Children enjoy the opportunity to rattle, move, or put together any object that they can manipulate. They often show preferences even at this early age for certain toys or dolls. Language is used primarily to communicate basic needs for food or for attention.

Generally three year old children can select an object such as a square from a series of geometric forms, although they cannot draw or copy a square until a year later (Brittain, 1969). There is no evidence to indicate that practice in perceiving shapes is of any value to preschool children, for they do not particularly improve in ability to select objects or shapes even after being given practice in this task. Even extensive help in showing youngsters how to draw a square does not improve their square-drawing ability.

When preschool youngsters look at pictures, recognizable objects are eagerly pointed out, but this may be quite different from getting an understanding of the picture itself. At the age of four or five years, children can identify familiar objects in pictures, but they enumerate them one after another and do not relate them to one another in any way; not until age seven do children attempt coherent, logically related interpretations (Vernon, 1965).

Preschool children learn in an active way rather than in a passive way. Bradley and Bradbard (1981) attempted to teach three preschool classes concepts of space and quantity. Those children who were taught with a manipulative method were enthusiastic, whereas the nonmanipulation children had to be coaxed to participate. Young children's active interaction with the environment, their touching, seeing, manipulating, are all part of their total development, and their cognitive and perceptual growth are closely entwined. Preschool children have little concept of time; to a great extent, the world has little past or future; rather, it is. Often children will express strong preferences, but these preferences change rapidly, and the nursery school teacher will sometimes find that she is hated one moment and loved the next. Pictures on the wall are not art in the usual sense to preschool youngsters. Art is what they make themselves. However, nursery school children usually do not remember their own drawings or paintings after a few hours, and it could not be expected that they can develop any aesthetic awareness as adults understand it. It may well be that sensitivity toward living is based on the continual interaction between children and environment. The degree to which this interaction is encouraged and

THE DEVELOPMENT OF AESTHETIC AWARENESS

FIGURE 53.

Young children's sensitivity to their environment includes curiosity about how things look, smell, feel, taste, and sound. Onions are more than a food, since youngsters are intrigued by their ball-like quality and the noise made by their dry skins.

stimulated can be an element in developing the urge and attitude toward exploring and investigating other forms and in voicing preferences or being able to discriminate differences more easily at a later age. Preschool children are probably at the most crucial age for the development of a sensitivity toward living.

The Elementary School Child

There are great changes in physical and mental development between kindergarten and sixth grade. The changes apparent in children's creative art as they mature are also evident in aesthetic development. Most first-grade youngsters can give simple descriptions of pictures, naming the objects that are pointed out to them, if these are recognizable as objects, and can identify colors if they are not too subtle. However, the description is limited to the objects in a painting and does not extend to any interaction between objects. That is, first graders are able to identify things they recognize but not the mood or atmosphere, nor are they able to discuss the message that a particular painting might have. It is not until later that a picture can be seen to have a story or interaction within the frame itself. Vernon (1965) indicates from her research that it is not until ten or eleven years of age that children can interpret what is happening in a picture, what the people are doing, and so forth. This inability to see relationships roughly parallels the ability in drawing, for first graders will draw objects, but these objects are related in their pictures only by being placed one beside the other, and it is not until about ten or eleven that overlapping begins to appear.

Children in the elementary school do not recognize paintings or other works of art in the same way as adults. Although adults may enjoy the work of a particular painter, such as Picasso or Cezanne, because of the particular style or the colors, tonal quality, or atmosphere, this is not true for children. As Lansing (1983) has said, it is discouraging to hear teachers discussing expressionism with youngsters who are only beginning to read. A study by Gardner (1970) found that first, third, and sixth grade children were generally insensitive to the painting styles of various artists. However, ninth graders did significantly better in selecting another painting from several shown that was like the ones that they had just seen. The younger children tended to match paintings by subject matter, such as a little boy or a church that happened to appear in one of the sets. Most children, up through sixth grade, are insensitive to line variation or shading in drawings (Carothers and Gardner, 1979). In a study including a group of nineteen year old students, the conclusion was drawn that only in the adolescent and postadolescent years do a majority of children give responses that reveal their awareness of the formal aspects of paintings (Gardner and Gardner, 1973).

It would appear then that development plays an important role in children's understandings of the arts and their aesthetic judgments. But there have been questions raised about this conclusion. Rush and Lovano–Kerr (1982) decry the lack of art programs that have continuity and sequence and feel that students' seeming lack of aesthetic sense is due to a lack of instruction; they do not agree that developmental level determines students' ability to comprehend aesthetic aspects. Let us examine this issue a little further.

Very young children can distinguish differences between geometric forms, and preschoolers have no problem in selecting a small object from large ones—even though they may call it the "baby" one—so it should not be a surprise that six year old children can distinguish the differences between line drawings of houses done with a simple, thick line from those with much shading (O'Hare and Westwood, 1984). However, saying that this means that six year olds are able to make stylistic comparisons of paintings may be putting meaning into an identification task that is not there. Aesthetic awareness deals with feelings, compositional arrangements, attraction, and an analysis of the work in relation to the viewer. Terms such as *unified, muted, sad, delicate, garish, balanced, restful*, and so forth, which are used to describe works of art, are meaningless unless there is a reference for these terms outside the work itself. It is not until a child has lived eleven or so years that these terms can be abstracted from the concrete; that is, it is not until then that a word such as *rough* can be understood when applied to a flat surface of color. It is at this time that the vocabulary of aesthetics can begin to be relevant to children. Adults who are concerned about the teaching of aesthetics need first to provide children with the basis for a meaningful understanding of themselves and a rich store of experiences for understanding their world. Only then can the art one finds in museums and art galleries in New York, Paris, Madrid, or other distant places, reproduced for children to admire by a half dozen printing firms, be understood or discussed meaningfully.

Ample evidence indicates that it would be a difficult task to develop in elementary school children an awareness of differences in artistic style. No doubt, with proper rewards and proper punishment, such stylistic differences could be mastered by fifth and sixth grade children. Probably their interest in the fine arts would be lost in the process. There seems to be no reason why this area of learning cannot be postponed until the age of twelve or thirteen, when such learning becomes easier. This does not mean that aesthetics as such should be ignored in the elementary school; rather, a different kind of program should be developed, and this will be discussed later.

An adult concept of aesthetics has no meaning for very young children. Kevin, a nursery school child, is not aware of the aesthetic qualities of, for example, a lamp. A lamp is to turn on when it is dark. Lamps look like the lamp in his house, his lamp that he can turn on by pulling the chain. When he encounters a lamp that is quite different—one with a large, translucent shade instead of the small metal bulb cover and a button to push to turn it on—he may be surprised to find that it, too, is a lamp. This discovery stretches his concept of "lampness." If the lamp is too unlike lamps he has known, it may be rejected just on this basis. If it is unfamiliar, it is wrong. Liking or not liking a lamp may have very little to do with its aesthetic qualities.

For first grade children, the liking or disliking of our lamp may not be based quite so much on the familiarity of the lamp; by now children have had a good

FIGURE 54.
Which salt shaker is best? To young children, it probably is the one most like the one they use at home.

deal of lamp experience, and the lamp concept has grown to include a wide range of lamps. Not liking may be more because the bulb is burned out, or the paint is chipped, or the shade is scorched and not because of some aesthetic qualities. One study (Holland, 1955) found a developmental progression in the responses of children to some plates, glasses, wallpaper, and so forth; in grade one, many responses referred to the self, whereas responses relating to color, design, and shape showed a great increase from grade one to grade eight. It would probably not be until nine years or so that children would be able to deal with the abstract concepts of lampness: its function, its utilitarian qualities, its ease of cleaning, or its sturdiness. And it probably would not be until eleven or twelve that the aesthetic qualities could be evaluated aside from the concrete qualities of the lamp. And, of course, a question comes to mind: why would anyone want children to mimic the "good taste" of an adult anyway?

There is a difference between aesthetic preference and aesthetic judgment. Most youngsters can tell which picture they like best if given a choice, but the ability to judge one picture as better than another is a different problem. Some youngsters are able to predict quite well what the teacher wants, but this may

THE DEVELOPMENT OF AESTHETIC AWARENESS

be quite different from their own likes and dislikes. Child (1964) asked elementary school pupils from grades one through six to choose which they thought experts would consider best. Youngsters up through the fourth grade disagreed with the expert choice and had a strong preference for the "poorer" of the pair of pictures. After fourth grade the children continued to disagree, although the disagreement was not as great. It is rather interesting to note that these youngsters not only picked the poorer picture but thought that the experts would pick the poorer picture too. Child followed this experiment by a training session with fifth and sixth grade youngsters. He found that it was possible to improve their guesses as to what the expert judges would select as the better pictures but found that the youngsters' own preferences remained unchanged. Although these children had many weekly sessions of seeing slides, including a wide assortment of landscapes, portraits, still lifes, sculpture, abstract art, and so forth, the study indicated that this exposure had no effect on children's preferences. In fact, the results were completely negative. On the whole, children show a systematic tendency to prefer the work of art that is considered poorer by experts. In a later analysis, Child (1983) suggests that children are responding to different features of the pictures than those to which the experts are responding.

Evidently it is a lot easier to change what children say than what they think. This might be expected, since children in school are usually marked on how closely they agree with the textbook or with the teacher and not on their thinking abilities. An interesting study was done in England by Rump and Southgate (1966) with three groups of children aged seven, eleven, and fifteen. They found that 77 percent of the children agreed with their teacher's stated preference for pictures if the teacher was present. However, 71 percent disagreed with their teacher's preference when the teacher was not there! Rump and Southgate also found that the children preferred representational pictures, and the younger children preferred simple items or pictures with few elements. The older high school age children had a definite preference for the more complex pictures. In a study with 255 children in first, second, and third grade, Ramsey (1982) also noted the preference for cartoons and photographic styles of illustrations.

There is no reason to believe that the development of discrimination in paintings should be different from the discrimination of objects or thoughts in other areas of cognitive processes. Children are satisfied with making representations that are symbolic and definite about their environment and do not include in their drawings light and shade, differing atmospheric effects, or variations in color relationships until about the age of twelve. Machotka (1966) did a study analyzing the basis on which children evaluated paintings. This study indicated that children like pictures of increasingly clear and realistic representation until about age eleven. Although younger children would establish an emotional relationship to a painting, it was usually in terms of a personal relationship, such as liking a picture of a person because it reminds them of their father; it was not until the age of twelve that an emotional relationship was established with a picture that was outside the youngsters themselves, that is, with the atmosphere or character of the picture as a whole. Machotka related this change to a decrease in egocentrism, which occurs at about the age of eleven, when thought loses its dependence on concrete data. Taunton (1980) asked groups of children four, eight, twelve, and sixteen years of age and some college students their preferences for 24 pictures, which had been categorized according to subject matter, space, and realism. The results showed that subject matter was most important for all children up to twelve years of age and that realism was an important consideration for all except the four year olds. Another study (Hardiman and Zernich, 1977) also found that realistic paintings were preferred up to eighth grade. In a later study, including 360 subjects from grades three, five, seven, nine, eleven, and college, Hardiman and Zernich (1982) concluded that ". . . the single most influential variable in shaping preference responses of untrained subjects for visual art stimuli . . . is associated with a high degree of realism" (p. 36).

Many factors within the environment probably will influence elementary school children in their likes and dislikes, their ability to discriminate, and their development of aesthetic awareness. As children mature, the changes in their cognitive processes enable them to respond to and evaluate art more efficiently (Marschalek, 1983). Franken and Diamond (1983) studied the developmental trends in picture recognition and memory in subjects from three years to adult; as children grow older they become better at recognizing, differentiating, organizing, and remembering information for later use. Memory ability develops slowly until age twelve. Schools undoubtedly play an important part in this developing aesthetic awareness, but it may not be as important to guide this development as it is to encourage it.

The Secondary School Student

This is a period of developing critical awareness, and although no sudden changes have occurred, young adolescents have increased in awareness of themselves as members of society and have left the egocentric stage behind. One would therefore expect that there would be some changes in the ways in which adolescents perceive their environment and possibly an increase in aesthetic

PLATE 10.

"I Am in a Lightning Storm," painted by a six year old child.
Colors are used subjectively, according to their emotional or
aesthetic value, rather than with an attempt at naturalism.

PLATE 11.
"The Forest," painted by an eighth grade girl. At this stage of development, aesthetic considerations can become important, so that the child may no longer be interested in a literal representation but instead seek to convey a mood and emphasize design qualities.

growth. However, this does not seem to be the case. Rather, young adolescents seem to be on a plateau and do not seem particularly committed to art in any form. This does not imply disinterest in art, but rather that development cannot be easily measured, and there seems to be no observable growth or change in art products during these years from twelve to fourteen. In a study of eighth-grade students, Frankston (1963) concluded that whether or not the students took an art course had no effect on the quality of their art performances. He found no differences from one semester to the next in the quality of the work the students produced, whether they took an art course or not. And he also found the same lack of change in quality in their poetry writing. In a later study, Frankston (1966) tried different methods of teaching adolescents and found great inconsistencies in the individual performances but, again, no changes in group performance level.

In another study of the same age group, Brittain (1968a) found that there was general agreement between the adolescents and their teachers as to which drawings were of high quality. Unlike the teachers, these students showed a strong preference for complexity and technical proficiency in drawings. It may be that children at this age are becoming much more aware of their environment generally, though not to the point of being able to sort the variety of experiences into what might be termed acceptable and unacceptable. It is clear that eighth-grade youngsters enjoy seeing art that they themselves would like to be able to do. It may be that this is a key to a good deal of aesthetic preference and that growth in aesthetic preferences is achieved as youngsters grow in their own abilities to portray the environment. Day (1969) found in attempting to teach some art history to eighth graders that those students who had concurrent studio experiences performed better and gained more knowledge of the subject matter in art history than those students who did not have a studio art class. Possibly the introduction of some discussions applicable to the production of art might begin to make sense to this age.

Only a minority of high school students take an art course. Although there are occasional classes that are required of all high school students in the humanities, these too are rare. Schools turn their backs upon the importance of aesthetic growth at the time when its development can best be promoted. High school students enjoy the opportunity to engage in abstract thinking and are no longer tied to concrete operations. Coordination and drive are such that great gains can be seen in art products, but sometimes these skills are misguided, and students may mimic or duplicate works of art that they consider great. The ability to discriminate is probably at its peak, and although individuals differ considerably, this is probably the best age at which to deal with problems of aesthetics.

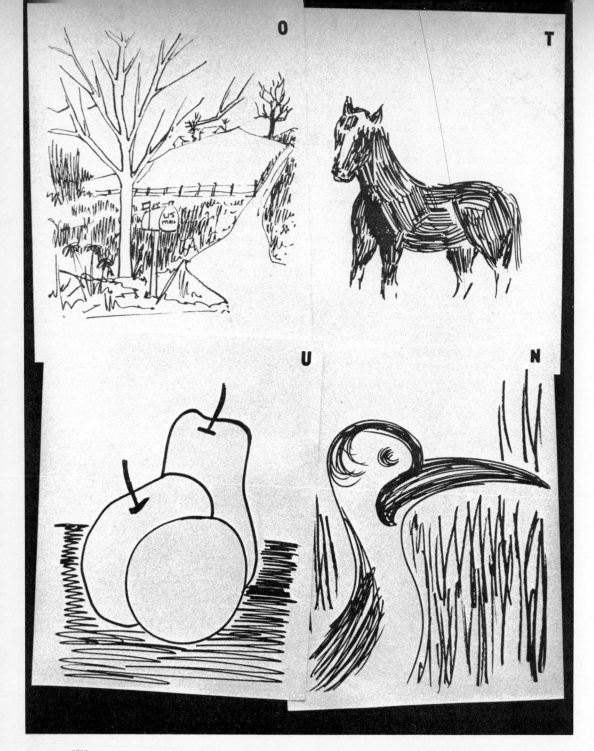

FIGURE 55.

Adolescents preferred the upper of these sketches, the landscape and horse; but teachers seemed to like the lower ones, the fruit and bird. A horse seemed more appealing than a bird to this age, and the detail of the landscape was preferred to the simplicity of the fruit.

A Program for Aesthetic Growth

Children have joy in exploring, investigating, and expressing their feelings about their environment. Possibly the best means of developing aesthetic awareness is through sharpening youngsters' sensibilities and strengthening their power of self-expression. Aesthetics should not be confused with the appreciation of art. Aesthetics can be a basic way of relating oneself to the environment. That is, looking at, responding to, feeling a part of, being aware of textures and forms, reacting to differences and similarities, liking or disliking an object, noticing differences in organization—all are part of the aesthetic response and part of aesthetic growth.

FIGURE 56.
These youngsters may accept their surroundings as normal, without question. The common recurrence of such scenes reflects society's lack of concern with aesthetic sensitivity.

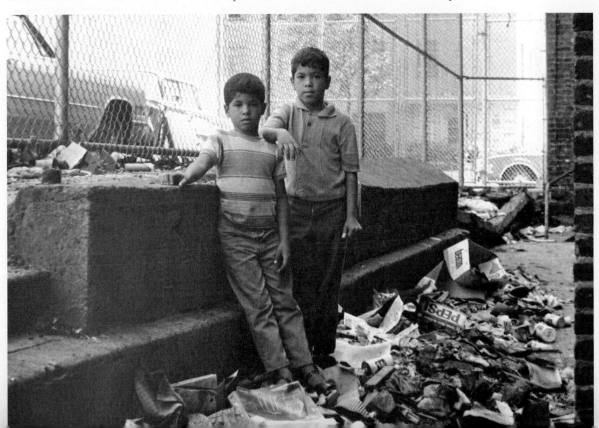

We are constantly reacting to our environment. Young children do this as well as older people. What we have experienced in the past makes us respond in given ways to the present. We respond to an object or event in terms of past experiences rather than in terms of its actual qualities. Contemplation of a work of art evokes many responses; these may be both positive and negative. Subject matter certainly can have a reference within one's past experiences; young children particularly respond to pictures in terms of such subject-matter content. However, colors, forms, and even the atmosphere of a particular work of art can evoke responses that the viewer cannot immediately understand or verbalize. The art of the past is a tradition invariably broken whenever new directions in art are taken. The purpose is not to honor the work of past or present artists, nor is it to teach the vocabulary of art, but rather the purpose is to encourage and develop aesthetic growth.

To a great extent, then, the understanding of art and aesthetic awareness should be combined in a program specifically aimed at the developing child. This should become a natural part of interacting with the environment. Attending selectively must precede the processing of information (Marschalek, 1983). Inattention to environment can be overcome, but attention is an achievement requiring effort (Parsons, 1971). Experiences in large and small enclosed spaces, the opportunity to comment on changing colors in a sunset, pointing out and enjoying the variety of textures in clothing or the feeling of expansiveness in open areas all have the primary purpose of developing youngsters' self-awareness and a sensitivity to the immediate environment. Children need the chance to develop ideas and examine them and to realize that their own opinions about their environment are important. In discussing the problems of developing a specific curriculum in aesthetics, Broudy (1971) emphasizes these problems: changes in attitude are harder to bring about than changes in belief; there is less consensus on criteria for evaluation than for truth; and we know less about teaching for appreciation than teaching for understanding.

The Preschool

The pleasure in looking at a brightly colored leaf in the fall and listening to the birds in the spring are experiences that can be readily shared. It is relatively easy to encourage the type of growth that we have been discussing at this age. But encouragement need not be passive on the part of the teacher. Children can respond to questions about whether the clay is hot or cold, whether the paint is too thick, whether the color red is their favorite, whether the painting should be hung high or placed low on the bulletin board, or whether they like the feel of

THE DEVELOPMENT OF AESTHETIC AWARENESS

FIGURE 57.

Preschool children are at a crucial age in developing aesthetic awareness, for they develop attitudes toward the environment and a sensitivity toward living that will remain with them as they start their formal schooling. It is important to encourage the youngster's participation and involvement in learning experiences.

the smooth piece of maple. To be able to look at, recognize, and respond to objects is an important step in aesthetic growth. The discriminatory skills are part of the whole cognitive process and therefore young children cannot be expected to go beyond their intellectual level in developing ways of looking at their environment. Moreover, looking at, feeling, and talking about objects make children much more conscious of this activity as worthwhile.

Preschool children are eager to share their treasures, and these treasures may take strange forms. A nursery school teacher would not be surprised to observe children saving buttons, fingering pebbles, liking stubby pencils, or having favorite socks. It is important that small children have the opportunity to examine and save part of their environment. Explaining why these things are chosen is not as important. A sensitive teacher will provide a place for children's collections, for it is important to children that these be honored. Sometimes group experiences can be meaningful, such as looking at unusual fossils, branches with interesting bark or leaf development, or pictures and reproductions that some youngsters have found appealing and worthwhile. Children's moods come directly to the surface; sadness or joy are obvious; feelings fill the whole mind and body, with no self-conscious awareness. Too often such exhibitions of expression are treated as if they should be repressed. "Stop doing that. Stop acting like a child. Behave yourself." Probably the biggest role a preschool teacher can play is a supportive one in the children's development of self-awareness and in the joy and pleasure they get from their environment.

The Elementary School

In looking at reproductions of contemporary paintings, children in kindergarten and first grade usually enjoy finding familiar objects and generally seem oblivious to the artistic qualities therein. However, sixth grade children, particularly girls, seem to be much more aware of the mood and atmosphere of a picture or the feeling that color or forms impart to the viewer. But then, this is to be expected since children in their own drawings follow this developmental pattern. Children in first grade will be drawing objects placed one beside the other, and the use of color is more to identify the particular object than to impart a mood or feeling to the viewer. Sixth graders will be drawing objects that overlap, there may be many base lines or a feeling for space, and the color may be purposefully applied to give a feeling of anger, hatred, joy, or serenity. Using 128 subjects, aged four to twenty, Ives (1984) studied the development of children's ability to express mood in drawings of trees. Children were asked to draw happy, sad, and angry trees; even some four year olds made drawings that were judged successful. Expressive ability advanced slowly, peaking at age sixteen, with complex abstract expression.

Children react to and express their feelings with whatever instruments or words they have mastered. Sometimes children can mimic words without understanding their meaning and sometimes these words sound quite amusing when they come out in songs, prayers, or in the "pledge of the legions." Recognition of great works of art at an early age may be possible, but the understanding and aesthetic awareness of these pictures would be missing. Abstract concepts of beauty and ugliness cannot be comprehended by young children. A

THE DEVELOPMENT OF AESTHETIC AWARENESS

FIGURE 58.

Relating to art and finding aesthetic pleasure in examining and reacting to representations are based on concrete experiences. Gathering autumn leaves brings an appreciation of the variety of their forms, textures, colors, smells, and sounds.

good example of this is a study by Liedes (1975), where first grade children were asked to bring in things they thought were beautiful and ugly to share with their classmates. The things they brought were based on personal feelings: beautiful things were clean, smooth, and shiny, such as figurines and jewelry; ugly things were broken, dark, or rough, such as bones and dirty stones.

A picture is merely a conglomeration of lines and forms and colors that have little meaning unless we can identify with the artist's purpose. In some contemporary art expression, the product itself becomes destroyed, or is practically nonexistent, placing the focus entirely upon the experience. Simple questions such as "How do you feel about this picture?" or "What part do you like best?" may be enough to get students involved. This comprehension is geared to the individual and not to an evaluation of a painting itself. "Why do you suppose the artist painted this? Suppose you had painted this picture; what would have been your purpose?" would be one method of focusing upon the process rather than on the product.

It would be a difficult task to plan a detailed curriculum for aesthetic education for the elementary school, especially since the end product of the instruction is not at all clear. However, attempts have been made. There are numerous commercially produced programs designed to teach a variety of art learnings. These may be designed to teach art appreciation or art history at each grade level. Sometimes they are fairly elaborate, with a running commentary available for teachers to use, along with slides or reproductions for each period of history or theme presented. Most of these programs do not require that the teacher have a background in art, but seem to utilize the teacher only to say the printed words and to show the pictures. One text (Lansing and Richards, 1981) bluntly states that elementary teachers are ill prepared for teaching the history and appreciation of art, and the book provides ways to talk about art with children so as to build their art vocabulary.

There is the question of whether slides or reproductions of real works of art can provide the same responses as do the originals. One study (Hardiman and Zernich, 1984) asked college students to respond to four realistic and four semi-abstract original paintings, as well as slides or color reproductions of these paintings. Although the students differed in their preferences, the mode in which these were shown made no particular difference. This raises serious questions. Do college students, and younger people too, respond to pictures as if viewing originals, or are our methods of teaching the arts through reproductions becoming canned, removed from real people and real emotions, in somewhat the same way that we can view accidents, acts of war, and terrorism on television with a passive attitude, much the same as when viewing violence in a fictitious program? The problem arises when we realize that children may confuse the real with fiction and passively regard both.

We need to do more than show pictures to children, more than provide them with a vocabulary so that they can respond properly. Artists are real people, reacting to the world, expressing feelings, manipulating colors, experimenting with form, doing the same things that children do. Until children understand this bond, the arts are passive and the mode of presentation is irrelevant.

It seems logical that children can identify and enjoy pictures that they can relate to. Past generations of teachers have selected the sweet pictures for children to appreciate, but it is a rare adult who still remembers the artist who painted the little girl and her dog that all third graders were supposed to identify. It makes good sense to stress that viewing a painting should be an enjoyable experience, not merely the source of facts to be learned. There is no reason why students must echo words of the teacher. Children should be able to select pictures to share with each other. Sometimes schools purchase original works of art for the classroom. These originals or reproductions should be picked out by the children who are going to view them. The teacher, too, should be able to have some say in the selection of such works of art. Since this is a democratic society, the elementary school provides a good opportunity for the development of likes and dislikes and for the increasing awareness of one's own attitude toward the arts, with a full realization that as a child grows, tastes and ability to respond to the environment will change.

The Secondary School

Young adolescents find a vicarious expression in popular music. Possibly there should be popular art for these youngsters too. However, some art teachers are much more concerned about propagating their own standards, and the likes and dislikes of the students tend to be ignored. It is adolescents who begin to spend money on jewelry, art objects, and interesting trinkets. They need support in their ability to make choices. Exposure to and awareness of some of the variety of forms available and the suggestion of alternate outlets for this interest in collecting artifacts could well be a starting point in making aesthetics meaningful.

The developing interest in art that can be seen in the junior high school should be encouraged, but not necessarily in the direction of the usual chronological approach to the evolution of modern art. There are many cultures that have expressed themselves in ways that may be closer to young adolescents than is the sophisticated art of nineteenth and twentieth century Europe and America. Some of the art forms from Africa, early American folk art like scrimshaw and quilts, and Eskimo sculpture can create great interest, because they express in a direct manner some of the same feelings and emotions that these youngsters are experiencing. Since this age is much more verbal, discussions and examples of a variety of art products can be stimulating, particularly if this is a part of a creative art activity. Care should be taken that these examples are seen as a means of stimulating discussion and of broadening possible avenues for action rather than as examples to be emulated.

Senior high school students are in an advantageous position for understanding some of the problems facing our society in its ignorance of aesthetic values. However, the temptation should be resisted to cram aesthetics down the throats of the unsuspecting students. Their own knowledge, interests, and environment should be the starting point. As much can be learned about aesthetics from

FIGURE 59.
Direct, bold art from other cultures has an honesty that appeals to junior high school students. (Mask of Wood, Ivory Coast. Collection of Ithaca College; gift of Mr. William Brill.)

seeing alternate methods of organizing pieces of scrap metal into a sculpture or from cropping photographs for enlargement as can be learned from armchair lectures about balance and repetition in a slide of a Mondrian painting.

From previous studies (Day, 1969) it seems learning in the cultural aspects of the arts can be enhanced by active participation. It makes sense. Someone who paints enjoys looking at paintings; if you have tried to throw pots, you enjoy a good piece of pottery; the weaver likes to examine interesting textiles. Basically, aesthetics, art appreciation, or art history needs to be part of the active, creative search for expressive symbols, for solutions to problems in artistic construction, or for pleasing combinations of form and texture. If these areas are treated in isolation, high school students can quickly relegate this learning to the same category as some other subjects: something that needs to be done for school, but not anything sufficiently exciting to be considered outside the school itself.

THE DEVELOPMENT OF AESTHETIC AWARENESS

An illustration might be a student who is trying to express in paint resentment against an apathetic society, but it just does not seem to take form. How have others painted anger? Some paint with gory details like Goya, some with distorted symbols like Picasso, some with heavy and bold lines like Rouault, and some with only form and color. The student's frame of reference is thus expanded and the history of art is put into a meaningful context.

Problems in sculpture, photography, design, crafts, graphics can all be approached in similar ways, using the past as a reference for the future, but not as something to be imitated. Too often all that students see in the way of art is the commercial variety—ads for cars, beer, cigarettes; or the pseudo-art that seems to fill every discount store—garish-colored, framed reproductions of saccharine subject matter, plastic reproductions of marble figurines, radios camouflaged as model automobiles, or lamps growing out of the backs of ceramic cocker spaniels. If these are the references for their own art, then the discovery of the serious art of the past may be a source of new perceptions. Care must be taken that the teaching of the arts does not ignore the personal history or the cultural background of the society of which the students are a part.

FIGURE 60.

The type of trinkets available in many discount stores may be the major contact many students have had with "art," greatly influencing their taste.

Often museums initiate programs designed to attract students to their facilities, and many offer special programs for children on Saturday morning. Book publishers and film companies make available instructional materials that can sometimes be of help in organizing a well-rounded study of art. Philanthropic organizations, foundations, and even state and local art councils have been known to assist in the funding of ambitious projects that are aimed at bringing the arts into the community and the lives of school children. Additional funding from outside sources is not necessary when the school administration is committed to fostering aesthetic experiences for its pupils. Moreover, students are usually more ready than the staff for such activities, since flexibility, innovation, and interdisciplinary thinking are necessary in order to break with the traditional school programming. Almost every state has some kind of traveling exhibition; a few bring performing artists into the classroom.

The community itself, regardless of its size, offers a vast resource of aesthetic opportunities. Beyond the obvious, such as museums, art exhibits, music and dance concerts, libraries, and theaters, other nearby resources should not be overlooked. Historical societies are active in nearly every community. Local architecture, in the form of churches, courthouses, and new and old homes, is often a good source. Parks provide good means of looking at landscaping, and their monuments give a tie to the past. Bridges can be both structurally and aesthetically interesting. Local photo shops not only offer materials but can also offer some information. Sometimes post offices or other public buildings have murals from the 1930s. The local radio and television studio can be an excellent source of exploring both the technical and aesthetic problems of program production. Many have experienced the feeling of awe inside a large church, but a feeling that is somewhat comparable without religious inferences can be had before large machinery, such as in a mill, factory, or utility company. At the same time, a watch- and clockmaker, a jeweler, or a cabinetmaker can provide the source of a different kind of appreciation, as can contact with private collectors or performers.

Some may question whether these experiences are really in the area of developing aesthetic awareness. However, developing sensitivity toward painting may not be as important as developing sensitivity toward life. A high school student who enjoys the work of a fine craftsman, who is sympathetic to the problems of the graphic designer, who appreciates the feel of fabric with the local dressmaker, and who is fascinated with construction methods of the local contractor is also ready to appreciate the fine arts.

Summary

Aesthetic awareness is part of the total growth pattern of children. It is not the imposition of standards or rules, but rather the development of their ability to discriminate and make choices. Beauty is something that changes with time and culture, and the opportunity for youngsters to express their own feelings and emotions about things around them is more important than the development of taste according to today's standards.

Clive Bell (1914, p. 249) had some rather amusing advice to give about art and children that makes sense even today. "Do not tamper with that direct emotional reaction to things which is the genius of children. Do not destroy their sense of reality by teaching them to manipulate labels. Do not imagine that adults must be the best judges of what is good and what matters. Don't be such an ass as to suppose that what excites uncle is more exciting than what excites Tommy."

Possibly what is necessary in the development of aesthetic awareness is not an appreciation of a particular picture or object, nor is it the teaching of particular adult values or a vocabulary to describe works of art. Aesthetic awareness may be brought about through an increase in children's awareness of themselves and a greater sensitivity to their own environment. There are numerous factors involved in aesthetics, and it is not a simple problem to deal with. Certainly the cognitive behavior of individuals, their affective behavior, and the interaction between themselves and their environment all play a part. The background of students, their socioeconomic level, the cultural factors of the time, their exposure to mass media, their ability to be flexible in thinking, and their standing in the classroom all influence the development of aesthetic awareness. It should be understood that aesthetic growth does not necessarily refer to art; it also refers to a more intense and greater integration of thinking, feeling, and perceiving. It thus may bring about a greater sensitivity toward living, and therefore it becomes a major goal in education.

Related Activities

1. Ask a seventh grade class which of a series of quite dissimilar pictures they would like to hang on the walls of their houses. Ask them which one their parents would like. Then ask which one their art teacher would like best. Does this

give any indication of how they see the adults' taste as different from their own?

2. In a drug or variety store, select a few inexpensive containers that are well designed. Select several poorly designed items. On what basis did you make your selections?

3. Ask a second grade class to bring to school something that is beautiful and something that is ugly. Compare their concepts of beauty and ugliness with your own.

4. Look around your own community and make a note of those buildings that are of the most modern design. Who owns these buildings or what function goes on inside them? Locate some new buildings that are more traditional in design. What are these buildings used for? Can you draw any inferences?

5. Select examples of paintings that are related to a particular period of art. Explain why these are representative of their time, referring to subject matter, technique, and mode of representation.

6. Select one large reproduction that shows some distortion of everyday objects, such as a painting by Modigliani or Chagall. Ask some first, third, and sixth graders to tell you what they think about the picture. Keep track of their comments and their acceptance or rejection of the distortion.

5

Art in the Elementary School

Classroom Procedures

Art is usually considered an important part of the elementary school program. Art activities, however, are scheduled in a variety of ways. Several years ago it was fairly common for an art teacher to push a cart of art materials from one elementary classroom to another. The art teacher worked on a fairly close schedule, and often children would be waiting impatiently for their turn to have art. It is much more common now for a classroom to be set aside for art activities. There are many advantages to this. It seems better to have one room messed up with paper clippings on the floor or clay on the desks, so that the janitor does not have to spend time cleaning several rooms. Also, the art materials are on hand and the activities can be varied, with several different projects going on at the same time. However, Silberman (1971) has decried the fact that art is something separate from ordinary classroom life and is something you go to another room to study or to do.

Sometimes, in an elementary school with a more flexible program structure, the art room is open for any child who has finished his work or who has the free time to come in and work for fifteen minutes or a couple of hours. In some schools the morning hours are scheduled with the more academic subjects, such as mathematics or reading; the afternoon is free for children to select one or more activities, so that children may come and go from the art room at will. Often children's art experiences will be provided by the elementary classroom teacher. Occasionally there is a schedule where an art consultant will spend several days in one room and then move to another location, to provide for a concentrated art experience.

There are many reasons for these different patterns, most of them economic ones. The most important consideration should be maximizing the value of the art program so as to provide a meaningful experience in the arts, with ample opportunity for the youngsters to express their own relationship to their environment. Classroom procedures should focus upon encouraging all children in a very personal way. A teacher's function becomes one of developing children's self-discovery and stimulating depth of expression. The atmosphere that is conducive to artistic expression, an environment that will foster inventiveness and exploration, is not the same type of atmosphere that is favorable for memorizing multiplication tables. In the latter activity students must concentrate on areas outside themselves; they are dependent upon the teacher for recognition of their efforts and must, with the rest of the class, deny giving vent to their feelings. Creative expression is the direct opposite of memorization. Where individual inventiveness, expression, and independence of thinking are crucial, an entirely different classroom atmosphere needs to be established.

A teacher who wants to foster individual expression in the classroom, who wants to encourage initiative and spontaneity, and who wants to have children motivated to produce freely, will have to accept creative behavior. The teacher must encourage children to be full of curiosity, to be able to poke fun at themselves and others, to have original ideas of their own, even to question the teacher's direction; at the same time the teacher must discourage children from feeling withdrawn, quiet, retiring, and dependent upon the teacher for direction and approval. Every child should be encouraged to look upon learning as a self-initiated activity. Children who are personally involved in an activity may be oblivious to those around them and are not easily distracted. Sometimes a whole class will become so involved that a classroom will be surprisingly quiet. At other times there may be a great deal of activity and noise as youngsters share ideas and materials. In a summary of Piaget's work, Ginsburg and Opper (1969) conclude that children should argue, converse, and defend their opinions in a classroom atmosphere that supports social interaction.

FIGURE 63.

The activities within the classroom must be planned in such a way that social interaction takes place. Exchanging ideas, arguing, and defending one's position are important in the learning process.

An art class is often confusing to the outsider anyway, because of the problem of having numerous materials distributed and picked up. A great deal of responsibility can be assumed by the children themselves in handling the art materials. Actually the art experience is more than merely using the art materials in the drawing or painting process; learning takes place in finding how paint is stored, learning how to mix the paint so that it is of proper consistency, and learning how to clean up after the painting is completed. Cleaning and storing the brushes and putting the painting itself away to dry are all part of the experience. Although very young children will have difficulty with paints, even nursery school children can help, and there is no reason why the responsibility for paper distribution or putting away crayons cannot be assumed by the youngsters. The teacher who prepares the materials and then assumes the responsibility for cleaning up afterwards is more in the position of a housekeeper than a teacher. There is some danger in encouraging students to think and do for themselves, although this danger exists only for the teacher who feels insecure.

Older and younger children can engage in many activities together, but usually younger children are oblivious to the ten and eleven year olds. These older children can often be a great deal of help in passing out paints, helping the six year old clean up spilled water, or getting paper off the top shelf. Some elementary schools have the fifth and sixth graders take responsibility for helping with school activities. Some children will work in the library, some in the school office, and some in the art room. The janitor can be of help in knowing sources of materials, salvaging scraps of wood, or helping to hold two pieces of wood together while they are being nailed.

Classroom procedures should be kept flexible enough to allow each child the opportunity to deviate from the group activity. Specific suggestions for motivating children to express their feelings and emotions will be included in later chapters; however, if a particular project does not appeal to some of the children, there is no law that says that all children must be occupied in the same activity at the same time. Working with paper in a variety of ways, such as cutting, tearing, crumbling, or using paper to express some particular feeling by piercing or folding it might very well lead some children into escaping from the artistic investigation and using the paper for making folded airplanes. This might be a particularly interesting way to upset a teacher, but such use of paper for airplanes can be an exciting project in itself; certainly encouraging these children to make changes in the design of the folded paper—by adding a paper clip to the nose, by using a different type of fold, by trying a variety of weights of paper, and by experimenting with these forms in the hall—can channel the energies and independent thinking of the creative child into a constructive art project. Denying the desire to make such airplanes by treating the child as disruptive and taking disciplinary action would not only be frustrating to this child, but would also deny the rest of the class the opportunity to deviate in the future from the prescribed procedures that the teacher might arbitrarily assign to the class.

Although undoubtedly every teacher would like to work with small classes, apparently there is no reason to believe that the size of class has much influence over the quality of the drawings of children. Lansing (1956) in working with fifth grade children found that class sizes ranging from 18 to 40 produced no significantly different effects upon the creative drawings of these children. Rutter (1983) surveyed a large number of studies relating to class size and came to the same basic conclusion. It is only when working with handicapped or disturbed children, where individual attention is crucial, that smaller classes become important. There have been studies done in other fields that indicate that the teacher is the important variable. It is only when a class gets too large, probably over 40, that even the best teacher has difficulty. A poor teacher is boring whether the class size is 5 or 100.

Any procedures used in the classroom should encourage rather than discourage creativity. Children seated in rows with hands folded, waiting for something to happen, waiting for the person in front to pass the paper back, waiting for someone else to use the paint, lining up to wash hands at the sink, or patiently waiting for their turn at the easel may experience long enough delays to make real creative expression difficult when the time finally comes to put a line on paper. In some cases, putting supplies in several locations, grouping youngsters with four or five others who share the same interests, not having everyone working at the same project, and encouraging children to change activities without waiting for teacher approval will allow greater flexibility.

Those children who have a good deal of energy and who are freer in their responses may need to have these energies channeled into acceptable form; at the same time the passive, quiet child may need real encouragement to overcome a fear of failure; such a child needs success experiences, so as to go on to develop independent thinking and to discover the joy of self-expression. Providing encouragement for creative behavior and rewards for independent thinking can go a long way toward developing an atmosphere conducive to creative activity. The classroom procedure can help in this respect, but it is only one factor among many that can provide the background for a meaningful art experience.

FIGURE 64.
The atmosphere in a classroom that is engaged in art activities is quite different from the atmosphere that is present in the classroom when usual academic subject matter is taught.

The Importance of Materials and Skills

The proper materials and the development of skills are an important part of art expression. It is only through the use of the art material that any expression can evolve. Just as words are important in verbal communication, and the structure of sentences and paragraphs are important in written work, the artist must develop the skills and techniques necessary to communicate through art and must have an understanding of the materials in order to be able to utilize their intrinsic qualities.

Important as skills and techniques may be, however, they must always remain the means to an end and never become ends in themselves. It is not the skills that are expressed, but the feelings and emotions of the artist. To concentrate only upon the materials that are used in art, or upon developing particular skills utilized in an art expression, ignores the fundamental issue, which is that art springs from human beings and not from materials. Exercises in penmanship were once popular in our school systems, and children would spend a considerable length of time making neat ovals or copying from moralistic poems so as to perfect their writing abilities. This is no longer true; now there is a great deal of concern that youngsters need to develop a will to express themselves with the written word.

FIGURE 65.

The procedures in working with new materials should be explained briefly. Even in working in the woodshop youngsters are much more anxious to do than to learn how to do.

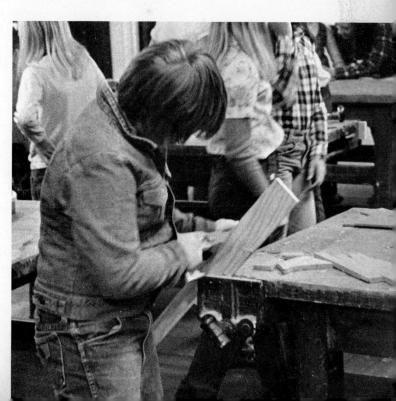

In art the same factors hold true. Merely understanding the differences between art materials and the development of particular skills will avail the child nothing unless the need and urge for expression are there first. The expression of the self, the urge to put down experiences that are meaningful, the desire to put into artistic form the frustrations or joys of life, must all be present before skills can be developed. Encouraging this expression is the crux of an art education program; the mechanics of art are secondary and can be explained when the demand for this knowledge comes from the youngster. Many magazines related to the arts carry advertisements from art supply companies. These can give the impression that using a variety of stimulating and expensive art products assures a successful art experience for children and at the same time makes teaching easier and more enjoyable. Hamblen (1983) points out that art supply companies have a vested interest in making sure that schools buy art supplies, and therefore they often provide workshops and services to teachers so as to promote their products. However, materials don't have to be expensive and in some cases don't even have to be purchased. Once the desire for expression is awakened, the urge for greater knowledge about the use of materials will follow.

Techniques and Procedures

Frequently an artist's work is recognized by the particular technique used. This is often an unconscious approach to the use of materials and is highly individual. With children this can also be true. Some youngsters will paint boldly with a great deal of spontaneity, whereas other children will be more concerned with detail and may concentrate on the outline of the forms they are making. A technique develops according to the individual's own needs. A procedure, on the other hand, consists of the different steps necessary in using a specific material. There are, for example, general procedures in making an etching. These are the preparation of the plate and acid used for etching, the methods of controlling the etching process, the ways in which the ink is applied to the plate, and so forth. These procedures can be explained to older students, and it is often necessary to have considerable experience before the procedures become so automatic that etching can be used for expression. Needless to say, a procedure such as this would be too complex for children.

Any material that is used with children must fit their needs for expression. The procedure in using these materials can often be discovered by the children themselves, but simple explanations or demonstrations of certain procedures may facilitate the use and care of art materials. For example, ten year old children will find pleasure in a discussion of a variety of ways that tempera paint can be used. Colors can be mixed either in a tray or directly on the page, colors will mix on the painting if the undercolor is still wet but not if the undercolor has dried, paint has a different quality depending on whether it is thick or mixed with water; these suggestions may open other possibilities to the youngster. The facts that brushes store better with the handle down and that jar tops must be tight so that the paint will not evaporate are also part of the painting procedures. Much of this is not particularly appropriate to the nursery school child, who needs the paint thick so that it does not run down the paper in uncontrolled mistakes; the tightening of jar lids is probably best done by the teacher. A sensitive teacher can constantly take clues from the children as to when particular procedures would be valuable to discuss or when these children would benefit from finding new ways of using familiar materials.

Art Materials and Developmental Stages

The range of materials that can be used for art is almost unlimited. Some of these are the traditional materials such as pencils, clay, paint, and so forth. Then there are other materials that are often used for art, although their main purpose is for some other function. These include wood, collage materials, and plaster. A third category might include materials that are unrelated to art but that sometimes have a unique contribution to make and can be utilized in various ways in art experiences. These include such things as packing boxes, fishnets, and pieces of discarded water pipe.

Artists, seeing beauty or a message in almost any material, have given the impression that anything can be used for art expression. However, when working with children, materials are not sought out for their unique characteristics or the qualities that make them particularly expressive for the professional artist. Rather, youngsters see these materials as being what art is all about, in somewhat the same way as they accept a pencil to write with and a book to read. Therefore, much harm can be done to children unless their developmental level is taken into consideration in selecting materials used for art expression.

Let us look, for example, at watercolor as one art material. Watercolor is transparent; it has a flowing, merging quality; it mixes easily and can be made into fine gradations. Watercolor also changes easily in its characteristics, and it has a vibrating quality that lends itself to atmospheric effects. This material would be used quite differently by a scribbling child, a child of eight years of age, a youngster of twelve, or a sixteen year old.

A three year old who is scribbling would have real difficulty with water-color, because scribbling is primarily a motor activity. The lines produced with the wet brush would have to be interrupted as the child would frequently need to dip the brush into the water and paint. The paper would fill with brush strokes, and lines would run into one another, merging into a blur, into an indistinguishable mass of colors in which kinesthetic activity and the child's urge for control would become invisible. For a child who is beginning to name scribbles, this blurred mass would be frustrating and discouraging.

An eight year old has developed symbols that are repeated, signifying the concept of order that the child has established within the environment. Objects are painted definite colors, such as green for grass and trees and bushes; the child knows that these objects are green and continues to paint them this way with satisfaction. Differences in light or shadows do not influence these colors, and any unintentional changes are meaningless and frustrating in the desire for mastery. An accident cannot be repeated and an unintentional change is a mistake. What often seems of aesthetic quality to adults would mean a spoiled picture to an eight year old child.

ART IN THE ELEMENTARY SCHOOL

A twelve year old has found a niche within society, loves to read fantastic stories, and enjoys discovering new things and having the opportunity to experiment, so that what formerly appeared as an accident in painting might now be considered stimulating. The flowing, merging quality of watercolor is well suited to this age, and the youngster may experiment with the accidents that occur when wet paint runs on the paper and merges with other colors in unexpected beauty. A colorful sky will be made more so by the introduction of reds and greens, which can be quite dramatic.

A sixteen year old has become much more critical. Usually there are definite intentions about how the product should look. In some cases the changing effects of distance and atmosphere will be the primary intent, in which case

FIGURE 67.

A young girl has drawn her teacher's plant, clearly indicating that she knows the shapes of the leaves, all of which are drawn as two-dimensional, with no leaf overlapping another, although some are in front of the bowl.

watercolor may be an excellent medium. Another student may not find the same interest in portraying nature but may want definite concepts expressed in flat tones; watercolor may be an obstacle to this kind of expression. Not all students will want to use watercolor. For some it may be frustrating, but for others it may be an excellent art material.

The teacher should know the variety of choices available in art materials and introduce them at the appropriate stage. Every material must make its own contribution. If a task can be done more easily and effectively by using something different, then the wrong art material has been used. The teacher should know that every child will develop a personal method of working with materials and that any help from the teacher can only be valuable if it provides the opportunity for greater awareness and greater flexibility. Several materials can be used at one time within a classroom, thus providing an opportunity to develop various possible approaches to expression. It is not the material itself that needs emphasis, for art materials must be seen as avenues for expression and not as ends in themselves.

Art Materials in the Classroom

Certain mechanical, routine methods of handling art materials make the art program much more effective. Children at all levels can take a great deal of responsibility for their own art materials. Occasionally a teacher will become so involved with the distribution and cleaning-up processes that there is little time to stimulate the children to depth of expression. Having children take over some of this responsibility not only frees the teacher from the routine of passing out paper, distributing scissors, and cleaning up paintbrushes, but it also provides an opportunity for children to become more aware of an art activity as a total experience that is primarily theirs. Although art materials in daily use should be left within easy reach of children, certain materials should be stored out of sight. These are not necessarily the expensive materials but rather those that can have special meaning at special times (styrofoam balls for mobiles, shiny paper for holiday decorations) and those that are potentially dangerous (large glass jars, thin strands of wire, sets of cutting knives). A violin virtuoso handles the violin like something sacred not only because it is of material value, but because it is the means of personal expression. A true artist develops a kinship to materials, and some of these feelings can certainly be developed within children.

In no instance should the lack of materials stand in the way of a good art program. This is not to say that such basic materials as clay, tempera paint,

154   **ART IN THE ELEMENTARY SCHOOL**

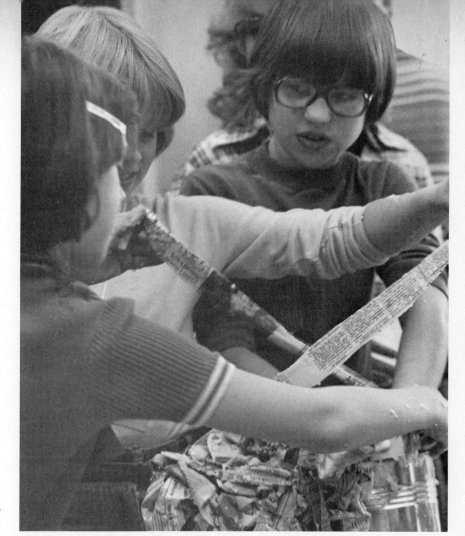

FIGURE 68.
The art program can make use of free or inexpensive materials. Old newspapers are the basic ingredient in this papier-mâché animal being constructed as a cooperative effort.

and paper can be dispensed with. What is meant is that adding sheets of copper foil, gummed paper, clay glazes, and cans of spray paint do not in themselves insure a good art program. Children themselves can provide many inexpensive or free materials, such as old newspapers for making papier-mâché, cloth for making collages or banners, boxes for making animals or dragons, and bottle caps and straws for making decorations. The art materials are important to an art program, but they play a secondary role; the materials are not as important as the way in which they are used. Because children at each developmental level have different needs and different capacities for for using various media, specific suggestions for art materials will be included in following chapters.

A vital part of any art motivation is the moment before the transition into expression. If this becomes lost, we lose an important part of the creative atmosphere. A girl who is stimulated by a discussion of shopping in the grocery store, and who is eager to portray her feelings about the canned goods stacked way above her head, the smell of the produce, or the excitement of picking out her favorite cookies, should not have to wait for six children in front of her to pass the paper back before she can get started. The materials should be ready for immediate use once the child is ready for them. Sometimes if the presence of the material would be a distraction, children can be gathered in a circle in a different part of the room for a discussion beforehand.

Every material should be thought of as meeting the needs of children and not as dictating a particular type of art lesson. Although children should be given the opportunity to discover and utilize the particular quality inherent in every material, no undue concern should be shown if the child uses this material in unexpected ways. If a second grade boy crumples his sheet of paper, do not condemn him to inactivity. A question like "Didn't you like that piece of paper?" may be better than trying to scold him for his actions, and the child himself may not be able to understand why he felt like crumpling paper. So now, for this child, a material like clay might be more appropriate, for it can be twisted and crushed without destroying the material itself.

The Teacher of Art

In teaching art to children the most important element is the teacher, for the teacher has the important task of providing an atmosphere conducive to inventiveness, exploration, and production. If we could imagine a very poor teacher in the elementary school—one who is ineffective, unimaginative and uninspiring—we would undoubtedly feel sorry for the children. At least we would know that they could get a great deal from the reading material in the class; the history book and the English reader would be there for them to use; and they would probably be able to develop some competencies in arithmetic. In art, however, there could be some real damage done; a poor teacher might be worse than no teacher at all.

There are ways that teachers can provide a proper atmosphere for creative activities, and there are ways that the environment can be organized to provide optimum conditions for art activities. The teacher of art should be a warm and friendly person. Cogan investigated the relationship between teacher behavior and the amount of required and self-initiated work performed by pupils (Levin

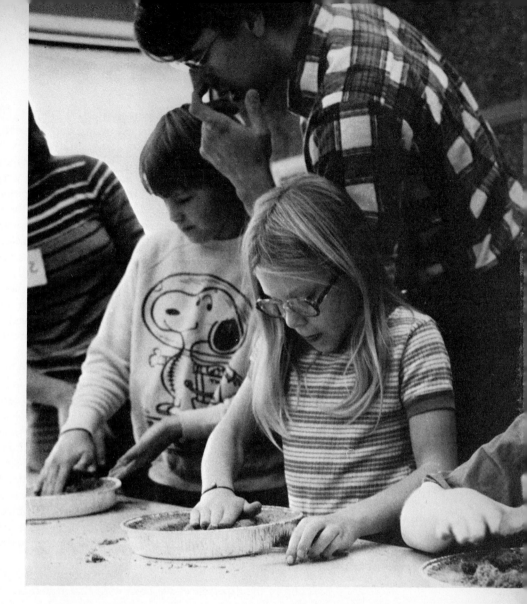

FIGURE 69.

An interested teacher shares the youngster's thoughts and gives support to their individual creative expression.

et al., 1957). Nearly a thousand junior high school pupils were surveyed; in almost every classroom positive relationships were found between the extent to which the student described the teacher as warm and friendly and the amount of self-initiated and required work produced. Averaging the amount of work that students did for each teacher clearly showed that the more friendly and warm teachers had pupils who produced more work. Other teacher characteristics can also be important, but apparently there is no other set of behavioral characteristics that is universally valuable in a school setting, since different teachers affect different children in different ways (Washburne and Heil, 1971).

THE TEACHER OF ART

There is some basis, then, for saying that a warm, friendly attitude toward students does foster productivity. In a study done with eleven year old children, Lippitt and White (1960) tried to find out what effects adult leaders had upon the behavior of children if the leaders behaved in ways called *authoritarian*, *democratic*, and *laissez-faire*. The authoritarian leader was one who issued orders and directions and gave praise or criticism; the democratic leader gave guiding suggestions, asked for children's opinions and judgments, and joked on a friendly basis; the laissez-faire leader gave out information when asked but did not take an active part in giving out directions or in stimulating self-guidance. Leaders changed groups part way through the experiment; the group behavior included a great outburst of horseplay by those children who were released from the authoritarian leader. But one interesting point was the finding that the children under a democratic leader showed the greatest expression of individual differences while at the same time showing less irritability and aggressiveness toward fellow members.

Learning does not take place in a completely relaxed environment any more than it does in a tightly structured setting. There is a middle ground where problems are seen as real, where interaction between teacher and children is open, and where thinking is expected. A study (Belcher, 1975) that examined scores on a creativity test found that students either in a game-like environment or in a stressful situation produced lower scores than did students who had been encouraged to do well as if in a normal test situation. In checking the creativity test gains of elementary classroom pupils, Wodtke and Wallen (1965) studied the methods of classroom control of seventy-seven female teachers, some of whom preferred a highly ordered and controlled classroom and could not tolerate behavior that did not fit into the pattern of order and control. It was found that a high degree of control by the classroom teacher had a detrimental effect on verbal creativity.

A work of art is not the representation of a thing but rather the representation of the experiences we have with that thing. Because experiences will change not only from year to year but from day to day, art expression becomes a dynamic, ever-changing process. The teacher, too, must be a flexible person, able to revise plans and to capitalize upon the enthusiasm and interest of the children. When the teacher is accessible and democratic in nature, youngsters can express themselves freely, both in words and in artistic expression; but it also is vital that the teacher be able to provide the flexible format so that the expression can be formed into an art product. To some extent this becomes a two-way exchange. Not only is the supportive atmosphere necessary, but flexible channeling of the youngster's feelings, ideas, and perceptions must culminate in an artistic form for the process to be meaningful.

PLATE 12.

"Walking Man," drawn by a five year old girl. Inability to control the flowing quality of watercolor made this girl unhappy. The colors may be pleasing to look at, but notice how the color has gone beyond the hair and hands and has also run down the paper, all of which was seen as a mistake by the child.

PLATE 13.

"Barns," painted in watercolor by a twelve year old girl. She has been able to control the paint to make a decorative and aesthetically pleasing composition, without concern for arbitrary rules of perspective, proportion, or design.

PLATE 14.

"Harbor," painted by an adolescent girl. For some older teenagers the merging, flowing quality of watercolor produces atmospheric effects that can be quite pleasing.

Identifying with the Child

Art must be important for the artist. This is obvious at the adult level, but it is also true for children. Youngsters must feel that what they are doing is important and that this activity is relevant to their needs. It may be difficult for a teacher to recognize and to face a discrepancy between an adult way of thinking and that of the pupils. What can be an exciting experience and a learning situation for an adult might not be appropriate for children's needs. The teacher, therefore, must be able to identify with the students. It is important that art activity be theirs and not the teacher's.

A child who shows signs of inhibitions in art or lacks the confidence for self-expression cannot be helped by a teacher who limits art instruction to the use of materials or to the problems of space relationships or color harmony. For example, a three or four year old who is afraid of becoming involved in scribbling may just put a few lines down in the corner of the page. Telling such a child to draw larger will not be of much value, even if accompanied by threats such as, "You may flunk nursery school if you do not draw larger." Instead, the teacher needs to identify with this child in such a way that the teacher too can feel the big, blank piece of paper as a threat.

The scribbling must become meaningful, and in this case one could ask the child, "Suppose you were in a big, empty room. Would you stand in just one corner or would you run all around the room? No one is there and you can do what you like. Wouldn't it be fun to run all the way to one side of the room and then to run back to the other? Now, look, here is a red crayon and suppose this sheet of paper is a great big empty room; how do you suppose the red crayon will act? Do you think the red crayon will just sit quietly in the corner? I don't think so either. Let's see how the red crayon runs around the paper." The tiny motions would thus become enlarged meaningfully because the reason for the large motion would become important. Few children could avoid the temptation of making large strokes all over the paper.

Although this may be an example that is obvious on the scribbling level, identification with the youngster and the problems that he is facing is necessary at any level. A fourth grade boy who says he cannot draw himself throwing a ball does not need the mechanics of figure drawing or an example that the teacher might make for him to copy, which could even widen the gap between his experience and his ability to express it. He needs an understanding of his own experience: "Show me how you throw a ball. What did you do with your arms, your legs? Let's try it again. Now you threw it up high. What did you do with your hands? Where did you look? Now throw the ball to me again." Such questions, interspersed with a friendly exchange of comments, should develop

FIGURE 70.
Most nursery school children enjoy scribbling and consider art activities to be one of the good things about going to nursery school.

in the youngster confidence to express these experiences, and the urge for such expression will be strong enough to overcome his lack of confidence.

It is also important for the teacher of art to identify with the youngsters who are successful in their achievement and who can express themselves easily. It is more important to recognize and share this joy of expression and pride in accomplishment than it is to point out that there are some corrections needed in proportion or that the hand has six fingers instead of five. The product is important for the child while drawing. One teacher was observed who told her second grade charges that the drawings would not be saved on this particular day and that they should throw their papers in the wastebasket on the way out. Obviously this teacher did not identify with these children, and it must be confessed that this observer felt that the attendance sheet she had been working on ought to join the youngsters' drawings in the wastebasket. The self-identification of youngsters with their own work can be a valuable experience, especially when the teacher can identify with the pupils so as to provide the proper motivation and environmental conditions for meaningful expression.

ART IN THE ELEMENTARY SCHOOL

Identifying with the Medium

A teacher who has never experienced the qualities of wood, who has never run a finger over the grain or sanded a board to a smooth finish, a teacher who has never been frustrated with the splintering of wood or been pleased with a joint well made will have difficulty motivating and inspiring the youth who has failed to solve a poorly conceived problem in working with wood. To think in terms of the material is an important part of the creative process, especially during the adolescent years. A teacher who has never gone through the process of creating in a specific art material may never understand the particular type of thinking that is necessary to work with clay, paint, or whatever. The teacher must have been truly involved in *creating* with materials, not in dealing with them in an abstract way by reading or mechanically carrying out some project.

This does not imply that an elementary school teacher needs to be an artist. But a teacher of children should have been involved in real creative experiences and competent in some area of expression. In some cases a new material can be worked through with a class, with the teacher becoming involved in the activity. However, as children grow, the final product becomes increasingly important to them, and with the increased emphasis being placed on the product itself, thinking in terms of art materials becomes an integral part of the teaching process.

An artist might seem to be the most logical person to teach art. It would be simpler if we said that a painter should teach painting, since art encompasses a great number of vocational areas. Most painters are striving to make some sense out of what they have experienced; that is, they try to put some feelings or emotions into a new configuration or try to place some visual matter in a pleasing, or in some cases a shocking, relationship. Each artist has a personal point of reference, and because of this we find that each artist paints in quite a different way. It is probably true that some artists are striving for recognition and tend to follow any current fad, even if this means making hamburgers out of an old pair of pants or taking one's bookshelf and painting it gold. However, the artist is supposedly attempting to make sense out of our strange, diverse, confusing, and contradictory world.

Now this sounds surprisingly like what children are doing in the elementary school. They too are using themselves as reference points for artistic creation. They too are trying to make some sense out of the environment and are putting things into relationships. Essentially, then, the child painter and the adult painter are both striving for the same goals, the main difference being that each has a unique reference point and experience to draw upon.

Since there is no body of factual knowledge in art necessary for the child to learn and retain, a painter's technical knowledge is not needed in the elementary school. At the secondary school level this technical knowledge could be valuable. There may be some point in saying that a competent painter might help throw out some of the tricks and busy work that are often called art. Looking at what galleries are presently exhibiting, the painter would probably cherish and support the spontaneous, free expression of children and look down upon triteness and repetition. However, what might seem spontaneous and free painting by young children might just as easily be random exploration, and as children grow older they develop a real need for order and repetition, which is reflected in their drawings and paintings. This decrease of spontaneity is actually a step toward the development of abstract thinking, an important factor in creativity. Therefore, a classroom teacher might seem better equipped than an artist to understand the developmental differences. But the education and training of the usual elementary school teacher does not include a real understanding of children's art as a prerequisite to receiving an education degree. In fact, an understanding of the normal development of children's art is often sadly neglected. Instead, a new teacher may have several projects for every occasion and for every holiday—projects that may have no relation to live, thinking, feeling children.

Whether or not a person working with young children calls himself an artist or a teacher may be incidental. An artist may be autocratic, know what is important to teach, and be sure what paintings by children should look like. An elementary school teacher may be like this too. What is needed instead is an artist or teacher who is warm, friendly, and democratic, someone who wants to help children develop their own concepts, is genuinely interested in what children paint, and has no preconceived notions of what each product should be like. The focus should be on developing sensitive, aware children. Art can be thought of as a continual process of creativity, because youngsters work at their own level to produce new forms with a unique organization, with countless minor problems of adapting subject matter to two- and three-dimensional surfaces. Each art activity should be planned to maximize the opportunities for creative thinking in art experiences.

Art has a far greater potential in the development of children than is now accorded to it. Until we can shake loose from tradition, until we can stop giving approval to what we, as adults, would like to do, until we can shake ourselves out of the grasp of habit and the status quo, we shall assign a meaningless role to art education in the elementary school.

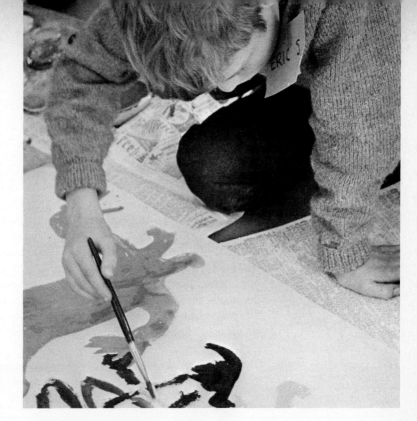

FIGURE 71.
Each child should be given the opportunity to paint his own ideas and feelings. It is the child himself who is the basis of art expression.

Motivation in the Classroom

The urge and excitement that children can bring to an art activity is dependent to a great degree upon their motivation. This motivation may come from several sources. A natural drive for expression can be seen in children when they are filled with enthusiasm for a particular topic. At other times it falls upon the shoulders of the classroom teacher to stimulate the interests of the children and to provide a motivational framework so that the art experience appears to have been designed especially for each child.

It would be quite impossible to say that any one approach to motivation is good for all children. At some times it might be best to have the children divided into interest groups or working on small projects; at another time the children might work with a variety of different materials but on one topic; at another time children might be working individually on a variety of topics. The method depends upon individual needs, and a sensitive teacher should know when these differences are important. First grade youngsters often have group experiences, such as visiting a fire station, that may excite a whole class so that they all want to put down on paper their reactions to such an experience. However, even here some individuals will become involved in particular parts of this experience. Some children may be excited about the big fire truck, others about the size of the wheels, length of the hose, the sleeping arrangement, or the pole that is used to slide down to the waiting truck. Although group motivations can be used effectively, it is still the individual's mode of expression that is important.

At times the motivation within the classroom can develop an enthusiasm that becomes contagious. Occasionally fifth-grade youngsters can develop such enthusiasm over a group project that it seems like the most important event in the world. Probably a variety of approaches best insures that each youngster is free to use his own mode of expression. The purpose is to translate the motivation into meaningful, purposeful creative activity, not to force a particular topic.

FIGURE 72.
These youngsters have become enthusiastic over the project of decorating the room for a party. Sometimes such art activities can be the most important thing that happens in school.

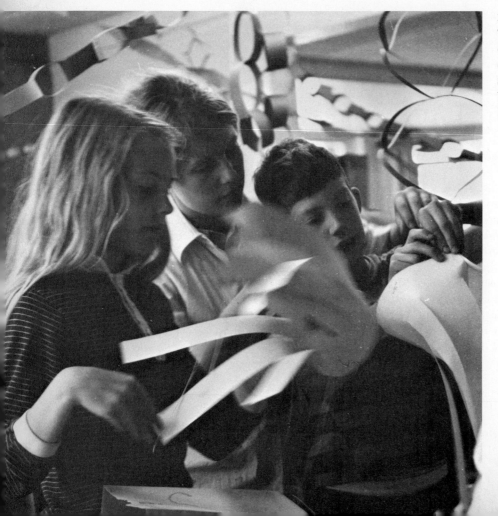

Extending the Frame of Reference

The principle of extending the frame of reference constitutes an important learning device in education. Start with the youngster's thinking, feeling, and perceiving, and extend these one step farther. This provides the opportunity for an expansion of possible directions in which he can move and that would be a logical extension of his own thinking. If, for instance, a kindergarten boy has drawn a picture of his mother and, as is usual, shown this off with pride, it is possible to extend his thinking into the environment in which the mother might find herself. "Where is your mother? Is she all alone? What is she doing?" Needless to say, such questions are aimed at enlarging the experience that the youngster has with the subject matter and are presented with warmth and interest in what has been accomplished. All relationships with youngsters should be supportive.

At times a child may become inflexible in his drawings, repeating a symbol without much alteration. This symbol may be of something that has particular appeal or is envied. A fourth grade boy might seem to draw just impersonal, generalized trucks. "Stop drawing those silly trucks" will not help; rather, it will show Johnny that the teacher is not interested in what he is drawing, or the skill he has developed, or (by inference) him. Instead, it is better to start where Johnny is and to extend his frame of reference.

"What kind of truck is that? Is it carrying a load? How many axles does it have? Are the tires big? Where is it going?" Sometimes this will be more than enough to stimulate Johnny's thinking, so that the truck symbol takes on the meaning of a particular truck, with a special cargo, driving to a definite destination, on a certain road. However, if this seems to be insufficient, it may be necessary to find other reasons why he draws trucks. The teacher should identify with Johnny. The truck then becomes the important focal point of a discussion. Does his father drive a truck? Or an uncle? Has he seen a truck like that, and would he like to drive one himself? Would he enjoy climbing into the pickup truck that the vice-principal owns or sitting behind the wheel of the district's dump truck? Has he counted the lights on the top or the number of lugs that hold the wheels on? Does he know whether the truck burns diesel fuel or how much horsepower it has? A genuine interest in trucks may spark a good deal of discussion, and the adult may learn much about trucks.

To some extent every drawing or painting becomes a natural means of the youngster's extending his own frame of reference. The elements in a drawing tend to be additive, that is, they provide an extension of thinking to related

FIGURE 73.

This picture of heavy machinery was drawn by a boy who obviously took a great deal of interest in the mechanical details of the equipment.

objects, which are then combined into a new form. A drawing of a person can often extend into the drawing of the ground, trees, houses, roads, and so forth. It is this relatedness that can sometimes lead youngsters to continue their drawings on the reverse side of the page, as if the paper were continuous but folded. It should be mentioned that a child ought to be in a position to reject any adult effort to get him to include a greater number and variety of objects in the drawing or painting. Every child does not have to be totally involved in every drawing, but every child should sometimes be totally involved in some drawings. We will discuss later how to involve the child who seems continually uninterested in art activities, for it may be this child who most needs the motivation of the teacher.

Motivation and Development

To motivate a child, a teacher must know that child. There are certain characteristics of each age that make it different from any other. Not only is it important to realize that what may be an exciting art material for the twelve year old can be a confusing material for the scribbler, but it is also important to realize that at each stage of development the youngster actually has a different relationship to the environment. The interest that a high school youngster may have in the structural design of a building will not be shared by a first grade youngster even though this topic is of interest to the teacher. The pleasure that a junior high school youngster derives from making a poster protesting new dress regulations in the school will obviously not be shared by a third grade boy who gets great pleasure from close examination of a caterpillar. To identify with the needs of a particular youngster may not always be easy, but the desires of the teacher must not overwhelm the needs of the children.

A child who is scribbling at the age of four may begin to name some of the parts of the picture. Lines may move up and down across the page and the child may identify this as a dog running. The youngster has made a big discovery: that the motions of running are similar to the up-and-down line that can be seen on the page. A sensitive and aware teacher must understand that this can be a satisfying experience, identify with the youngster, and share in the discovery. This line is of kinesthetic origin and it would be ridiculous for the teacher to try to motivate the child with visual imagery. To talk about a dog in visual terms, discussing the color and size and the proportion of the head to the body, would be meaningless. The well-intentioned teacher may seize upon this discovery as a chance to show the child pictures and illustrations of dogs and may even try to point out the differences between breeds of dogs. But this will all be wasted effort.

Not only is it necessary for the teacher to identify with the general needs of a youngster, but also with the specific needs of a particular individual. It may be that one child feels inhibited in motor activity. Another child may appear particularly timid and fearful of using materials. Still another may have a very short attention span and never become truly involved in the art process. It is important that the child's general as well as specific needs are understood, for without this background the teacher's motivation may never reach the child.

FIGURE 74.
We cannot expect every child to be thoroughly engrossed in every art activity; however, every child should occasionally be totally involved in some art experience.

Motivation and the Insecure Child

Most children in our classrooms express themselves readily in art activities. Occasionally, however, we find an insecure child who has a fear of even putting a line on paper unless it is given prior approval by the teacher. These children often express the feeling that they cannot draw or that they do not know how to do it; often they want the teacher to show them how or to draw something for them. Obviously, these are the children who need the art experience the most; to ignore this plea for help or simply to say that the youngster really *can* draw is no motivation whatever. If a boy says to the teacher that he cannot bring himself to express his feelings or emotions on paper, it is obvious that this is a statement that should not be contradicted. There may be children who feel at a loss unless they are given clear guidance and direction. This reliance upon adults can in some instances have a very negative influence upon the youngster's thinking; in other cases the child may have been rebuffed in his own attempts at self-direction and may retreat into a world in which his sensitivities and emotions will not be hurt further.

There are instances of children who are overwhelmed by the school situation. One second grade boy was reluctant to draw, and his teacher loudly explained that there was no point in expecting any art work from him. With encouragement, he did produce a timid drawing. Yet later, out of the classroom, this quiet child was extremely verbal and expressed great enthusiasm for his drawing. The school environment was a problem for this youngster, and this seeming inability to draw was reflecting his insecurity.

Sometimes a child will have difficulty in identifying with what she does. Such a child laughs nervously and self-consciously about her own products, for she is continually dissatisfied. She has to please others. Her own experience is less important to her than the product. The final product is only the result of the process, which is a complex learning experience that brings together the thinking, emotional, and perceptual processes resulting from preceding experiences. If the child cannot identify with her own experiences, the final product will show this.

A third grade boy who says "I can't draw" knows he cannot draw. "What can't you draw?" Perhaps he cannot draw a camel because he has never seen one, which would be quite understandable. But often the problem is deeper than that. "What do you want to draw?" If this third grade youngster says that he does not want to draw anything, then the teacher must find out what experience has been meaningful to him, or in some cases sensitize him to experiences he has had so that these can become meaningful. "What did you do yesterday?" The problem is one of making the youngster more actively aware of himself as a part of the environment and of stimulating this awareness. Some youngsters actually feel that they have done nothing interesting and can go through life partially sealed off from the outside world.

"What did you do yesterday? Did you just stand up all day? What did you do? Remember, remember exactly where you were yesterday afternoon. Oh, you had to work around the house. What did you do? Oh, you helped wash the car. Was your father with you?" Now here is something definite to talk about. The child has indeed had some experiences that you can discuss and share. Although to the child this may be just another boring day, the washing of the car can be a focal point for a discussion that needs to be carried on with warmth and interest on the part of the teacher. It is important that all of the senses be involved in such a discussion so that the youngster can relive the experience in even more detail than he experienced this originally. "Did you take the car to one of those car-wash places? Oh, you washed it at home. Was it very dirty? Did you use a hose? Oh, you used a bucket and a sponge. Was the water cold? Did you get yourself wet? Was the car so dirty that you had to change the water? Did you draw any pictures on the dirt before you washed it? Did your hands get all puffy from the water? Did your back ache when you were through? Did you have to change your clothes after it was finished? Let me see your hands. I can see that your fingernails are clean; you must have gotten them well soaked. Did your father do very much? Did the bucket of water spill? Were your feet cold when they got wet? Did the car look better when you were finished?"

The particular motivation will vary depending upon the age of the child. Sometimes with young children it is a help to have them go through the motions of how they washed the wheel covers. The older child will be able to identify more with the father and share with him the pride of having a clean car. In any case, it is important to make this motivation meaningful to the youngster himself and to stimulate the sensory experiences, what he has seen and felt, as well as stressing his own contributions to the activity.

Although we do not have many very insecure children in our classrooms, it is of vital importance that children who are completely bound up in themselves and have difficulty interacting in any meaningful way with their environment be given special attention in art. This is one area of the school program that can truly be based upon the youngster's own experiences, and any motivation should be of such a nature that it provides the opportunity for flexible, meaningful growth.

Numerous experiments have been done to assess the effectiveness of various motivational methods upon children's drawings. There is no doubt that the intensity and personal involvement of the motivation play a most important part in the quality of an art product (McVitty, 1954; Lansing, 1956; Clements, 1964). To a great extent there is a parallel development between the quality of experience that the youngster is trying to portray and the quality of the final product. The higher the quality of the one, the higher the quality of the other. The motivation is a vital element in this process.

FIGURE 75.

The teacher is an important element in children's creative expression, providing motivation and encouragement. Creative expression cannot be dictated in an aloof manner by an uninvolved adult.

Integrated Learning Experiences

Too often within the school learning program, experiences are isolated. At 9:27 the arithmetic books come out, at 10:14 it is time for recess, at 10:33 the music teacher arrives, at 11:05 it is social studies time. This fragmentation of the learning process into isolated segments creates an artificial situation. A child does not grow in single subject matter areas, nor does each area remain isolated in life outside school. This early specialization has isolated some of the subject matter areas from life to such a degree that the subjects have lost contact with society. We can even see this at the upper levels of education, where there is great discrepancy between social and scientific achievement.

Sometimes art is used in an attempt to correct this difficulty, usually with superficial results. Integration in learning means that the single subjects lose their identity and form a new unit within the student. Teachers often think that if history is illustrated, an integration between these two subjects takes place. This is sometimes referred to as correlation, as, for instance, where the students may be studying the American Indian in social studies and drawing wigwams in art. Sometimes this is successful. When third graders draw a picture before they are instructed to write something, they produce an increased amount of work (Cecere, 1966). All too often, however, an injustice is done to both areas. After an extensive survey of studies of the relationship between art and reading, Groff (1978) concluded that there is no experimental evidence to support some teachers' enthusiasm for the idea that including art in the program helps children learn to read. Because art is usually looked upon by the child as an attractive experience, and some of the social studies, arithmetic, or writing exercises are less favorably viewed, the correlation of these subject matter areas with art may have a negative value for the art experience. It is a little like mixing medicine with orange juice—both can be rejected.

It is possible that an integrated experience can develop in a school setting, but the separate parts must lose their identity and the individual child must feel that there is a meaningful whole with which to identify. Integration occurs within the individual. The child is influenced by emotional responses and perceptual sensory experiences. If the youngster can become totally involved in the learning process, then real integration takes place.

For example, history is often taught only in terms of dates and events. The Pilgrims landed in 1620. Plymouth Rock is somehow important in the event,

FIGURE 76.
The Pilgrims would never recognize this child's interpretation of the Mayflower, complete with engine room, refrigerator, and bathroom.

and a ship called the *Mayflower* was there, too. A request for children to draw this event is a meaningless activity. On the other hand, if children can empathize with the experience itself and focus upon this involvement, the activity may be a meaningful one.

"Have you ever been on a boat? On what kind of a boat? Were you ever in rough water? How did it feel? Do you know how big the *Mayflower* was? That's really pretty small! Did you realize that they had to come all that distance by relying on sails? How many sails were there? Do you know what happens when it is windy? The boat tilts way over and where do you go? Yes, all the people have to go to the other side! Do you get wet? Do you think you would like to stay down below deck? Do you know how long the Pilgrims were on this little sailing ship? That's a long time! Just suppose you had been on that ship all that time! Then you finally see land! Is everyone anxious to get off the ship? Are there any docks built? Oh, you have to get into a little rowboat! How do you go over the side? Hold on, don't slip on the way down! We still have to row to shore! Stay all together! What shall we do when we first land? Build a fire? So we can all keep warm!"

The children must feel the air and the waves, and even taste the salt on their lips. The experience must be *their* experience. The Pilgrims are no longer figures marching across the pages of the history book, but are recreated in the child's own experience. The picture that may result from such an experience can be anything that is of particular interest to the child. It may be the motion of the ship itself, with lines going up and down, or it may be the portrayal of an incident with which the child particularly identifies. Meaningful integration occurs in the youngster through such a motivation, which creates an atmosphere that is conducive to self-identification and self-involvement. To involve the child in the learning process and to make these isolated subject matter segments have meaning must be an important goal for the teacher. The art experiences that the youngster has had can provide the means of accomplishing this. To some extent, then, art can be the core of the learning environment within the school. Integrated learning does not happen by merely shuffling subject matter around—such integration can take place only within a child.

Grading the Child's Art

Probably no child has ever failed a grade because of poor marks in art. One often finds, however, that marks in art are required for report cards at various times. These report cards may take many forms, such as a letter to parents; at other times the grade is actually a numerical score, which is supposed to show the percentage of achievement in art. The usual practice is to use some sort of external standard, but this deals only with the product and completely neglects the individual child or the effect that the creative process has had. At the high school, each project may be graded, and the teacher goes through the process of averaging the grades, which may make it sound somewhat more objective.

This is probably not the place to question the value of giving any grades at all to children, but it is important to state that grading in art has no function. This is particularly true in the elementary school, where the youngster has no conscious awareness of making art in any manner other than that which is natural to him. At this level it would make more sense to grade the teacher, for it is the teacher who has been able to motivate the children to do excellent work, or has not been able to motivate some youngsters, or who may have failed to involve a few youngsters at all in the art activities.

Unfortunately, many teachers are expected to grade art, which throws added importance upon the end product. This is harmful to the child because it turns attention away from creating to concern for the picture itself. It can be particularly discouraging for a youngster who is beginning to become involved in creative activity if the art work is graded as a failure.

Often high marks are given for works of art that the teacher admires and other works of art are graded lower on the same arbitrary basis. Neatness and fine line control are frequently important is such a grading system, so that the youngster who paints more freely and who draws more boldly tends to be penalized. Sometimes, of course, a teacher who is very aware of trends in contemporary art may reward children who accidentally produce the type of art that is currently in vogue. Both methods are equally meaningless to the child.

The evaluation of an art product can take many forms. Sometimes it is a display of the so-called best pictures; or perhaps each picture or drawing will receive a reward: a letter grade, a gold star, or a written commendation. Whatever the form, these rewards disrupt the learning process. In a survey of studies related to reward and extrinsic incentives, Condry (1977) found ample evidence that offering rewards reduces efficiency and diminishes interest in a project. He concludes that such rewards, even for children as young as five, undermine self-confidence, for in such cases the ". . . activity is of a lower quality, contains more errors, and is more stereotyped and less creative than the work of comparable nonrewarded subjects working on the same problems" (p. 472). Even a group of female college students working under conditions of external evaluation were found to produce less creative art than a comparable group working without such evaluation (Amabile, 1979). In another study second grade youngsters were given a choice of shape-matching tasks, of simple, intermediate, or complex difficulty. Those who were to receive a reward if they played had a strong preference for the simplest version. When given a chance to do the activity again, the rewarded children were less interested (Pittman, Emery, and Boggiano, 1982).

In spite of the overwhelming evidence available that rewards, in the form of grades, gold stars, or special recognition, are negative motivators, there are some people in the arts who feel that evaluation of students is important

(Hoepfner, 1984; Day, 1985). The argument given is that art is a discipline that can be taught sequentially and that student progress needs to be monitored. For example, children can be graded on whether they achieve the goals set for them, such as if they can mix colors of different values or if they are able to overlap objects to represent space. This is rather sad since those who subscribe to such evaluation—and sometimes school administrators feel this way too—do not understand the essence of art or the importance of this area to the children's growth. It is easy to mimic the externals, the mechanics of art; it is easy to leave children out of the thinking and to put art into the same category as old handwriting exercises, making swirls in a nice round hand but with nothing to say. Needless to say, the mixing of colors or the overlapping of objects may bear no relationship to expression. For some children the "I can't draw" exclamation will be verified in the teacher's grade book.

There should be one place in the school system where marks do not count. The art room should be a sanctuary against school regulations, where youngsters are free to be themselves and to put down their ideas and feelings and emotions without censorship, where they can evaluate their own progress toward their own goals without the imposition of an arbitrary grading system.

Workbooks and Coloring Books

There is general agreement that coloring books too are detrimental to children's creative expression. These books usually have an outline of some form or other, such as a cow, or a dog, or a complete landscape. The youngster is supposed to color within the lines, and some youngsters seem to enjoy this activity. This enjoyment may be because these youngsters do not have to think for themselves. The dependency upon someone else's outline of an object makes children much less confident in their own means of expression. They obviously cannot draw a cow as good as the one in the coloring book. Parents, however, are becoming much more aware of these problems, and blank pages can be purchased in tablet form for youngsters to use. Self-made lines are more meaningful, and children who mark all over a coloring book do not do the same type of marking over their own drawings.

We can decry the use of coloring books for children, but some of the same objections can be raised to the paint-by-the-number kits that adults use. Just as a poem can be copied without understanding the message, the rhythm, or the metaphor, painting a picture with a paint-by-the-number kit is an automatic procedure that merely reinforces one's own inabilities.

It is rather surprising to find that workbooks and worksheets are used so extensively without the research to support their use as an educational device. Sedlak and Sedlak (1985) claim that the worksheet is the most commonly misused type of instructional material. However, in spite of the lack of educational support, the worksheet is used universally, particularly in the early years of schooling. Of particular concern here is the extensive use of stereotyped images for children to color. It is remarkable that, after kindergarten and first grade, children would have any incentive to make their own drawings; instead, it would seem that the self-confidence of young children would be crushed. Until some educational justification for worksheets can be documented, it would seem inappropriate to continue their use.

Workbooks used in arithmetic often greatly resemble coloring books. One arithmetic book has a child draw 76 repetitions of a stereotyped rabbit, 88 repetitions of a bird, 62 of a kite, 80 of a balloon, and so forth. Such repetition is meaningless. A study by Heilman (1954) indicated how dependent some children can become upon these workbooks, for the data revealed that the general growth pattern through creative work was seriously influenced by these workbooks. However, Daniel (1958) compared drawings by 90 children whose parents said they were frequent users of coloring books to drawings from 90 children who never or rarely used coloring books; he found that the quality of the drawings seemed more affected by the child's mental age and socioeconomic level than by coloring book usage. Possibly parents who value art experiences are buying coloring books for their children, whereas those parents who do not feel that art is important are not; this can confuse the findings. In some experiments conducted by Russell and Waugaman (1952), 63 percent of all children who had been exposed to coloring book birds lost their original concept of bird and changed their drawings to resemble the workbook stereotype. Even preschool children's drawings can be adversely affected. Yates and Fisher (1980) had children spend only two sessions completing dash-line drawings of a stick figure, the rear view of three rabbits, and a stereotyped house. Their study indicated that if the children's own drawings were similar, they were influenced, but otherwise the patterns were rejected and the children continued to use their own symbols.

Often the excuse is given that workbook exercises are fundamental to learning arithmetic concepts or to developing recognition of a letter. However, a thesis by Johnson (1963) indicated that tracing over a letter up to ten times was of no value in recognizing that letter later. There is no evidence that these laboriously colored balloons and kites actually help to develop either number concepts or reading abilities. And, typically, the children already know the concepts that

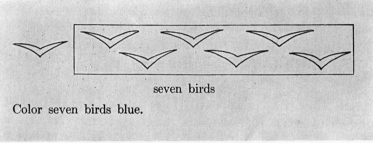

seven birds

Color seven birds blue.

FIGURE 77.

Coloring books affect a child's creative expression. (Courtesy of Dr. Irene Russell, Research Bulletin, The Eastern Arts Association, Vol. 3, No. 1, 1952.)

(Top) This bird shows one child's expression before he was exposed to coloring books.

(Center) Then the child had to color a workbook illustration.

(Bottom) After coloring the workbook birds, the child has lost his creative sensitivity and self-reliance.

supposedly are now being taught. Although no one will admit it, one of the main reasons for using these workbooks may well be that they give the classroom teacher a chance to have some rest while the youngsters fill in the appropriate number of birds or color the proper kites green.

Surprisingly enough, dittoed sheets are still occasionally handed out for youngsters to color that may have outlines of George Washington, a Thanksgiving turkey, a Halloween pumpkin, an Easter rabbit, or a Christmas tree. One particular example showed Pilgrims standing in front of their log cabin holding blunderbusses which had not been invented yet; actually, Pilgrims lived in huts made of sticks and vines until they built clapboard houses, because "Neither the English nor the Dutch built log cabins at first, and apparently did not even know how to do so. . . ." (Stewart, 1954, p. 152). Sometimes art projects also smack of the same absurdities, as when youngsters are given copper foil to press over some preformed design to mount for Christmas presents. Even May baskets preplanned by the teacher for the first grade youngsters to cut out fall into the category of being detrimental to creative expression.

Art instruction that includes these kinds of activities is worse than no art at all. Such predigested activities force youngsters into imitative behavior and inhibit their own creative expression. These activities make no provision for emotional growth because any variation the child makes can only be a mistake; they do not promote skills, because skills develop from one's own expression. Instead, they condition the child to accept adult concepts as art, art that the child is unable to produce, therefore frustrating normal creative urges.

However, sometimes teacher aides or helpful parents, who know little about art or children's thinking, will bring a cute project to class for children to complete. It is rather difficult to know what to do under these circumstances, but an occasional turkey made from a pine cone and pipe cleaners won't be devastating. One report (Mitchell, 1982) on a compensatory education program found that the para-professionals wanted to use pre-made patterns, but the teachers were more interested in the process of art. The school failed to recognize the significance of the art product to parents. The aides had predicted correctly: the adult-designed art work was displayed more frequently in homes than were the finger paintings and child-designed collages. Education and understanding take time.

Copying

It has generally been accepted that children should not copy anything. The arts are supposed to be a means of one's own expression and not a superficial copy of someone else's thought and ideas. Copies for the most part are done with no understanding of the structure or meaning of what is imitated. Adults copy things too; it is not just children. One often sees ashtrays copied from leaves, oil paintings copied from postcards, or drawings copied from photographs. These facsimiles are shallow and copy only the superficial qualities of the original. It is not an easy thing to transform an actual three-dimensional shape onto a two-dimensional surface. However, it is an intellectual challenge that most youngsters confront without question. Where to place parts, the space to be utilized, the quality of line to be used, the parts to be emphasized or left out, all make this a serious mental challenge. A copy is merely a duplication from one surface to another without the involvement of the problem-solving capacities of the mind. However, Wilson and Wilson (1982) feel that there are some advantages in providing children with a method of artistic expression and sometimes a greater awareness of detail. They feel that some copying is unavoidable. Unfortunately, here the emphasis is on the final product, not on the thinking processes. Smith (1985) had children do a series of comic strips. She found that most children invented their own imagery and their own themes based upon their own experiences, but a few children relied upon existing cartoon strip images. Leeds (1984) points out that, through history, artists' training included a good deal of copying. It is only in the twentieth century that innovation and invention have taken precedence over duplicating the masters. She feels that today the artist and the child are both free to express the self without the pressure to conform to the style or demands of others.

It indeed would be a blow to a child who is struggling to represent an object and finally has had some success to have a well-meaning adult say "Here, copy this." For young children this would be easily rejected, but for the nine or ten year old, the feeling that an adult does not see the child's expression as being valuable could be a devastating blow. We need to provide children with the confidence in their own expression. There is no right way of drawing or painting. The success of artists who have rebelled against tradition and against their own culture is well documented. There is no place for mindless copying of others' art in a meaningful art program.

Exhibits and Competitions

Exhibits in the classroom are usually held for the children who enjoy seeing their own work displayed. For some children this becomes particularly important. Those who are not able to achieve in other ways can see themselves as

FIGURE 78.

The stimulation children receive from one another can contribute to a creative atmosphere. This sharing of thoughts and enthusiasm is quite different from copying from one another.

members of the class in good standing when their art products are displayed with everyone else's. Generally, the work to be displayed should be selected by the children and hung at their eye level. The preparation for an exhibit can often be an exciting occasion, and when properly guided, children can take over most of the work of hanging the pictures. Classroom exhibits should be frequently changed, for youngsters quickly lose the intimate relationship to their own work, and it is senseless to display work that was done weeks or even months earlier.

An exhibit for parents may be a different problem. Here the reason for the exhibit should be clear. Often the purpose is to educate the viewer rather than to display pictures for parents to admire. It is possible to combine these two functions, but such exhibits take a good deal of planning. Often signs help in conveying the message; a carefully labeled exhibit will be able to explain itself. It is better to have a small exhibit stressing one theme such as individual differences, the variety in expression of a particular topic, or a sequence of drawings showing changes in development, than to have an exhibit that is too large to be easily seen and that may be too hastily put together.

Competition in art is of two types. Natural competition is inherent in every classroom situation, where youngsters have a natural desire to improve upon their own achievements. Forced competition is usually imposed upon a class or group of children, and prizes are often given as rewards. Growth is a continuous competition with one's own standards and achievements, and this is a most natural and healthly form of competition. Children in the lower elementary grades are usually unaware of any competition in art, for their drawings and paintings are merely a means of expression. Each child differs from every other, and usually there is no feeling that one drawing or painting is better than another. The situation changes somewhat as the child grows older and as the final product becomes more and more important. In the upper grades of the elementary school, the stimulation children receive from each other's creative work is a valuable contribution to their own flexibility. The youngster is usually exposed to many different styles and modes of expression, which can be rejected or adapted. Such natural competition is not based on external standards. This sharing of ideas is not to be confused with a copying of forms by the insecure child, where the problem is quite different because the youngster is copying a configuration without any understanding of the process behind it.

Occasionally forced competition is unwittingly brought into the classroom. Sometimes the teacher may state that the best pictures will be saved for an exhibit, or the local P.T.A. or Chamber of Commerce will offer a prize in a good-hearted manner to the best picture illustrating how our town can be made more beautiful. Michael (1959) found in an experiment with high school art students that giving a prize for the best painting significantly decreased the aesthetic quality of students' work. A judge of an annual competition of children's art said that each year some children copied the winner of the preceding year in the hope that they would be awarded a prize too. This type of competition is bad for the winner and the loser. The losers know that they do not have the artistic ability to achieve and they therefore lose interest in art expression. The winner has achieved recognition in art and therefore loses the incentive to investigate and explore other means of art expression. Of course, there was the case of the boy who could not understand why his picture was entered in the competition, because he did not think it was as good as he wished it were; it was even harder for him to understand why he was awarded a prize. Some schools pride themselves on the number of prizes their students have won in various art exhibits. The results tend to be superficial, with a stress on techniques and an overemphasis on outcome. All this overpowers serious involvement by the child. No jury can take into consideration the meaningfulness of an art work to its creator. Even on the adult level the winner of a competition may not be looked upon as a great artist ten years later. Such forced competition has no place in our school system.

Summary

Child art is highly individual. No two children express themselves entirely alike. One of the vital aims of art education is to bring out the individual differences that make up each child's personality. To suppress these individual differences, to emphasize the final product, to value one youngster over another, goes against the basic premises of creative expression. The influence of the teacher is crucial in creative activities. The teacher's enthusiasm, interests, and attitude are all reflected in how children view the arts. Children need to know that their thoughts and feelings are important and are treated with respect. Art is an activity that needs no external reward. It may be that the hesitant, insecure child who feels withdrawn from other class activities can find satisfaction and acceptance in creative expression.

It should not be forgotten that the goal of an art program is to develop the thinking, feeling, and perceiving of each youngster. It is not to produce products. It is not to produce little artists. It is not to indoctrinate children into a predetermined way of viewing art. The materials and the technical skills follow expression; they do not precede it.

Related Activities

1. Collect the drawings from an elementary school class. Ask a classroom teacher, an art teacher, a college student, and a child to grade these drawings, as for a report card. Ask how these judges determined the best and poorest. How do the various ratings compare? Which, if any, seems to be the most valid approach?

2. Plan and display an exhibit of the children's art work with a definite purpose. Organize the exhibit so that it presents a feeling of unity. Identify and label the specific age, grade level, medium, and subject matter or motivation.

3. Observe two separate classrooms of the same grade. Predict on the basis of the teachers' interest and enthusiasm in art activities how the products will differ. Collect drawings from these classrooms on two occasions and compare. Note differences in amount of detail, color use, amount of action indicated, and extent to which the total area of the page is used.

4. Make a survey to determine what competitions are presently being sponsored in a local school in music, art, and so forth. Gather information from teachers and students and discuss the effects of these competitions upon the classroom behavior, the time consumed, and the results of the competitions.

5. Check to find an elementary school that divides its classes according to achievement levels. Compare the drawings of the children in the "fast" classes with those in the "slow" classes. Are there any differences in method of representation? In the number of details used?

6. Pick out one child who does not appear gifted in art. Over a period of several months, give special attention to his art performances. Show an interest in his products, encourage him, praise changes in his expression, exhibit his paintings, show him you enjoy what and how he draws, give him confidence to explore new materials, ask him if he would like to be an artist. After the experimental period is over, compare his products with those done previously. Do you still consider him not particularly gifted?

6

The Beginnings of Self-expression

The Scribbling Stage
Two–Four Years

The Importance of Early Childhood

The first few years of life are the most vital in a child's development. During this period, learning patterns, attitudes, and a sense of self begin to be established. Art can contribute a tremendous amount to this development, for it is in the interaction between a child and the environment that learning takes place. Although we usually think of art as starting with the first mark that a child puts down on paper, it actually begins much earlier, when the senses first contact the environment and a child reacts to these sensory experiences. Touching, feeling, seeing, manipulating, tasting, listening—in fact, any methods of perceiving and reacting to the environment—are essentially background for the production of art forms, whether it is on a child's level or on that of a professional artist.

Although vocal expression begins very early in life, the child's first permanent record usually takes the form of a scribble at about the age of eighteen months or so. It is the beginning of expression, which leads not only to drawing and painting but also to the written word. It is unfortunate that the very word *scribble* has negative connotations for adults. The word may suggest a waste of time or at least a lack of content. Actually, the very opposite is true, for the way in which these first marks are received and the attention that is paid to them may cause young children to develop attitudes that will remain with them as they start formal schooling.

The Development of Scribbling

Scribbles tend to follow a fairly predictable order. They start with random marks on a paper and gradually evolve into drawings that have content recognizable to adults. But between the ages of about eighteen months and about four years, when the first visual image appears, a great deal of development takes place. It is rather surprising, therefore, to find that only recently has much research been done on these early drawing attempts. Generally speaking, scribbles fall into three main categories. These are disordered scribbles, controlled scribbles, and named scribbles.

Disordered Scribbling

The first marks are usually random. They vary in length and direction, although there may be some repetition as the child swings her arm back and forth. Often a child may look away while making these marks and still continue scribbling. The line quality often varies considerably, with somewhat accidental results. A typical disordered scribble is shown in Figure 80. Various methods are used to hold the crayon or pencil. The crayon may be held upside down or sideways; it may be grasped in the fist or held between clenched fingers. The fingers and wrist are not used to control the drawing instrument. It is important to realize that the size of the motions shown on the paper is relative to the size of the child. If an adult swung his arm back and forth, he would cover an arc of about three feet; a child would tend to draw an arc only about twelve inches long. Because scribblers have not yet developed fine muscle control, usually only the larger sweeps will be repeated. We have to remember that the child scribbles with what are big motions for her, although to an adult the result may appear to be on a small scale.

It is important to mention that scribbles are not attempts at portraying the visual environment. To a great extent the scribbles themselves are based upon the physical and psychological development of the child, not upon some representational intent. Making the haphazard array of lines, however, is extremely enjoyable. A child will be fascinated with this activity. It is very important to have the opportunity to scribble. Sometimes scribbling will be done in the dirt, on the walls, or on furniture if the proper tools and place are not provided.

Parents may try to find something in these early scribbles that they can recognize, or sometimes a well-meaning grandparent will attempt to draw something for the child to copy. The two year old typically cannot copy a circle, although some two year olds are able to copy a line. So while a child is still in the stage of disordered scribbling, drawing a picture of something "real" is inconceivable. Such attempts would be similar to trying to teach a babbling baby to pronounce words correctly or to use them in sentences. A parent would not ask a babbling child to repeat the Gettysburg Address, even though this may become important at fifth grade. The stick figure or apple drawn by an encouraging parent can be just as ridiculous. Such imposed ideas are far beyond the comprehension of a child at this developmental level and may even be harmful

FIGURE 80.

In this disordered scribble, the pen has not been lifted from the paper. The child's repeated motions result in a record of a kinesthetic activity.

to his future development. However, an interest in what the child is doing is important, because the child has to feel that this avenue of communication is an acceptable one.

Children of this age have little visual control over their scribbling, which parents should regard as an indication that they are not yet ready to perform tasks that require fine motor control. They are going to be sloppy eaters, they are going to have trouble with buttons, and they will not be able to follow directions based on visual cues. Very young children may find a crayon more interesting to look at, feel, or even taste. However, two year olds usually have no such problems, and scribbling activity quickly becomes a real means of expression. All children begin with scribbling, whether they are Chinese or Eskimos, Americans or Europeans. It is quite apparent that scribbling is a natural part of the total development of children, reflecting their physiological and psychological growth.

Controlled Scribbling

Children will discover that there is a connection between their motions and the marks on the paper about six months or so after starting to scribble. This is a very important step, because now children have discovered visual control over the marks they are making. Although a casual glance may show no difference in the drawings themselves, gaining control over the motion is an important accomplishment.

Most children approach scribbling at this stage with a great deal of enthusiasm. When they discover the coordination between visual and motor activity, they are stimulated to vary their motions. Now the lines may be repeated, and sometimes they are drawn with a great deal of vigor. These lines may be drawn horizontally, vertically, or in circles. Occasionally we find dots or small repeated patterns, since children now are able to take the crayon off the page. Children can become very engrossed in scribbling, as the girl is in Figure 83, sometimes with their noses practically glued to the paper.

Children will now spend about twice as long drawing and occasionally will like to try different colors on the paper. They often like to fill the page, while earlier they even had trouble staying on the paper. They still experiment with a variety of methods of holding the crayon, though by the age of three they usually come close to an adult grip. They now understand more about trying to copy a line or a cross but will not refer to the given model and usually strike off in unpredictable directions. By the age of three, children can copy a circle but not a square. The scribblings now become much more elaborate, and children will excitedly discover a relationship between what they have drawn and something in the environment. There may still be very little relationship between the drawing and what is drawn.

This control over the scribble is also reflected in children's control over other parts of the environment. Mother, who six months earlier could not get Alice to button her jacket, now finds that she insists on doing it for herself. She understands and enjoys practicing this new ability. The physical growth rate is very fast from one to three; a body image is developing, hand preferences are emerging, and the real integration of visual and motor apparatus is beginning, although this integration is not really complete until early adolescence (Cratty, 1970). Because control of motor abilities is an important achievement, we can certainly understand that calling attention to some interesting patterns in a drawing would not be particularly helpful; at this stage children's intentions do not go beyond moving the crayon, and the enjoyment is essentially from the kinesthetic sensation and control of the drawing tool. The adult's role is increasingly important now, because children will often run to an adult with these scribbles, eager to share their excitement. It is this sharing of an experience that is important and not the scribble itself.

FIGURE 81.
This controlled scribble shows a variety of motions, with increased use of small muscles.

Naming of Scribbling

This next step is an important one in the development of children. This is the point when children start to name their scribbles. They may say, "This is Mother," or "I am running," although neither Mother nor the child may be recognized. This naming of scribbling is of great significance, for now children's thinking has changed. Before this stage they were satisfied with marks that resulted from motions, but now they have connected these marks to the world around them, a change from kinesthetic thinking to imaginative thinking. This stage usually occurs at about the age of three and a half years. The importance of the change can be simply understood if we realize that, as adults, most of our thinking is in terms of mental pictures. If we try to think back as far as we can, our memory will not likely carry us further than this naming-of-scribbling stage. It is at this point, then, that children develop a basis for visual retention.

As children begin to name their scribbles, an important transition takes place. The line becomes more than just the result of a motion; it becomes the edge of a form. This transition is a dramatic one, for as adults we usually draw a line to connote the contour or to symbolize distinguishing features of an object. Up to this point, scribbles have been the result of kinesthetic activity, and children sometimes name these scribbles with reference to a physical activity, such as running or jumping. It is not long before the line has a visible reference, and the space enclosed within lines begins to take on meaning; what has been empty space now can be understood as symbolizing substance.

The drawings themselves have not changed remarkably from early scribbles. Although children may now start with some idea of what they are going to do, they are also influenced by what they have done. So, as children make marks on the page, these marks may have a visual reference for them, which in turn affects the drawings. Whereas earlier they sometimes could see a relationship between what they had drawn and some object, now they draw with intent.

Although children at three and a half have usually arrived at the stage of naming of scribbling, they will often enjoy the sheer physical motion; if given a new drawing tool, they spend a considerable length of time in trying out this instrument to see how it feels, in much the same way as an adult would do. The amount of time that youngsters spend on drawing will increase even more, and the scribbles become much more differentiated. They may be well distributed over the page, and the marks will sometimes be accompanied by a verbal description of what is going on. This conversation is not directed at any particular adult, but often seems to be a communication with the self. Not all children

FIGURE 82.
A four year old girl has drawn with intent. The lines enclose space, creating forms that adults can almost recognize.

do this, by any means, but it seems apparent that drawings now become a record of how children feel about parts of the environment, and the way they draw makes the scribbles an important means of communication.

Sometimes at this stage children will announce what they are going to draw, or sometimes drawings will evolve from the first exploratory marks on

THE BEGINNINGS OF SELF-EXPRESSION

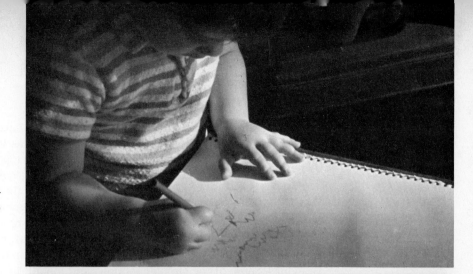

FIGURE 83.
Scribbling is a serious, meaningful activity for young children. Notice the determination and concentration that have gone into this drawing.

the paper. It is quite clear that although parts may have some intent as they are being drawn, children have no preconceived notion as to what the finished scribbling will look like. A line that is drawn at the top of the page may be called a tree but may end up being given a different name before the picture is completed. The wavy line may be a dog running or the child making giant steps. These lines are not always symbols of visual impressions, but can be representations of a nonvisual nature; roughness or hurry-up lines are just as important. The point is that the scribbles and lines that may appear meaningless to adults do in fact have a real meaning to the children who are making these drawings. Some of the circular motions and longitudinal lines may seem to tie together to make a person, but adults should not try to find a visual reality there or try to give scribbles their own interpretation. There may be a real danger in parents or teachers pushing children to find some name or some excuse for what they have drawn. Rather, teachers and parents should give confidence and encouragement in this new kind of thinking.

The Meaning of Color

The experience of scribbling, then, is mainly one of motor activity. At first satisfaction is derived from the experience of kinesthetic motions, next from a visual control of these lines, and finally from the relationship of these lines to the outside world. Color, therefore, plays a decidedly subordinate role in the scribbling stage. This is particularly true when children are establishing motor coordination. The choice of many colors can sometimes divert children from scribbling. They need to be able to distinguish their marks from the rest of the page. Therefore, it is necessary to select drawing materials that will provide a strong contrast. Black crayon on white paper or white chalk on a blackboard are to be preferred over colors that may not give this contrast.

Most research indicates that discrimination of objects by form comes earlier than differentiation by color. Casey (1979) was able to have one year olds respond to form differences, but color differences aroused little curiosity. One study (Melkman, Koriat, and Pardo, 1976) asked children to match a given colored shape with one that was like it either in color or form; they found that two year olds matched objects on the basis of form, three year olds more often matched on the basis of color, but four year olds again matched on the basis of form. It is interesting to note that four year old children are beginning to make

FIGURE 84.

Tempera paint must be a thick mixture so that it can be controlled if the youngster will be painting at an easel. Here we see a two-fisted approach to painting.

recognizable shapes at a time that coincides with this increased awareness of form.

Some work has been done in attempting to relate color and form to the personality of children of nursery school age. A well-known study by Alschuler and Hattwick (1947, 1969) attempted to relate the paintings of some one hundred and fifty nursery school children to certain of their behavioral characteristics. In a two-volume report, support was given to the assumption that in painting,

THE MEANING OF COLOR

children express their emotional experiences and adjustments. Those children who consistently painted in warm colors manifested free emotional behavior in warm, affectionate relations; children who preferred blue tended to be more controlled in their behavior; and children who used black tended as a group to show a dearth of emotional behavior. However, some questions have been raised about these conclusions. Corcoran (1954) found evidence that three year old children used colors in sequential order when painting at an easel. That is, the colors were used from left to right or right to left on the easel tray, regardless of what the colors were. Apparently, Alschuler and Hattwick did not control for the placement of colors in their study. Biehler (1953), in a study with nursery school children, found that they tended to apply colors in direct relationship to how these were placed on the easel tray. This might indicate that painting at this age is more a mechanical activity than an emotional one. Scribbling apparently tends to be concerned with a striving for visual control. Color as part of the scribbling process in painting is mainly exploratory, and the use of particular colors may be related more closely to how the containers of colors are arranged than to deep-seated emotional problems of the child.

Changes in color can sometimes be used purposefully in the naming of scribbling stage, for here colors may have some meaning. Colors can also be fun for the child to work with. However, it is of far greater importance in the scribbling stages that children be given the opportunity to create lines and forms and to develop some facility with drawing tools.

Environment and the Developmental Process

With increased attention focused upon early learning and a good deal of concern being shown for the need to develop methods of working with young children, their art experiences are of increased interest. It has been shown that even during the first few months of life children exposed to an enriched visual environment develop faster than children who do not have anything interesting to focus on, such as mobiles hanging over their cribs (White and Castle, 1964). Children raised in an atmosphere of sterility and deprivation apparently fall far behind normal development in all phases of their growth (Bronfenbrenner, 1968). A passive, neutral, sterile environment for young children is not the ideal setting for development. A study of 93 young children (Bradley, Caldwell, and

THE BEGINNINGS OF SELF-EXPRESSION

Elardo, 1979) found that the competence of children twelve to twenty-four months of age increased when mothers encouraged and challenged their abilities. A rigorous "parents as teacher" project, involving four school districts and 380 Missouri families for a period of three years, instructed first-time parents in child-rearing practices. The children of participating parents scored significantly higher on all measures of intelligence, achievement, verbal ability, and comprehension than did comparison children (Maeroff, 1985). The interaction between children and the environment is the crucial element in learning.

Programs for disadvantaged children are often started at a very young age. Some experimental programs have focused on the behavior of mothers; others have started when youngsters of three or four arrive in the nursery school setting. Some of these programs are called enrichment programs, in which children are exposed to a great number of activities that are expected to provide

FIGURE 85.
Watching the effect of gravity as a marble rolls down a tube may not be exciting for adults, but for a preschooler this simple task is an involving experience and one that needs an adult's passive support.

some of the background that youngsters in nondeprived homes would normally experience. A number of these activities are essentially art activities, with youngsters involved in painting, drawing, manipulating clay, or working with two- and three-dimensional forms. The theory behind most of these programs is essentially the same: that the interaction between children and environment needs to be increased so that children actually see, hear, smell, taste, and use all their senses to make this interaction process meaningful. Although there are high expectations for these preschool programs, early evidence indicated that such programs did not have any lasting effects. However, a study (Darlington et al., 1980) of children in seventh grade showed evidence that those children who had been in a preschool program fulfilled school expectations significantly better than a comparable group who did not have this advantage.

One study on the drawing development in preschool children (Goertz, 1966) found that experience in working with art materials accelerates the developmental level of a child's drawings. Probably the attitude of parents toward a child's drawing is indicative of the attitude of the parents toward the child. An interest in the drawings may indicate an awareness of the necessity of providing experiences in all spheres.

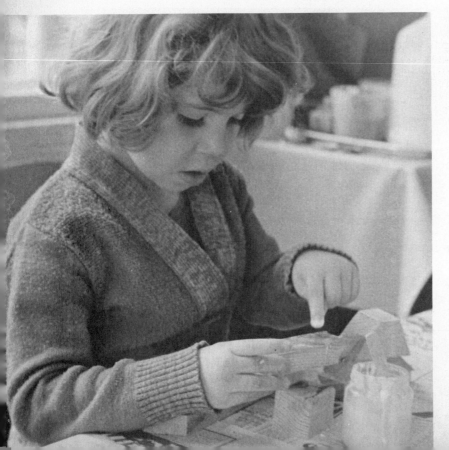

FIGURE 86.

Learning to glue can be a challenging experience. Keeping fingers from sticking together can be as much of a problem as making two pieces of wood stick together.

In a study of preschool children's attention, Bee (1964) expected that children who were not easily distracted would have parents who would leave them alone to solve problems. However, this was not borne out. What she found, in fact, was that children who were easily distracted had parents who offered children ready-made solutions, whereas the children who were not easily distracted had parents who gave them suggestions only for means of finding their own solution. Apparently it is better to interact with children, to help them find ways to solve problems, rather than either to leave them alone or to provide specific answers. Art in itself is a constant problem-solving situation. This is true at the preschool level as well as at older ages. The parent or teacher who provides the task and the solution may be doing as great a disservice to children as parents or teachers who stand back and let children create on their own. What seems to be needed is someone who can provide alternate suggestions, give encouragement, and make children feel that their efforts are worthwhile.

Rosario and Collazo (1981) made lengthy observations in two preschools; the teachers they observed defined art as the highly structured projects which emphasized the importance of completing the activity, but these teachers seldom called art the child-initiated activity and seldom saved it.

Some teachers feel it important that young children experience success in art. After all, these teachers say, it is difficult for three year olds to manipulate scissors and to control a pen or pencil. Such teachers plan projects that they feel will have a good chance for success: a valentine heart will already be cut out, or grape leaves will be duplicated so children can paste precut purple circles on the paper to represent bunches of grapes. Needless to say, these projects are doomed to failure if the children cannot produce what the teacher wants. Some children fail more than others.

There is also the feeling that some materials are easier for young children to use. If children are having difficulty drawing a person, they may be given precut body parts to assemble, with the assumption that even very young children should be able to assemble pieces into a recognizable figure. However, when children were asked to draw a man, make a man from clay, and paste pieces together to make a man (Brittain, 1979), there seemed to be no difference in the representation regardless of material. In a follow-up study (Brittain and Chien, 1980), children between two and five years of age were asked to draw a man, were given colored paper circles and rectangles to make a man, and were also given colorful pieces of paper clearly representing body parts to make a man. Again there was little difference. If a child could draw a person, he could paste one together; if he scribbled, he pasted geometric shapes or body parts randomly distributed about the page and showed no concept of man.

A

FIGURE 87.
A change in material does not produce a change in the child's concept of a human form.
Here are the works of two children; the scribbling child (A) showed consistent lack of
organization, and the child who drew a head-feet representation (B) repeated this concept when pasting paper forms.

These children easily identified body parts, but assembling the shapes into a
cohesive whole was beyond their abilities. It is not a problem of eye–hand coordination or physical dexterity since, although the pasting task was easy, the
pasted man was no more successful than the drawing. For most children up to
the age of four, and for some even later, the task of conceptualizing a total
configuration is beyond their cognition. The children were not aware of failing
to complete the figure accurately. As far as they were concerned, they had done
the task satisfactorily. They seemed content with pasting pieces of paper on the

THE BEGINNINGS OF SELF-EXPRESSION

B

page, regardless of the fact that the results did not look like an adult concept of a person. It was found (Brittain and Chien, 1983) that if a child had difficulty identifying a body when it was pointed to on a sheet of paper along with randomly spaced arms, legs, and a head, the child would tend to ignore the body in making a drawing and include only the head and legs.

In the transition from recognition to reconstruction, perceptual awareness is transformed into a concept. Recognizing that scribbles can sometimes have form that is similar to objects in the environment means that these objects can now be indicated by a symbol. This is a big step—being able to think of objects and to reconstruct them or symbolize them.

In the early stages of development, motor activity plays a more important role than language in the discovery of reality. To represent this reality, a child between two and four develops the ability to make something—a symbol, a word, or an object—stand for something that is not present (Ginsburg and Opper,

ENVIRONMENT AND DEVELOPMENTAL PROCESS

203

1969). This does not imply that the child attempts a visual representation of objects or lacks sufficient motor control to draw a visual representation of objects. Rather, concepts beyond the self have not fully developed, nor has the child a full visual–motor integration. The nursery school child operates within touch space; that which is touched and manipulated has more meaning than what is passively viewed or what is distant and incompletely perceived.

Scribbling as a Reflection of Growth

The growth process is continuous but not smooth. This can be seen in the physical growth of children. Although we can say that children of a certain age have an average height of so many inches, there are great differences in individuals; sudden spurts of growth, especially during adolescence, demonstrate that growth is extremely uneven. In the scribbling stage this is easily seen, for scribbling can be considered a reflection of the physical and emotional development of children. Just as there are differences in growth, there are also great individual differences in the scribbling of children.

Holladay (1966) documented the drawing abilities of children from two through five years of age. He collected unmotivated, spontaneous drawings, and also had the children attempt to copy numerous forms. A record was kept of the way drawings were made, including type of grip, choice of crayon, drawing time for each child, and so on. He was able to show seven different stages of scribbling, from undifferentiated scribbles to decorative scribbles. Dempsey (1971) examined the drawings by children three to four and a half years of age and recorded their verbalization of the meaning of these scribbles. In both the Holladay and Dempsey studies, it appears that these scribbles have symbolic meaning to the child after three years of age, even though an adult cannot get an understanding of this meaning just by looking. We have to listen, too; but the words that the child uses to describe these scribbles, as Piaget (1955) has pointed out, utilize personal meanings that are not necessarily the same as for adults and emphasize the difference between the thought processes of the scribbling child and the adult. Cognitive development and language development are related intimately. In a review, Houssiadas and Brown (1980) document the sociolinguistic research on children's language development from early egocentric speech to later social and communication uses of speech. There are clear indications that language development is far from complete at age five (Palermo and Molfese, 1973).

FIGURE 88.
This girl pays close attention to her scribbles as she develops her motor skills and forms concepts.

The ability to copy geometric forms is sometimes used as a measure of young children's developmental level. Although the circle can be copied by most children at the age of three, it is not until four that a square can be copied successfully. Identifying these shapes seems to be no problem for the preschool child. Cratty (1970) has determined that the perceptual abilities mature in a predictable manner, with very young children understanding the vertical dimension first, followed by recognition of the horizontal, with the diagonal being the last dimension to be understood. Scher and Unruh (1982) tested subjects aged 6, 10, 14, and adult and found that these understandings continue to improve with age. The scribbling child will not be able to copy a diagonal, since this is a task that most children can accomplish only after five years of age. Even training does not seem to bring any noticeable change in this ability. As mentioned

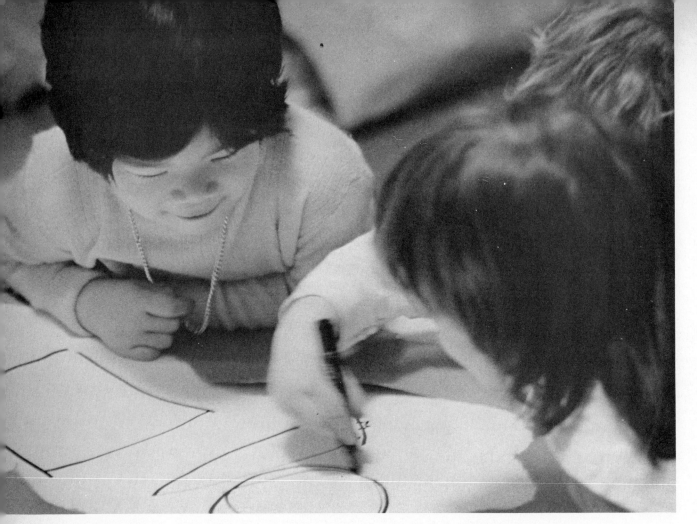

FIGURE 89.
It is not possible to teach children how to copy a square; but, by the age of four, the development of this skill is a proud accomplishment.

previously, Brittain (1969) attempted to increase young children's ability to copy squares. He found it impossible, although he tried all the usual procedures of having children trace around cardboard squares, showing them feltboard squares, helping them to construct squares from straws and clay, making squares from paper strips, and pointing out square shapes in the nursery school. In a further study Brittain (1979) found that if the edges of the 8½ by 11 inch paper the children usually used were trimmed to a triangular shape, it

THE BEGINNINGS OF SELF-EXPRESSION

PLATES 15 AND 16.
"Scribble in Line" and "Scribble in Mass," painted
by nursery school children. Enjoyment and exuberance in painting can be seen in the lines that record
the child's arm movements over the whole paper;
the large areas filled with paint indicate a child's
pleasure with color for its own sake. In neither case
is representation attempted.

PLATE 17.

"Cow," drawn by a four year old girl. A naturalistic representation is not important to the child; rather, this picture shows her concept of a cow. She has drawn the face as she would a human face. Her cow has a large number of legs, what appear to be horns, and a swishing tail.

was even more difficult for children to copy a square; but the triangle was easier on the triangular paper, although children normally cannot copy that shape until they are five. It may be that, when copying a square, children use the edge of the paper as a reference; the paper's four sides and right angles could be making the task of drawing squares easier.

Sometimes nursery school teachers feel it is important to teach children how to copy squares and triangles, since these shapes are useful in forming letters. But the evidence indicates that it is frustrating for both children and teachers to spend time trying to develop copying skills, when this ability seems to come naturally at a later date. Even calling these shapes a different name, such as calling a triangle a witch's hat, did not make it easier for children to copy them (Trisdorfer, 1972). The process of drawing is a learning experience in which children devise ways to depict their world on a two-dimensional surface. They will learn to draw circles, squares, and triangles without adult pressure.

To a great extent the differences in levels of scribbling reflect physiological and psychological changes in the child. On the average, children start scribbling at about the age of two and continue until they are about four years of age. If there is a marked discrepancy, the child is either above or below average. This is not lack of talent. In some cases a child may regress when given a new drawing tool or when afraid or unsure. In our society, intelligence is seen as the quality of a child's performance relative to that of all children of the same age. A child who performs tasks typical of an older child tends to be considered more intelligent. Since scribbling is a reflection of the child's development, here is an indication of the child's intellectual growth, particularly at a time when the usual group-type intelligence tests are not usable. Therefore, the kindergarten child who is still in the scribbling stage will not be able to perform at the level usually expected of kindergarten children. In first grade the same child could not learn to read. It is obvious that the understanding of scribbling can help us to understand children.

Teachers should look at the scribbles of children as part of the total child. The beauty often seen in preschool children's art may be because, as adults, we see these markings as a free, uninhibited approach to painting, whereas actually this beauty may have very little to do with the child's intent. Some individuals even go farther in this interpretation and look at children's drawings as an indication of inner feelings and inhibitions. An adult looking at an ink blot can often see within this blot figures or forms that recall personal references. Adults can also look at scribbles in the same way and see certain forms or shapes, but this has very little to do with the child's meaning.

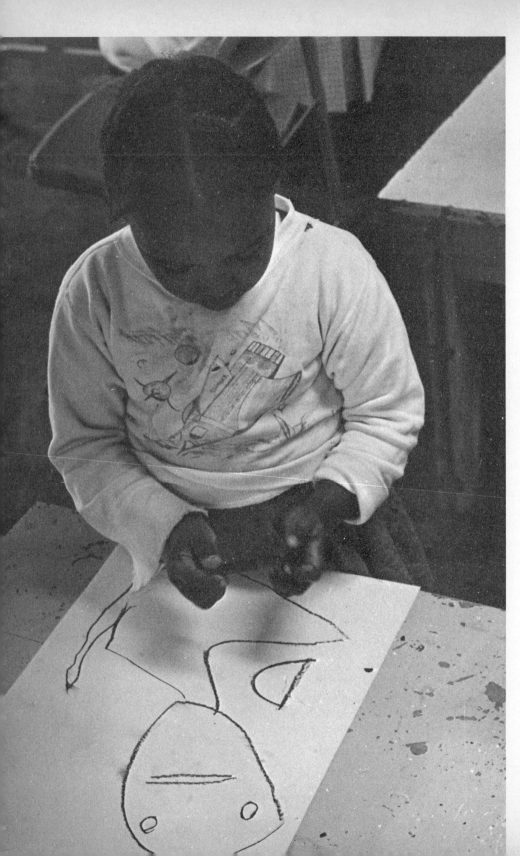

FIGURE 90.
During the scribbling stage, children should have the opportunity to develop a pictorial concept of a person, with drawing instruments they can control.

Art Motivation

Usually in the first stages of scribbling no special motivation is needed except to provide the child with the proper materials and the encouragement to go ahead with the activity. Most children will eagerly cover two or three sheets of paper with scribbles. The very young child will continue at this activity for no more than a few minutes. The child of three may be involved for as long as 15 minutes. The four year old child, who now names scribbles or who has been introduced to a new material, may keep at this activity for 20 to 30 minutes. No clock should dictate the length of time a child may spend in self-expression.

Scribbling should not be interfered with. Sometimes a nursery school teacher will see a child painting a picture that accidentally turns out to look quite like a piece of modern art. It is a great temptation to stop the child at this point and "save the picture." However, the child will not understand this interruption; the child should decide when a picture is completed.

Occasionally one finds a child who seems to be afraid of scribbling. There may be several reasons for this hesitancy to engage in a creative activity, from being told "no" by parents when scribbling in the past to a more deep-seated problem of anxiety or fear in a particular situation. Establishing mutual trust is important, and it is sometimes necessary to make the art experience into a tempting activity. Providing the child with a mound of easily workable clay might be a good start. "Is it cold? Can you squeeze it? How high can you make it? Can you push your finger through it? Can you make it smooth? Can you make it lumpy? Once a child gets involved in the clay, other means of expression will come more easily as the child develops confidence. Colored chalk or a new fiber-tipped pen may be enough to make a youngster eager to draw. Most children will scribble quite eagerly after motivation. Certainly a parent or teacher should encourage this important developmental activity.

When a scribble is named, we have a clue to a child's thinking. This new direction, the relationship of scribbles to the environment, should be stimulated. The child's thinking can be motivated in the direction already indicated. For example, when the child says, "This is Daddy," it is possible to stimulate a greater awareness of Daddy. "Is your daddy tall? Does he have big feet? Does he ever lift you up? Do you ever feel his whiskers? Do you like your daddy?" The purpose here is to encourage imaginative thinking. The motions that are made on the paper are satisfying, although they may not be recognizable to adults;

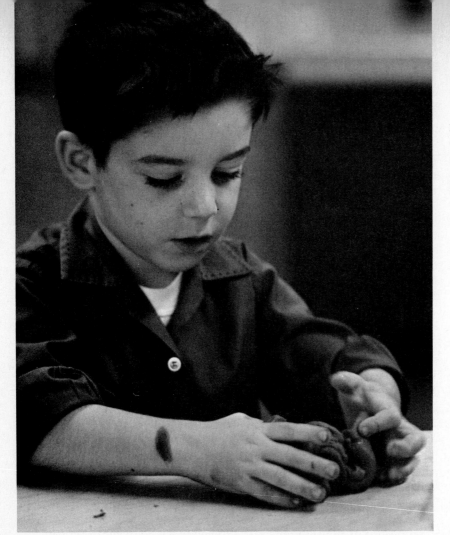

FIGURE 91.
Clay is a three-dimensional
material which can be
pushed, stretched, squeezed,
and pounded.

some lines may represent a feeling of lifting or the texture of whiskers or even
be symbolic of being held. The inclusion of many senses is important. If the
child says she is going shopping, such things as smells, sounds, and personal
involvement—her own part in the shopping experience, her likes and dislikes
for this activity—can all be included in the discussion. But the child should also
feel free to ignore these comments and be satisfied simply with the motor activity and the scribble.

During the very first stages of scribbling, no particular motivation is necessary, whereas any topic the child suggests during the last stage of scribbling is
suitable to extend the thinking process. Most important in all stages is the
adult's understanding and encouragement. Creative children scribble indepen-

dently. Children who constantly ask questions, wondering how to use the material, asking the way things should be done, are also the ones who are most easily influenced by the work of others. If one child starts with big, round motions, they will start to imitate this.

Ideally, each child should be self-motivated and feel satisfaction with the process of creating. Because scribbling is the beginning of creative expression, it is especially important at this time to give the child the confidence to work independently. It is sad but true that projects planned for the scribbling child occasionally undercut their self-confidence—projects that are too difficult for a young child to accomplish without help, projects that are conceived by and for adults.

Art Materials

Any art material used with children must fit their needs. Since during scribbling a child needs to practice and experience kinesthetic sensations, the materials used should encourage free expression without the intrusion of technical difficulties. Watercolor, for example, is a very poor medium for this age because the colors tend to run and flow easily. The child is unable to gain control over the material or to follow visually the motions on the paper and can therefore become discouraged. The usual type of pencil is also unsuitable for the scribbling child because sharp points prevent gliding along the paper, and of course the points break easily.

There are numerous art materials that *do* lend themselves to the needs of the child at the scribbling stage. A big, black, unwrapped crayon is excellent and easily obtained. White chalk on a blackboard or a fiber-tipped pen with black ink are also excellent drawing materials. Any art material should facilitate expression rather than be a stumbling block.

Because of some adults' feeling toward scribbling, sometimes old newspapers, the back of wallpaper samples, or wrapping paper are used for the scribbling child. Although these materials may be used in the art program at a different developmental level, these materials have no place in the nursery school or in the kindergarten. Drawing a dark line over a printed news page is much too confusing, the back of old wallpaper tends to be rough and prevents the easy flow of a crayon, and wrapping paper does not provide good contrast with the drawing medium. A 12 by 18 inch size light-colored or white paper is best for crayon; a larger 18 by 24 inch size is best if paint is going to be used.

Tempera or poster paint can be used to advantage. The paint must be mixed to a fairly thick consistency so that it does not dribble or run down the page. The opportunity to use paint can satisfy some of the emotional needs of the scribbler better than a crayon. The result is obvious joy in exploring a range of colors. A horizontal surface is best for a child to paint on, since the problems of running paint are thus minimized and the child can work from all sides of the paper. However, in situations where space is at a minimum, it is better to use an easel, or even to fasten paper to the wall, than not to give a painting experience at all. Large, fairly absorbent paper, three-quarter-inch bristle brushes with the handles not too long, and some variety of thickly mixed tempera paint provide a wonderful opportunity for an emotional outlet and a truly artistic experience.

Clay is also an excellent material for this age. Handling a three-dimensional material provides the opportunity for the child to use fingers and muscles in a different way. Beating and pounding the clay without any visible purpose is a

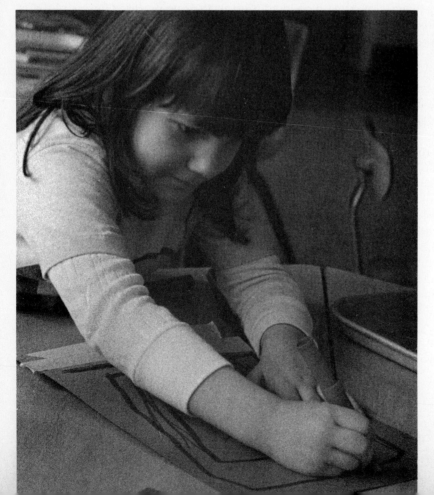

FIGURE 92.
Every child needs the experience of drawing and painting. One great advantage of nursery school is that these activities are part of the curriculum.

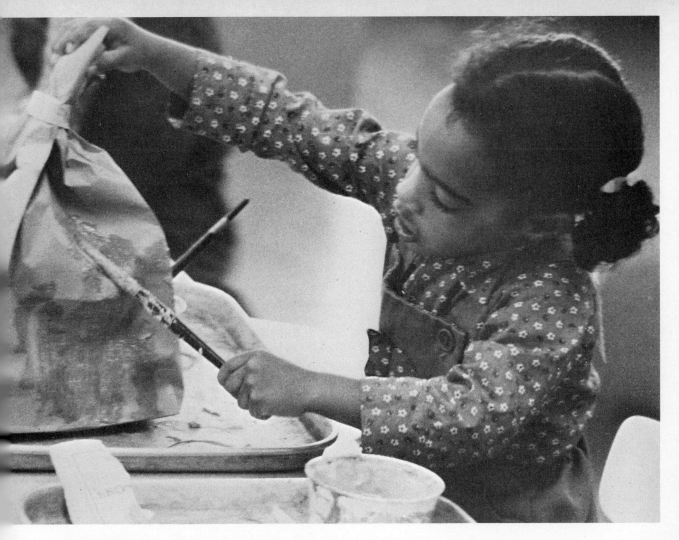

FIGURE 93.

The teacher's purpose in this activity was to make puppets, but it was satisying enough just to paint the bag green. Art activities need to be carefully geared to the ages of the children.

parallel stage to disordered scribbling. Forming coils and balls without attempting any specific object is parallel to controlled scribbling. At some point the child may pick up a lump of clay and, perhaps with accompanying noises, call it an airplane or say, "This is a car." The child has changed from kinesthetic thinking to imaginative thinking. The clay should not be so hard as to be difficult to work with or so thin that it sticks to the fingers. Clay of proper consistency can be stored in a plastic bag for an indefinite length of time. Since the scribbling child does not have good control over small muscles, the clay chunk should be large enough to be grasped with both hands. A grapefruit-sized piece of clay is probably adequate. Since the child is exploring and manipulating the material in a kinesthetic way, there is no need to let the clay harden or even to think of firing these products.

Providing an opportunity for children to become aware of color and texture by handling various collage materials is of value. Although it is interesting for the child to select some materials and then put them into some sort of assemblage, the continual use of collage materials may stand in the way of the development of perceptual–motor skills. However, the occasional use of collage materials is certainly worthwhile. A box of different materials, bright bits of paper or fabrics of varying textures, can be exciting to rummage through. One study (Amabile and Gitomer, 1984) compared the differences between letting preschool children select their own materials for making collages and telling preschoolers which materials to use. The collages by children who selected their own materials were judged more creative by eight people who didn't know which group the collages came from. The opportunity to choose, to decide for oneself, seems a necessary part of the creative process even at this young age.

In some nursery schools and kindergartens, finger paint is a favorite material. There is some reason to doubt the advantages of using this medium now. Just as we would hesitate to have a very young infant handle and use a crayon if the prime enjoyment from the crayon was scratching it or chewing on it, we should hesitate to use finger paint with the scribbling child, who tends to be concerned with its sticky consistency. If the purpose of art materials is to provide the opportunity for self-expression, then the misuse of materials may interfere with the activity for which the finger paint was originally planned. There is also evidence from experiments and direct observation that the young child may sometimes regress into an earlier stage of behavior. Finger paint, because of its very consistency, may remind children of these former stages and retard development temporarily. You may easily see this effect by watching children. If they are more concerned with the sticky consistency and with smearing the paint all over than with using it for expression, then they are not using finger paint to satisfy the desire to control their kinesthetic movements. However, for tense, timid, or fearful children finger painting may provide an important outlet even when used in such a manner.

There is no place in the art program for those activities that have no mean-

FIGURE 94.
The child's purpose in painting is not picture-making. Experimenting with new materials can be an end in itself.

ing for the scribbling child. Occasionally a nursery school or kindergarten teacher may plan certain art activities such as pasting, lacing, tracing, folding, or cutting; these are designed for a particular end product, such as May baskets, Pilgrim silhouettes, cute snowmen, or projects for Halloween, Christmas, or Mother's Day. Such activities are worthless and should never be included in a program planned for scribbling children, because they only point out the inability of children to perform on a level foreign to their understanding and ability. Sometimes teachers have an interest in discovering new and novel activities for children. Any new material should be looked upon with a great deal of care to make sure that it can further the natural development of children. It must not obstruct their ability to gain control over the material; rather, it should promote creative expression.

Summary

For an understanding of young children, it is of great importance that scribbling be recognized as part of the total growth pattern. During this stage, children's intellectual and emotional development are reflected in their creative work. Most children pursue scribbling vigorously and yet are flexible enough to change their motions with new experiences. They enjoy kinesthetic development through their scribbles and gradually gain visual control over these markings. Creatively, they will be independent and not easily distracted.

Young children freely explore their environment through a variety of senses, and some of these experiences are reflected in their scribbles when they begin to name them. The drawings themselves have a healthy variety, beginning before two years of age with a series of random markings, changing to continuous or controlled motions about six months later, and becoming much more complex when children begin to name what they have drawn. In working with paint, these stages closely parallel work with crayon, and color will be particularly enjoyed when they begin to name these scribbles. Also, they usually enjoy working with a range of three-dimensional materials.

This period of life is extremely important for developing attitudes about oneself and in establishing the feeling that the world is an exciting and interesting place to live in. The roles of the teacher and of the parent become very important in helping children develop these attitudes. The nursery school teacher is in an excellent position to provide the opportunity for children to grow by means of art experiences, to help them develop the confidence and sensitivity important for self-expression, and to provide a range of materials and the environmental setting for creative activities. Most important of all is to provide the stimulation and motivation necessary for developing an increased awareness of the environment and to provide the encouragement and approval for the creative act. All these responsibilities rest squarely upon the shoulders of the parent or teacher.

THE BEGINNINGS OF SELF-EXPRESSION

Related Activities

1. Collect examples of art work from a nursery school or preschool group of children. Observe the variety of expression. Try to classify the scribbles according to disordered, controlled, or naming of scribbling stage. Compare the drawings for use of space, control of line, boldness or timidity of motion.

2. Collect the scribbles of one child over a period of several months. Date each drawing and note any remarks the child made while drawing. Keep a notebook in which you record observations on length of attention span, materials used, amount of concentration or diversions, type of motions used, and the emotional reactions of the child. Compare these notes with the child's motor coordination when eating, dressing, and so forth. Draw conclusions from the three sources of information (the scribbles, the notes, and the behavior) as to the child's growth during this time.

3. Find out the effectiveness of your motivation during the period of naming of scribbling by comparing one scribble done when the child was left completely alone with another made when you motivated the child in the direction of his thinking.

4. Observe children working with clay. See if those children who make forms or shapes also give these forms names. How does this relate to the scribbles of these same children?

5. Watch children paint at an easel several times. Make a list of the amount of paint used and the order of use. Shift the order of paints in the easel trough and see if there are any changes in the paintings. Experiment with two or three different consistencies of paint each week. Repeat this for several weeks to see if the children make any comments or if there is any relationship between paint consistency and length of time spent painting.

6. When a child starts to name his scribbling, does he introduce certain lines or motions for certain objects or experiences? Collect scribbles and keep notes on the changes in the scribbles when naming begins. Observe the development of a form for a person.

7

First Representational Attempts

The Preschematic Stage
Four–Seven Years

The Importance of the
Preschematic Stage

A different method of drawing has begun—the conscious creation of form, the beginning of graphic communication. This stage grows directly out of the last stages of scribbling. Although the drawings themselves may not look particularly different to the adult, this stage of development is very important. The marks and scribbles have lost more and more of their relationship to bodily movement, and these marks are now controlled and related to environment. Scribbling was mainly a kinesthetic activity, but now the child intends to represent something. This provides a great feeling of satisfaction.

These new drawings are important not only for the child but also for the parent or teacher, who now has a tangible record of the child's thinking process. This gives the adult a concrete object to see and discuss with the child. It also provides clues about all those things important in the child's life. Usually by the age of four, children are making recognizable forms, although it may be somewhat difficult to decide just what they are. By the age of five these marks are usually quite distinguishable as people, houses, or trees. By the time the child is six, these shapes and forms have evolved into clearly recognizable pictures with a theme or purpose. However, there is much variation among children, and even the material influences how they draw. Several factors may influence the kind of drawing that is done at any particular moment, and these will be discussed.

Characteristics of
Preschematic Drawings

Usually the first representational symbol attempted by children of this age is a person. Typically, the person is drawn with a circle for a head and two vertical lines for legs. These head–feet representations are common for five year olds. It is not surprising that the first representations are of people. The importance of

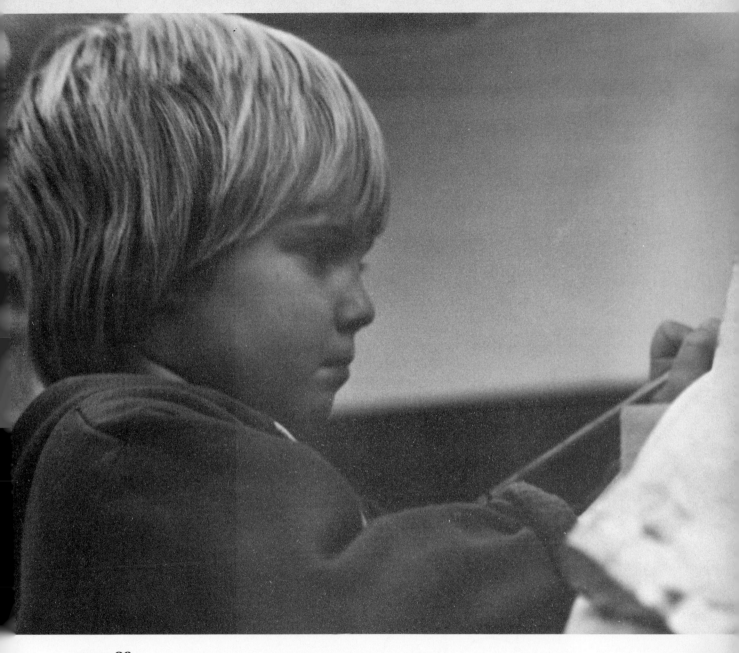

FIGURE 96.
As children grow older, their drawings reflect the development of an ordered thought
process.

CHARACTERISTICS OF PRESCHEMATIC DRAWINGS

221

people in most children's drawings remains quite evident throughout childhood. It is not as clear why the head–feet representation should be the first method that children use to portray people, but there is general agreement that they are not trying to copy. Showing five year old children pictures of people or having them look at people while they draw does not change the way they draw. It may be that children are actually drawing themselves; if we were to try to draw what can be seen of ourselves when looking straight ahead, the representation would probably be a somewhat nebulous circle for the head with legs and arms attached. This assumes that children are involved primarily in the self; their egocentric view of the world is actually a view of themselves.

Another point of view is that the head–feet representation is what children actually know about themselves and is not a visual representation at all. The head is where all eating and talking goes on. Piaget (1960) found that some six year old children thought that the thinking process goes on in the mouth. Certainly the eyes, ears, and nose make the head the center of sensory activity. The

FIGURE 97.
The basic essentials of a person are included in this young child's drawing. In this case the toes seem especially important.

addition of legs and arms makes this center movable and may indicate a really functional being. However, children know a great deal more about the body than they portray, for most young children can quickly identify body parts.

Freeman (1980) feels that children start with a head as the top and continue to draw down further until they stop at the legs; he calls this end-anchoring. Another view is that the first representational attempts result neither from visual stimulation nor from a concept, but are a representation of the method by which a child perceives. For example, the sense of touch in actually running the hands over an object may be as important at this stage as visually seeing this object or understanding its function. At any rate, the first drawing of a person should not be looked upon as an immature visual representation, for it is fairly obvious that a drawing is essentially an abstraction or schema from a large array of complex stimuli and demonstrates the beginning of an ordered thought process.

The head–feet representation is elaborated on with the addition of arms sticking out of the sides of the head, the addition of what seems like a belly button between the legs, and the eventual inclusion of the body. There are many variations in this development, and by six years the child typically produces a fairly detailed drawing of a person.

Although it is not clear just how the person symbol originates, the universality of the circle for the head and the two lines representing legs gives support to the notion that this is somehow biological in nature; that is, all children, either through their sight, hand control, or cognitive development, make surprisingly similar configurations for a person. This is true for children from cultures as diverse as Australian Aborigines and United States middle class (Brittain, 1985). Golomb's studies (1977) of the representational development of the human figure found no differences attributable to socioeconomic or cultural influences.

The drawn symbol is not particularly influenced by the real world. Pointing out to a child the discrepancy between a drawing of a person and how a person really appears does not influence or change the symbol. It is as if the symbol is a shorthand notation for an object, more generic than specific. In examining drawings by five and six year old children, Barrett and Light (1976) noted that children invariably draw a door on their symbol for a house. They had children draw from a model of a house without a door and also told a story about a magical person living in a house without a door and asked the children to draw the house again. They found almost no effect on the drawings of the youngest children and noted little change in the drawings by the six year olds. The authors felt that the information was entirely ignored by those children who were drawing symbolically. Apparently a house has to have a door.

FIGURE 98.
"A Man," drawn by a four year old child. The first representational attempts develop naturally from the child's scribbles.

While children are forming new concepts, representational symbols are constantly changing. They will represent a person differently today from the way they will represent a person tomorrow. This is not only true of drawings of a person but also of the representation of houses and trees. But, by the age of seven, children will have established schemas and drawings will become less flexible.

The Meaning of Color

During the stage of the first representational attempts, children begin consciously to create forms, and it is those forms themselves that become important. This does not mean that children in the preschematic stage are not aware of color, but it indicates that the ability to make forms of their own choosing dominates their thinking.

In drawings and paintings done by these children there is often little relationship between the color selected to paint an object and the object represented. A person may be red, blue, green, or yellow, depending upon the appeal of the various colors. To an adult these color relationships may seem a little odd. In fact, one study (Marshall, 1954) compared adult schizophrenics with normal five year olds and found the use of color with these two groups quite comparable.

This does not mean that colors do not have significance to children who are using them. Lawler and Lawler (1965) found that nursery school children of about the age of four selected yellow crayons to color a happy picture, whereas the same picture was apt to be colored brown if the children were told a sad story about it. It would not seem strange, then, for a child to select a favorite color for painting a picture of his mother, especially if he feels a warm emotional attachment. There are often other reasons for the particular selection of a color for an object. Some of these are simply mechanical in nature. That is, the color selected may be thicker and less likely to run, or perhaps the red has not been used, or maybe the brush used for one of the colors has a longer handle. Children may have deeper psychological meanings in their color choice, but these meanings tend to be highly individualized, and adults would be put in a difficult position to try to interpret what these colors mean.

For children of this age, the use of color can be an exciting experience. Although they have no desire for exact color relationships, they can and do enjoy using color for its own sake. This is particularly true when using paint, where rich masses of color can be painted quite fluidly. It is obvious that criticizing the use of color or pointing out the correct color for objects would interfere with freedom of expression. Ample opportunity should be provided for continued experimentation so that children can establish a relationship between their own emotional involvement with color and its organization on the page.

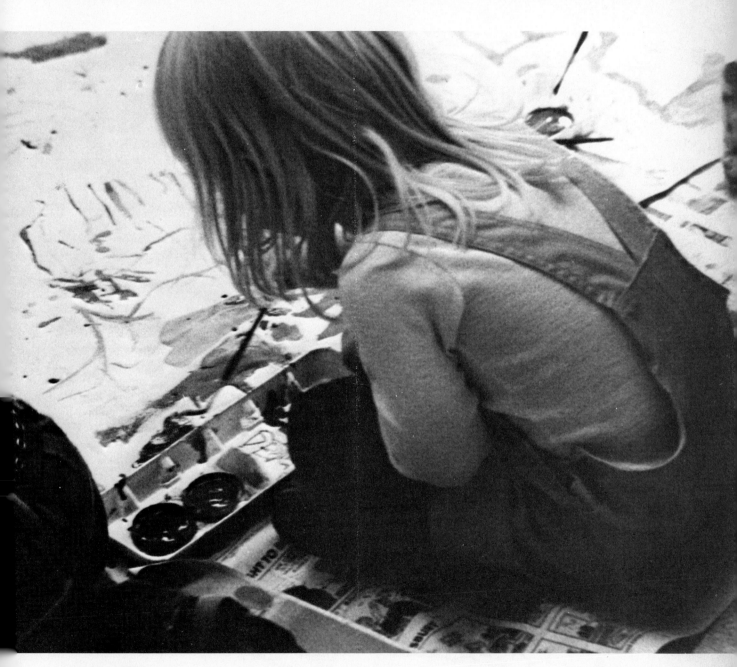

FIGURE 100.
Children enjoy painting as they explore and experiment with color.

The Meaning of Space

The representation of space in drawings or paintings by adult artists differs widely, depending not only upon the individual but also upon the artist's culture. Our own society tends to look upon the representation of space as being appropriately shown by the use of perspective, a mechanical perspective with vanishing points and horizon lines. This has not been true for other times or other cultures; for example, an Oriental concept of space shows objects in the distance drawn higher on the page. Many contemporary artists have rejected mechanical perspective of space in favor of representing subject matter honestly on a two-dimensional surface. It can be readily seen, then, that there is no right or wrong way to portray space in a drawing.

FIGURE 101.

Here is a house, with the important door, and a variety of objects scattered both inside and outdoors. Connie has drawn what is important to her. The tricycles, a swing, a seesaw, and what may be a sandbox are shown around the house.

In the first representational level, children's drawings show a concept of space quite different from that of adults. At first glance, objects tend to be represented somewhat randomly in space. However, closer inspection will show that children conceive of space as what is around them. That is, objects will appear above, below, or beside each other in the way children understand them. They do not see themselves standing on the ground with other objects also on the ground beside them. Possibly this could be better understood if we were to quickly look around the room and list the things we have seen. "There is a table, there is a light, here is a chair, and I am in the middle." No objective spatial relationship has yet been established. Space, therefore, is conceived of as revolving around the self with no relationships between objects. During the stage when children code the location of things in relation to their own position, they are not yet able to specify the location of things in relation to adjacent landmarks. According to Harris (1977), only later, as children develop, will they be able to determine location according to landmarks as well as by relating it to themselves.

Since the child is the center of a personal environment, in what might be called a stage of egocentrism, those experiences that are directly related to the self are the most meaningful. Just as children draw what is around them in an apparently random fashion, their comments tend to be loose-jointed and disconnected. If a five year old is asked what happened at a birthday party, the reply does not follow any logical sequence; instead, the child's remarks may be more closely tied up with their emotional significance than with any orderly array of events.

If objects in drawings are unrelated to each other, it is an indication that the child does not have the ability to relate letters to each other, or to learn to read, or to cooperate socially. There is no point in trying to teach this child how to read (Sibley, 1957) or how to comprehend the logical relationships of numbers. Although children can learn early how to count (Pentz, 1965), or to recognize words, there is no genuine understanding of content. Right and left confusion is typical. Cratty (1970) indicates that by five years, the child knows there is a right side and a left side but is unable to identify them accurately. At six, there still is some indecision in identifying them. At seven, there is accurate right and left judgment and a judgment of visual space with the self as a reference point. While right–left confusion persists, there will be difficulty distinguishing between "b" and "d," some letters will be written backward, or words will be written from right to left. Expecting such a child to perform school or art tasks before appropriate maturation proves discouraging to child and teacher alike. A kindergarten teacher can readily tell from a child's drawings

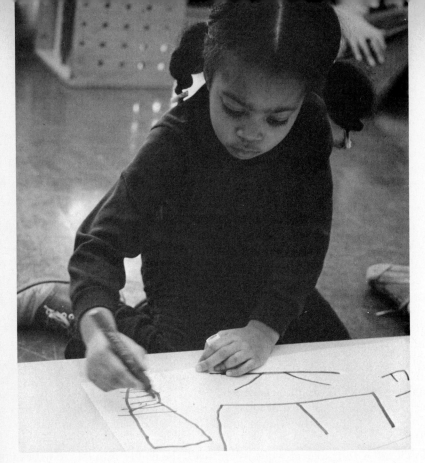

whether the child is ready to participate in tasks that require spatial coordination. Forcing tasks on children who are not yet ready may lead to undesirable actions and attitudes, and these negative attitudes may last longer and be more important in the end than doing the task at the moment.

A child learns space concepts by personal involvement, by actually climbing over, hiding behind, running beside, or sitting on top of. Worthington and Typpo (1980) found that preschoolers learned these concepts significantly better through activity than by verbal means. As children grow older and have had experiences to relate to, words have more meaning. One study (Herman, Kolker, and Shaw, 1982) found that young children depend more upon motor activity to learn about space than do older children. A child may even confuse his own thoughts and feelings with those things around him. If a chair falls over, there is concern about the chair's being hurt (Piaget, 1960); it is almost as if the child were the chair. The size of objects, the subject matter selected, and their placement on the page are to a large degree determined by value judgments. Portrayal of space reflects the child's whole thinking process.

Liebermann (1979) asked nursery school children to put a series of photographs into proper order. The photographs, taken at the children's eye level, showed four views of the nursery school, from the entrance to where the children hung their jackets. Although all of the children identified objects in the photographs, it was impossible for those children who were in the early scribbling stages to put the photographs in order, but those children who were drawing recognizable objects had no difficulty in putting these in proper sequence. Apparently understanding of ordering or of sequencing (or what Piaget calls seriation) begins with the manipulation of objects, or in this case photographs, before it becomes evident in drawings by children. Piaget (1976) conducted a series of experiments dealing with seriation, in which children tried to arrange a set of objects according to size. He believed that understanding the relationships between sizes comes during the process of manipulation or follows the successful completion of the task. By age seven, children had acquired an operational scheme to use and could order objects consciously. It is not surprising, therefore, that children's drawings in the preschematic stage show little relationship of one object to another, with a pleasant disregard for size relationships.

When 98 children of this stage were asked to draw a house with a tree behind it (Kalyan–Masih, 1976), they had no success in making their drawings look visually correct. Those children under four tended to make scribbles; those under five ignored the instructions and drew the house and tree alongside each other; and those about six often placed the tree above the house, or drew the

FIGURE 103.

Drawing one object behind another presents a problem. Several examples of the drawing strategies used by young children to portray a tree behind a house are shown (adapted from Strommen, 1983).

house directly over the tree so both could be seen, or put the house on one side of the paper and the tree on the other. None of the children under six used an adult concept to solve the problem of how to represent the house with a tree behind it. Even when children are shown how an object can be partially hidden by another, they are incapable of drawing this. Cox (1978) asked 130 five, six, and seven year olds to look at and draw a red and green ball, one behind the other; the most common drawing showed one ball above the other. To attempt to teach children of this age an adult concept of space representation would not only be confusing, but might actually damage children's confidence in their own creative work. There would be no comprehension that their representation was other than correct. The child's pictorial concept of the environment is just as valid as an adult's.

The Development of the Four to Seven Year Old Child

Some children start school at the age of three or four, in either a community or church sponsored nursery school; the kindergarten child is usually five or sometimes six years old; formal schooling for all children has begun by first grade. The preschematic stage, then, tends to fall between the time when some children enter nursery school and the time when all children begin formal education in the first grade.

Children differ tremendously during this age. They are products of differing backgrounds; just as parents vary, so will each child. The psychological literature indicates that this is a time of great intellectual growth, and family factors such as the number of siblings, amount of television watching, or even the diet can influence a child's energy and attitude toward learning. The background that the child comes from, then, cannot be ignored. In a study of kindergarten-aged children in Finland (Liikanen, 1975), it was found that those parents who had more artistic and creative interests had children who scored higher in fluency, flexibility, and originality in a battery of tests. However, all children of this age tend to be generally curious, full of enthusiasm, and eager to try tasks, particularly those that involve manipulation of materials. Children are often anxious to express themselves, although not in logical ways. Apparently, they develop a logic of their own, and although they may be full of questions, of

FIGURE 104.

This drawing progresses all around the page, with what appear to be two suns and several people arranged in egocentric order

"Why?," they seem to see the world as being how it is without realizing that they themselves can make changes in it. The world tends to revolve around them, and their knowledge is obtained through firsthand contact with the environment. The preschooler plays alone or alongside other children rather than with them, and often their conversation is more a reflection of their own thinking than the development of a social grace.

The art of children follows the same developmental patterns as other aspects of growth. In fact, the study of children's drawings can give us great insight into the reasoning behind their actions. It may be well to mention that although there are general trends and a clearly predictable development in drawings, these do not come automatically. Rather, they evolve slowly in spurts, and at times children will regress to an earlier stage. Growth is never a smooth process.

Preschematic Drawings as a Reflection of Growth

Drawing is much more than a pleasant exercise for the child. It is a means by which to develop relationships and to make concrete some vague but important thoughts. Drawing becomes in itself a learning experience. Although children can recognize and name numerous objects around them, these objects can be somewhat peripheral to their functional thinking. One study attempted to compare how five year olds recognized missing or deformed arms and legs in incomplete pictures of people (McPherson et al., 1966). They found that five year olds drew anatomical parts with much more accuracy than they recognized them. Apparently a picture is not as important to look at as it is to draw. It may be that through the drawing experience children are beginning to establish some sort of conceptual organization. This experience is not one that can be imposed. That is, attempting to teach certain artistic skills or techniques to children of this age will not help them to use drawing and painting in a meaningful way.

As children develop a concept of reality in their art, adults can better understand the thinking processes of these children. This is an age of great flexibility and change in drawings; it is also an age of rapid changes in the mode of thinking. We are not discussing thinking here as the quiet contemplation of a problem; rather, we are considering total intellectual development, which at this age is nicely infused with fantasy, reality, and biological responses to the environment.

A child who has reached the chronological age of four or five, and whose drawings are still based on motions, has not advanced intellectually to an average stage of growth. A series of drawings by a five year old child would normally include some representational attempts. The more differentiated these attempts are, the more highly the intellectual processes have been developed.

FIGURE 105.
Making a drawing can be an exciting experience; putting down in a concrete way the images of his world, Ale is developing concepts and communicating with himself, an important aspect of learning.

FIGURE 106.
This six year old boy has added a body to
his head-feet representation. Body and
legs both relate to the head but not to
each other.

Generally, the more details included in a drawing, the greater the child's awareness of the world. Our whole concept of intelligence is based primarily upon
this assumption. The greater the intellectual development, the greater the
awareness and use of the various facets of the environment. It is fairly obvious,
then, that the child who has not yet developed concepts of the environment at
the age of five is retarded in intellectual growth.

One of the important attributes of this preschematic stage is the child's flexibility and frequent changes in concepts. A child whose drawings are merely

repetitions of the same symbol without any deviations may use that symbol to hide behind and will exhibit in other behavior a tendency to withdraw or to hide behind social stereotypes. A child who reacts toward meaningful experiences or objects in an emotionally sensitive way will show this emotional sensitivity in art work by exaggerating certain special things. For example, John walked barefoot in the grass after the rain; the obvious delight of this kinesthetic experience shows in his emphasized toes, almost to the extent that we, too, can feel our toes in the cool grass (Figure 107). A child who becomes so absorbed in part of a drawing may concentrate on important details and ignore

FIGURE 107.
"Walking in the Grass After the Rain," drawn by a six year old boy. The picture shows the intense feeling of wetness from the grass on the boy's toes.

the rest. Since growth in perceptual discrimination is very rapid at this age, drawings also change rapidly; some children by the age of six or seven draw parts of objects that interest them in great detail, although not always in proportion.

Drawings reflect a child's development honestly, but sometimes adults can be misled by words children use. Adults may mistake the use of words for an understanding of these words and try to carry on a conversation with a youngster, assuming the child's meaning of the words is the same as what an adult would mean. One teenager recalls that a song she learned in nursery school about springtime had a phrase in it that warned her to "watch out for the first crocuses popping up from the ground." The teenager remembers that she was scared stiff for weeks because she was afraid crocuses popping up from the ground might bite. She still does not like crocuses.

Perception means more than just the awareness of the visual appearance of objects; it includes the use of all the senses, such as kinesthetic or auditory experiences. Later, when a child establishes more than the mere meaning of an object, visual differentiation will begin. For example, look at Judy's drawing in Figure 108, where only geometric forms are used. All such geometric details convey a meaning only in context. The way things are represented is an indication of the type of experiences the child has had with them. The image Judy has of herself and of things around her will change as she becomes more aware of the significant characteristics of these objects. The same situation exists in color at this age, for a child uses color for the sake of color itself. It does not imitate the subject matter.

Salome and Reeves (1972) attempted with some success to improve the visual discrimination of some four and a half and five and a half year old children with several training tasks, involving discussion, visual aids, and exercises containing information about contour lines. However, there is a lack of data on the long-term effect of such training, that is, in six months or a year. It is usual to find that any special attention given to a group of children has favorable results, particularly if there is enthusiasm and a feeling of significance for the project at hand.

The development of creative growth within the context of art education is one of the prime justifications for art experiences for any age group. During this stage of first representational attempts, the creative child uses independent concepts and will not ask how to draw a mouth or a nose. The child's own concepts can readily be distinguished from those taken from other sources by their free and flexible use. In a group the creative child remains uninfluenced but may show interest in what others are doing. The creative child spontaneously

FIRST REPRESENTATIONAL ATTEMPTS

PLATE 18.

"Mommy and Daddy," painted by a four year old child who has just left the scribbling stage. Color is used only to outline shapes. The mode of representation is quite rudimentary; heads are indicated by circles and household objects appear as ambiguous shapes.

PLATE 19.

"I Am Playing in the Leaves" is a typical head-feet representation, drawn by a kindergarten youngster. This drawing includes only the child's active knowledge of a man. His increased physical control would distinguish his picture from one by a gifted younger child, although the concepts might be similar. Notice that the leaves were colored in with such eagerness that the hands and feet were painted too.

PLATE 20.

"I Can Stand on My Head," painted by a five year old girl. Young children paint and draw from their own experiences, reflecting their exuberance and joy of living.

FIGURE 108.
Notice in this drawing the use of lines for symbolizing the legs and parts of the faces.
The heads and feet are circles and the bodies are somewhat rectangular.

paints or draws or manipulates materials and does not create only when encouraged to do so. A creative first grade girl was motivated by the Christmas
story to paint the manger scene (Figure 109). Notice how she has shown the top
view of the basket so we can look inside but has shown the side view of the
stable. An angel is just arriving on the scene from the left, carrying the star.

Young children enjoy talking to others but are not as concerned about being
understood. Kindergarten children certainly need to talk, but sometimes a

PRESCHEMATIC DRAWINGS AS A SIGN OF GROWTH   239

FIGURE 109.

Plan and elevation are combined in this drawing of the manger scene by a six and a half year old girl. The basket with the handles on each side has been tipped up so we can look inside.

whole class will be forced to listen to a single child, which seems such a waste. Communication is important to develop; this can be done in small groups, sharing experiences, bringing something special to talk about, or explaining a drawing, but not to an entire bored, eager-to-talk but not eager-to-listen class. Usually five year olds know what they have drawn and expect it to be obvious to everyone. One study (Korzenic, 1975) found that kindergarten children blamed the viewers if they could not understand what the drawing was about; it was not until second grade that children began to realize that their drawings might not really communicate to others.

240

FIRST REPRESENTATIONAL ATTEMPTS

Particular skills, whether manipulative or cognitive, seem not very conducive to acceleration. A child will not be able to copy a triangle before five years of age or a diamond, which seems even more difficult, until about seven. Although attempts have been made to increase this ability (Brittain, 1969; Rand, 1973), they have not been successful. Probably attempts at increasing particular skills are doomed to failure because they ignore two fundamental considerations. The first is the erroneous assumption that practice on a task, no matter what the task, will improve the skill in accomplishing that task. The prerequisite experiences needed may be missing; until those are developed, the particular task is meaningless. For example, if one *were* to really go about establishing a program, such as one to teach three year old children how to draw a cube in proper perspective, it would require a lot of pre-cube experiences: a year of scribbling to establish visual–motor control; a year of manipulation of objects to acquaint the youngster with two- and three-dimensionality; a year of two-dimensional drawing to establish drawing abilities; a year of physical expressiveness to perfect the understanding of left and right, up and down, front and back. Now the youngster would supposedly be ready to learn how to draw a cube, but would also be nearly eight years old!

The second consideration that may be overlooked is the cognitive one. To accomplish a particular task, a comprehension of the task itself is necessary. Piaget and others have provided evidence that learning is tied to maturation—a physiological, biological functioning that is predetermined in each individual. Within this restriction there can be great differences, but the development of concepts such as that necessary to draw a cube would not come until well beyond our four to seven year age span and not until the child has developed the ability to deal abstractly with the concept of dimensionality.

In spite of the preceding considerations, many art educators feel it important to try to teach certain artistic skills. Although it is unclear why five year olds should not be allowed to enjoy expression at their own level or why they need to develop some skill at five that will come naturally at seven, some educators try hard to do just that. Castrup, Ain, and Scott (1972) list several skills that four and five year olds could do, such as distinguish some colors, identify some geometric shapes, hold a crayon correctly, and so forth and some they could not do, such as draw one line thicker than another, use the proper amount of paste, or point to a dull or bright color. The study stated that difficult skills would be given added emphasis in their program. How sad, focusing upon what children can't do instead of being supportive of their own creative expression. It has been suggested that one reason children lose their spontaneity and pleasure in art is because they go to school where art is "taught." In some cases there may be good justification for that statement.

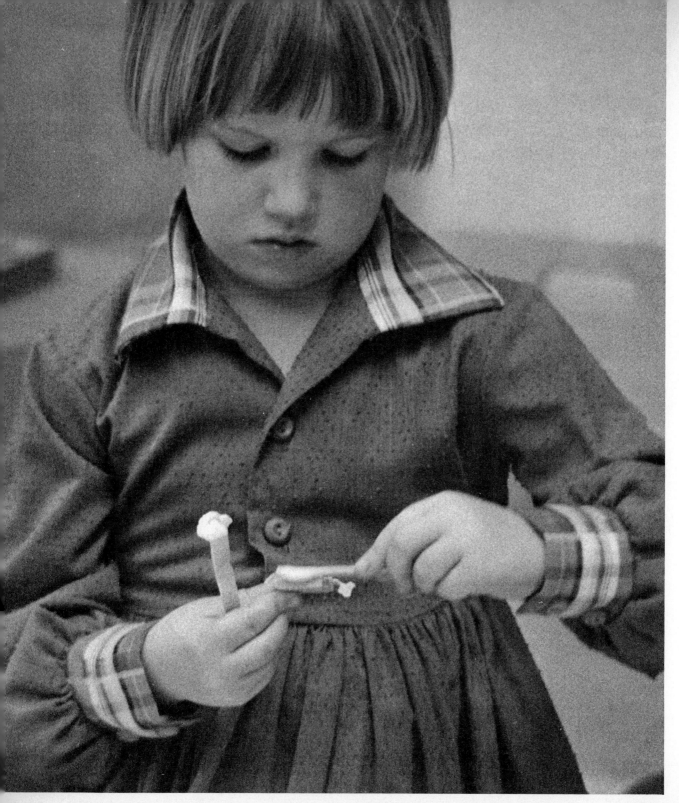

FIGURE 110.
Knowing how much paste to use must be learned by experience. This kindergarten girl is
discovering how much paste she needs for her project.

Art Motivation

Any motivation should make the art experience much more than just an activity; it should stimulate children's awareness of their environment and make them feel that the art activity is extremely vital and more important than anything else. To merely follow an adult's instructions for working with materials or to be handed paper and told, "Draw what you want," or even to have a range of material and activities to do over a period of time—any one of these can result in busyness yet fail miserably in being a meaningful learning experience. A child cannot be expected to gain in knowledge and confidence and in sensitivity toward the environment if there is a barrier between adult and child. The teacher as well as the child needs to feel that this is an important, meaningful, and stimulating experience.

The atmosphere for art experiences is also important. The way something is said can be more important than what is actually said. A study of the influence of a nursery school environment upon children's drawings (Reichenberg–Hackett, 1964) found that children's drawings made in a supportive–permissive atmosphere were rated higher than those made in either an authoritarian atmosphere or in a laissez-faire atmosphere. Cratty (1970), in reviewing research on the relationship between child behavior and adult attitude, concluded that strictness on the part of adults brings anxiety and noncooperative behavior on the part of children. Other studies support the conclusion that the attitude of the teacher is vital to the learning experience. When the adult shows an interest, provides an atmosphere of support for the activity, and acts as if there were nothing more important in the world than the drawing experience, then the environment is ready for art. The two other extremes, that of standing back and not particularly caring what children do, or the authoritarian role of dictating what must be done, apparently have a negative influence upon drawing and therefore a negative influence upon children.

The four to seven year age is an important one in the area of perceptual growth. One study (Spitz and Borland, 1971) found that children between the ages of four and eight showed remarkable growth in the ability to recognize familiar objects from line drawings that had a portion of the drawing deleted. Although four year olds had difficulty in identifying the objects, the ability of adults was not much greater than that of the eight year olds on this task. In another study of young children, Birch and Lefford (1967) concluded that

FIGURE 111.
The young child does not need to be taught how to draw and paint; this comes as naturally as learning how to walk or speak. Proper motivation should assure the child's involvement, so that art expression is a vital activity.

between five and eight years appeared to be the period of most rapid improvement in perceptual analytic ability. It would seem, therefore, that these years are the ones in which to develop the ability to look, examine, and take pleasure in a visual awareness of things in the environment. This perceptual growth is not difficult to encourage. Pointing out the bright colors in the fall, sharing an interesting looking stone, looking at footprints in the mud, having youngsters find a smooth-barked tree and then a rough one, looking for prickly weeds in the grass, noticing how the sun feels hot on your back, listening to the sound of the wind, or noticing the smell of the garbage truck are all perceptual experiences that can be encouraged.

One of the best means of stimulating children's relationship to things around them is to start with the function of the various body parts. The results will show readily in the drawings by children at this age. For example, six year olds who draw only a line for a mouth can be motivated to include teeth and other facial features by stimulating an awareness of teeth in a topic such as "Brushing Your Teeth in the Morning."

"When do you get up in the morning, children? What time do you get up? At seven? How long does it take you to get dressed? Does your mother call you? Do you have a clock radio? How long does it take you to get dressed then? Does your mother have to help you? Do you have to catch a bus? Where do you have your bedroom? On the second floor? All by yourself? After you are dressed, are you ready to catch the bus? No? Oh, you haven't eaten your breakfast yet? But you forgot! You went to breakfast without brushing your teeth! Oh, you brush your teeth after breakfast! Don't you have to hurry? Especially if it's raining? Oh, you brush your teeth anyway! Why? You mean it's bad to leave all that food in between your teeth all day? Do you brush your teeth every morning? How do you hold your toothbrush? With just two fingers? Oh, you hold it this way! Do you brush your teeth back and forth? Oh, no; you mean you do it up and down? Why? Did you ever get your toothbrush caught between your teeth? Does it hurt? You have to be a little careful when you brush your teeth, don't you! But did you forget the toothpaste? Some people don't use toothpaste! Do you? Let's think how we brush our teeth. Let's really brush them good and clean! Now are we all set to go to school? Oh, no; not with all that toothpaste still in there!

Now, we are going to draw a picture about how we get up in the morning and go to the bathroom and brush our teeth."

All children should now have a feeling for brushing their teeth, and one boy may even have a pain where he got his toothbrush caught between his teeth. But every child will be conscious of teeth, and each drawing will include teeth

FIGURE 112.

The small body with the elongated arms is dwarfed under the huge head and toothbrush
in this drawing by a seven year old boy.

as an active part of the child's awareness. We can compare former drawings
with those drawn after the motivation; if an enrichment of the form concept
has taken place, the teacher was successful.

The motivation for a similar lesson can be achieved by engaging the children in an actual experience. One example might be to pass out a bag of crisp
apple chunks to munch on. "Is it hard? Do you really have to bite with your
teeth?" Any such motivation should include as many senses and sensory experiences as possible and should stimulate thinking, feeling, and perceiving.

The length of motivation may depend upon several factors. If the children
have just engaged in an actual experience, a short discussion may be quite sufficient. However, in some cases the motivation may take longer than the actual
drawing or painting. Discussing how a child feels in the rain, how the rain feels

FIRST REPRESENTATIONAL ATTEMPTS

on one's face or the clothes one has to put on, and stimulating an awareness of the sensations of walking with boots on, or even how feet feel if they are wet inside boots, may take a longer time.

In some cases the motivation may be concerned primarily with the material itself. When first working with clay or collage material, the experience with the actual qualities of the material will be most important. "How does the clay feel? Is it hot or cold? Can you push your finger into it? Does it bend easily?" This type of question may be the only motivation necessary to stimulate children to a greater awareness of their own senses.

A motivation based primarily upon recall of something in which the children have all been involved should provide the opportunity for all children to express feelings and emotions in an individual way. No attempt should be made to censor their creative expression, but rather we should try to stimulate the greatest variety of responses. The atmosphere for the particular topic should be generally established by a discussion, for example, of going to school. "Where do you go to school? What time do you go to school? Do you walk? Do you ride a bus? How do you get on the bus? Do you hold on to the door when you climb in? Is the first step a high one?" Topics for motivation should therefore include the *where* and *when*, the *what*, and the *how*.

Subject Matter

The most important consideration, in selecting topics for children in the stage of first representational attempts, should be the meaningfulness of the activity. The more involved children become in the art activity, the more they identify with what they are doing, the more they are actively using their senses, the more the project is really their own, the more meaningful it is. At this age, it is particularly important that any motivation or any subject matter be related directly to the children.

This is an age that shows great gains in awareness. Even as the head–feet representation of a person is usually the first symbol a child makes, this interest in people continues to be central in drawings—not people living in igloos in the Arctic, not Swiss children in the Alps, but the child's own family and especially himself. Basic subject matter stresses an awareness of body parts, such as "The Time I Hurt My Knee," "I Have a Cold and My Nose Hurts," "I Have a Stomach Ache," or "I Am Brushing My Teeth." Several activities include the body and are good topics, such as "I Am Drinking My Milk," "I Went to the Dentist," or "I Am Eating Breakfast." Just presenting a topic is not enough, for the child needs to become involved and actively aware of the details.

Size relationships can also be stressed. "My Family" is a topic that brings an awareness of the size of each family member, from father to little baby sister and maybe even the cat. Other subjects might be "My House Is Big" and "I Am Pushing the Shopping Cart." The flexible use of symbols should be encouraged with topics such as "I Am Putting on My Clothes" and "I Am Tying My Shoes." Another type of topic, such as "I Am on the New Swing at School," or "I Am Crawling on My Stomach," or "I Am Standing on the Table" provides for an awareness of the self in relation to space and objects.

Children often have subject matter within themselves, requiring no motivation or further encouragement for it to spill out. Every kindergarten teacher realizes that if Michael's cat has kittens, this news will come out in arithmetic class, during social studies, or maybe when he bursts into the room first thing in the morning. Ample opportunity should be given children to express on pa-

FIGURE 113.
In this drawing a rural boy imagines himself driving a tractor. Notice the special significance given to the hands and the steering wheel.

FIRST REPRESENTATIONAL ATTEMPTS

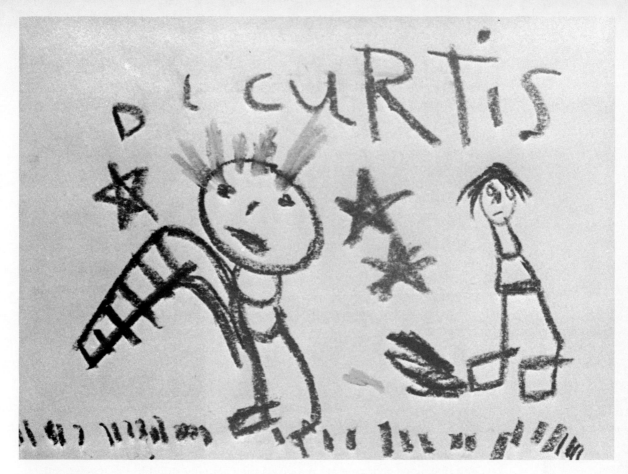

FIGURE 114.

"I Am Playing in the School Yard," drawn in chalk by a five year old boy. Apparently the teacher only watches while the youngster plays on the slide, for the child has drawn the teacher without arms.

per their feelings and emotions. Some of these feelings will be quite apparent to any adult. Such topics as "The First Snowfall," "The Storm," "An Approaching Holiday," "A Big Fire" are all subject matter that cannot be ignored. Some subject matter will be a great deal more personal to the individual child. Such topics as "My New Baby Sister," "I Got Hit by a Car," "I Got Lost in the Store," "My House Caught on Fire," or "I Have New Shoes" all provide appropriate subject matter for any age. The child who produced Figure 114 explained that his teacher, represented by an armless figure, watched while he played on the new slide in the kindergarten play yard. When the child is eager for expression, art should certainly not be limited to a specific time of the day or regimented to a particular topic.

Another subject matter is the art material itself. Any art material should play a subordinate role in an art experience, and children's own expression should be of predominant importance. However, at this age children have been exposed to only a few art materials, and in some cases their experience with these materials may have been restricted. The prime reason, then, for using an art material as subject matter is to promote a positive attitude toward material and to insure the greatest amount of exploration and flexibility in its use. Such experimentations should be related directly to the children and should not be concerned with any adult consideration of "artistic qualities." The use of an art material as a subject matter should therefore take the form of exploring and experimenting with the various qualities of clay, tempera paint, or other materials.

Art Materials

The process of creation is of greater significance than the final product, which means that an art material should be selected that meets the needs of the age group for which it was planned. Because children at this age are excited by the ability to represent what is meaningful to them, any art experience should provide the opportunity for developing mastery of the material itself. Constantly introducing or changing art materials may actually stand in the way of children's mastering the material enough to express their own feelings, their own reactions to their senses, and their own intellectual concepts of the environment. Any art material should truly be an art material. Expression itself is not limited to any age group, so any material used with children should be of such a nature that it is possible to use this material throughout life. There should be no "cute" art materials for nursery school or kindergarten children to use, because these provide no opportunity for continued growth.

As with younger children, thickly prepared tempera paints, used with a bristle brush on a somewhat absorbent, large, heavy sheets of paper, are excellent materials for this age level. Absorbent paper (about 18 by 24 inches) is recommended because it prevents the paint from running. A low, flat table provides the best surface on which to paint; the floor can also be successfully used. If the limitations of space do not allow painting on a horizontal surface, easels or a bulletin board can be used. Here, however, the paint should be of a thick enough consistency so that the child can control the paint without the frustration of dripping accidents.

FIRST REPRESENTATIONAL ATTEMPTS

Good quality colored crayons and smaller sheets of paper (12 by 18 inches) are also excellent materials. The crayon should be large and unwrapped. Too often a new set of wrapped, sharply pointed crayons is looked upon as a treasure to keep rather than as material to use. Unwrapped crayons can be used on the sides and ends, unlike pencils.

Pencils may provide the opportunity for some children to draw in detail. The usual kindergarten pencil works quite well. A study comparing crayon and colored pencils used by children in kindergarten (Salome, 1967) indicated that drawings made by crayon tended to be rated higher on several measures, but some youngsters spent more time and were able to include more detail with pencils. It is more important that children be given the opportunity to draw, even if they have to use a pen or poor pencil, than not be given the opportunity at all.

Clay is an excellent three-dimensional material for the preschematic stage. As in drawings, there is a constant change of modes of representation. Pulling out all meaningful parts from the lump of clay and adding parts together to make a form can both be observed. A child who starts with a lump of clay and

FIGURE 115.

A person made from clay closely resembles a drawing by the same child. Note that this five year old has added hair to the head-feet symbol; in fact, lots of hair.

pulls parts out from the whole usually does not go into as much detail as a child who starts with separate parts and then puts these together. But either method comes naturally from the child and is acceptable. Moist clay can be easily stored in plastic bags, and water can be added as needed to maintain the proper consistency. Plasticene, which is essentially clay with an oil base, is much more expensive than clay, may stain, and the consistency cannot be altered.

FIGURE 116.

"Indians," drawn with a felt-tipped pen by a seven year old girl. This material lends itself to a bold, direct presentation of thought. Every art material has its own characteristics and specific values.

In addition to these basic materials, there are many other materials that are quite suitable for this developmental level. These include colored chalk, fiber-tipped pens, colored papers, collage materials, scissors, and other materials that truly give the child an opportunity to develop flexible concepts. Tricky use of materials should be avoided, such as dripping paint, pasting cereals, printing, and using stencils, or using materials in methods that are foreign to the child's own intentions. Activities such as mass-producing little stereotypes for holidays and seasonal events only make children feel inadequate and lose confidence in their own self-expression. As long as the search for a concept of form and space is predominant, the desire for decoration generally does not develop.

Summary

The art of children in the stages of first representation is a direct reflection of children themselves. Not only are the drawings and paintings a record of concepts, feelings, and perceptions of the environment, but these drawings and paintings also provide the sensitively aware adult with the means for a better understanding of children. In our discussion the concern has been primarily to see art as one of the essential components in total development.

The art of children also provides an opportunity to promote growth through the area of art education. Here we mean something a great deal more significant than changing the outward appearance of the drawings themselves; we are concerned with the total process of creating. We cannot positively affect children's behavior by giving them patterns or procedures to follow in order to achieve a "better-looking" product. The change in the product itself should come about through the changes in a child's thinking, feeling, and perceiving. It is through the *process* that changes in behavior or changes in growth patterns develop. It is also through the process that meaningful changes take place in the product.

The art motivation for this particular age group concentrates upon children's experiences whether actually, in fantasy, or in vicarious experiences. Art plays a crucial part in the educational system, particularly in the area of perceptual growth, the developing awareness of those things around us through all the senses; through creative growth, the development of characteristics of flexibility, imaginative thinking, originality, and fluency of thinking; and also through emotional growth, the ability to face new situations, the ability to express feelings, both pleasant and unpleasant. Art also provides the opportunity for growth in the intellectual, social, and aesthetic areas.

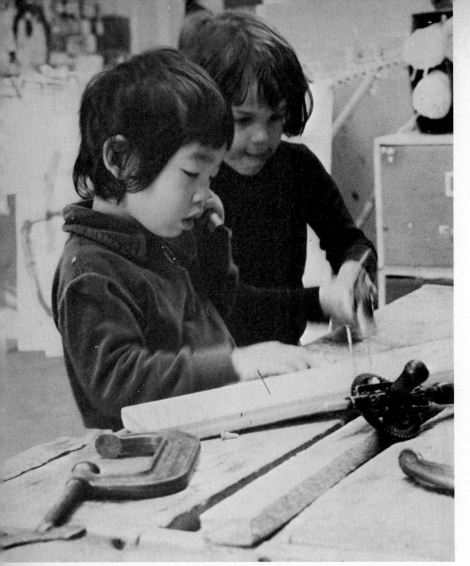

FIGURE 117.
Children enjoy using adult tools. The opportunity to explore, investigate, and invent new forms through art activities is an absorbing experience.

The majority of children who are beginning to attend school will be in the stages of first representational attempts. It is therefore imperative that their introduction to art experiences be a meaningful one. A great deal of what goes on within school is dictated by adult society; however, children are not miniature adults, nor do they think in adult terms. Art can provide the opportunity for growth in several vital areas and the opportunity for children to investigate, invent, explore, make mistakes, have feelings of fear and hate, love and joy. Most essential, they should have all these experiences of living as individuals who can, should, and will think for themselves.

Related Activities

1. Collect drawings over a period of time from a child who is still scribbling and trace the evolution of the first representative symbols. Keep in chronological order, and then see how the symbol for a person develops.

2. Collect drawings that include symbols for the mouth. Stimulate first grade children by a motivation built around chewing peanuts. Compare the drawings done before and after the motivation to see what changes, if any, have taken place in the symbol for the mouth.

3. Observe the activity of a group of kindergarten children during their free play and during organized games. Relate the amount of parallel play to the discussion of the use of space in drawings. What are the differences or similarities between these two activities?

4. Compare the development of representational symbols in drawings with symbols in clay. Photograph the clay products to keep a record of the development in clay to compare with the drawings.

5. Observe a child who is making his first representational symbols. Keep a verbatim record of his comments for several different fifteen-minute periods. What relationship is there between his verbal and his graphic expression?

6. From a collection of paintings by five year olds list the objects that are painted with a visually established color–object relationship. List those objects that are painted with no visually established color–object relationship. What might cause some of these choices of color?

8

The Achievement of a Form Concept

The Schematic Stage
Seven–Nine Years

The Importance of the Schematic Stage

After much experimentation, a child has developed a satisfactory symbol for a person and for familiar objects. We call this symbol a schema if it is repeated again and again whenever no intentional experience causes a change in this symbol. These schemata are highly individualized. For some children the schema can be a very rich concept, while for others it is a fairly meager symbol. Differences in schemata depend upon many things, but just as no two children are the same, no schemata are identical. Although there is no magical time for the formation of a schema, most children arrive at this stage at about seven years of age. The schema for an object may be determined by how a child sees something, the emotional significance attached to it, kinesthetic experiences with or touch impressions of the object, or how the object functions or behaves.

A pure schema in a child's drawing occurs whenever a child's representation confines itself to the object: "This is a tree." "This is a man." However, when a child intentionally alters a form, it is no longer a pure schema, and we know that the child has portrayed something of particular importance. As Stacey and Ross (1975) point out in their study of six year old children's memory of their own drawings, children of this age can produce alternative schemas for objects and events when asked to do so. This is of special importance to the teacher, who can determine the effects of teaching by comparing the usual schema with any deviation.

The mental images a child has of objects in the environment are the result of a thinking process; the drawing on the paper is the symbol of that mental image, the symbol standing for the object. The art product, then, is an indication of the way the child comprehends and interprets space as well as objects. For example, a child may usually draw a house without including a chimney. But in the winter, when it is cold and there is talk of Santa Claus coming down the chimney, the schema may change to include a chimney. Although the schematic stage normally starts at age seven, some children will develop a schema earlier than this for certain things, such as people, whereas other children will remain longer in the preschematic stage.

THE ACHIEVEMENT OF A FORM CONCEPT

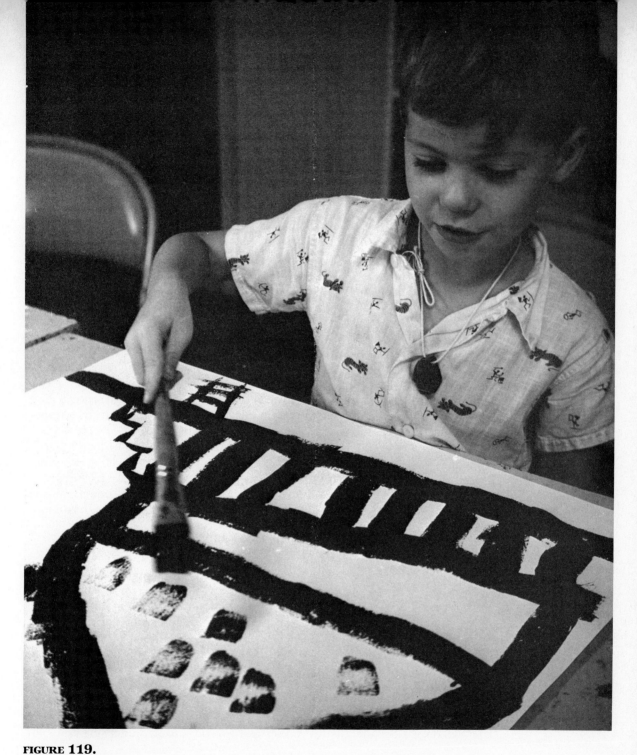

FIGURE 119.
By the age of seven, most children have developed schemas for elements of their environment. This boy has an elaborate schema for a house.

Characteristics
of Schematic Drawings

Human Schema

At about the age of seven, the drawing of a human figure by a child should be a readily recognizable symbol. The portrayal of body parts depends on the child's knowledge of them. Not only will there be a head, body, arms, and legs, but also some of the various features. The eyes should be different from the nose, the symbol for nose should be different from that for the mouth, and there should be hair and sometimes even a neck. Usually, the child includes separate symbols for hands and even fingers and of course a different symbol for feet. Often clothing is drawn instead of the body. The average schema for a seven year old includes most of these items, and for some children the symmetry of the body, the two arms, the two legs, the two eyes, the two ears, is important. In a study of children in Trinidad, Ives and Rovet (1982) found that children portrayed certain items in front view (men, houses, owls) and certain other items in side view (horses, boats, cars); stationary objects were drawn with a front orientation, and objects in motion were frequently (but not always) drawn in side view. Engel (1981) explains that the most salient view, the most readily recognized, is used by youngsters.

The schema usually consists of geometric forms that lose their meaning when separated from the whole. Sometimes ovals, triangles, squares, circles, rectangles, or irregular shapes are used for the body, and all kinds of shapes are used for legs, arms, and clothes. In Figure 120, "My Family," notice how the girl repeats her schema for each member of the family. This child is not attempting to copy a visible form, but rather her concept has developed from many factors: her process of thinking, her awareness of her own feelings, her perceptual sensitivities, and her own special interests and priorities. The human schema is therefore highly individualized and is used when the child requires a generic symbol for a person. Even when asked, kindergarten and second grade children do not draw people looking at each other. Ives and Houseworth (1980) asked kindergarten, second, and fourth graders to draw two people, two horses, or two dogs. Generally the two horses and two dogs were drawn side view. But

THE ACHIEVEMENT OF A FORM CONCEPT

FIGURE 120.
Four nearly identical schematic figures represent this girl's family. All are looking
straight forward, rather than relating to one another.

when asked to draw the two people talking to each other, it was only the fourth
graders who drew the people facing each other; the younger children repeated
their usual schema—two people looking straight forward.

Space Schema

There is now a conscious awareness of a definite order in space relationships.
The child no longer thinks, "There is a tree, there is a man, there is a car"
without relating them to one another, as was typical during the preschematic
stage. A child now thinks, "I am on the ground, the car is on the ground, the
grass grows on the ground, mud is on the ground, we are all on the ground."
This consciousness, which includes all objects having a common space relationship, is expressed by putting everything on a *base line.*

The base line is universal and can be considered as much a part of the natural development of children as learning to run or skip. In a study of over five
thousand drawings, it was found that only 1 percent of the children included
the base line at age three, that by age six more children included the base line
than did not, and that by eight years 96 percent of the children included the
base line in their drawings (Wall, 1959). These percentages are nearly identical

FIGURE 121.

In this drawing, Amber has shown an understanding of size relationships and a more flexible schema. David is in his crib, and all the family seems happily posed for us.

to those found in drawings by a thousand children, all representing the topic "eating" (Brittain, 1985). The base line indicates the relationship between the child and the environment; this line can apparently represent not only the ground on which objects stand but can represent a floor, a street, or any base upon which a child is standing. This line might be thought of as a travel line, somewhat like a map, with objects appearing in order along the line. Siegel et al. (1979) had children take trips through a model town and then asked them

THE ACHIEVEMENT OF A FORM CONCEPT

to construct the layout from memory. They concluded that the understanding of space is determined by the perceptual and motor mechanisms by which it is explored.

In creative products of primitive cultures the base line was often used as a means of indicating motion. It may be that the origin of the base line is the kinesthetic experience of moving along a path. The use of the base line is also very apparent in the art of some complex cultures, such as in the carvings on the tombs in ancient Egypt, or the vase decorations of ancient Greece, or the

FIGURE 122.
"Eating Ice Cream." A typical base line and skyline frame the action, with the important sun partly above the skyline. The legs of the smaller figure are especially long, to reach the ground.

FIGURE 123.

This detail from a Peruvian bowl with an incised design shows the figures moving along
a base line, a practice common in cultures widely separated by distance and time.

cylinder seals of the Hittites, where pictorial matter is arranged on a line for a
narrative purpose. When children use their art as communication, it may be
natural to think of objects coming one after another on a line.

It is quite obvious that in nature neither objects nor persons actually stand
upon a line. When questioned, children invariably identify this base line as
being the ground. A counterpart to the base line appears in drawings as a sky
line, drawn at the top of the page; the space between this and the base line is
identified by children as being air. Adults usually think of the sky in pictures as
coming down to ground level; however, this is actually an optical illusion. Not
only does the sky never actually meet the ground, but of course there is no tan-

THE ACHIEVEMENT OF A FORM CONCEPT

gible sky, only an accumulation of air over a dark background. The concept of the sky above, ground below, and air between is just as valid as the concept that the sky and ground meet. Both are illusions. At this stage of development the child has little awareness of how to represent the three-dimensional quality of space, although occasionally some abstract lines are substituted for depth.

The Base Line
as Part of the Landscape

When a child is drawing or painting an outdoor picture, the base line can be used to symbolize the base on which things stand and at another time to represent the surface of the landscape. In the painting in Figure 124 one base line symbolizes the level ground while another represents the mountain. Apparently, the child wishes to indicate that this second base line is elevated over the plain. It can readily be seen that the mountain is still meant as a base line from the fact that the flowers stand perpendicularly to the mountain. Even the figure is related to its base line. It is as if the base line were a length of straight wire with flowers attached to it. If the wire is bent according to the kinesthetic experience of going up and down, the flowers attached to the wire stand out perpendicularly, just as in this drawing. It is not the mass of the mountain that is

FIGURE 124.
"I Am Climbing a Hill," painted by a seven year old boy. The hill is an upper base line which is bent, representing the experience of climbing up and down.

of significance but the line itself, which goes up and down. When children in this schematic stage draw a building, the chimney is typically drawn perpendicular to the line of the roof, which serves as a base line, just as the line of the mountain became a base line.

In Figure 125, entitled "Fruit Harvest," two base lines represent an orchard. The child himself is shown on the lower part of the paper picking apples off a tree. Above him is the sky and above that another base line upon which his father appears driving a wagon full of apples. Notice the schema the child has for apple tree. Notice also the size of the apples on the tree as compared to the size of the apples in the basket. The ripe apples have great importance on the tree, but once they are in the basket they become less important. One can get a real feeling for the freshness of children's expression from this, and it is this freshness that many adult artists strive to emulate. The bird in the upper corner becomes important, too, for apples pecked by a bird must be discarded. The showing of two base lines usually is a later development and is a step toward

FIGURE 125.
"Fruit Harvest." There may be more modern examples, but this classic painting demonstrates many aspects of representation typical of this age.

THE ACHIEVEMENT OF A FORM CONCEPT

perspective in drawings. However, this is strictly a two-dimensional representation, as can be seen by the fact that the sky is represented in both halves of the painting. Children of this age rarely draw anything that is not directly related to the base line, even if two or more base lines appear in one picture. A better understanding of "Fruit Harvest" may be had by seeing the top portion as a more distant row of trees in the orchard, beyond the lower or closer trees.

In this picture everything functions and has meaning. The child wants to say, "This is an orchard"; therefore, he is not satisfied by merely drawing one tree. "The apples on the tree are the most beautiful ones, because I want them, but I have picked some into the basket. I am just now reaching for one. Those in the basket are no longer single apples; they are the dozens of apples I have collected. Daddy is carrying them to town. Birds are pecking on the apples. We don't want the birds." The child relates himself actively to his environment. He is on the ground, the basket is on the ground, the apples are in the basket, the tree is on the ground; and farther away, the wagon is on the ground, the horse is on the ground, and the bird is in the air with the sky above. The picture signifies the child's understanding of himself and his environment.

Other Means of Space Representation

Although the base line usually represents space in drawings and paintings, occasionally a meaningful experience forces a child to deviate from this type of schema. These are subjective space representations. *Folding over* belongs to this category, expressing a space concept by drawing objects that appear to be upside down. Figure 126 shows the process of folding over; the child has depicted himself waving to the ferry. After the child drew himself waving with his handkerchief, standing on one side of the bay, he decided to draw the boat. He drew it apparently upside down. But it is not really upside down. This child was leaning on the floor and, after drawing himself on one side of the base line, he walked around his paper and drew the other side of the bay and the ferryboat. You can even see where the ferryboat is landing. This concept can best be understood if the paper is folded along a base line on which the boy is standing so that the child stands upright and faces the boat. By folding the other side of the bay upright also, we get a model of the scene and suddenly realize the interesting concept of the two skies, one at the bottom and the other at the top of the paper. Actually this is a perfectly valid concept: the child feels that both sides of the bay are important because his experience is that of being in the center of the scene.

FIGURE 126.

"Norfolk Ferry,", painted by an eight year old boy. This painting is an imaginative example of representing space by "folding over."

There is an advantage to have children work on the floor or on low tables,
so that the drawing or painting can be approached from all directions. In Figure 127, "I Say Hello to My Friend on the Other Side of the Street," drawn by a
nine year old partially blind boy, the principle of folding over is used in a different manner. In this drawing the sides would be folded down rather than up
to show the opposite sides of the street.

Sometimes children will not use a base line as the ground, but instead put
objects or people in a circle, such as around a table. Figure 128 shows a family
eating with each member of the family viewed separately, as if from the center
of the table. Possibly the edges of the table could be understood as a substitute
for a base line, but an important consideration is that the child includes a variety of viewpoints in one drawing. The scene is not to be viewed from outside

THE ACHIEVEMENT OF A FORM CONCEPT

FIGURE 127.
"I Say Hello to My Friend on the Other Side of the Street." These children frequently called to each other at the street crossing. Here the base lines are at the edges of the paper, in contrast with their location in the previous illustration.

FIGURE 128.
The child has drawn from several points of view with family members seated around the table, which is tipped up to show the plates.

the picture plane, but rather each person is seated at the table, seen from directly in front of that person, and in each case the person is smiling pleasantly back at us.

Subjective space experiences can result in mixing plan and elevation. The drawing "Eating Out at Joe's" (Figure 129) shows the table tipped up on its side so that the checkered tablecloth can be seen. The plates and tableware are perched on the table edge; however, the chairs and diners are drawn side view. This combination of plan and elevation describes the important elements, although it is little related to a naturalistic representation.

Another drawing that combines plan and elevation is "Amusement Island" (Figure 130). The child visited an island on which were all types of amusements, people playing cards, hot dog stands, and so forth. There were boats for rent, and in such a boat the child took a ride around the island. The drawing shows a top view of the island, because it is important to show that water surrounds the land. Since the child rowed around the island in a boat, it is important that this, too, be portrayed. Each of the events is shown as a separate activity. It is a listing of events, with each table folded over or the boat tipped

FIGURE 129.
The knife, fork, and spoon are ready to be used but are drawn with the table edge as a base line. The light fixture overhead seems to be turned on.

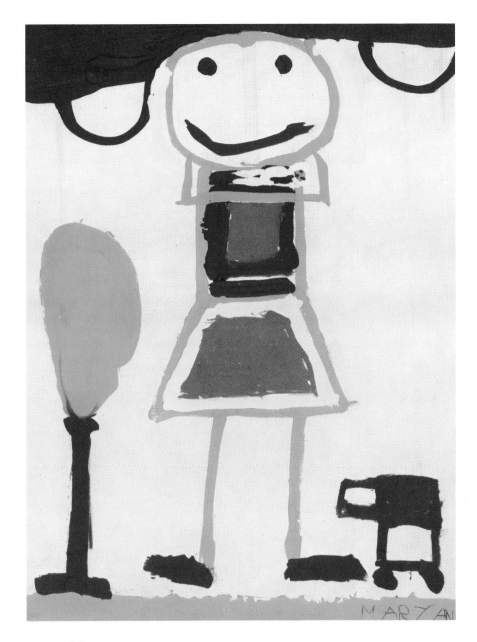

PLATE 21.

"I Am Standing in My Back Yard," painted by a six and a half year old girl. Notice the developing signs of the child's awareness of the relationship between objects and color; the grass is green, the sky is blue, and the girl's hair is yellow. She has painted herself much larger than the tree; the relative sizes show the child's egocentrism at this stage of development. She is holding a doll in the picture, and a doll carriage is on the right.

PLATE 22.

"Lightning and Rain," drawn by a seven year old girl. Here the relationship between objects and color is more firmly established: sky is blue and lightning is yellow. Large hands grasp the umbrella, which does an effective job of keeping the child dry.

PLATE 23.

"Spring," drawn by an eight and a half year old child. There is a sky line at the top, a base line at the bottom, and a pond in the middle which has been folded up to show the water, cattails, and the turtle who lives there.

FIGURE 130.
"Amusement Island," drawn by an eight year old boy. The boy had gone around the amusement island in a row-boat.

to explain what went on. Here it seems as if three edges of the paper have become three separate base lines. Similarly, it is not unusual to see all four sides of a house portrayed at one time or to see all four wheels drawn on an automobile. What a child includes in drawings and paintings is a direct reflection of subjective experiences. There is obviously nothing wrong with these representations. By observing this creative expression, the sensitive adult can gain insight into a child's relationship to the world.

X-ray Pictures

There is another interesting, nonvisual way of representing different views that could not possibly be seen at the same time. A child may depict the inside and outside of a building or other enclosure simultaneously whenever the inside is of greater importance. Apparently unaware of the impossibility of such a visual concept, the child mixes up the inside and outside, becoming so involved with the inside that the outside is treated as if it were transparent. In Figure 131, the illustration "Coal Mine" shows an X-ray representation in which both inside and outside are shown. A girl realized the significance of the mine shaft and tunnels and became quite absorbed in the interior of the mine and how the coal was

FIGURE 131.

This is a picture of a coal mine painted by a nine year old girl. She has shown both the inside and outside features of the mine in one representation.

produced. Note that the mountain surface is treated like a bent base line, with the house and trees placed perpendicular to it. It is not surprising to find that the child was the daughter of a coal miner living in a company house near the mine a generation ago.

Space and Time Representations

Space and time representations include in one drawing different time sequences or spatially distinct impressions. Just as children invent ways of showing two- and three-dimensional objects, sometimes by using plan and elevation at the same time, so they also invent ways of showing events that occur in sequence. Apparently, children have different reasons for developing these space and time representations, and an understanding of them is important because they can provide a rich source for motivation.

One purpose of space–time representation is to tell stories. This is why several episodes are represented in one sequence of drawings. The pictures may be

THE ACHIEVEMENT OF A FORM CONCEPT

FIGURE 132.
The x-ray method of representation is not unique to young children. Other cultures, other times, have felt this was an appropriate means of representation. This typical x-ray painting on bark of a Brolga Bird was made by an Australian Aboriginal.

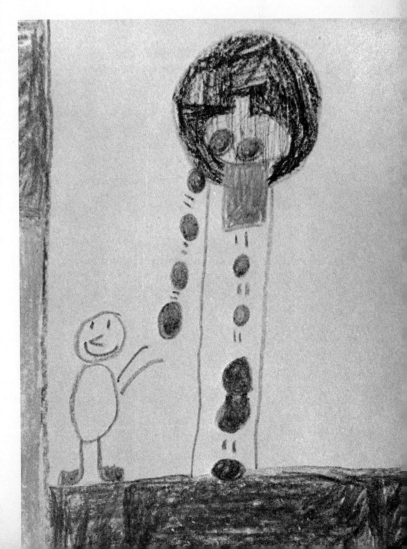

FIGURE 133.
"Playing Basketball" shows how the youngster throws a ball through the hoop. The path of the ball is portrayed by a series of ball shapes, almost as if we were seeing the scene in slow motion.

FIGURE 134.

The Bayeux Tapestry tells the whole story of the invasion of England, from the preparations to the final victory. This section shows three base lines, with the dead soldiers and horses below, the fighting knights on the second base line, and the warriors defending the hill on a third base line. (from artist's sketch of the Bayeux Tapestry, circa 1080)

separate, like those in a comic book, although they may not be divided by a line. Journeys, trips, travel episodes, or other events that require a sequence of time belong in this type of representation. The series of separate pictures shows a complete event, so the topic is usually the same. Not only children have utilized this method of space–time representation; a classic example is the Bayeux Tapestry, telling the story of the Norman invasion of England in 1066.

Placing the various aspects of a particular experience next to one another in one space is a method of portraying its distinctive qualities. For a typical example, refer to Figure 135B, the drawing entitled "Searching for the Lost Pencil." The figure on the left both is looking for and has found the pencil. The boy uses the next figure to express putting the pencil into his pocket with one hand, while the other hand no longer has any function. In other words, by means of two figures he has represented four different time phases. In a sense he could have given one figure four arms, as has been done in medieval manuscripts, but this would have contradicted his concept of a man. He was so involved with his experience—searching for the pencil, finding the pencil, picking it up, and putting it into his pocket—that he drew all these events.

Significance of Variations in the Schema

If the schema is the concept of man and environment that the child has developed, then every deviation has special importance. Rarely does the basic schema itself change, but rather variations can often be noticed in sections or parts.

274

Three principal forms of deviations are: (1) exaggeration of important parts; (2) neglect or omission of unimportant or suppressed parts; and (3) change of symbols for significant parts. Children are not conscious of these exaggerations; rather, they create size relationships that are "real" to them. The origin of such deviations lies either in autoplastic experiences (that is, the feelings of the bodily self or muscular sensations), or in the relative significance the particular part has for the child.

Figure 135 displays many types of deviations. First we see a schematic representation of a man that the child drew when simply asked to draw a man. Thus, in this drawing no intentional experiences are represented. In comparing this schema with the drawing "Searching for the Lost Pencil" (Figure 135B), note that the arms and the hands express the searching and groping about for the pencil. The enormously lengthened, groping arm and changes in the shape of the symbol for hand in the first figure show how the representation has been modified by the experience of reaching. "With this hand I have just found the

FIGURE 135.
(left) This is a child's schema for "A Man." No particular experience is portrayed.
(right) "Searching for the Lost Pencil." Notice how the schema has been changed to show how the child looked for and found the pencil.

pencil." The arms show a double line, indicating their special functional importance. Notice, too, the exaggerated pencil, showing the importance it had for the child when he found it. "With this hand I put it in my pocket," the child says, and points to one of the arms of the second figure which, in fact, represents the same person. The arm putting the pencil into the pocket is now far less emphasized and is represented by a single line only; the second arm of the figure, no longer having a function, has shriveled to a mere stump. The pencil has been reduced in size now that it has been found. An experience of bodily sensations is also shown. The left figure in the drawing is supposed to be bent forward, and this is expressed by means of shorter legs, a lowered head, and an elongated neck. The figure on the right is standing upright while putting the pencil into his pocket, and since the sensation of bending down is no longer important, the head and the neck diminish in size and the figure looks more like the schema. We may also speculate that the introduction of a base line in the second drawing might be caused because of the awareness that the pencil is on the floor and therefore it is important to show the floor.

In examining variations in schemas, Goodnow (1978) asked 320 children from nursery school age to fifth grade to draw a person picking up a ball. The younger children showed the least change from the usual schema; they placed the ball near the figure, lengthened an arm to touch the ball, or drew the ball raised, but left the body unchanged. Sometimes the first and second graders would have the figure side view, but it was not until third grade that most of the drawings began to show the figure itself bent. In a second study, Goodnow asked children to draw two people, one walking slowly and the other running fast. There was no particular difference between these two figures except for altering the legs.

Disproportions nearly always result from some definite intention or experience, though this does not mean that the experience is necessarily conscious. There are no "inaccurate proportions," since such an adult judgment is the result of a visual comparison. Because the child is not aware of making these exaggerations or omitting parts, correcting such drawing would only confuse the child. The pictorial representations of children follow laws of their own. In some cases the subjective space representations may look confusing or incomprehensible. Although a child should never be forced to justify or interpret a painting, most children are more than eager to discuss their involvement in the experience that motivated the picture. An awareness of the variety and an understanding of the meanings of these types of space schema give a greater insight into the inner thought processes of children. A sympathetic and under-

FIGURE 136.
"Playing Football." Only the arms of the figures have been changed from the boy's usual schema. The jumping figure is raised above the base line.

standing adult can learn a great deal by showing an interest in how and what a child thinks.

The Meaning of Color and Design

The child discovers naturally that there is a relationship between color and object. It is no longer a random choice or emotional relationship that determines which color is selected for objects in a painting. The child now draws the environment more objectively and has developed definite space relationships. In color, too, the child has discovered a similar definite relationship. Just as the schema for a person is repeated again and again, so also are the same colors repeated for the same objects.

The establishment of a definite color for an object and its constant repetition are part of the continuing development of the child's thinking processes. The child now has the capacity to categorize, to group things into classes and to

FIGURE 137.

As children paint, they develop color-object relationships; they now establish schemas for colors as well as for objects.

make generalizations. "What color is the sky?" "The sky is blue." "What color is grass?" "The grass is green." To the visually discriminating adult the answers might vary, depending upon whether it is a hazy day, or there is a stormy sky, or whether the grass is dry and brittle or fresh from a spring rain. To Carlos, however, just to be able to realize that the color in his painting is the same as the object that he is painting is an important accomplishment and a satisfying experience. He has begun to find some logical order in the world and is establishing concrete relationships with things around him.

Although there are common colors used by most children for particular objects, each child develops personal color relationships. The origin of the individual's color schema is probably to be found in a visual or emotional concept of color. Apparently, the first meaningful relationship with an object can determine a color schema. If the child's first impressions were of a muddy back yard, and through repetition this concept has become firmly established, then all ground will be brown, regardless of whether there is grass over it or not. This color schema will not change unless the child has an experience in which a change in color becomes necessary.

In Plate 21, "I Am Standing in My Back Yard," the child has established definite color–object relationships. Notice that the eyes, lips, and hair, and also the grass, tree, and sky have been painted in very direct, bold colors that seem to indicate that the child "knows" the color of these objects. Plate 22, "Lightning and Rain," is drawn with crayon. Notice that the sky retains its blue color although it is raining. Criticism of the use of color in these two pictures would only be upsetting to the children. Also the happy accident when colors run into one another, which may stimulate an adult, can be very frustrating to a child, who is unable to capitalize on these accidental happenings. For the child such accidental happenings are just mistakes. The color schema is an indication, therefore, of the developing ability for abstract thought and shows that the child can generalize to other situations from these experiences. This is an important step in the developmental process.

A certain third grade boy had a new classroom teacher, one who felt that her youngsters needed more opportunity to paint. He was amazed to learn that she wanted the children to mix their own colors, because never before had they been allowed to mix poster paints. He spent the entire hour mixing paint and, to his delight, discovered brown, all kinds of brown. So his jars of brown paint were carefully stored for him to use as soon as he could make time for art again. Sometimes children will make such discoveries when mixing paint. Wondering how this happened and trying to do it again can be exciting. When there is no green paint, but plenty of blue and yellow, children may find that color mixing is a challenging experience. This is quite different from telling children to mix a couple of drops of blue into the yellow to get a cool green. At this age there is little awareness of subtle variations in hue.

The evidence indicates that children of this age have no concern for any formal aspects of art; art for them is chiefly a means of self-expression, and they are not aware of the beauty in what they do. However, adults can see many design qualities in what children of this age paint or draw, taking a great deal of interest in this native or innate design sense. This was not true a century ago.

One of the important attributes of design is rhythm, and this rhythm is often to be seen in children's paintings in their repetition of form. Looking over drawings or paintings by children of this age will quickly show that the way children deal with space contributes greatly to this "design." This is a natural part of development. Children paint spontaneously, and the repetition of forms or schemata is done unconsciously, whereas an adult artist uses repetition and manipulates forms on a conscious level. The teaching of design fundamentals would be detrimental to the spontaneity and freedom typical of children's drawings.

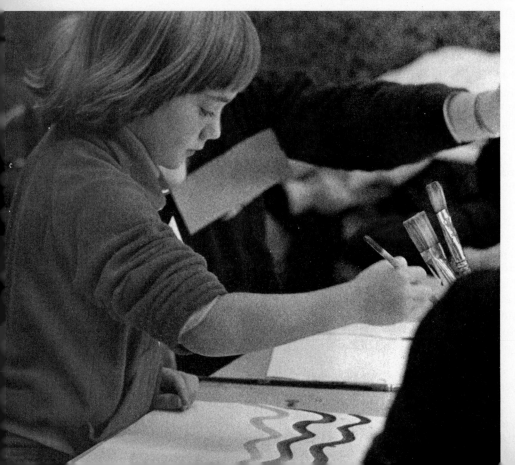

FIGURE 138.
While experimenting with colors, this girl has spontaneously repeated the same wavy line, displaying an innate design sense.

The Development of the Primary School Child

Drawings reflect the child's total being; the emergency of a definite schema has many implications and can give an understanding adult some valuable insights into the child's development. For example, Maxine no longer represents objects in relation to herself but now begins to represent objects in some logical relationship to one another. When younger, she drew a house or a tree or a toy in juxtaposition, without any objective order. Now, however, Maxine includes herself in her concept in the same way that she includes the tree, the house, or the whole environment. This experience—"I am on the street, the house is on the street, John is on the street"—is a decisive step in the psychological development of the child. Her egocentric attitude changes, and this is reflected not only in her drawings but also in her total development. The child seeks to find order in the environment and to develop formulas for proper behavior (Piaget, 1959). These may make no sense to an adult but can often become very important in a child's life. Most of us can remember some of the laws governing our behavior at this age, such as avoiding stepping on the cracks in the sidewalk for fear of dire consequences, or performing some private ritual if two children said the same thing at the same time, or touching every desk in the row before sitting down to insure good luck. These laws and rules for behavior make a schema of sorts in another area of the child's development.

The development of the schema also signals a change to a more cooperative attitude (Wall, 1959). The differences between the preschematic and schematic stages can easily be recognized by observing children in a kindergarten and then comparing their behavior with that of children in second grade. Kindergarten children play and work together only when urged to do so. One child will be going in one direction imitating a train, another child will be sitting self-concerned in a chair, whereas a third will be playing in the sand, scarely noticing the others. Their conversation will also be ego-involved. Although they apparently are talking to one another, they seldom listen to, or seem to expect a reply from, those near them. Their talk is usually tied up with their own play and seems to be more concerned with explaining what is going on to

FIGURE 139.

"Daddy is Coming Home." This child shows great awareness of his environment, with the car parked outside, the father coming through the door, and the family inside the house waiting to greet him.

themselves rather than to others. This is clearly indicated, as we have seen, in the spatial concept of children during that age. However, with the development of the schema and a definite order in space, the child begins to relate to others and to feel as part of the environment. Before the development of the schema is not a period for cooperative games. An awareness of others and of others' feelings will not be understood, whereas during the schematic stage the ability to share and understand others' feelings is beginning to develop.

THE ACHIEVEMENT OF A FORM CONCEPT

The introduction of the base line in the schema has other important implications for the understanding of children. Since a child can now see logical relationships between objects in the environment, it is possible to begin to think of a meaningful reading program. In reading it is necessary to relate letters to one another in order to form a word symbol. Sibley (1957) gathered reading readiness scores, teacher estimates of reading potential, and several drawings from three kindergarten classes. The following year when these same children were in first grade, reading achievement scores and the first grade teachers' evaluation of their reading skills were obtained. It was found that the reading readiness and reading achievement scores were closely related, which would be expected since the material the children were tested on was similar. However, the drawings gathered from the kindergarten children were a better predictor of how well they would be reading when they got to first grade than were the estimates of the kindergarten teacher! Dyson (1982) notes that there is a thin line between drawing and writing. Young children frequently mix up these terms, suggesting that the processes are similar to them; they use pictures, letters, or numbers to symbolize parts of their environment and view print as symbols, too, rather than as representing the sounds of speech. Another study utilized art in a program to develop reading skills. Platt (1971) has developed a method using drawings by children as the basis for teaching reading, in which children put together their own reading books by making drawings with the names of the objects added. Mills (1973) developed an art program for first grade Appalachian children that sought the inclusion of details by activating the children's passive knowledge. Mills concluded that the reading ability of these children was measurably improved.

Others report that art helps in the reading program, but a survey of some studies relating art to reading (Groff, 1978) concludes that concrete experimental supporting evidence is missing. It appears that intellectual ability influences both reading and art ability; art exercises tied to some reading lesson to make it more palatable are not going to result in measurable reading improvement and may have a negative effect on art. Stein (1972) compared the effectiveness of three programs: a reading readiness program, a program involving a number of creative art activities for kindergarten children, and a control group. On a later reading readiness test, there were no significant differences between these groups; however, the control group of children, who helped plan their own activities and were read to a lot, scored higher on the posttest.

It was found that trying to teach nursery school children how to make squares and triangles was a frustrating task (Brittain, 1969). However, after waiting a year, most of these same children could do the copying tasks easily.

Some of the same factors may be important to consider in this seven to nine year age range. It is usual to teach skills or to develop competence in reading or mathematics by merely taking the desired educational outcome and dividing it into small, teachable components, but apparently this method does not work. Trying to improve visual discrimination, motor coordination, memory, or understanding of spatial relations seems unrelated to improvement in children's reading ability (Larsen and Hammill, 1975). It might be expected that training in visual discrimination would have a positive effect on children's drawings, but a study of drawings by six to ten year olds (Miller et al., 1977) before and after

FIGURE 140.
The boy who drew this picture of himself has a developing awareness of size relationships and order. The objects on the table are arranged in a line for us to see.

twelve weeks of perceptual training showed no more differentiated drawings than a control group who had no such training. Some of the visual discrimination tasks demanded that children trace around objects or color in certain shapes; happily, the aesthetic quality of the children's drawings did not seem to be adversely affected. Although we focus upon the process in art, and realize that the product is only a record of that process, sometimes it is easy to forget that reading is also a product, reflecting a child's thinking process. In art as in reading, trying to improve the product without an understanding of children's thinking and the experiences that influence the process makes teaching toward adult goals meaningless.

Schematic Drawings as a Reflection of Growth

Within any classroom there is a large range of individual differences. It is not unusual to have a third grade class composed of children whose IQ may range from 75 to 125. This means essentially that the mental age of these children will range from the six year level to the ten year level. There is also a wide range of physical differences. In looking at the drawings by children in this same third grade, we can also expect to find a comparable range of individual differences. A few drawings and paintings, in fact, may be more typical of either a first grader or a fifth grader. We have come to expect the child who is more developed intellectually to be in general more developed physically, and because art is a reflection of total development we can expect artistic achievements to follow the same general pattern.

One of the indications of the child's growing intellect is an increased understanding of the surrounding world. Objects may be meaningful or meaningless to the child, depending upon emotional relationships and intellectual comprehension. Piaget and Inhelder (1971) believe the continual assimilation of external factors is necessary for the development and modification of concepts. Learning, growing intellectually, depends upon the ability to take into the system new information, which can be combined and integrated with existing concepts. This new information is gradually internalized and, once assimilated, provides new concepts and an altered schema. Whether or not the world has

FIGURE 141.
"Playing Checkers," painted by a seven year old boy. The checkerboard has been tipped up because it is important to see the top view when playing.

become meaningful partially depends upon the degree to which the child has formulated concepts. It is to be expected, then, that the child will express in drawings a definite symbol for those things that are repeatedly represented. In the drawing of the children playing checkers in Figure 141, we can see where the child repeated his schema of a man for both figures; however, the sizes as well as the motions of the figures differ. Notice that the nose and the eyes are expressed with the same symbol, just a dot. Yet obviously these parts have different functional characteristics.

The *active* knowledge of the child reveals his understanding of and interest in the world about him, and this is what is expressed in drawings. Our checker playing youngster shows little awareness of these details. His eyes have no eyebrows, lids, or any other details, nor are the nose or mouth indicated by more than a mere generalization. The only concept that shows some detail is the concept for hand, which consists of the palm and five fingers. Of course, our checker player may not have been very involved in this particular picture; several drawings would be useful to help us understand him better. However, the field of art can contribute a great deal to a child's growth by stimulating an awareness of the things around him. "Do you have to watch the moves carefully in checkers? Are you hoping your partner will not notice that he can jump you? Do you keep track of how many men you have left?" The clarifications of concepts and the stimulation of an awareness of details can be a big step toward

THE ACHIEVEMENT OF A FORM CONCEPT

developing a greater awareness of eyes. Children are a product both of their heredity and of their environment, which means that we should strive to make their environment as rich and stimulating as possible. Figure 142 was drawn by a boy after a trip to a firehouse. He not only remembered the rubber boots and pole but became very involved with the fire truck and was particularly interested in the hose and ladder. Such overlapping is unusual for this age.

FIGURE 142.

"At the Firehouse." The boy felt as if he were a fireman. At the left is the back of the truck with its hose and ladder.

The area of emotional growth can often be neglected in a classroom. A child who has hurt a finger usually gets immediate attention from the teacher and often from a nurse or even a physician. A child with hurt feelings, however, usually has no one to whom to turn for help in patching up wounds. It has been well established, however, that emotions, feelings, and attitudes can affect a child's learning. The opportunity to express in socially acceptable fashion the feelings of anger, fear, and even hatred not only produces a release of tensions but also allows the child to discover that constructive use can be made of one's emotional involvement. An experiment (Francis, 1973) was done with 143 third grade children, which has given support for the assumption that creative activity can provide the atmosphere for reduction of frustration. Here purposely frustrated children were given a chance to make fierce animals out of clay, while a control group colored and cut out dittoed tulips. Although some of the children's teachers were more creative than others, which confused things, the "fierce animal" experience groups did better in a subsequent learning experience.

When a schema is used in a rigid fashion, it may actually be an escape from facing one's own feelings and emotions. On the other hand, the flexible use of the schema is an important requisite for true self-expression. The very nature of the schema makes it likely to be considered a stereotype if it is repeated without any personal involvement. Flexibility in thinking should be given special attention during this period. Usually many changes and deviations in the schema can be observed, especially if the child's reactions can be expressed without fear of being censored. Exaggerations, neglect, or omissions are not only typical of this age but indicative of a child's healthy emotional reactions. It is not normal for a child to concentrate on one part of the figure to such an extent that the body appears only as an appendage; however, continued and extremely distorted exaggerations are quite rare.

Art not only provides an opportunity for the release of emotions but it can also provide the child with an opportunity to use these emotions constructively. Schools have to limit the degree of emotional outbursts that can be accepted within the society of a classroom. Outbursts of anger, frustration, envy, and sheer joy are usually not tolerated. Even so, the usual bland classroom goes far beyond this and strives to make an emotionless environment in which only the intellectual pursuits are worthy of consideration. Art should encourage a greater emotional involvement in a healthy, tension-free environment.

The social growth of children can also be seen in their creative productions. Children have become less ego-involved and more aware of themselves in an objective way; the use of the base line signifies that they are beginning to view themselves in relation to others. Self-identification with their own experiences in creative work is one of the prerequisites for establishing contacts outside the self. It is necessary to identify one's own actions and to feel responsible for, and to have some control over, these actions before one can develop a greater group consciousness. For example, in Figure 141 our checker playing friend went beyond the immediate self by establishing contact with another person, as well as the rest of his environment. The awareness of things around the self, which have no immediate relationship to the central experience, shows a high level of social growth, although he did not include any particular characteristics of the lamp or the window.

Related here is the child's development in perceptual growth. The mere portrayal of a symbol for an object indicates little perceptual awareness. Since perception includes many of the ways in which a child becomes aware of the environment, perceptual development is of prime importance. Textures, sounds, smells, tastes, and visual shapes and forms can all be shown in a variety of ways in drawings. Developing a sensitive perceptual awareness is crucial; it is the interaction between a child and the environment that establishes the amount or kind of learning that takes place.

Toward the end of this schematic stage, drawings are increasingly influenced by visual perception. Sixty British children, from five through nine years of age, were asked to draw several common objects, including a cup. Then each child was able to hold and manipulate a straight sided mug, with a handle and an applied flower design. Next the child was asked to draw the mug with the handle turned away, out of sight, and the flower toward the child. The handle, which is characteristic of a mug, was drawn by the five, six, and seven year olds but was dropped by most eight and nine year olds, whereas the flower was drawn by only a few of the younger children and one third of the eight year olds, but by all of the nine year olds (Freeman and Janikoun, 1972). This change in drawings illustrates the children's shift from drawing what they know about an object (their concept) to drawing what they see (their percept).

Freeman (1980) found that children had even more difficulty drawing a transparent glass mug. Davis (1983), however, found that if children were asked to draw a pair of mugs, with only one having the handle turned away, the task was easier. If an object is named before drawing (Bremner and Moore, 1984), children tend to include the hidden feature, but otherwise it is apt to be left out. Children do not want their drawings to be ambiguous and therefore include handles, which are a defining feature of cups and mugs. Freeman suggests that it is unwise to merely judge the success of the final drawing products, but instead we should consider the children's systematic efforts to solve tasks, as children try different strategies and change their repertoire of rules.

Drawing can't be considered as a manual skill to be learned in isolation. The object that is drawn has some meaning, which may be more important than its visual aspects. Children draw in different ways, depending upon the meaning of what is drawn, even if the result appears the same; adults do it too. To borrow an example from Van Sommers (1984), try making a quick sketch of a short ladder resting on its side; then try making a Roman numeral three. The ladder will be drawn with the horizontal lines first, whereas the III will be made with the vertical lines first, even though the finished drawings cannot be distinguished from one another.

Light and MacIntosh (1980) asked 64 six and seven year old children to draw a small model house placed inside a transparent glass beaker and to draw the same house placed behind the beaker. From where the child sat, the visual image looked virtually identical. However, the drawings differed considerably. All of the children drew a beaker shape or circle surrounding the house when the toy house was placed inside; but when the house was placed behind the glass, most children drew the two separately, with the house above or alongside the glass. Apparently the information about the two conditions was most important to the children, and the visual impression they received of the house and glass played a minor role in its depiction.

To some extent even physical growth can be seen in the productions of children. A child who is physically active is much more likely to indicate movement and action in figures than is a child who lacks physical energy; continuous exaggeration of the same body parts may indicate some defect. The child who drew our friends playing checkers was hard of hearing and typically emphasized the ears, as in Figure 141. Seven to nine year old children are more able to handle art materials effectively; there should be less concern about paint being spilled, and youngsters will use smaller details in their paintings.

Aesthetic growth does not start at any particular age. The lack of aesthetic growth can be seen in pictorial representations that are disorganized, either in thought and feeling or in execution. The child has no use for rules of aesthetics. It is the effect of art experiences and processes upon the individual, not the final product, that contributes to aesthetic growth. If Robert casually starts drawing somewhere and either does not have enough space to place everything he wants to draw or discovers he has nothing to add and too much blank space left, he obviously lacks a sensitive awareness of the relationship between his paper and what he is expressing. We need to involve the whole child. "Imagine that your

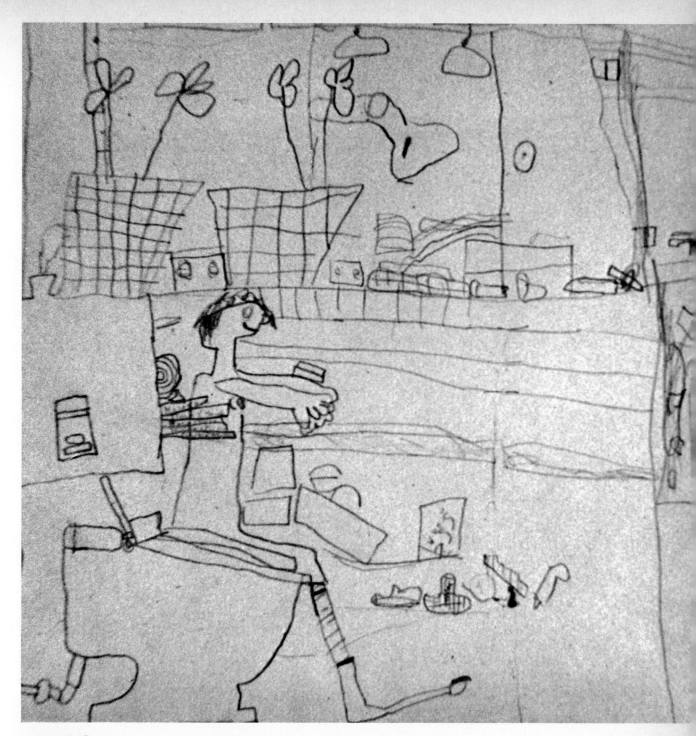

FIGURE 143

"In the Bathroom." Notice the awareness of details in this drawing; even the tiles and water pipes are included. The child has a rich concept of his environment.

paper is a treasure map of a large island. What will you need on this map? Harbor? Boats? Trees? Mountains? Swamps? Lakes? Streams? Graveyard? Stockade? Where would you hide the treasure?" A motivation should make a child more sensitively aware of the material used and the message he wants to convey. It must be stressed, however, that there are no set rules that can be applied to all individuals. What is harmoniously right for Robert may not be right for another. Just as artists are striving for variation and innovation in design, we should also expect and encourage large differences in children's work.

Art Motivation

The kind and type of motivation a teacher should use at the different age levels grow out of the needs of the children during each particular stage of development. The task of the teacher is to stimulate children's consciousness and awareness so that they are not satisfied with making rigid symbols. A whole class discussion on a particular topic can be exciting, as group contagion may provide a positive force for creative activities. However, sometimes small group or individual motivation is important, depending on the particular subject at hand. Discussion should include consideration of *we* (I and somebody else), *action* (what we are doing), and *where* (actual description of the place, not depth or distance). It is important to create an exciting atmosphere that is flexible and open to suggestions from children. Any motivation should develop and stimulate an intense desire to create a meaningful picture and should encourage children to be flexible in their approach to both materials and subject matter. Every motivation should have an introduction, culmination, and summary. So, a topic such as "We Are Playing on the School Grounds," would begin with a general introduction. "When do you play? Didn't I just see you playing outside a short time ago? When do you usually play on the school grounds? When? During recess; I see. Where do you play? Do you use the whole playground? What do you play? Do you just stand out there and look at each other? Oh, you play tag! Yes, I have played tag, too. How do you play this game? You have to run! Do you run fast? Do you keep yourself nice and straight and tall? You mean you can't run fast that way? You have to bend forward when you run; why do you bend forward? If you run fast, would you fall on your back if you didn't lean forward? Johnny, show me how you run fast! Yes, you really do have to lean forward! If you leaned too far, what would happen? You would fall on your knee! Oh, some of the gravel even got stuck in your knee once—that made it all

THE ACHIEVEMENT OF A FORM CONCEPT

bloody; yes, I know it hurts. Sometimes your body wants to go faster than your legs can. If you didn't bend forward at all, you would fall backward and hurt your head. . . . I guess it is better to hurt your knee than your head! How about your legs? Do you have both legs in front at the same time? No, that's like a rabbit! You are right, we cannot jump like rabbits and go very fast. Could both legs be on the ground at the same time? What happens when you run? Oh, one leg is in the air. Isn't that funny! One leg is in the air, did you ever think of that?" When children are stimulated to a greater awareness of their own actions, they develop a more flexible schema for a person. Now the children can actually sense their legs and feet on the ground and have become personally involved in the motivation. "Does everyone know how to play tag? We have all played tag! Let's draw how we play on the school grounds."

In any motivation such as this we must be sure that every child is personally involved. However, there should be a wide range of topics so that all children have the opportunity to express their own particular interests. There should be the feeling that the motivation was individually planned for each child.

FIGURE 144.
Children create from their own experiences. Any motivation will result in a variety of responses from children, depending upon their backgrounds and awareness.

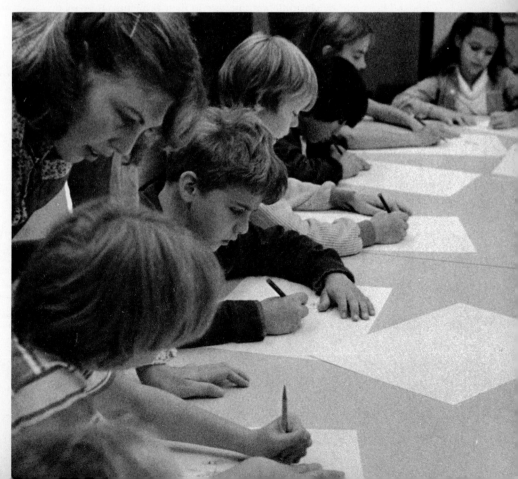

Subject Matter

Ideally no subject matter would be needed if all children were free of external pressures to perform in certain ways and could draw, paint, and construct whatever was important to them. However, our society is filled with messages from teachers, parents, peers, television, and radio to behave in certain ways; and there is conflict between what children can do, what they are supposed to do, and what they would like to do. In art, children are not forced to conform to external standards. The art experience has many tasks: it must truly be the youngsters' expression, and it must also be a growing, expanding awareness experience that can help to extend the youngsters' frame of reference.

FIGURE 145.

Girls and boys may display different interests in their drawings. Here a boy shows an awareness of, but not an understanding of, the mechanical features of this tractor.

Many topics come to mind in which action plays a major role in encouraging a flexible use of the schema. Starting with the *we*, adding the *action*, and following with the *where* includes the essential aspects of the experience. Many topics come from the children themselves without much effort, such as "Playing on the School Grounds," as mentioned, or "Running To Catch the School Bus." Others might be "We Are Climbing a Tree," "We Go on a Hike," "We Are Jumping Rope," "We Are Playing Hockey," "We Go Sledding," "We Are Planting Bushes Around the School," "I Am Wrestling with My Friend," and so forth. Some topics can provide for the use of profile and front views, such as "A Tug of War," "Playing Games on a Rainy Day," "Watching the Parade," "I Am Eating Pancakes with my Brother," "The Dentist Examines My Teeth," or "I Am Being Taught How To Swim."

Several topics are excellent for a variety of space–time representations. These would include "How We Cleaned Up Around Our Neighborhood," "We Visited the Crowded Shopping Center," "Our Trip to the Bakery," or "We Made Cookies for the Holiday." Discussing various aspects of the experience will encourage some children to include many elements in one drawing, but other children will portray the one part that seemed most important, like eating the cookies after they were baked. X-ray pictures will be produced if both inside and outside are important in some experiences. This would include drawings of "Our Class Visited a Newspaper Office" or "Our Trip to the Dairy"; other topics might be "Shopping in the Hardware Store with My Father," "We Are Staying in a Hotel," "The Time I Was in the Hospital," or "Riding in an Elevator."

Just as it is important to develop a flexible, functional form schema, it is also important to develop a flexible approach to color. Although it is obvious that some of these topic areas overlap, the following may give some suggestions for developing color concepts. It is possible to see how effective a motivation is by comparing the use of color after a particular motivation with the use of color before motivation. Many topics lend themselves to color awareness, such as "The Workmen Are Painting Our House," "I Like Ketchup on My Hamburger," "We Got Our Shoes Covered with Mud," "The New Grass in the Yard Is Beginning To Grow," or "We Are Raking Leaves in the Fall."

Another area of importance to consider for subject matter is the private world of the child. This includes topics that have emotional significance, such as fantasy and dreams. When a child paints things of deep personal concern or reveals certain desires and conflicts, it should be remembered that any subject matter is acceptable. Although the teacher may show interest in the representations, under no conditions should any moral judgment be made about the content of these pictures. Personal involvement would be high for a topic such as

"The Time I Was Most Afraid" or "I Had a Horrible Dream." But emotions can also be sublimated in topics such as "I Am Making Believe I Am a Fierce Animal," "If I Were Teacher," or "I Am the Richest Person in the World."

One other area of subject matter that should be considered is the topic of the particular material itself. The principal reason for concentrating on the material is to insure that the child has an opportunity to investigate their possibilities and uses materials in a flexible fashion. Unfortunately, some children will use this nonrepresentational theme as a means of retreating from a creative expressive experience. This lack of involvement can be seen when children merely explain "I am just making a design." However, getting to know how paint runs or how a drawing instrument behaves is important for further expression. Making a collage, using crayons in different ways, making tall things with holes out of clay can be both interesting and worthwhile.

Art Materials

The selection of an art material, its relevance to a particular group of children and their needs at a particular time, and its preparation and handling are all important considerations. Any art material should facilitate the self-expression of children and not be a stumbling block. When children have become eager to create after a meaningful motivation, the art materials should be ready for their use. How frustrating to get all excited about painting "How I Broke My Leg While Sledding" and then have to sit still waiting for paints! Often the material can be prepared and distributed with the help of the children, and then the motivation can take place in another part of the room.

Three things are important in developing methods of working with materials. First, the teacher should know that every "help" in showing the child a "correct" method will mean restricting the child's individual approach to materials. There are many ways of working with art materials; and, as mentioned previously, time should be taken to explore many procedural possibilities. No child should be stopped in the middle of a creation to be shown the "proper" way to hold a brush, use a crayon, or fill the paper. The teacher's job is to introduce the appropriate material at a time when a child is most ready to use it.

Second, every material must make its own contribution. If a task can be done in a different art material with a better effect, the wrong material has been used. A material is wisely used only if it fulfills the purpose for which it is intended. Thus, nothing should be done in clay if it could better be painted,

FIGURE 146.

An art material must meet the expressive needs of the children. During the process of creating papier-mâché heads, youngsters can remain flexible as the product continually changes as it is constructed, hardens, and is finally painted.

and nothing should be painted if it could be done better in clay; likewise, nothing should be done in clay or paint if it could better be done in wood. Therefore, it is important that the teacher know the qualities of the material being used so that the best material will be used for any particular expression.

Third, the teacher should not force too many materials on the children. An art program should be based on experiences and not be planned on the basis of one material after another. At a time when the child is eager to create and is full of intuitive power, too many different media may not only be wasteful but can often prove distracting as well.

The child of seven to nine years is not concerned with the representation of distance. What is most characteristic now is that the child has found a form, space, and color concept, which through repetition develops into a schema. At times these repetitions develop a designlike quality. The child should be able to repeat the same colors for the same objects at will. An art material that does not afford the opportunity to experience mastery or self-assurance is not a good medium for this developmental stage. The consistency and texture of poster paint or tempera serve this purpose best, but crayon or colored chalk can also be used successfully.

There is no reason whatsoever for introducing water color at this time. Water color is transparent, runs, and at times results in happy accidents. The transparency of water color serves best to paint atmosphere and landscape but does not lend itself to repetition or to painting the designlike qualities so typical of this age. Since the child is more concerned with expressing ideas than with visual stimuli, these happy accidents can turn into sad disappointments. The child is striving for order and attempting to put knowledge into a working form. At older age levels, when the urge for repetition is not important, water color will serve to inspire the child. It is quite apparent, then, that an art material should be selected because it can contribute to the child's development and should not be introduced merely for the purpose of changing a material.

Larger paper can be used at this age, to give children more freedom than smaller sheets provide. Since they have developed better coordination, and their arms have grown longer, the larger sheets may fit their needs better. Also, brushes made of hair can now be used along with bristle, because children have developed a greater awareness of detail.

Clay is not just another material. Since it is three-dimensional, it stimulates another kind of thinking. The unique characteristic of clay is its plasticity. Because of this plasticity, clay can be used most advantageously with children of this age, for the very nature of the material will facilitate the flexible use of concepts. Whereas a drawing demands a simultaneous concept of one event

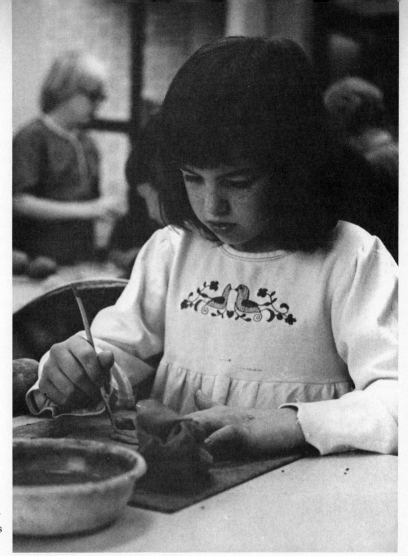

FIGURE 147.
Each art material has its own characteristics, which call for different kinds of expression.

(with the exception of the space–time representations), the process of modeling with clay permits a constant and continual changing of form. Figures can be added or taken away or changed in their position and shape. Therefore, action can be included in any motivation. A comparison of the three-dimensional qualities of clay with space in nature could result in an attempt at small scale model making, which is not a creative activity but simply the development of a technical skill and has no place at this age level. However, children may include objects of the immediate environment spontaneously. An example of this might be a child who models a picnic scene, making visitors come and sit down, and actually moves an arm up to indicate eating.

Two different methods of working with clay can be observed. One is that of pulling out from the whole and the other is that of putting single parts together. In Figure 148 are examples showing these two different modes of expression, each method revealing a different kind of thinking. Pulling the clay out from the whole means to have a concept of the total, however vague, from which details will be developed; this method is called the *analytic method.* In the other method a child puts single representative symbols together into a whole, building up a synthesis out of partial impressions; this is called the *synthetic method.* Either pulling out or putting together is welcomed, for this is not merely a superficial means of achieving a form, but grows out of the child's thinking. Some teachers feel that it is wise to discourage modeling by the synthetic method of putting details together, because such modeling cannot be

FIGURE 148.
In the synthetic method of modeling (left), single pieces are put together. In the analytic method of modeling (right), single parts are pulled out from the whole form.

fired in the kiln. It is true that such pieces cannot be fired easily because of the danger of air bubbles and because the parts may separate in the firing process, but it is an adult concept that clay products made by children should be fired.

There are, of course, a number of materials in addition to those mentioned that can meet the needs of this age group. Colored paper, oil crayons, fiber-tip pens, collage materials, paste and scissors, many natural materials such as twigs or pebbles, and even a large, soft pencil can be used to advantage. Care should be taken to insure that the child has an opportunity for a depth of art experience and that new materials are not introduced just to stimulate the teacher. Ideally, art materials should provide the opportunity for both a variety of experience and a depth of expression.

Summary

To some extent the products of this schematic stage appear more rigid than the drawings and paintings of younger children. However, children's thinking processes are now structured in such a way that they can begin to organize and see relationships in the environment. This is not a step backward. Children are also beginning to structure their drawings and paintings so as to allow some basis for change and reorganization. Creative thinking is not disorganized thinking; rather, it is the ability to redefine and reorganize familiar forms and elements in a flexible manner. Abstract thinking is based entirely upon symbols, and during this stage children take initial steps toward this development.

It is essential that children be given constant encouragement to explore and investigate new ways and methods. Occasionally children will try to copy each other, particularly if one child has just received praise and another wishes to have this praise too. Putting a positive emphasis upon differences and praising nonconformity and experimentation will encourage creative thinking. Children's own creative efforts should be accepted regardless of how meager the product appears. Ideally, each child should be eager to create, with the teacher's role being the important one of encouraging depth of expression and a meaningful experience. The child who clings too closely to stereotypes, or repeats a particular schema too often, or is constantly looking for suggestions is the one who needs the attention and special guidance of the teacher to bolster self-confidence and to provide positive experiences in self-expression. At this age the opportunity to establish the self as an acceptable being who can think and express these thoughts, whatever they are, becomes most important. Because the child

FIGURE 149.
"I Am Rowing the Boat."
Clay can provide the opportunity for developing spatial concepts and understandings. It was not important that this product could not be fired.

is searching for a pattern or structure within the environment, the self-concept as developed at this time may be an important factor in future learning abilities. This is not the time for rigid instruction in art rules. Marantz (1981) suggests that what we should be examining are children's freely produced images, such as finger marks on foggy window panes, stick-made scratches in seaside sand, and doodles drawn in spilt chocolate milk. To develop a positive self-image, to encourage self-confidence in expression, to provide the opportunity for constructive divergent thinking should certainly be basic aims of the art program.

Related Activities

1. Collect drawings of a man done by a first grade class. Find how many different symbols are used for nose, mouth, body, arms, and so forth. What percentage of these children are using geometric shapes for their expression? Compare with drawings done by a third grade, to see if the percentages change.

THE ACHIEVEMENT OF A FORM CONCEPT

2. Find one child's schema for a person. See how this is repeated over a period of several weeks. After a strong motivation centered upon some physical activity, notice the deviations in the schema. A week later, has the child's usual schema returned?

3. In observing the behavior of children of this age outside the classroom, can you detect any social schemata? Are there fixed rules for games? Are there set patterns for certain activities? Are there set songs or chants for such games as jump rope? Is there any evidence of adults' pressure for these patterns, or do they come from the children themselves?

4. How many children in a first grade use the base line in their representations? Compare the percentage with a second grade class.

5. Collect samples of X-ray drawings, folding over, and space–time representations. Why were these subjective representations important to the child's expression? How would adults portray the same event? Which is the more adequate portrayal?

6. In examining children's drawings and paintings, show how the use of color parallels the establishment of a schema in form. What are some of the differences found in color schemata for common objects?

7. Keep a list of the different reasons for exaggerations, omissions, or neglect of parts as shown in drawings. Illustrate each from examples of children's work.

8. Plan and carry out an experiment similar to that of Freeman and Janikoun (1972). Gather drawings of a common object with distinctive features from a third grade class. Determine how many children have a more visual representation and how many still draw their concepts. How do the differences in their drawings relate to other activities of these children?

9

The Dawning Realism

The Gang Age
Nine–Twelve Years

The Importance of the Gang Age

One of the outstanding characteristics of this age is that children discover that they are members of society, a society of peers. It is during this time that children lay the groundwork for the ability to work in groups and to cooperate in adult life. The discoveries of having similar interests, of sharing secrets, of the pleasure of doing things together, are all fundamental. There is a growing awareness that one can do more in a group than alone and that the group is more powerful than a single person. This age is the time for group friendships and peer groups or gangs. The word *gang* has taken on negative connotations within today's society, but we as adults may have some very happy memories of the gang of kids we went around with when young. This age shows an increasing development of social independence from adult domination, a learning about social structures in a personal way. This is an essential part of the developmental process and an important step in social interaction.

Groups or gangs are commonly of the same sex. Boys ignore girls, and girls despise boys. It is a time when youngsters go camping, belong to groups that have rules of their own, and take greater interest in group sports. Boys may build elaborate hideouts from boxes or stray pieces of lumber, and not infrequently lead wars against girls. Girls begin to pay attention to clothes, enjoy parties, sit with their own group, listen to a stereo, invent their own secret codes or languages, and not infrequently lead wars against boys of their own age, although often secretly admiring an older junior high school boy.

These important feelings of an awakened social independence are often in direct conflict with the desires of parents or adults who do not want to give up the close supervision and guidance of their children. It is mostly for this reason that adults consider this stage of development as an undesirable one that often interferes with their own lives. Instead of giving support to this awakening feeling for group cooperation and the discovery of social independence, both parents and teachers often try to counteract it. Instead of showing sympathetic and warm understanding of their children's desire for group life, they often oppose it, not realizing that by such actions they only drive their children into secrecy. Increasing problems face the teacher: students are less motivated to study and show greater disrespect for authority (Duke, 1984). The negative attitudes of adults may be responsible for some of the causes of delinquency.

Children's increase in size, skill, and strength provides opportunities for them to become more independent. It is not unusual for ten year olds to earn their own spending money by running errands or doing small tasks. Although adults may now find it easier to carry on a discussion with them, children who become dependent upon adults for approval tend to lose status in their group or gang. A fifth grade class may have a wide spread in abilities, with some children reading at third grade and others at seventh grade level. Their art products will also vary. Some girls will have reached puberty, some children will have had tangles with the law, and some will have gained recognition for their skill in dance or music. This is an exciting age.

FIGURE 151.
By this age, there is great variety in children's abilities. The boys seem to have grouped themselves together in the rear, and the girls are together in the front.

FIGURE 152.
Children of this age continue to exaggerate certain important elements in a drawing. An eleven year old girl here portrays her experiences in the bowling alley.

Youngsters of this age are becoming increasingly aware of their real world, a world that is filled with emotions, but emotions that are hidden from adults; a real world with friends, plans, and memories; a real world that belongs only to them. There is sometimes confusion in the use of the term *realism*. Often it is confused with the term *naturalism*. However, these terms can be self-explanatory so long as it is remembered that naturalism refers directly to nature and realism refers to what is real. Nature can be looked upon by many people. Their backgrounds, reactions, or emotions do not affect what is there. Nature may be snow on the ground, a hot summer day, or any part of the environment—it is this way whether we look at it or not. What is real, however, is firmly rooted within each individual. One can be inspired by the beauty in nature, be disgusted with the selfishness of man, or be full of hope for the future—and all of these are very real.

Characteristics of Drawings During the Gang Age

This age may be the most dramatic and healthy period of discoveries, as seen in children's creative work. The schema is no longer adequate. The concept of the human figure during the earlier schematic stage was a generalized person. Now the child is eager to express characteristics of sex and to show differences in clothing. Greater awareness develops at this age; the modes of representation of the preceding stage are no longer suitable.

In earlier stages of drawing the separate parts of these drawings were not self-explanatory, but were composed of geometric shapes. A part removed from the whole lost its meaning. Now, however, geometric shapes no longer suffice; when a child draws a nose it looks like a nose whether it is on a face or not. Children move to a form of expression more closely related to nature although it is still far from a visual representation. For example, children do not yet draw their clothes with folds or wrinkles. The drawing is not a result of careful visual observation, but rather a characterization of what is seen. Children gain a feeling for details, but often lose a feeling for action, and a greater stiffness can be seen in representations of the human figure.

Although at the age of nine most children still exaggerate the size of the human figure, studies have shown that this exaggeration tends to disappear during this stage of development (Lowenfeld, 1952). Children begin to substitute other means of expression to show emphasis, such as an accumulation of details on significant parts. The greater awareness and concern for detail can even extend to making a left hand quite different from the right. This can occasionally make the total look distorted. Sometimes this exaggerated concern will even make a boy exclaim that he has "goofed" if he has not drawn the proper number of buttons on his shirt. This growing awareness of the visual appearance of objects has little to do with naturalism, as can be readily seen in drawings and paintings, where there is no attempt at showing light or shade, the effect of motion, or atmospheric effects. Rather, children characterize the environment by indicating its distinguishing features.

X-ray drawings, and drawings using folding over, are now criticized by the children themselves as being unnatural. That type of representation is primarily subjective, so children who are becoming more aware of nature no longer consider such a mode of organization appropriate. Girls of this age often focus a great deal of interest upon drawing horses. Now that the anxiety about animals has disappeared, children will project their own feelings into this animal form. For some the horse becomes a symbol of running, dashing freedom that is part of the joy of growing up. Boys identify more with cars, and it is not unusual for boys with questionable mathematical ability to be able to spout statistics about the horsepower and displacement of the latest engine design. Sometimes it even seems as if the boy *becomes* the car, making shifting noises as he draws, just as

FIGURE 153.
Children now are acutely aware of those things that are of personal importance. This drawing includes all of the essential details to identify this as a baseball player.

FIGURE 154.
As his big sister steadies him, this ten year old shows how he is learning to ride a bicycle. His awareness of the details of the bicycle, even from the back, would make an adult envious.

the girl can seem to *be* the horse. The emotional and psychological concerns of children of this age demand constructive outlets, and at any age the feelings and concerns of an individual are the basis of true art expression.

The Meaning of Color

There is a consistency in the way expression changes. Children move from a rigid color–object relationship to a realization of the properties of color. Now they distinguish between a bluish-red sweater and a yellowish-red sweater. This greater understanding of color differences cannot be called a true visual awareness because children do not indicate the changing effects of colors in light and shade or the effect of atmosphere upon color. Some children will find that the

FIGURE 155.
Children of this age are gaining control over the expressive media and are more concerned about mixing the proper shade of paint.

sky has a different blue from the blue of the river or the lake, and some will find that the tree is a different green from the green of the grass. A child in this stage of development who still uses rigid color–object relationships does not have sufficiently refined visual sensitivity to notice the differences that distinguish a green shrub from a green lawn.

There is no place in the elementary school for the teaching of color theories by means of color wheels or other such aids. Such teaching only disturbs spontaneity and makes children insecure in their own developing sense of color. Color consciousness can be increased by emphasizing personal reactions. Children enjoy colors and are now capable of greater sensitivity toward differences and similarities; eager explorations through fall leaves or sudden realization of the constantly changing sky colors should certainly be encouraged. Any discussion of color, therefore, should focus upon experience and not upon the "proper" use of color in a particular painting.

THE DAWNING REALISM

The Meaning of Space

During this stage, nine to twelve, the child is gradually moving away from a dependency on the concrete and is now beginning to deal with abstract concepts. Art is not merely the representation of objects, but rather is the reaction to and expression of concepts of those objects. The ability to arrange several images on a piece of paper so that they have a relationship to one another means that the child is able to deal with these objects simultaneously, rather than merely to arrange them in a line, as in the previous stage of development. The tree no longer stands in isolation beside the house but becomes a shade for the house, although just where the shadow is cast is still not fully understood. And the man no longer stands aloof beside the house, but is now seen in relation to the tree and may be coming out of or going into the house. In a study of

FIGURE 156.

These children playing ball overlap the mountains in the distance, but are on a common base line with the house and tree. The grass in the foreground has become a horizontal surface in which flowers grow. The sky is no longer just a line and includes clouds and a bird as well as the sun.

English children, Kutnick (1978) found that young children drew their classroom in a static fashion: that is, making symbols or drawings that merely indicated the presence of the pupils and teacher. However, a transition took place between the ages of nine and ten, when children moved to an active representation, with drawings portraying the actual roles of pupils and teacher.

Just as greater awareness of the self and the environment leads a child to realize that geometric forms are inadequate to represent the human figure, the symbolic use of the base line concept changes to a more naturalistic representation and the child discovers the plane. The change from a single base line to the use of the plane is usually a fairly rapid one. The stage of transition can be seen in drawings that include several base lines, where the space between these base lines is filled in. We can only speculate on how the child physically discovers the plane: perhaps through increased physical activity and developing curiosity. One can picture a first grader walking to school, carefully following a prescribed route. Compare this with a fourth grader who acts as if the sidewalk were there to ignore, who is much more interested in walking on the wrong side of the hedge, kicking a can in the gutter, or going around in back of some of the houses to see if something interesting is happening. At any rate, the base line begins to disappear; the trees and houses no longer stand only on the edge of this line. Although for some children the base line mode of space representation remains in frequent use, the space below the base line now takes on the meaning of ground.

For the most part, prior to this age children have very little understanding of maps, particularly of geographic maps of foreign countries. This may seem unusual, since nursery school children can make what are essentially maps from blocks and then drive toy cars around from one location to another (Blaut and Stea, 1974). However, a vertical, two-dimensional configuration covered with cartographic symbols is generally not understood until a youngster is eleven or twelve years old. Gerber (1979) divided children from fourth to ninth grade into four groups based upon their map-reading skills. Drawing ability was one of the significant factors that differentiated between the group that could understand maps and the group that had difficulty. Possibly one way to improve or develop map comprehension would be to have children make maps of their own spatial experiences. Until a logical map of "the route to school" can be drawn, it would be useless to try to teach map reading. There are numerous studies dealing with children's development of cognitive maps, their recall of salient features, and their ability to represent space, following exploration in familiar neighborhoods and locales (Anooshian and Young, 1981; Biel, 1982; Hazen, 1982; Herman, Roth, Miranda, and Getz, 1982; Herman and Roth, 1984).

FIGURE 157.

The ten year old girl who made this drawing used multiple base lines. The limbs of the elaborate tree overlap the foliage, and the sun is peeking out from behind a cloud.

The sky is no longer drawn as a line across the top of the page. It now extends all the way down to what at the beginning may be a base line but which gradually assumes the significance of the horizon. The child has not yet become aware, however, of the meaning of the horizon or developed a conscious visual perception of distance. With the sky all the way down, the child soon realizes that a tree growing from the ground will partially cover the sky, hence a beginning consciousness of overlapping. A more naturalistic

CHARACTERISTICS OF DRAWINGS DURING THE GANG AGE 315

FIGURE 158.
Here a boy obviously enjoys driving this interesting car. A beginning awareness of overlapping can be seen, as the car partially covers the large building, but the small house is raised so it can be seen.

representation has been achieved, as can be seen in the buildings behind the car in Figure 158. It is exciting for children to discover that objects can overlap; this awareness can be utilized by the sensitive teacher. That one object can cover another is important, because it implies a recognition of the interrelationships between objects.

The child of this age is now beginning to think socially, to consider the thoughts and opinions of others, but it is a slow shift away from egocentric thought. Understandings of interrelationships, of causality and interdependence, are only starting. Piaget's experiment (Piaget and Inhelder, 1967), in which he asked children to identify pictures of a model of a mountain taken from a viewpoint other than their own, has been carried out in a modified form by Laurendeau and Pinard (1970). They experimented with 700 children and found that, on the average, children are eleven before they can free themselves from their own point of view and successfully select pictures that show how a scene would look if they were in a position other than their own.

It would seem logical then that an eleven year old would portray a scene differently from, for example, an eight year old. An eight year old might show a scene such as "eating" from several points of view, as if looking separately at each person sitting around the table. An eleven year old would more likely por-

316   **THE DAWNING REALISM**

tray the same scene from a single viewpoint, as if observed from another part of the room, and with an attempt at perspective. Hooper (1977) asked second, fourth, and sixth graders to sit at a table, which had been arranged with dishes and flatware. It was only in the sixth grade that most of the children could successfully select from several pictures the one that correctly showed how the table would look from different positions. Hooper also asked the children to draw a table and to draw "eating." There was a significant relationship between drawing development and the ability to identify how another person might see the table from a different position. Young (1984b) cautioned that age alone does not automatically bring an understanding of the use of perspective to represent three-dimensionality. He found, with his sample of 61 eight to fourteen year olds, that the increase in this ability was not smooth. Young also found, as did Hooper, that being able to perceive another's point of view comes before being able to utilize perspective. Children of this age enjoy drawing tasks that require problem-solving abilities but are not eager to learn formulas or to assimilate rules for "proper" representation of perspective. As part of an art lesson, several fifth grade classes were given a paper on which was a predrawn trapezoid. The children were asked to imagine that this was a playing field and to draw a fence around the field. Three typical but varied solutions to the problem are shown in Figure 160.

FIGURE 159.
The girl who drew this picnic struggled with the perspective but was able to represent the scene from a single point of view.

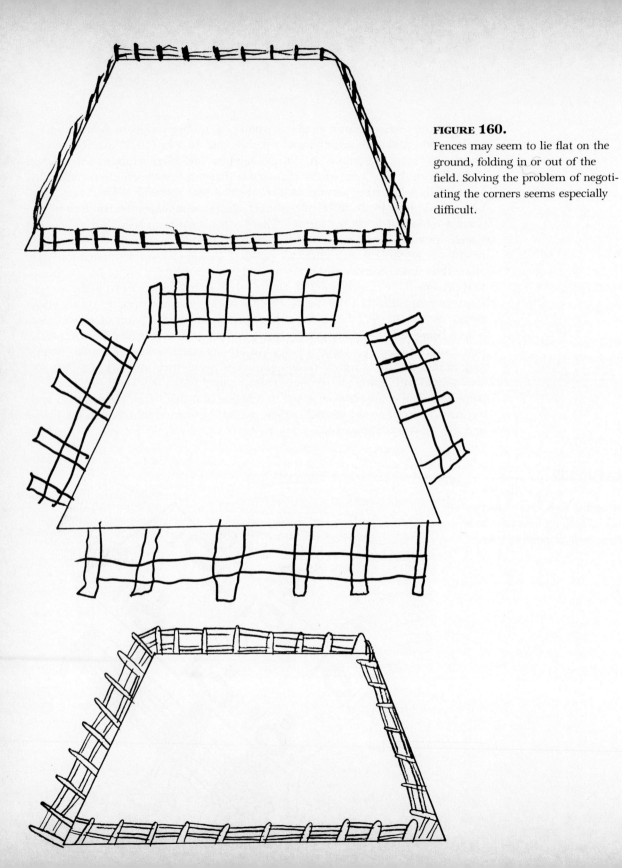

FIGURE 160.
Fences may seem to lie flat on the ground, folding in or out of the field. Solving the problem of negotiating the corners seems especially difficult.

PLATE 24.

"We Are Exploring the Surface of Venus," a four by eight foot mural painted by a group of ten year old boys. In a project such as this, where imaginative subject matter is used, diverse ideas are welcomed by the group and cooperation is encouraged. No one boy could have done the mural by himself.

PLATE 25.

"My Doctor." Although apprehensive about a trip to a doctor, youngsters recognize this as a necessity. Here a boy has faced his fears and produced a humorous picture, including the dreaded shot needle. Cut paper and crayon are combined to make a flat representation.

PLATE 26.

"Standing in the Rain," drawn by an eleven year old girl. Color, use of space, and wealth of detail combine to give an aesthetically pleasing whole. Here a growing visual awareness is coupled with a child's directness and freshness.

The Meaning of Design

As children now discover the meaningfulness of their environment and begin to relate this to themselves, it becomes most important for education to give them a feeling for what is honest in our environment and what is insincere and imitative. At this age it is vital to stimulate children's thinking and provide them with opportunities to discover the natural beauty of materials that are found unspoiled within our environment. This means developing a feeling for differences in rocks, pebbles, shells, barks, moss—all the wealth to be found in nature. Children of this age are normally collecting a variety of objects anyway, from bits of string to toads, as any parent of a nine year old can testify.

The sincerity of beauty as found in nature should be stressed, because this is a natural extension of the child's own direction at this age. Much modern society now has a heightened awareness of ecology, and children need but little encouragement to develop a concern for their environment. Collecting a pile of pebbles can be very exciting. Discussing the different shapes and different colors, noticing how the water has worn down some edges, or seeing how the light tries to shine through some varieties but not others—such discoveries can awaken perceptual sensitivity. These explorations require a relaxed atmosphere, for such learning cannot be rushed. Occasionally children will enjoy putting their collections into some form, such as putting the pebbles into a little sand in a box and pouring plaster over the back of them to make a mosaic, or arranging material in a collage. Becoming sensitive to the qualities of a material is of great importance; children on their own improvise combinations of materials that do not necessarily serve a useful purpose. Discovering the beauty of natural materials need not be limited to woods and streams alone. Even scrap material can have beauty hidden in it. Rusty iron, or wrinkled paper, or even mold and mildew can be pleasing to look at if one is able to redefine values and not think of them as discarded and rejected parts of a sometimes oversterile environment.

It may seem as if undue emphasis is being placed upon a knowledge and understanding of materials, while the area of design may appear to be bypassed. However, there should be no separation between the material and its function or between crafts and design. The inspiration for working with materials should come directly from the structure and nature of the material itself. Establishing relationships between a child and materials will be crucial in enabling the child intuitively to create designs that utilize qualities inherent in the materials. In the world's greatest cultures, workmanship and skill have been inseparable from design.

FIGURE 161.
Toadstools may not be universally popular, but the design qualities of their caps need not pass unnoticed.

Drawings and paintings by children in this stage of development begin to show a greater awareness of clothing. This developing awareness of pattern and decoration does not provide an excuse for the formal teaching of design. The formal rules of grammar are not taught to a two year old child who is only beginning to speak, nor are the formal rules of balance, rhythm, or half-drop repeats taught to a child who is beginning to discover patterns within the environment. A project such as designing a decorative border for a tea towel has little relevance, and it is entirely unsuitable to plan a design carefully on paper for possible transfer to some other material with which the child is not involved. Learning the nature and behavior of materials is important not only educationally but also ethically, because it will promote a feeling for sincerity and truth in design.

THE DAWNING REALISM

The Development of the Gang Age Child

During this stage children have come to wonder why things work the way they do and about their own being. They may now raise questions about areas that not very long ago they felt were unquestionable. Children are becoming increasingly critical of others and of themselves, and some will begin to hide their drawings from an inquisitive adult or else make some disparaging remark about their efforts. Children of this age also develop a sense of justice and may object violently to actions that "aren't fair." There is also an increasing concern with sex differences; although publicly the opposite sex is treated with a great deal of disdain, privately there are awakening feelings of curiosity and affection. Ten year olds have gained a fair amount of information about the working of the world, both natural and social, but to a large extent this tends to be isolated, concrete learning. Much of the information that has been drilled into them in the classroom therefore tends to be meaningless. The fact that the Pilgrims landed in 1620 is readily repeated in a test, but whether 1620 was before or after the last Ice Age is not clear. Some of the concepts children develop by this time continue with them through adult life. This is even true of their drawing characteristics. Studies have shown that there is surprising similarity between drawings by children during this stage and drawings by adults who have had no formal art training.

This is also a period when children are beginning to develop a self-concept, an understanding of themselves as independent individuals. Developing a positive self-concept is essential in order to establish personal attitudes and is closely related to the ability to learn. One experiment attempted to change the self-concept of thirty boys who had just completed sixth grade (White and Allen, 1971). During a summer program half of the boys were enrolled in a traditional nondirective counseling group, and half were in an art counseling group, where numerous art activities were carried on that were designed for expression of feelings and the boys were encouraged to verbalize about their art products. The results were surprising: " . . . the art counseling approach was more effective in bringing about self-concept changes among pre-adolescent boys than was the traditional nondirective counseling program." The authors state that during a follow-up study 14 months later, the growth effect of the program was still evident.

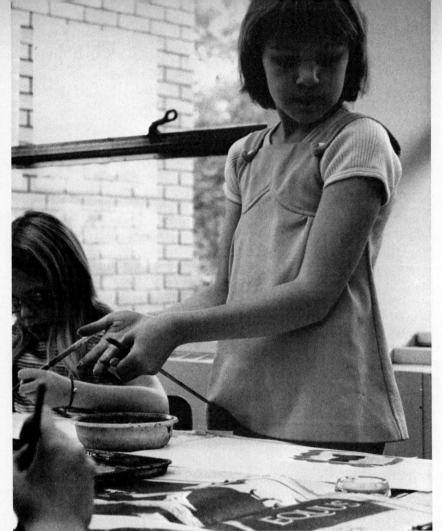

At this age children have not yet developed full control over their emotions,
and often a seemingly minor incident will be of extreme importance to a
youngster. This intensity of feeling can be utilized within the art program. The
emotional relationships a child develops with various segments of the environment can be expressed either directly or symbolically. Topics centering around
religious themes, individual justice, or the expression of love or hate may involve
a youngster completely. In such cases exaggeration or overemphasis of particular parts within a composition will be noted. Color in such cases can also be
used symbolically, as in painting a face green. Such distortion is very acceptable, and support should be given to the free use of exaggeration and distortion
for emotional effect.

FIGURE 163.
Fairness and cooperation now are basic considerations. Two boys confer and decide how their group art work should proceed.

Gang Age Drawings as a Reflection of Growth

The ability to break away from the schema and to perceive and be attentive to the variability within the environment is typical of this age. To a great extent, however, these children do not remove themselves from their own observations. That is, their drawings and paintings show quite clearly that they see things through their own experiences and assume that this "reality" is the way things are. Children can sometimes be critical of the drawings of others and even of their own drawings if these do not live up to their own interpretation of what is real. They have not yet achieved an objective, naturalistic viewpoint. It should

FIGURE 164.
"Man with Umbrella," painted by a ten year old boy. For some children the base line and the exaggeration of meaningful parts, such as the enlargement of the hand holding the umbrella, continue at this age.

THE DAWNING REALISM

be emphasized at this point that there is no value judgment implied in discussing the various stages of children's development. The concern here is simply to understand these differences and to become more sensitive to the great variety of artistic expression.

Intellectual growth is indicated by how much a child has departed from schematic representation and feels the need to characterize particular objects, figures, and the environment. A child of low mentality neither becomes aware of the changing environment nor discovers those characteristics that make it possible to individualize objects or figures. Plate 26, "Standing in the Rain," was drawn in crayon by an eleven year old girl. The schema has practically disappeared except for some facial features: note the repeated symbol for the nose in the three central figures and the sharp nose form in the rest of the figures. One of the distinctions of this stage is that parts of a drawing can now be subtracted from the total without losing their meaning; no longer do geometric forms suffice. It can be noticed in "Standing in the Rain" that the feet or facial features would remain as recognizable parts even if they were removed from the context of the drawing. It is also very apparent that the child has departed from her base line representation and has a distinct feeling for the plane. The inclusion of such details as puddles, houses with windows, raincoats with buttons and belts, boots of various colors, and umbrellas of various patterns clearly shows that this child is very much aware of her environment.

Notice for comparison the drawing "Man with Umbrella" in Figure 164, where the awareness of detail is much less. Could intelligence alone cause such differences in representation? In comparing "Standing in the Rain" with "Man with Umbrella," might not lack of motivation be a real consideration? A closer look at these drawings can give a better understanding and some insight into thinking processes. Lack of motivation may cause great differences in drawings, but this is a matter of functional intelligence, how one actually acts and performs. In some cases a potentially brilliant person may never be motivated to utilize this potential. It might be more precise to say that these two children have differences in their functional intelligence that may be caused by several unknowns. Clearly the teacher must promote in children a greater sensitivity to a changing environment and awareness of their own thinking, feeling, and perceiving to help them develop their fullest potential.

To some adults, intellectual growth connotes only improved mathematical and reading skills. But in some cases it shows up in an art-related activity. Fourth grade children were given a multiple seriation task, which required them to arrange colored circles in a rectangular array according to increasing size in one direction and color differences in the other (Watson, 1979); thus it was necessary to keep in mind two dimensions simultaneously. Those children who had a strong mental grasp of the whole did not need to check visually where each circle should go. Poor readers tended to rely on trial and error, and some children never could see the relationships. Success in such tasks is strongly related to reading comprehension and is not achieved through instruction.

Art experiences aid the development of emotional growth. Within our society, all too often, children's emotions and feelings are squelched. This is particularly true of boys, who at an early age are told not to be sissies. Even within a group of age-mates a boy usually has to conceal his true feelings in order to remain "manly." To be able to express sensitivity and to develop in emotional growth, children need to identify with their own experiences in their art. Children who constantly depend upon stereotypes are unable to express their true feelings.

Schools themselves can often produce a great deal of anxiety. The smaller boy may be ridiculed, or the tallest girl may feel embarrassed to find that she is now taller than any of the boys and sometimes even her teacher. It is a rare classroom that does not contain some periods of boredom, listening to explanations repeated for the slower learners or reading what seems like irrelevant information; some periods of frustration when important questions go unanswered; periods of fear when the homework is left undone; periods of terror at test time. There is no evidence that tests motivate children of this age. An Australian study (Campbell, 1975), using a large sample of sixth graders under test and nontest conditions, found that these children had little motivation to learn spelling lists when tests were to be given; instead, tests tended to reinforce a fear of failure in girls and to increase impulsive risk-taking in boys. These emotions can sometimes be expressed in drawings and paintings, although these may be hidden in notebooks or appear as highly embellished doodles.

Social growth, during this period, is one of the outstanding facets of development, yet when something interferes with this new feeling of social belonging the child may withdraw and remain an outsider. Whether or not the child identifies with a group can be recognized by two indications from creative work: the content of the work and participation in group work. The girl who drew "Standing in the Rain" (Plate 26), is aware of people and has made the children different sizes. However, every figure is looking straight ahead and seems to have but little relationship with the others. The figures appear more like a group of individuals who happen to be standing next to each other. To some extent, however, the topic may have been responsible for this lack of a common feeling of participation. The illustration indicates that the child has identified strongly with the scene and with the people involved but has not shown much

FIGURE 165.

In this drawing a sixth grade boy is listening to his stereo in his bedroom. He includes bunkbeds, posters, and dresser in his refuge from the adult world. Art should be based upon the child's experiences and environment.

interaction within the group. Not only is a particular setting portrayed, but there are differences in clothes, an awareness of everyone's being in the rain, and in turn the rain, boots, and puddles indicate an awareness of the child's own relationship to her environment.

The ability of children to participate in group activities can be seen when children work together on murals. Children of this age usually have the urge to work in group activities, but it may be the child who withdraws from such activities who needs this social experience most. To a great extent democracy is based upon social action. Children who avoid the group and who are unable to relate to their own experiences in drawings may need some support from the teacher in order to develop greater social awareness. Experiences such as being in charge of a section of a mural may be of value. Certainly the individual's contribution to the group should be recognized, and a sensitive teacher can insure that each child is able to participate.

A mere photographic imitation of the environment does not express the interaction between the artist and the subject that is perceived. The child who drew Plate 26 ranks high in perceptual growth. The child's growing visual awareness and her awakening feelings for nature are part of her perceptual growth. One of the first indications of a child's visual awareness is the inclusion of the horizon line and painting the sky to meet this line. The child has become very much aware of distance, even though no sky is indicated. Another aspect of visual perception is the child's awareness of overlappings, and here there is not only overlapping of people but overlapping of objects. There is also a visual awareness of differences in color, although, as expected during this age, there is no particular awareness of light and shade. The hemline continues to remain straight, at least in this illustration. The child has an advanced awareness of detail, which can be observed in the raincoats, in the background buildings, and in the way the boots fit around the legs. Certainly the encouragement of perceptual sensitivity is a vital part of any art experience.

There are also indications of aesthetic growth in this picture. Notice the conscious awareness of design in the umbrellas. Aesthetic growth can be seen in the way children relate the subject matter to the qualities of the material with which they are working. They are now much more aware of the nature of clay, paint, or crayon. Utilizing the intrinsic qualities of a material is a characteristic of aesthetic sensitivity. Children who work with clay as if it were a flat drawing material are not aware of its distinctive qualities. Apparently, our artist who drew "Standing in the Rain" was very much aware of the possibilities crayon could afford.

One of the most important areas of growth to which art can contribute is that of creative growth. During this stage of development there is a great deal of pressure put upon children to conform not only to the wishes of adults, but also to the demands of the group. To function creatively, however, one must first be able to function as an individual. The encouragement of the individual child's own approach to working out problems is vital, which means that imitation and conformity to patterns must be discouraged. A child's creativity can be seen in the desire for experimentation, exploration, and invention. A child who is rigid needs to be encouraged to find new and different ways to use materials. Commenting upon the interesting stipple or the effect of one color being placed over another will be positive steps in the direction of supporting creative growth.

Art Motivation

Adults often have pleasant memories of childhood; however, most of these memories are of happenings and situations outside school. Probably each of us has memories of this particular time. One adult remembering this stage had the following to say:

> If I remember back at my childhood—now, you see, if I remember back at this stage, it must have made a very distinct impression on me, but I remember very distinctly how we converted a small, little, oh, island into something, into a wonderland. When I was a child we were in a gang—a wonderful gang—and we would sit on a footbridge over a small stream, I am quite sure it was not larger than a few feet, but when we went over this bridge it appeared to us like, oh, miles long, you know, going over the bridge and entering our land which no one knew. This was fascinating. We made a building there at the highest point—there was a little hill, and we made our own money, of course, we collected the money, you know, for entrance into this island. I can still remember that we had pockets full of paper money which we ourselves printed. And we had there, we found bones of a dead animal and made a little sign saying, "These are the bones discovered of an animal two thousand years ago," and we really looked at it as we put it there in a certain order, and you know, this was something magic to us. And another place was the Snake Point where we had spread out a dead snake which we found, and when we went there we really got goose pimples. This was the Snake Point, let's go to the Snake Point, and then, you know we collected gravel and built little paths, and these were then real paths, you know. We had a hideout when it rained, so this island was really something magic.

Imagine if we could promote in school these same intense experiences. All too often school is considered a place to "behave," a place to endure. But school should be a stimulating, exciting place, where natural drives of children are not only accepted but utilized to develop stimulating education that is meaningful for the students.

Motivation now should capitalize upon youngsters' greater independence in order to give support to their self-esteem. An art experience must provide an opportunity to express a growing awareness of sex, to develop a greater awareness of self, and to satisfy a new curiosity about the environment. It must also inspire the child to use cooperation with others to achieve results. To inspire

FIGURE 166.

A cooperative venture in building construction, including plumbers, riveters, and crane operators, is drawn in great detail by a fifth grade boy, with many erasures and corrections.

cooperation, two methods can be used. The first or *subjective* method of cooperation deals with representations of individual experiences of cooperation, or the representations of scenes in which cooperation is important. Much depends upon the way such motivation is presented to the group and the atmosphere the teacher develops during the motivation. Such topics as "Helping the Flood Victims" or "Cleaning Up After the Storm" can be presented very dramatically. When it is possible to identify with a large undertaking in which a child can feel like part of the group effort, a topic will inspire cooperation. "Whose house is under water? Suppose you were living there and we could watch how the water rises and rises! How would we feel?" The youngsters need to identify with the flood victims. They should also identify with those people who are responsible for social welfare. Such activities as drawing the firemen during the big fire or the policeman during the evening rush hour can also effectively stimulate greater social cooperation.

The second or *objective* method of cooperation deals more directly with group work itself; a whole group works on one project. Here also the type of motivation will determine its success. Group work can be quite simple in its planning, such as having each child make a fierce animal of clay and then assembling these animals into a large zoo. Straws or sticks can serve as bars, and the children will enjoy making signs for the various parts of the zoo. Group work can become quite elaborate, with a class dividing up into several working

FIGURE 167.
Here a group of youngsters are involved in constructing a three-dimensional city. Much planning and discussion goes into this activity, but the finished project is much larger than one child could do alone.

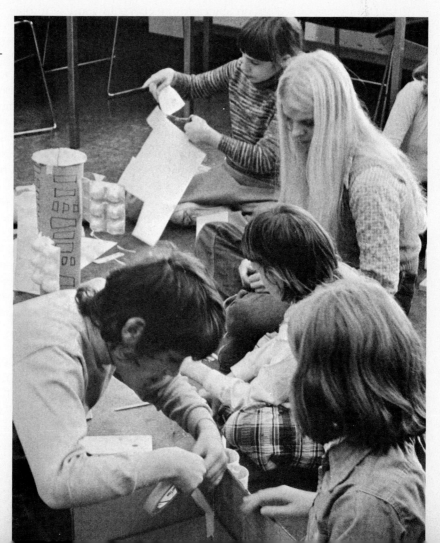

units. An example might be making a mural of a city. "What makes a city? Yes, houses and stores and factories. But we cannot have them all mixed up together! How would you like to live right next to a factory? Yes, we need to have some zoning laws. We will certainly need the residential district. How many children would like to work on the residential section of our city? There are so many different kinds of buildings that people live in! Now we have the industrial area for our factories. How many would like to work on this section? And, yes, the shopping area, too. But there are more than just stores in the commercial district! What other districts do we have? Oh, yes, playground and recreation area, fine! Does everyone know what section he is going to be working on? You had better pick a leader to help your group decide what kind of buildings you are going to need. You say we still need a school district? Oh, I think the residential area committee should worry about that. Why, Ed and Maria, you are not on any committee! Would you like to plan the background for our city? Should we have a stream or river near the city? Do you think we should have some mountains, fields, or forest land around?" Probably a material such as colored paper would be quite suitable for this topic. A large background paper or board would be needed. It should not be expected that a cooperative enterprise like this will be a smooth, quiet operation. Democratic action may not be easily learned, but it is an essential part of our way of life.

When the various committees of the city have completed their districts, the city can be assembled. A lack of trees may be apparent, or some small houses may be needed, and maybe nobody has remembered to make cars and trucks for the streets. In such a way all the children can become involved in the activities. It is probably best to staple or tack the various buildings in place so that these buildings can be readily moved from one spot to another. There may be a sudden cry of dismay as Hannah finds that someone has placed a church right over her house. This provides a fine opportunity for some explanation of overlapping, now that overlapping can be understood. "Did you ever go to a movie and find a nice seat where you could see the screen, and right in front of you a lady with a big hat sits down and now you can see nothing? Is that good? Would it be all right if a little boy sat in front of you? It wouldn't matter if a little boy sat in front because you could still see and people could still see you. Overlapping is fine, but one should not completely cover the other. Maybe your small house can go in front of the church since the church could still be seen. And look, a tree can go in front of the house." The child has developed a fair amount of understanding when she can accept a minor role for one of her buildings, but maybe she can feel better when her tree goes in front of someone else's building. Every individual, every child in the class, should think, "I could not have accomplished by myself what the whole group has done." This is the heart of cooperation.

Here the teacher is a catalyst and plays a subordinate role. It is a far harder task to stimulate and encourage children to learn, produce, and explore on their own. An easier method of producing products would be to authoritatively assign projects and have the "best" method for achieving results already worked out beforehand. But to provide a rich, meaningful experience for children, such authoritarian methods must be discarded. It is much more important to increase children's interest in the materials of expression, it is much more important to give a sense of discovery, it is much more important to provide an opportunity to determine personal relationships with the world than to worry about how "artistic" particular products look. Any art motivation must insure that children have ample opportunity to develop their own method of expression. There is a need for group activities, but these group activities should never press for conformity or submerge individual interests.

Subject Matter

Both boys and girls at this age can develop an interest in particular, individualistic subject matter. At one time it was possible to say that girls would spend a considerable length of time drawing flowers, fanciful figures, and particularly horses and that boys would spend an equal amount of time drawing airplanes, guns, and particularly cars. However, as society changes, so will the products of that society. If boys are not pushed into a male stereotype, it may be that more of them will develop an interest in flowers, and, conversely, that girls may become more interested in the mechanical aspects of their environment. But it seems that sex differences exist in drawings. Majewski (1978) found that, while girls did not draw more delicately than boys, they did draw more scenes of the environment, more smiling people, but fewer sports pictures. Freedman (1979) found that in non-Western cultures the interests of boys and girls, as seen in their drawings, were not the same as in Western societies. Brown (1979) asked 366 children from five to eleven years old to draw a person. A few of the five year old boys drew females; but from eight years on, boys drew only males. As might be expected, most young girls drew females. By nine years, 28 percent of the girls were drawing males, and 100 percent of the boys were drawing males. One could speculate why, when asked to draw a person, girls begin to draw

FIGURE 168.
A ten year old girl's drawing of herself displays the traditionally assumed feminine interests in hair style, pattern in clothing, and flowers.

males at nine and ten, but it is important to realize that this seems to be normal.

Whatever the particular interest of these youngsters, this interest can be capitalized upon in the art program by expanding the frame of reference. The child's subjective relationship to the environment provides the subject matter; as the child changes, so does art expression. The following suggestions are based upon the characteristics of this developmental level. These topics are meant to be only suggestions; it is assumed that they will always be adjusted to the particular classroom and to the particular group of children involved. Topics, then, are not to be considered as assignments, but as areas of interest that can be pursued with enthusiasm by both teacher and children.

To stimulate subjective cooperation, to develop the feelings of being a part of a group, and to identify with group activities, some topics might be "Gathering Wood for Our Campfire," "Decorating for a Party," or "Building a Clubhouse with My Friends." It is also important to stimulate cooperation through identification with the forces of social preservation and maintenance by understanding the duties and responsibilities, with an emphasis on how it would feel to be the telephone repairman, the policeman in five o'clock traffic, the nurse on the night shift in the hospital, or a member of the crew repairing a broken water main.

THE DAWNING REALISM

There are of course many ways in which a group can work objectively together for group cooperation. Small groups of children can work together on such a project, and the final product should be large enough and complex enough so that each child contributes and so that no one child could possibly do the whole project alone. Some suggestions for group projects might be "Making a Circus," "Sale Days at the Shopping Plaza," "Making a Dairy Farm," "Picking Berries and Making Ice Cream for a Festival," and "Exploring the Surface of Venus."

With the disappearance of the base line, ample opportunity should be given children to explore the possibilities of using the plane. Since there is an increasing awareness of differences in sex and a greater attention to detail, the children should be allowed to express these. It should be stressed that all subject matter should be meaningful and relate to the child's own experiences. Suitable topics might include "Sitting Around a Table for Supper," "Planting a Garden in the Spring," "Watching the Parade Come Down the Street," "Skating on the Pond in the Woods," "Playing Baseball on the School Grounds," and "Keeping Cool at the Fire Hydrant." With the beginning awareness of overlapping, discussions will arise normally during the painting procedures. Specific topics might include "Looking Out the Window of the Crowded School Bus," "Sitting in the Stadium," "Looking at Clothes in the Store Window," and "Performing in the School Assembly."

FIGURE 169.
When students occasionally draw from a posing classmate, the teacher should encourage the students to imagine the feelings and emotions of a specific situation as well as the visual aspects.

There is one very important subject matter area in art that should never be overlooked, and this is the subject matter that is within each child. In some cases this subject matter may be very apparent, such as a child's love for working with tools; sometimes, however, it can be hidden beneath the surface, as in quiet feelings of rejection. There should be ample opportunity for these extremes to be expressed. Not only should the joy and pleasure of creating be given free rein, but deeper emotional feelings and subconscious drives should also be given a chance to be faced. Some materials lend themselves to such expression of the inner self better than others. Finger paint provides a direct release for such feelings; working in clay can provide the opportunity for frustrations to be eased. Ideally, every child should express thoughts and feelings freely, but in some cases the understanding support of a sensitive teacher is necessary to guide strong feelings and emotions into artistically constructive channels.

Another large area of subject matter in art is related more to the increased familiarity with the nature of materials and the development of skills. These experiences with different materials may not have a specific subject or topic to represent, but the purpose and reason behind each of the activities should be made quite clear to the youngsters. As these children are becoming more outspoken about themselves and about adults, they need to have a knowledge and understanding of the purposes of any project. A number of craft activities can be included under this heading, although care should be taken to insure that their direction and planning rest with the children involved. This means that activities such as those that are preplanned by the teacher or those that are cute or tricky are inappropriate. Some suggestions for projects in this general area are making a collage for fingers to feel, making a funny animal from papier mâché, putting together an object from wood, making a mosaic from pebbles and plaster, making imaginative animals in clay, experimenting with macrame, using shiny paper for decorations, and weaving with grasses for a wall hanging.

Art Materials

A material is good only if it contributes to children's needs and helps to express their intentions. Although there are unlimited materials available for the use of children, care should be taken that those chosen lend themselves to expression and do not restrict children's originality. If a material is by its very nature restrictive or inhibiting, it should be discarded. Some strange creations have resulted from some misguided "arty" programs. Such things as marshmallows on toothpicks, wilted phonograph records, decorated light bulbs, lamps made from old ginger ale bottles, or egg cartons decorated with macaroni and gilded can make a mockery of an art program.

Children have advanced beyond the use of geometric forms and base line representations. With the discovery of the plane comes the need to fill in spaces, as, for example, in the representation of the sky, which is now usually painted down to the horizon. Although crayons can be used on their sides to fill large areas, a better material for this purpose is poster or tempera paint. Since children now have greater control over the paint, it is no longer as necessary to have the paint mixed to a thick consistency. In fact, children themselves can add water to the paints to make them the consistency that they prefer and can also be responsible for refilling their own paint containers.

Because they are more concerned with detail than formerly, some children will want to use a hair brush in addition to the bristle brush. Although children of this age differentiate their color–object relationships, using different greens for grass and trees, it is not necessary to increase the number of colors available. Actually, having a limited number of paints encourages children to creatively mix colors. Good crayons also mix, but this is more true with poster paint. If children are given a limited scale of colors, they are encouraged to invent their own colors if they feel the desire; if they do not feel the desire for greater color differentiation, it is useless to give them a larger color scale anyway. Actively engaging in mixing colors for a particular reason is much more desirable than having a variety of hues that are passively accepted.

Colored paper is a basic material for this age. It provides a natural means of overlapping and is appropriate for the early stages of cooperative projects. Another essential material is pottery clay, which can be used for many three-dimensional projects. This clay can easily be stored in plastic bags and, of course, it can be used again and again. There are certain advantages to using materials that are considered adult art materials, and clay is certainly one of these. However, sometimes clay is used as a craft material to make such things as plaques and ash trays. Unless these objects meet a real need in the life of children—and not very many children between nine and twelve smoke cigarettes—these projects will be merely busy work. Pressing various textures into clay, or exploring the possibility of space and form, such as holes in clay, or repeating a pattern of lines in a clay batt may have some utilitarian value if the clay pieces are fired. However, the teacher must not put the emphasis upon the preservation of the final product. If children participate in the total process—from seeing the clay in its natural state to watching it come fired from the kiln—this can be a

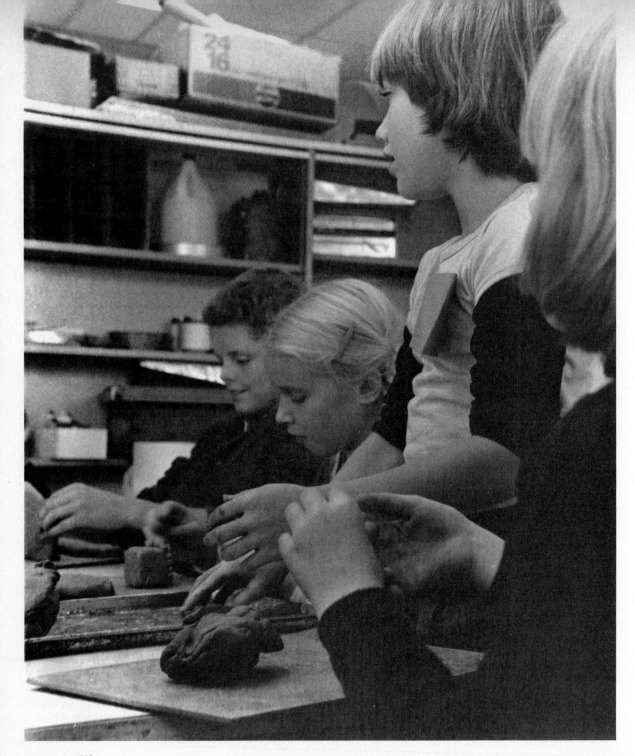

FIGURE 170.
Clay lends itself well to exploration and manipulation, because of its three dimensional
character and plasticity. Children enjoy the process; the finished product is secondary.

very worthwhile experience. Occasionally, however, teachers take the clay pieces away and have them fired. Then the finished product has no relationship to its creator; the color, texture, and consistency have been so altered that children can no longer identify their products. Under such conditions it is better to leave the clay piece unfired. Clay that has been modeled or made to represent some object, person, or animal is usually not fired anyway. This is because the importance of the activity lies in the process itself, and the procedure of firing can often cause these pieces to break apart. Most of the synthetically modeled pieces (those put together from single details) would not be able to stand firing. It is not worthwhile to sacrifice the child's individual thinking to conform to mere procedure.

Finger paint is a material that has not been considered to any degree before this stage. Now, however, it can be used for expression without the concern that children will be too involved with its textural consistencies. Needless to say, there should also be a good supply of other basic art materials. These include scissors, a stapler, paste, masking tape, and some woodworking tools. For craft work many materials can be used, such as wood, papier mâché, wire, cloth, and a scrap container with a wide range of straws, buttons, boxes, colored cellophane, and anything else that looks interesting. Children themselves will collect bark, rocks, pieces of wood, feathers, pieces of old chrome trim from cars, or whatever happens to attract them. Although some care should be taken to insure the safety of the children from such things as broken glass or sharp points, undue concern for sanitation and cleanliness may stand in the way of children's developing skill in hammering or cutting or of digging up a particularly pleasing pebble.

It is quite possible to stimulate a greater sensitivity toward common materials within the usual classroom setting. For example, a common material like paper has many possibilities. "What can paper do? How does it feel? Is it smooth or rough? Can you fold it or crease it? How does it look when it is crumpled? Notice how it tears. Is there any way to make it stronger? Can you make it turn or bend so that it looks happy? Can you make it feel sad?" Other materials can be treated in somewhat the same way, with the emphasis being upon the process of manipulation and exploring the material and not upon achieving a nice-looking finished product. There is no reason why all children should be equally occupied and interested in the same materials. Children at this age often develop great enthusiasm for working with wood. If simple tools are available, a great deal of interest can be generated in discovering the qualities of wood, and the physical exertion of hammering and sawing and nailing often gives positive release to bottled-up energies.

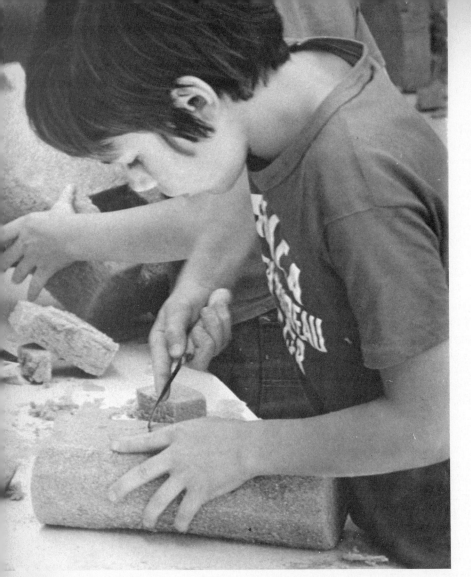

FIGURE 171.
Gang age children are eager to construct, build, and carve projects of
their own devising. They have no need
to follow someone else's plan.

A word should be said here about exposing insincerity in the use of art materials. All around us are examples of sham and falsehood in the use of materials. There is so much in the way of natural beauty for children to discover that
exposing the artificial flowers, the imitation stone floors, and the false chimneys
for what they are should be a part of these children's education. To a great
extent children accept the things around them as appropriate and unconsciously
may go on living in an insincere environment. To promote a more truthful society, it is not too soon to stress the sincerity of design.

THE DAWNING REALISM

Now that children have developed an interest in the possibilities of working with a variety of materials, they can be "pushovers" for a range of noncreative craft projects to be found on the market. Such items as precut leather tooling kits, easy-to-glue-together plastic objects, or mosaic kits that "anybody can put together" can be a real menace to normal curiosity and development. The teacher should point out that making a boat from scrap wood can be a much more enjoyable activity than trying to fit together some adult's preconceived

FIGURE 172.

In working on their individual projects, these youngsters are using paper, crayons, and paints, which continue to be excellent expressive materials.

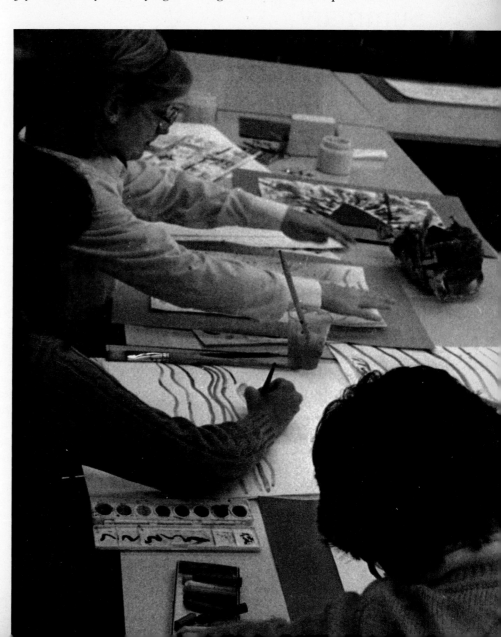

plastic model. If children could learn to get satisfaction from working with a range of common materials, and if misguided parents would stop praising products instead of children, the precut, already-thought-out "easy projects" companies would be out of business.

Summary

Art contributes much to total development. There are no short cuts to the development of perceptual abilities or creative growth. Although the range of individual differences can be very great, the end product should be seen only as an indication of individual development. Growth affects the products and also affects the aesthetic awareness of children; any standards outside the child are false. Standards of value should never come from the teacher, nor should group influences be so strong as to dictate a particular kind or type of product. One of the greatest needs of children during this period is to find themselves, to realize their own power, and to develop their own relationships within their own group. They all need to discover their own sincere relationships to the environment and to the people, objects, and materials that make up this environment.

During the earlier Schematic Stage children had a need to repeat the same symbol again and again. Now, however, the repetition of form will gradually disappear, and there should be a development of new forms or shapes that are not constantly repeated. Working in unfamiliar materials can often have a positive effect upon drawings and paintings. Children who have worked in collage materials may become much more aware of a variety of textures and forms and be able to transfer this awareness into a painting medium. Art should certainly give support for individual expression and creative thinking.

Having gained a greater understanding of this peer-group age, one can readily see how the teaching of particular techniques in art may stand in the way of children's exploring and experimenting for themselves. Adults help a great deal in the physical development of children by providing them with the proper nutrients and the place and encouragement for the development of the necessary physical skills; in the same way adults should provide the essential ingredients for children's artistic development—but they cannot do this developing for them.

THE DAWNING REALISM

Related Activities

1. Collect the drawings of a fourth grade class and tabulate how many children use the base line concept. How many use more than one base line? Have any children begun to use the space below the base line as a plane?

2. Save the drawings of a third grade child over a period of several months. Trace the development of the symbols used in representing forms. Compare with drawings from a fifth grade child during the same period.

3. Observe several group activities within a school setting at several grade levels. Which activities were the most productive? Which were most satisfactory from the child's point of view? Analyze the reasons why some activities were more successful than others.

4. Make a list of materials used in a fourth grade art program. Revise this list according to the appropriateness of these art materials for expression at this age level. Compare this list with what is appropriate at the kindergarten level.

5. Make a list of examples of children's growing awareness of design and textural pattern in their drawings. Pay particular attention to clothing and objects important to the artist. Are any differences observable between the sexes? How does the extent of awareness compare with academic ability?

6. Keep a record of which fifth grade children begin to make the sky come down to the base line. What is the first realization of overlapping beyond this initial step? Are these the same children who are also more socially developed?

10

Art in the
Secondary
School

The Role of Art

Art ought to play a very important role in the lives of students in the secondary school. Within the framework of our public school system, however, art usually plays a subordinate role, whereas within our society it is taking on greater importance. Art is more than pictures on a museum wall, more than the making of paintings or sculpture, more than the creation of our environment by building structures or planning and landscaping open spaces. These are the tangible evidences of art within our society, and those people who call themselves artists are the ones who design, build, paint, and cast. But art can also mean an attitude toward living, a means of formulating feelings and emotions and giving them tangible expression. It is a means by which sensitivities to experiences are heightened and refined. In a broad sense, art is both external and internal. The responsiveness to the things around us develops through a system of attitudes and experiences into new forms.

Even with such a broad point of view, it is quickly apparent that most school experiences are unrelated to art. The art classes currently offered in most public schools tend to emphasize the production of art rather than the development of artistic attitudes. When there is an undue emphasis upon producing a certain number of required projects, this may be detrimental to the process of thinking, feeling, and perceiving in an artistic manner. It is the process of art that is important, not the products themselves.

Some secondary schools offer what is basically an armchair approach to the arts, a study of art history and art appreciation. Although there is no reason to ignore this important area of our culture, it should not substitute for a course with actual involvement in creative activity. It is easier and much less expensive from an administrative point of view to have thirty or more students watch slides, take notes, and take multiple-choice examinations than it is to have smaller classes with students using expensive art materials, working on a variety of space-occupying projects in what is basically an experience in questioning, seeking answers, and confrontation with the self. The latter can be somewhat disturbing to a secondary school on several points. Grades are difficult to give; after all, a teacher will have difficulty identifying the talented student when it is clear that many artists who are recognized as great in this generation were not "talented" throughout their lifetimes. The basic premise of a painting or drawing course is individual expression, which in an academic

FIGURE 174.
These youngsters are finding that, far from being just another stuffy subject, art class can be a lot of fun.

environment can be a jarring note; the making of art may require being outside of the school environment and thus mean lessened control and supervision by school administrators. All of these factors might seem to rule out an art program committed to personal involvement. Or do they?

There is an increasing awareness of the need for developing not only sensitivities to our environment but sensitivities to the needs and feelings of others. This whole area is one which in the past has been ignored by our public school system. The usual secondary school curriculum is divided into small segments of subject matter, and these segments are usually justified on the basis of vocational or educational preparation. However, in our rapidly changing society, there are emerging professions and specific job opportunities that were not dreamed of thirty years ago, and youngsters in our junior and senior high schools may end up in jobs that have not yet been defined. There is a common attitude that "science has all the answers," placing great emphasis and reliance on technology. But there is also an increasing awareness of the fact that the study of science alone cannot provide the means to deal with values and attitudes. In a changing society those values and attitudes established by older generations are not values and attitudes that can be easily assumed by youngsters in the junior and senior high schools. The means of expression that are available and socially acceptable are strictly limited. Art may be the only field within the framework of the school system where the development of feelings and emotions is given proper recognition. The Carnegie Foundation for the Advancement of Teaching has stressed that the arts are not a frill but are an essential part of human experience, and has recommended that all students study the arts to discover how humans communicate through music, dance, and the visual arts (Boyer, 1983).

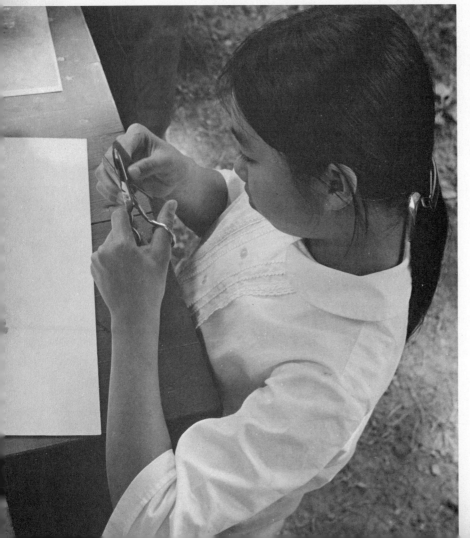

FIGURE 175.

At this crucial age of increased self awareness, students are critical of their own art products. Although some secondary schools do not offer art, there is a real need for an art program where students' sensibilities and sensitivities can be expressed openly, and learning in artistic media can take place.

Mills and Thomson (1981) report that, in 30 states, 50 percent or more of the high schools offer art sequences. Only a small fraction of students take art beyond ninth grade, even if available. But this dismal picture may be changing somewhat; it is reported that enrollment in arts electives is increasing in high schools, as much as 10 percent within one year in some localities. Much of this increased interest is due to the expanded offerings of mini-courses that capitalize upon the interests of students, for short courses of ten weeks or less. Schools frequently provide credit for art-related out-of-school work at community centers, alternative schools, multicultural schools, schools without walls, learning centers, and comparable special interest centers (Carnegie Council, 1980). Occasionally there is a required course in the humanities for all high school students, which attempts to combine art with other subjects to make a supposedly meaningful whole for these students. Intellectually, this may have some value, for the student needs to understand art as a reflection of the society and culture of the times, but the establishment of values and attitudes cannot be imposed from without. Personal involvement is essential to a feeling for art. On the other hand, some schools have changed very little in their attitudes toward art. It almost seems as if they feel it is the responsibility of the schools to indoctrinate students in conventional "good taste." Over a century ago, Quackenbos (1871, p. 182) advised that "Taste, being in a great degree the result of assiduous study and cultivation, requires long and careful training to attain perfection."

The Psychological Change from Elementary to Secondary School

Children in the elementary school typically paint and draw without inhibition. This can be seen especially at the nursery school and kindergarten levels. However, by the time they arrive at fourth, fifth, and especially sixth grade, children become increasingly aware of their own products. Spontaneous and uninhibited expression disappears, and by seventh grade a critical awareness has developed. This critical awareness is not limited to art products, for youngsters are now agonizingly conscious of themselves and their limitations within a society of peers. At this age youngsters begin to realize their unhappy position; they are now aware, thinking individuals but are not yet in a position to take any particular action to change their circumstances. These youngsters are hostile toward

FIGURE 176.
"Playing Tag on the School Grounds,"
painted by a six and a half year old
boy. Notice the exaggeration of the
arm that is doing the catching and
the omitted arms of the captive. The
environment is indicated only by a
base line.

their parents, disillusioned with school, and at times discouraged with themselves. It is not surprising, therefore, to find that they are also critical of their own art products.

To investigate the change in imaginative concepts in the school years, the topic "Playing Tag on the School Grounds" was assigned to three different groups: to a number of elementary school children of the first three grades; to boys and girls of the upper elementary school; and to students in the secondary school. There were approximately 300 subjects in each group. The topic was presented to the youngsters with no requirement that they draw it, and they were allowed to select other topics they preferred if they so desired. Ninety-five percent of the lower elementary school children made some attempt to represent this experience, whereas only 35 percent of the secondary school students tried to depict this game. The drawings were analyzed on two variables: the ways of expressing the experience of catching and being caught, and the spatial relationships representing the schoolground.

The elementary school children of the first three grades generally made no attempt at naturalistic representation. This was true both in the representation of the human figure and in the representation of the schoolground. The environment was almost entirely missing in the youngest group tested. Figure 176, done by a boy aged six and a half, is a typical representation. Here the boy has used an oval for the body and a circle for the head. Arms and legs are expressed differently in the two figures; although the arms of the captive are entirely missing, that of the captor is greatly overemphasized. Notice particularly the exaggeration of the grasping hand. Apparently only one hand is needed for tag. The legs of the captor are longer than those of his playmate, which may give some indication of the faster running ability of one child. Notice also that the schoolground is indicated only by a base line. The child's perception of space is not visually determined. The child's world of images originates with the self, with personal experiences and emotions, and is not involved with a naturalistic representation.

The second drawing, Figure 177, is a more elaborate drawing by a nine year old girl from the upper elementary school. This, too, is typical and shows quite clearly that the girl is aware of naturalistic details and her own relationship to her environment. The girls are wearing dresses; their hair is flying, a handy method to indicate speed; the schoolground is clearly indicated, surrounded by trees and a fence. The upper section of the picture serves as a base line for the school and swings. The lower section has a base line with the girls and what appears to be a slide resting on it. Also, some playground equipment has been placed between the two base lines. The addition of some "ground lines" has transformed this empty space into the school yard. One arm of the chasing girl is exaggerated, but otherwise the figures are quite stiff. There is a beginning awareness of overlapping, but for the most part each object stands separately, and the girls are looking at us rather than paying attention to where they are running. Although there is a greater awareness of nature, the drawing itself is not an attempt at visual accuracy.

The majority of the drawings of the secondary school students show an attempt at naturalistic representation. In a typical drawing, Figure 178, the student endeavored to make the running boys as naturalistic as possible; they are

FIGURE 177.
"Playing Tag on the School Grounds," painted by a nine year old girl. Here we see exaggeration of important parts. There are two base lines on which the children and school are placed.

fairly well proportioned, with arms and legs bent, and parts of the environment are drawn in a sketchy fashion with good size relationships.

The preceding study was based upon children's utilizing their past experiences, their familiarity with their school playground and its environs, the kinesthetic experience of actually playing tag, and the visual impressions that they recalled. The outcome was less an attempt at photographic imitation of a scene than a drawing of a concept. That is, the drawing showed the child's understanding of what was important about playing tag, and this was organized in a way that reflected a particular developmental level. It could be argued that these differences would not be present if children were to draw from objects directly in front of them. However, Willats (1977) had children from five to seventeen years of age draw a table with a radio, box, and saucepan on it. All children drew from the same point of view. Willats found comparable developmental stages; little overlapping was shown below the age of nine; various attempts at depicting depth and increasing use of overlapping occurred from nine to twelve; but the use of some kind of perspective was still only used by half of the fifteen to seventeen year olds.

This is not to suggest that children draw objects the same way whether these objects are visible or not. Hooper (1977) found that second graders drew a table in somewhat the same manner when they drew the topic "eating" as when they drew a table by itself. However, when sixth graders drew the table as part of an eating scene, they distorted the table, sometimes drawing it from overhead; whereas, when shown one, they more often drew the table with an attempt at perspective. It would be expected that most seventeen year olds would be consistent in their manner of representing the table, whether just drawing a table or illustrating "eating." The important point is that there is not

FIGURE 178.

"Playing Tag on the School Grounds," drawn by an adolescent. This picture is an attempt at naturalistic representation. Space is shown through the use of visual perspective.

a gradual awareness of a correct system of photographic representation. Rather, there seems to be a process, distinct from perception, which is responsible for a variety of methods of representation.

The Importance of Self-identification

To some extent, the period of development covered by the secondary school could be considered a time when youngsters find themselves. Children just entering middle school or junior high school have left behind the close attachments to parents. Up to now, however, children have been controlled, guided, and commanded by the older generation. At the other end of the secondary school system the adult emerges, ready to contribute to society. The six or seven years between these two stages can be characterized by a search for the self. "Who am I? What am I going to do with my life? What do I believe in?" These are all problems to be worked out during this period. Yet the school curriculum is usually planned so as to provide little opportunity for contemplation or soul-searching. Somehow, time for thinking is considered dangerous; the old axiom of a busy person being a happy one is forcibly applied to most of the secondary school population.

The art program in the secondary school ought to provide the means for this important self-identification. The adolescent is constantly bombarded by a world of advertisements stressing the importance of the proper hairspray, toothpaste, or deodorant, all of which can lead to success as measured by gaiety, activity, and attention from the opposite sex. By age fifteen, the average American child has spent about 20,000 hours watching television, more time than in school (Swerdlow, 1981). Value systems are greatly shaped by the world of television and popular music, both of which can be sexually suggestive, if not actually explicit, and can be confused with reality. Rigid conformity to the peer group peaks in ninth grade (Berndt, 1979); being seen in the "right" places, having the proper hair style or brand of jeans shows quite clearly that the individual is under tremendous pressure to belong. The peer group seems to function as a sorting house where the participants use one another not so much to compete as to compare; peers serve both as models and mirrors (Seltzer, 1980). When adolescents were asked to list the significant people in their lives, more same-sex non-related young persons were listed than any other category (Blyth, Hill, and Thiel, 1982).

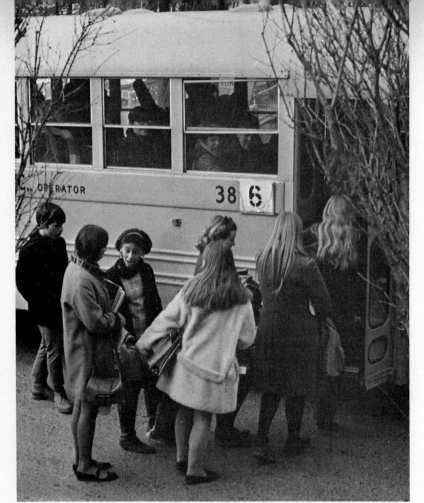

FIGURE 179.
Secondary school students often catch the bus by 7:30 in the morning and do not return home until 4:00 or later in the afternoon. The day is spent with their own age-mates and usually within the confines of the school grounds.

All of this means that teachers of this age group must capitalize upon the interests and concerns of their students. Most elective art courses ignore the problems of the students as people; yet it is from the needs, desires, and frustrations of adult artists that great art is made. Most students who elect art in the secondary school are not going to become artists. In fact, the limited learning that takes place within these elective art courses may need to be unlearned if the student does continue on to a professional art school (Brittain, 1961). The focus of these school art programs should be on the process of making art and not on the art product, and should be based on the needs and desires of the students themselves. To identify with oneself, to identify with others, to identify with a product and be able to say "This is mine," to be able to set problems and goals for oneself and to be responsible for the direction and method of expression—all these are important considerations in developing an art program for the secondary schools. The life of the student is not to be ignored. It is the resource upon which the program should be built.

Each person as an individual reacts and responds to objects on different levels. To ignore the responses and concerns of the individual students could cause a frustrating experience. The important consideration is to make the individual sensitive to the values, attitudes, and judgments in an appreciative experience. To impose set standards or to teach rules for discussing art may be irrelevant to the student. Certainly political, social, or cultural history may be a factor in the development of a particular work of art, but this will not determine whether it is enjoyed or rejected by the individual. Fourth, seventh, and eleventh graders chose the same words from a given list to describe some paintings, words such as: sad, calm, warm, and weird (Farrell and Rogers, 1982). Children see the same picture, regardless of their age, but their preferences will change with exposure and experience. With older students, there is evidence that mood or emotional state influences personal judgments of the quality of works of art; if one is depressed, pictures are more likely to be considered ugly (Hoege, 1984). It is important not to analyze and look at the art work itself in abstract or objective terms, not to repeat terms regarding art judgment, but rather to identify with the creator and with the problems and emotional relationships that the artist has had in completing the work of art.

To be more specific, the study of a mobile should not be limited to an appreciation of the work of Alexander Calder. Rather, nature itself can provide the understanding for this type of art in observing how a paper flutters when the breeze strikes it, or how the leaves of a tree create constant new patterns as the light changes, or how maple seeds or thistles glide as the wind carries them. Seeing the mobile in this context is much more meaningful than looking at the mobile only as an abstract art form. Identifying with the artist's experience in viewing the environment and trying to translate an aesthetic impression into a tangible product make the appreciation of art part of the experience of the student.

The importance of identifying with oneself at a particular moment should not be minimized. Painting or drawing is usually the most expressive type of art, but posters and montage provide an opportunity to deal with the social problems of our time. Where they are going and the problems of getting there are very real issues to senior high school students. For both girls and boys, the problems of sex and marriage are frighteningly close, and the prospect of finding and holding a full-time job is of increasing concern. The voting age is getting closer, and the will to do something constructive about the present condition of our country is a powerful driving force. Art has not limited itself to

FIGURE 180.
Art can take many forms, but the young-ster's own expression should be considered the most important element of any prod-uct. Solving the problems of joining wood is a learning experience.

the portrayal of the beautiful in the past, and the art of youngsters in the sec-ondary school does not have to be a portrayal of the beautiful today. It is much more important to provide a school environment in which serious expression can be encouraged.

The Development of Two Creative Types

At about the age of twelve or so, it is possible to see examples of two types of expression. One is called the *visual* type, and the other is usually referred to as *haptic* (from the Greek work *haptos*, meaning "to lay hold of"). Theoretically at opposite ends of a continuum, these types refer to the mode of perceptual organization and the conceptual categorization of the external environment. The visually minded person is one who becomes familiar with the environment primarily through the eyes and feels like a spectator. The person with haptic tendencies, on the other hand, is concerned primarily with body sensations and subjective experiences, which are felt emotionally. Most people fall between the two extremes. The very visually minded individual would be disturbed and inhibited if asked not to use sight but to become oriented only by means of touch, bodily feelings, muscular sensations, and kinesthetic functions. An extremely haptic individual, although normally sighted, will use eyes only when compelled to do so and relies upon the sense of touch and body self as the main means of becoming acquainted with and reacting to the environment.

The initial work in discovering these two separate means of acquainting oneself with the environment was done by Lowenfeld (1939), while working with the partially blind. He found that some partially blind individuals would use their limited sight to examine objects or when they expressed themselves in clay modeling. At the same time, other partially blind individuals would not use their eyes, but preferred to use the sense of touch. This led to his study of normal people, and here he found similar tendencies. Further work was done in measuring these qualities (Lowenfeld, 1945, 1966). Using 1,128 subjects, Lowenfeld found that 47 percent had clear visual tendencies, whereas 23 percent could be scored haptic, and 30 percent received a score somewhere in between. In other words, approximately half of the individuals tested reacted visually, whereas not quite a fourth reacted haptically.

Further evidence that some normally sighted individuals may relate themselves to the environment through the sense of touch was indicated in a study comparing blind and normally sighted blindfolded college students (Kennedy and Fox, 1977). When asked to identify common objects imprinted in outline, some of the normally sighted students did not mention visual imagery, but instead relied on shape and form; identification was obtained through the sense of touch and the object's function. In England, Millar (1975) studied figure drawings by sighted children under visual and blindfold conditions and compared these with drawings by blind children to try to determine the roles of visual and haptic feedback in drawing. By age ten the blind children used the same two-dimensional representations of body parts as did sighted children. She concluded that success in figure drawing does not depend only on visual experiences but comes also as a result of haptic perceptions.

Using an electroencephalogram, Walter (1963), in a study of alpha

FIGURE 181.

"Pain," sculpture by a sixteen year old blind girl who is visually minded. (A) The general outline is made. (B) The cavity of the mouth is formed. (C) The nose is added. (D) Eye sockets are hollowed out. (E) Eyeballs are put in. (F) Lids are pulled over. (G) Wrinkles are formed. (H) Ears are added (I) Hair is added. (J) In the finished product, all features are incorporated into a unified surface.

FIGURE 182.

"Pain," sculpture by a sixteen year old blind boy who is haptically minded. (A) The chin is constructed. (B) The teeth and tongue are put in. (C) The mouth is closed, hiding inside features. (D) The nose is added, eye sockets are made. (E) Eyeballs are put in from inside, head is closed. (F) Ears, muscles, and hair are added. (G) The head is finished. (H) All features remain isolated as partial impressions on final product.

H

THE DEVELOPMENT OF TWO CREATIVE TYPES

rhythms—the brain waves or electrical pulsations that are recorded with the mind at rest—discovered that in one group of persons these rhythms persist even when the mind is active and alert. He administered a test to 600 individuals that enabled him to distinguish between a visualizer (the M type), the non-visualizer with a persistent alpha activity (the P type), and a mixed type (the R type). Individuals with persistent alpha rhythms that were hard to block with mental effort, who had continuing alpha rhythms even when the eyes were open and the mind active, tended to have kinesthetic and tactile perceptions rather than visual imagery. Moreover, the visual type retains mental pictures of the environment and, according to Walter, thinks primarily in terms of visual images.

The visual type is the observer, who usually learns about things from their appearance. One important factor in visual observation is the ability initially to see the whole without an awareness of the details. Apparently, the visual type first sees a general shape of a tree, then the single leaves, the twigs, the branches, the trunk, and finally everything incorporated into the whole tree. Starting with the general outline, partial visual impressions are integrated into a whole image. The visually minded individual can analyze the characteristics of shape and structure of an object and be concerned with the changing effects of these shapes as they are influenced by light, shadow, color, atmosphere, and distance. How something looks is of prime importance, and even tactile sensations are translated into visual form. For such a person the complex and ever-changing appearances of shapes and form are exciting and pleasurable experiences.

The haptic type utilizes muscular sensations, kinesthetic experiences, impressions of touch, taste, smells, weights, temperatures, and all the experiences of the self to establish relationships to the outside world. The haptic person enjoys textures and feels objects pleasurably with the hands. Because art of the haptic is more subjective, there is no attempt at trying to translate these textures into a visual image. The artist becomes a part of the picture, and subjective values determine the color, sizes, and form of objects.

A thorough discussion of the haptic system was set forth by Gibson (1966). He documented the numerous means of perception that people have open to them in addition to the eyes. The skin feels, the touching of hairs carries a message, heat and pressure can be understood, and the size and shape of objects can be realized. Gibson's work indicated that objects can be identified and selected without their even being seen. Boffoly (1978) gave to 103 eighth graders a series of tests measuring 23 variables to determine how they responded to a variety of perceptual information. Using factor analysis, he found that three factors accounted for differences in how these junior high school students responded: 20 percent responded haptically or kinesthetically, 26 percent visually, and the rest responded in ways he termed cognitively.

There may be some relationship between the haptic–visual theory and a theory dealing with different modes of perception: Field-Independence versus Field-Dependence (Witkin, 1962). In an experiment with children's reading ability, Templeman (1962) found that there was a relationship between a first grader's creative type and the ease of learning; those children who were considered haptic had more difficulty in learning to read. Kagan, Moss, and Sigel (1963), reporting upon several studies on cognitive style, found results similar to aspects of haptic–visual types in what they termed the analytic and nonanalytic responses of children. Although the ability to discriminate between different shapes seems to be fully developed by six years of age, Gliner et al. (1969), in an investigation of the development of haptic and visual preferences of kindergarten and third grade children, found that more younger children, when feeling hardboard forms, distinguished between them by their texture, whereas more older children distinguished forms by their shape. Further studies of haptic aptitudes have been undertaken (Concannon, 1970; Heller, 1980; Kennedy, 1982; Simmons and Locher, 1979) but these have dealt primarily with tactile experiences of children rather than with haptic expression.

This documentation of the haptic–visual theory is less important than its implications for art in the secondary school. Realizing that extremes of either type are rare, it is important to understand that some children may be inhibited by references solely to visual stimulation. This is particularly important to keep in mind for those teachers who themselves may be strongly visually minded. If one thinks of an immediate response to the word "lifting," is the response a visual one such as "box" or "books," or is the response a haptic one such as "heavy" or "straining"? Suppose you were asked how many floors there are in a building that you have been in; would you answer by visualizing it and counting the floors, or by recalling the number of flights of stairs you had to climb? Or if you go quickly down a flight of steps, do you have to watch your feet so you won't fall, or do you get confused if you watch your feet?

Ast (1981) examined children's responses to two types of haptic–visual tests. Although these tests were designed originally for adults, it was thought that the third and fourth grade youngsters might respond in similar ways. However, such was not the case. It appeared these children had ways of responding to words that may have been learned in school, such as rhyming words or giving opposites, that tended to confuse some of the responses. Also, children's drawings are not as easy to categorize as adults'. Ast concluded that existing tests for

FIGURE 183.
Obviously one does not have to be blind (as in Figs. 181 and 182) to show haptic or visual tendencies. Here a twelve year old has constructed a head by starting with a lump of clay the general shape of a head; details were fashioned by pulling out or pushing in for the various features.

FIGURE 184.
Here a twelve year old has added separate parts to make a whimsical head. This is more typical of children who tend toward haptic expression.

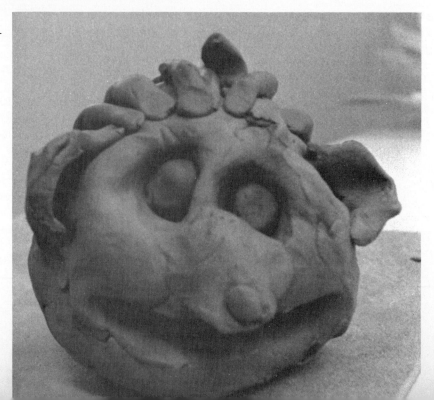

haptic–visual aptitudes are not particularly suitable for the early elementary grades. It is obvious that children learn in a variety of ways, and differences in cognitive style can influence the way that they learn. A good deal of school teaching takes place using visual stimuli; for some children this may pose a problem.

For some adults there is a continued inability to deal with visual stimuli. Some college students were asked to make maps of a familiar area (Hardwick, Woolridge, and Rinalducci, 1983); approximately one third of the students had great difficulty with this task, drawing maps that were largely unorganized and contained only a few landmarks, as if they could not visualize the area.

It is important to remember that teaching should encourage the expression of students, regardless of their mode of representation. There is no need to value one type of representation over another, because our culture provides the opportunity for honest expression of all types. Unfortunately, the teaching of art is usually in visual terms. However, even color is impossible to teach as a purely visual phenomenon. Although color can be described in terms of hue, lightness or darkness, and strength or intensity, there may also be many variations within an object itself, as reflected light or changes in contour affect the color. Color can also be described as bright, cheerful, and warm or cold, forbidding, and hostile. The representation of objects will differ depending upon the way in which they are viewed and the response of the individual to these objects. Both haptic and visual stimulation should be provided and both kinds of art should be welcomed.

An example of one type of expression is Figure 185. There is a concern for correct proportions and measurements, and the changing effects of light and shadows are necessarily a part of the visual image, which are qualities that are discovered with the eyes. Figure 186 is a more haptic type of representation. Here the human figure is used as a means of expressing emotions and feelings. Because different parts of the body have various functions and importance, the proportion given these parts assumes emotional significance.

The history of art is filled with examples of art of both the haptic and visual types. Michelangelo's "David" is a type of expression very different from a piece of sculpture from the South Pacific islands. Both, however, are true art expression and sincere forms of art. In the past, classic Greek sculpture was highly admired. Capturing the beauty of the visible form was considered a high achievement, and the religious art expression of the early medieval period was thought quite crude in comparison. However, these religious expressions were symbolic of deeply personal experiences; viewed with this in mind, the distortions and exaggerations of the medieval art take on an intriguing beauty quite different from the classic purity.

FIGURE 185.
"A Scene at the Police Station," drawn by a visually minded adolescent. Correct proportions, lights and shadows, and three-dimensional quality are important to the artist.

The experiences of the adolescent youngster can often provide intense motivation for visual awareness. The blazing flames of the sky at sunset, or the reflections of a shimmering image in a puddle, or dark silhouettes in the evening can be inspiring. At the same time, these youngsters can be deeply touched by the human qualities of life and become involved in the struggle of humankind; the sky becomes only a reflection of this struggle, while the puddle reflects merely poverty, and the shadows are symbolic of man's false façade. It is important to provide the range of stimulation that will make those individuals who are at either end of the haptic–visual continuum acutely aware of the problems of artistic expression, and this type of motivation will be equally meaningful to the individuals who are able to produce from both haptic and visual experiences. A visual type may dislike and reject such haptic works as unskilled and worthless, whereas a haptic type could interpret visual representation as superficial and unfeeling. Tolerance and acceptance of other modes of expression need to be learned by students as well as teachers.

The visual–haptic theory is important to understand, for it explains much development in art. Young children's art can be generally classified as haptic in nature, for the experiences portrayed are those that originate primarily with the self and include what might be considered touch-space. The increasing visual

FIGURE 186.
"A Scene at the Police Station," drawn by a haptically minded adolescent. The elements of this composition are determined subjectively; proportions, lights and darks, and space are of emotional significance.

awareness of children can be seen in their drawings and paintings, as discussed earlier. For the haptically minded, the emphasis on visual representation can be confusing and at times frustrating. The rewards in the elementary school may have gone to those children who were the most visually aware of their environment. Between the two extreme modes of expression are the indefinites, who are also of concern. Gutteter (1976) studied 200 adolescents, identifying those with haptic and visual attributes, but found evidence that students who fell between these groups lacked self-direction and were constricted in thought and action. In a study of 64 eleven and twelve year old English students in art classes, Weston (1984) found that his more haptic students had difficulty with perspective, tried to imitate the work of their visual classmates, and responded poorly to the teacher's offers of assistance. Weston noted that some of his students, classified as indefinites, also lacked self-confidence and even copied from others. Both of these studies point to the problems in art experienced by students who are neither very haptic or very visual. Possibly those students who are very haptic ignore or do not understand the problems of showing depth or the effects of light, and so forth, and therefore can be oblivious to teacher criticism or help with their art. It may be the indefinites with some haptic tendencies who feel inadequate, who have trouble following visually based instructions for drawing buildings, so that imitation without understanding results—a real blow to creative endeavors.

The teacher in the secondary school may be confronted with children who have rejected the world of visual art and decided, therefore, that they cannot draw or paint. The haptic art that can be elicited from such children, whose expression has previously been thwarted, is often emotionally charged. The sensitive teacher will find it difficult but worthwhile to stimulate students' natural means of expression.

Creative Expression and Brain Specialization

As scientific understanding of the biological functioning of the brain has increased, there have been corresponding attempts by psychologists and educators to apply the new evidence to their own areas of expertise. This has not escaped the notice of art educators. Of particular interest has been the discovery that mental activity is not a generalized process, but that certain localized areas of the brain specialize in specific tasks. "Maps" of the brain have been produced, showing which areas of the cerebral cortex are responsible for receiving sensation from and initiating movement in specific parts of the body.

Evidence for the location of sensory and motor specializations in various areas of the brain is relatively direct, through the study of stroke and accident victims. It has become apparent that the manipulation of language is located in the left half, or hemisphere, of the brain. Many other functions, such as the ability to recognize faces, to name objects, to perceive spatial relationships, and to perform mathematical operations, are similarly localized; whenever a specific type of task is performed or problem is solved, the area of the brain that specializes in tasks or problems of this type will habitually become active. On a very broad level the cerebrum may be subdivided into two major areas. The two halves of the brain are the right and left hemispheres, almost completely separated except for a bundle of nerve fibers running between the two halves. For a time surgical separation of the two hemispheres was used as a method of controlling severe epilepsy. Studies of these "split-brain" patients and more recent studies of the electrical activity of the brain (EEG), measured by the use of electrodes placed outside of the skull, have allowed researchers to determine which hemisphere is involved in different kinds of thinking. In split-brained individuals this may be accomplished by presenting problems to only one side of the brain at a time, by such devices as putting an object into one hand and hiding it from the other side of the body or by placing a visual signal where only one half of the brain will be able to perceive it. It is then a fairly simple matter to measure the performance of each side of the brain individually and compare them to see which has done better. Neuroscientists are finding a wide range of behavioral and chemical, as well as anatomical, asymmetries of the brain, (Marx, 1983).

The left hemisphere specializes in monitoring and controlling the right side of the body, processing words in writing and speaking, manipulating numbers, attending to details, and logical thinking. The right hemisphere specializes in monitoring and controlling the left side of the body, producing appropriate emotional states and recognizing and interpreting emotion in others, recognizing and humming tunes, and understanding spatial relationships (Goleman, 1977; Foster, 1977).

Since the left hemisphere has control of the right side of the body, and most people (about 90 percent) are right-handed, and since the left hemisphere contains the areas controlling speech, the right hemisphere being unable to communicate verbally in split-brain subjects, the left hemisphere is spoken of as being "dominant." To many people this apparently suggests a logical, verbal left

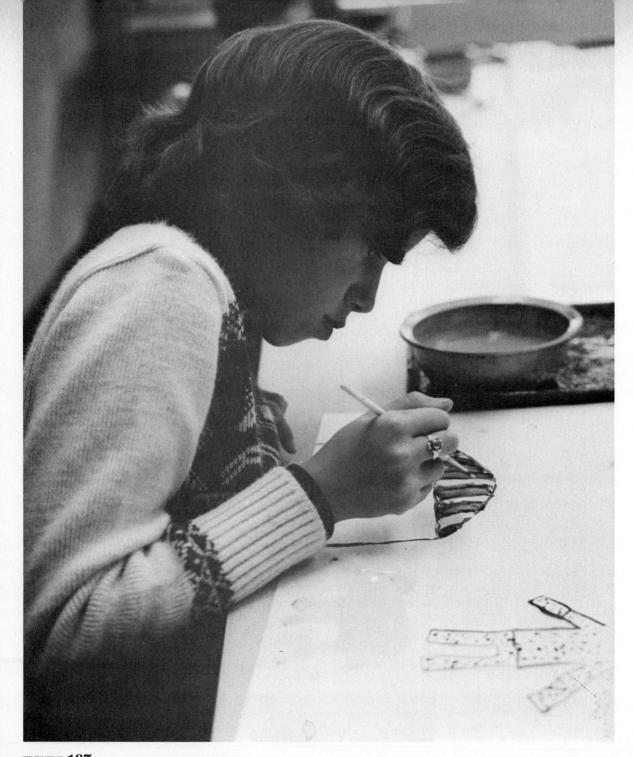

FIGURE 187.
Drawing and painting are sometimes thought to be related to the intuitive and the right brain. However, the arts demand as much from the intellect as from the emotions.

hemisphere lording it over a sensitive and artistic right hemisphere. These well-meaning people then propose to rescue the right hemisphere from its subjugation by giving it a greater share of the attention lavished on the left hemisphere by our traditional educational system. Artistic pursuits such as drawing, music and dance, and an emphasis on "creative" thinking are supposed to somehow strengthen the right hemisphere through exercise and allow it to take its place as part of a "whole" brain.

In reality, of course, the dichotomy drawn between the left and right hemispheres of the brain is at the same time an oversimplification and an exaggeration. Each hemisphere is divided into four lobes, with each lobe known to serve a different sensory or motor function; hindbrain and midbrain structures contribute to the processing of information necessary for higher mental functions (Springer and Deutsch, 1985). Judging by the strange deficiencies and inabilities of the victims of minor strokes, other specific skills may be just as highly localized as language has been shown to be. Further, the performance of most daily tasks requires a variety of skills, drawing upon the specialties of many areas. For example, the ability to correctly reproduce the sound of words is useless without the further ability to comprehend their meanings. Researchers studying split-brain individuals were hard pressed to find tasks that one half of the brain, but not the other, could perform (Gazzaniga, 1973), and EEG studies show only relatively higher amounts of activity in one half of the brain, not activity in one half and inactivity in the other (McCallum and Glynn, 1979). The fact that people can recover from strokes demonstrates that much more of the brain may learn a task or function than may habitually participate in its performance, although this learning may remain passive until called forth (Geschwind, 1979). The cells affected by stroke die and cannot regenerate themselves. Any recovery a patient makes is through surviving areas of the brain taking up new tasks. Higher mental functions involve a constellation of regions of the brain; various fields overlap, so that combinations of sensations become perceptions based on tactile, kinesthetic, and visual information about an object (Springer and Deutsch, 1985).

Creativity is apparently not one of the specialized areas of the brain. The notion that creativity is exclusively the function of the right hemisphere comes from making a false dichotomy between logic and creativity, or equating creativity with emotion. Creativity is a way of thinking, not a specific skill. Far from being localized in the right hemisphere, it appears that creative thought, like any other kind of problem solving, is a product of the cooperation of both hemispheres of the brain (McCallum and Glynn, 1979). A group of 175 community college students from Illinois, of both sexes and ranging from seventeen to forty-eight years of age, showed no significant relationship between cerebral dominance as measured by conjugate lateral eye movement, a test that discovers hemispheric dominance by observing which direction the eyes move after a subject is asked a neutral question, and creativity as measured by the figural section of the Torrance Tests of Creative Thinking (Doerr, 1980). In a study comparing the electrical activity of the hemispheres of the brain and handedness of a sample of students at a large midwestern university, Dorethy and Reeves (1979) found that art majors, contrary to expectation, were even more likely to be left-brain dominant than either art education majors or non-art majors.

Our school systems certainly do appear to be geared primarily toward the acquisition and use of verbal and logical skills, left-hemisphere functions, but this may be more a reflection of our innate abilities as humans than anything else. The area of the brain associated with the acquisition and correct use of language has been shown to be larger than the corresponding area in the right hemisphere, even in the fetal stages of development (Geschwind, 1979). Each hemisphere of the brain appears to operate almost independently until age two (McCallum and Glynn, 1979), and the final arrangement of hemispherical specializations, at least for language, is not fixed until about age eight (Geschwind, 1979). There is even some evidence for a larger left hemisphere in the great apes and Neanderthal man. As Marx (1983) has noted, no animal species, no matter how humble, lacks cerebral dominance. Far from being an evil of modern society, an emphasis on verbalization has been an integral part of our evolution and survival as a species.

Implications of Cerebral Dominance

The ethnic and environmental backgrounds of students vary, and some of these differences are obvious. Physiological and psychological differences are more difficult to determine, yet these influence behavior and learning. These differences, as well as the presumed intelligence of students, must all be considered when trying to involve students in learning, whichever hemisphere is dominant. Cerebral dominance relates to many areas of children's lives, both in and out of school.

Brog (1985) tested 128 students from grades 8 and 11 for hemisphere dominance and compared this information with their grade-point averages. Some educators have felt that perhaps children should be taught in different ways, depending upon which of their hemispheres is dominant. But Brog found no significant relationship between hemisphere dominance and grade-point average. Clare and Suter (1983) measured EEG alpha in normal righthanded subjects in order to study the degree of each hemisphere's activity during several tasks, including writing and drawing. As expected, there were task-related asymmetries, indicating some degree of hemispheric specialization for the tasks. Writing requires linguistic processing and drawing requires visuospatial processing, and the EEG asymmetries appear to be related to the fundamental information-processing requirements of writing versus drawing. Right-hemisphere EEG alpha did not differ between writing and drawing; free drawing involved greater left-hemisphere participation than did copying. Clare and Suter concluded from their experiments that drawing is not exclusively a right-hemisphere task, and that "fully competent performance of either of these tasks requires the integrated activity of both hemispheres" (p. 25). In a related study, Young and Bion (1981) tested 80 right-handed subjects, from five years to adult, in an attempt to determine the relationships between hemisphere dominance and picture recognition. They determined that once the identity of the pictured object is known, this information is available in some form to either hemisphere. Certainly the evidence indicates that creative activities are not necessarily those that involve primarily the right hemisphere.

Because each hemisphere of the brain seems to specialize in certain functions, there is renewed interest in the visual–haptic theory. Wieder (1984) has pointed out that some art educators are seizing upon the split-brain idea as justification for the teaching of art. He notes that visual/haptic, spontaneous/deliberate, cognitive/affective are all related to the left/right brain theory; but the existence of sharp distinctions is really only an assumption. Recent research seems to provide a basis for saying that one's hemisphere dominance should be a factor in one's haptic or visual aptitude. Gowan (1981) has already equated haptic aptitude with right-hemisphere dominance, although the evidence for this is not yet firmly established. One measure of brain dominance that has been used fairly extensively is the Dichotic Listening Test, which has many variations. The theory behind the measure is that information received in the right ear will activate responses from the left hemisphere and vice versa. Brain domination then would be indicated by which of two signals coming into the ears simultaneously would be registered. For example, if numbers were being programmed into both ears at the same time, and the person could mostly remember those heard by the right ear, there would be some indication that the left hemisphere is dominant.

Ten to twelve year old children's brain dominance, as measured by the dichotic listening test, was compared to their haptic or visual aptitude, as determined by the Lowenfeld test. The haptic–visual testing instrument was originally in German and was designed to test an adult population, so this may not be the most reliable way to determine children's haptic or visual tendencies. This difficulty has also been pointed out by Ast (1981), when the test was used with a younger population. But there does seem to be some relationship between responses on the dichotic listening test and haptic–visual tendencies, although the degree of this relationship is reasonably low. Tegano, Fu, and Moran (1983) found a significant positive relationship between right hemisphere dominance and divergent thinking abilities in 27 children who were given a dichotic listening test. Future studies with better testing measures may clarify the connections between the variables.

FIGURE 188.

Here a girl's responses to a dichotic listening test are being recorded for later comparison with her responses on tests of haptic-visual aptitude.

It is important that we realize that differences in the way children learn may have a physical basis and thus may not be easily changed. For some children, not only those who might be termed extreme haptics, school may be frustrating because of the emphasis on visual learning. Perhaps the "I can't draw" youngster is also the one who may have had difficulty in visualizing geometric problems or in other academic subjects where visual memory was important. The art room can provide the opportunity for a different kind of expression, an expression that may be lacking in fine visual qualities but forceful in terms of emotional impact.

Methods of Working in Art

Just as no two students are the same, their ways of working in art will also be different. This may greatly complicate matters, because the teacher is dealing with the many diverse ways in which youngsters approach an art experience. This can readily be seen in the way some youngsters tackle projects with enthusiasm, while others will begin the same project with hesitation. In some cases these attitudes toward materials or toward certain art activities may be a reflection of how a youngster feels that day; in others, these may merely be the manifestation of a long-term attitude.

In studies by Beittel (1966) and by Beittel and Burkhart (1963) two methods or strategies of learning in art were differentiated. These were called the *spontaneous* and the *divergent*. The spontaneous students began with a big whole that was devoid of detail, experimented with form, and took advantage of accidents. Their products looked quite free and tended to be nonvisual in nature. The divergent students usually began with fine drawings of details and added single elements together, developing an organization as they did so. Although this study was done with college students, these types can also be seen in the secondary school. There may be some relationship here to the visual–haptic theory, but Beittel has been more concerned with analyzing the way students draw than with the development of their modes of thinking. However, it is obvious that these are related.

In studying these two different strategies of working in art, Beittel provided a situation where students could see photographs that were made of their work in progress. Being able to look at these and clarify their own thinking and goals provided students an opportunity for self-motivation. The study indicated that self-discovered criteria were more effective and motivating to these students than were some external criteria. But the researcher also played an important

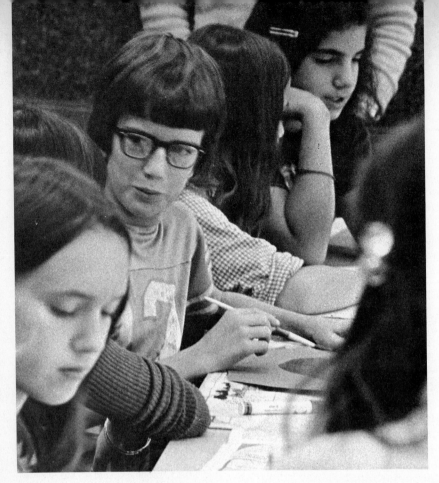

FIGURE 189.
Secondary school students show
great diversity in the attitudes,
the abilities, and the degree of
interest in art that they bring to
art activities.

part in these studies: the student had someone to talk to. Apparently, it was
important to have some means by which the thoughts and directions that students saw for themselves could be clarified; and the role of the teacher, or in
this case the researcher, was merely to listen. Beittel (1972) emphasizes the
powerful potential for learning that the "hindsight" method brings to the artist;
he urges that everyone engaged in art try to communicate to another person
just what was being attempted, so that self-understanding can take place.

Although these two methods of working in art are quite opposite from one
another, they also appear to be flexible (Beittel, 1966). At least some students
could assume the methods or strategy of the opposite type, for when told to
paint with the opposite strategy, their work changed. Surprisingly, this shift in
method did not mean that their paintings dropped in quality. There may even
be an advantage, then, in pointing out to students other methods or ways of
working once they have clarified some thoughts and directions on their own.

There is no reason to believe that the spontaneous method of working is any
more appropriate than is the divergent method. But the teacher's own method

ART IN THE SECONDARY SCHOOL

of working in art should not be imposed upon students. Continually drawing in one method could put students in somewhat of a rut, however, so they might indeed benefit from the realization that there are other approaches. As an example, consider a boy who is working diligently and with good control over his drawings. He may have excellent detail and add parts to his composition to make a whole. When drawing buildings, he may draw large and small buildings, with fine detailing around the windows, add smokestacks and sidewalks, and be mostly concerned with line quality. A discussion of where he is going and what he is trying to do can probably clarify some of his thoughts. However, if he becomes dissatisfied with this method of drawing, the suggestion that he draw something large and forceful, with rough edges, with a great deal of freedom and movement, using many ways of smudging and shading, may provide him with other approaches to art, which he can incorporate into his own method. Of course, the opposite procedure may work well with a spontaneous student. The concern of the teacher, then, is to expand the student's awareness

FIGURE 190.
Depth of personal experience is of prime importance in art activity. The meaningfulness of an art program can be measured only in terms of the individual.

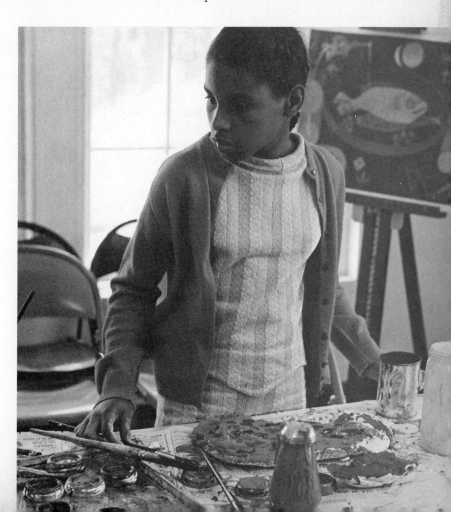

of the possibilities in art and to provide him the opportunity to evaluate and reevaluate his own direction.

There are many theories of how learning takes place in the arts. How these theories differ is less important than the fact that differences in theory exist. For the teacher in the secondary school it becomes imperative that each student be considered unique and that all ways of learning are encouraged. Environmental conditions or situations can be altered so that all students feel their art is respected. In a true art experience the inner self of the artist is displayed, with visions, thoughts, and feelings laid bare. One of the goals of any secondary school art teacher should be to provide an environment where these thoughts and this expression, however it is produced, can be treated with sensitivity and respect.

Creativity in the Secondary School Art Program

In recent years educators have shown increased interest and concern for the field of creativity. Many innovations have been made in the teaching of the usual academic subjects to provide for the creative responses of students. One method has been to provide problems that students must work through in order to arrive at axioms or postulates in mathematics, rather than having this information memorized in advance. In history, questions such as "What might have happened if the battle had been lost?" or "What would you have done if you were president?" are becoming more and more common. In art, there has always been the feeling that creativity is an essential part of the experience; but unless care is taken to insure that students develop a creative attitude and that the environmental conditions are conductive to creative growth, there is no assurance that art experiences in themselves will develop creativity.

The change from a natural, spontaneous manner of working with art materials, seen in young children, to one of a critical awareness of one's own actions calls for a well-developed plan for encouraging creativity. With younger children, it was a simple matter to encourage and foster the enthusiasm and freedom that seem to be part of life. In the secondary school, however, encouraging creative thinking must be an essential ingredient of the art program. Flexibility, fluency, originality, and the ability to think independently and imaginatively must not be left to chance.

FIGURE 191.

Rather than imposing subject matter, the secondary art program should capitalize upon the interests of students, even if the prime interest is food.

The art teacher must therefore plan for experiences that develop creative thinking abilities. It is not enough just to have students produce, even if these productions can be called art. It is important to develop the ability to think creatively, to learn how to create. For some students this may be a difficult experience, because many of them have achieved success by following the formulas or patterns of others. This may be true even of the highly intelligent youngster (Getzels and Jackson, 1962). There is a certain amount of risk involved in setting out on new and uncharted paths. This risk is not limited to the students; the art teacher too takes many risks in encouraging students to think for themselves. It is certainly a great deal simpler for the art teacher in the secondary school to follow a set syllabus and to develop an art program around easily graded projects. However, the excitement of discovery and the growth of the student in the process of exploration can be most stimulating.

Creativity is not fostered in an unstructured, chaotic atmosphere. However, a certain degree of ambiguity and diversity, or what might appear to be lack of organization, may be a better environment for developing an individual's own structure than an environment that is already predetermined and made neat and orderly by someone else's standards. The creative person has a greater tolerance of ambiguity (Barron, 1963), and a sterile working environment, both psychological and physical, lacks stimulation.

The usual classroom, and this often includes art classes, has a well-defined course of study outlined. The youngster is quite aware of this fact, and a common question is "What am I supposed to do?" Obviously students do not expect to be included in the planning of the activity. Any chance to escape or deviate from this predestined path is welcomed. The problem goes even farther, because the next logical question is "How am I supposed to do it?" This question is customarily soon followed by "Is this the way you wanted it?" For some students it may be somewhat uncomfortable to shoulder the burden of helping to make decisions rather than relying solely on the teacher. This may be especially true at the junior high school level, where there is an indication that creativity hits a low point (Kincaid, 1964). When children feel oppressed by a highly structured art program, they may "vote with their feet" and drop art classes entirely as soon as the subject is no longer required.

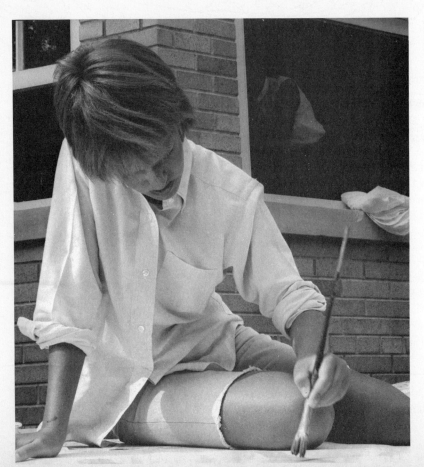

FIGURE 192.
Sometimes it is important to support the individual who wants to paint or draw alone. Art expression should be free of pressures for conformity.

Many educators are concerned about the tremendous pressure that peer groups have upon the individual in the secondary school, and with good reason. Studies have shown that individuals are very susceptible to pressures from their peers to conform. In a classic study, some college students, when asked to pick out the longest line from a series of lines of different lengths, went against what their senses told them and agreed with the group that had already selected one of the shorter lines (Asch, 1952). Apparently, most people are seriously affected and influenced by the decisions and judgments of others. Testing this in other ways, Crutchfield (1963) found similar results. It only takes a minute when observing youngsters in the junior high school to note the conformity and rules of dress and behavior that they impose upon themselves. Similar pressures will be found in the art room and will influence what is produced. On the other hand, the group can provide a great deal of stimulation and support for innovative thinking. The pressures of the group can be used positively if the atmosphere is such that creativity is recognized and the new, novel, or unusual is welcomed.

Although there are numerous tests for creativity, these have little value in an art room. Many things indicate creativity: how students perform, the degree to which they feel free to express themselves, the flexible way in which they use materials, the amount and number of things they can produce, their unusual approaches to drawing or painting, and the number of original or unique solutions that they provide to artistic problems. Standardized tests can only approximate this. It would probably be more valuable to know who is the least creative person in the art room, for this is the individual who needs the most support in creative endeavors. In some cases this may be the highly intelligent youngster who has overly high standards. In some cases it may be an extremely sensitive individual who is afraid of the unknown, who needs the support of an encouraging adult.

It is interesting and rather surprising to note that youngsters who have run into problems with the law and been put into institutions under the label of "delinquents" have apparently not been able to express themselves creatively. Burgart (1968) found that a group of delinquent boys ranked lowest on a creativity test, compared with other groups of school children and some nonschool groups. A study comparing creative thinking between delinquent boys and nondelinquent boys (Kuo, 1967) found that sixteen and seventeen year old boys reading at the fourth grade level tended to be nondelinquent if they scored high in measures of creative thinking compared with delinquent boys who scored low on the same measures. Another study (Anderson and Stoffer, 1979) found that nondelinquent boys scored significantly higher on tests of verbal creativity than did delinquent boys, although there were no differences in intelligence.

Apparently having the opportunity to express oneself in creative activity provides some means of reacting to the social environment in ways that are acceptable to that society. Possibly those who find they cannot create, who have found no satisfaction in building or producing, may react in negative ways. Unable to contribute in a positive manner, they destroy or deface what others have built. There may be more danger in having a passive view of life than in being aggressive about one's role. Gibbens (1968) reported that submissive, helpless, and unrealistic boys having an inadequate response to life were more apt to be reconvicted to jail sentence than those boys who rated as being aggressive, extroverted, and dynamic. It is clear that the problem is not one limited to delinquent boys. Everyone, particularly those who are confined to our school institutions, needs to have a means of self-expression, and this should be especially encouraged for those who seem disinterested and submissive. Art can play many roles, but the channeling of energies into productive outlets should certainly be stressed at the secondary school level.

The negative effect of grades, rewards, or other evaluation upon the creative thinking of young children has already been discussed. However, it is not only young children who are adversely influenced. The pressures to conform are particularly strong during early adolescence but also continue through young adulthood. Any reward or external evaluation apparently changes the focus of an activity from exploring interesting possibilities and satisfying oneself to trying to conform to others' wishes and to satisfying external demands, even if those demands are not understood. Pearlman (1984) told sixth graders that they could have an extra three points on their next mathematics examination score if they solved a problem correctly. Given the choice of a difficult or an easy problem, most children chose the easy problem. When other sixth graders who were not offered the extra points were asked to solve a problem, most of them picked the hard one. The same negative effects occur with older students. In examining the consequences of external evaluation on artistic creativity, Amabile (1979) told some college women that their work would be judged on creativity, others were told they would be judged on the technical aspects, and others were told they would be judged but with no particular focus. An additional group was told their work would not be judged. Fifteen artists rated the products and determined that the quality of the artwork of the nonevaluation group was significantly higher than that of the others. The negative effect of rewards may also be seen in the general population. Wilde and Murdoch (1982) reported that attempts to reward automobile drivers for accident-free records actually led to a significant increase in their subsequent accident rates.

It must be emphasized that the art teacher should never forget that the development of creativity is one of the basic reasons for art's existence in the sec-

PLATES 27 AND 28.

"Trees," watercolor paintings done by adolescent girls, illustrating two different methods of approach to the same subject. The artist of Plate 27 has utilized the flowing qualities of the materal with no concern for photographic representation. On the other hand, Plate 28 is built up out of carefully drawn details: leaves, branches, and flowers. Although an individual may identify more with either the subjective or the naturalistic approach, it may be valuable to encourage experimentation with both methods.

PLATE 29.
"Leaves," painted by an adolescent, is a free interpretation of leaves and greenery, evoking the essence of a forest. The adolescent is able to abstract from nature and enjoys making new forms.

FIGURE 193.
Great art has not portrayed only beautiful and elevating thoughts, but has dealt directly with commonplace activities, such as Van Gogh's "Potato Eaters." Even subjects such as chewing on celery can become a basis for creative activity.

ondary school. Creativity can be improved at any level; the most effective method starts with the unreserved acceptance of a student as an individual with worthwhile thoughts and ideas. Sometimes students go beyond the immediate assignment when they want to find out things on their own, unrelated to requirements or rewards. This is called intrinsic motivation. In gathering data on 455 high school sophomores, Lloyd and Barenblatt (1984) found that intrinsic motivation was closely related to academic achievement. The teacher must deal with the student simultaneously from an intellectual and an emotional point of view by providing a stimulating and supportive environment within the classroom.

The Art Teacher in the Secondary School

Unquestionably the art teacher has a favorable position in the schools. In part it may be because art has an aura of being somehow different from other subjects, which permits the art teacher more license. So teachers of art are often able to run a different type of classroom without the wrath of the administration falling upon their heads. In part this may be because it is difficult to evaluate progress in the arts and in part because art teachers are apt to be more creative individuals anyway. That is, art has a fascination for people who are willing and eager to express their thoughts and feelings in an imaginative way. It could also be argued that art provides the training for creativity in itself. Either way, the art teacher is usually looked upon as somehow different and may therefore be in a more enviable position than the usual academic teacher. Yet the art teacher may feel isolated in the school situation, since art teachers comprise only 3.1 percent of secondary school teachers (Boyer, 1983).

The art teacher has some other advantages. Youngsters *like* art. There is a delight in teaching a subject that has a natural attraction for youngsters. Although the art teacher must spend hours in preparation and planning, there are no dull hours of correcting essays or papers that plague other teachers at the secondary level. One would expect therefore that the art teacher's job should be a delightful one.

Although the art teacher may feel fortunate, the students view him in a rather different perspective. In an investigation into the character of early adolescent art, Brittain (1968a) found that the teacher is seen by the junior high school student as a potential threat. Most art teachers would like to consider themselves closer to youngsters than the average academic instructor, so this may come as quite a surprise. However, Brittain's study, surveying all junior high students in a small city, showed that students clearly rejected the teacher as a fit person to evaluate their work or to set standards for their performance. Apparently, the youngsters themselves decided whether they were successful on the basis of their own feelings rather than on the teacher's evaluation. This study also indicated that junior high school youngsters rejected the teacher not only as an evaluator, but as a source of ideas on what is important to do in art. When placed in the situation of having to perform art tasks assigned by the

FIGURE 194.
The art teacher can have closer rapport with students than do teachers of the academic subjects. This role should be one of concern, listening as well as talking, for art is not merely the teaching of factual material.

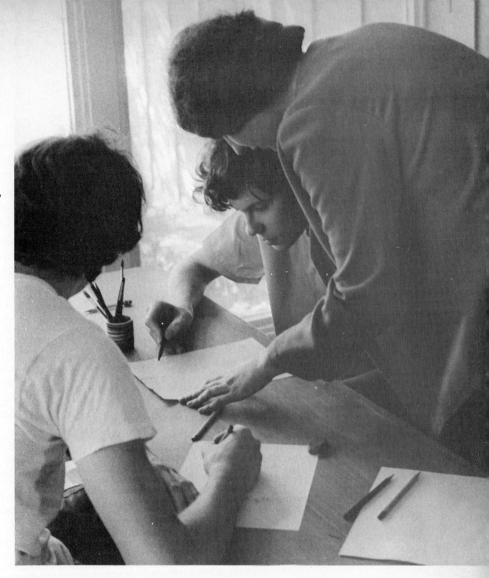

teacher, the students' own expression was thwarted. The only positive role that students saw for the teacher was that of providing new materials.

This is rather humiliating. Perhaps the traditional-style art teacher these youngsters must have known was concerned primarily with handing out materials. Obviously this method is still used in some elementary schools, and frequently one can find programs even in the junior high school that seem to be oriented primarily toward using one material after another. There may be good reasons, in fact, why the youngsters should treat such a teacher as a guardian of materials, rather than as a person able to help them with their aesthetic development and expressive needs. Part of the problem may be that adults do not attribute the same values to performance and behavior that youngsters do. Children seem to prefer to work or play in a group of four or five people, giving support for the organization of the classroom into small, workable units.

The teacher is both helper and judge of student competence, placing the student in an awkward situation (Newman, 1981). Although the teacher may be viewed as a threat and his values may be different from those of the secondary school student, the teacher's perception of students is very important. It has been clearly shown that individuals who are expected to perform creatively, and who are aware of this expectation, do much better than a group of people not so prepared (Hyman, 1964). The teacher's attitude becomes a crucial one in the classroom. A study by Rosenthal and Jacobson (1968) indicated that the teacher can also be influenced by how he expects the student to behave. Some 20 percent of the children from a certain elementary school were randomly selected and the names of these youngsters were reported to their teachers as showing unusual potential. Eight months later these "unusual" children showed great gains in intellectual performance on standard tests compared to the rest of the youngsters. The fact that the teacher expected the best may have paved the way for this to happen. Perhaps the most exciting and creative art class happens because the art teacher expects it to happen.

The usual teacher has many responsibilities in an art room full of students. These include a concern for classroom structure, the dissemination of materials, the need to save time for proper cleanup, and the presentation of some new material or method; so it becomes somewhat surprising to find that there is also time to talk to students. However, students may rarely have time to talk to the teacher. A study by Clements (1964) found that teachers rarely paused for student answers to their questions. In an average fifty minute art class, in which fifty-nine questions were asked, a total of only five seconds of pausing occurred. Clements looked upon the shortness of pupils' answers and the lack of time allowed for them to answer as casting real doubt on the value that art teachers attached to their students' opinions. Closely related to this is a study by Jones (1964), which showed that art students who replied to the teacher's questions in long statements had definite gains in the aesthetic quality of their products. It may be important in the teaching role to listen as well as to talk.

In addition to all his other responsibilities, the art teacher is expected to be a creative producer of art. Schwartz (1970) reports on a survey he did of 139 art teachers who almost unanimously agreed that art teachers should have personal creative experiences in order to be better able to provide these experiences for children. But, after all, one would expect art teachers to respond that way, just as a science teacher would expect a person who teaches science to have some experience in the field. However, the implications go further than that. Some schools had an artist in residence as an example of what a creative person does or is supposed to do. Financial assistance from governmental and philanthropic sources has supported this program. There was apparently great enthusiasm for the project in those schools that received funds. However, at the same time, there was little evaluation of the program. Would an electrician or telephone repairman bring as much excitement into the classroom? What is unique about the artist–performer? Are there any positive values that can be documented

FIGURE 195.

"My French Teacher," "My English Teacher." Secondary school students need to have the opportunity to express their feelings about their environment in socially acceptable ways. Although this may not be viewed with pleasure by the teachers concerned, this type of art activity is important for any student who has ever failed a test.

from the program? Is the art teacher supposed to be the artist–performer in schools that are not so fortunate as to have an artist in residence? To the last question there can be a definite "no." The classroom at the secondary level has plenty of creative potential in it without the teacher adding another element. Within the classroom setting the teacher is a teacher, and many problems of both human and environmental nature take precedence. Also, the particular approach a teacher has to working with materials might be construed as being *the* way of working, and this in itself could be inhibiting. But, away from the class, the teacher can be free to paint or construct art forms and to experience firsthand the rewards of creative activity.

Summary

Art has now become a means of purposeful expression for the secondary school student. No longer is a picture drawn without inhibition; no longer does self-expression flow freely; rather, a critical awareness of oneself as a member of society has taken over. For some students the development of artistic skills can be a challenge, but the youngsters who are haptically inclined may need support for their more personal expression.

The art teacher in the secondary school has an extremely important position, as he determines the direction and atmosphere for learning. He must have a genuine faith in students and be willing to accept their values as well as his own. He must provide an atmosphere where creativity can be fostered and where external evaluation is absent. He cannot be a threat to students. Certainly the freedom of the individual student in the classroom must in some cases be limited by the physical environment and by the limits of behavior that society imposes. However, the symbolic expression of these feelings need not be limited; the opportunity to put concerns, real or imagined, into constructive art forms should never be minimized.

At the time when there is an increasing concern for individual freedom and a discontent with existing social conditions, we must find ways to use the power of the mind creatively and to unlock the potential of every secondary school youngster. Theories differ as to why students paint and draw as they do. No matter what the final results of brain research may be, it is apparent that personal expression in art is important for all students. Art must play a major role in the school setting: to provide a means for the constructive outlet of emotions, for the development of creative thinking, and for the enrichment and cultivation of aesthetic awareness.

Related Activities

1. Compare the drawings of an eighth grade with those done by a fifth grade class. Point out the changes that show the development of a critical awareness toward creative expression.

2. Make a list of the characteristics of a boy who tends to be haptic. What would be his preference for subject matter, his manner of representation, his use of color, his use of proportion? Plan a lesson that would emphasize nonvisual responses.

3. Make a list of the characteristics of a youngster who has a preference for visual stimuli and plan a lesson, as above, emphasizing the visual elements.

4. Discuss the changing relationship between the child and his environment as seen in his representations of space. Point out how the use of space changes and how these changes reflect changes in development as the child grows.

5. In a free and open group discussion among secondary school art students, observe to what extent the group gives support to novel and creative suggestions and to what extent the group rejects original ideas. Would this vary with different groups?

6. Observe an eighth grade class working on an art project. Keep a record of the number and type of questions or comments made by the students. Keep a record of the teacher's comments and questions. Can you draw any inferences?

The Age of Reasoning

The Pseudo-Naturalistic Stage Twelve–Fourteen Years

The Importance
of the Pseudo-Naturalistic Stage

This period is one of the most exciting and yet one of the most trying in one's entire life. It is an age of turmoil and excitement for the child, although the term "child" now no longer truly applies. This is a time when girls start to develop mature sex characteristics and boys are wondering if they will ever grow hair on their chins. This age, sometimes referred to as the period of pubescence or preadolescence, is a time when youngsters find that they are not children but are equally sure they are not adults. It is a period of great individual differences; this is most noticeable in physical changes, but it is also true in the mental, emotional, and social areas as well. In the intellectual sphere, there is a developing capacity for abstract thinking. Social expectations change, bringing a new perspective of the world. The final push toward independence now begins. According to Harlow et al. (1971), there now is a crisis, a choice: either to venture out into the anxiety-arousing world of peers and achieve some mastery or to withdraw into fantasy.

The organization of schools for this age youngster varies. Often it is the junior high school—grades seven, eight, and nine—that stands as an entity. But sometimes grades five, six, seven, and eight are put together into a middle school. Teachers of young children often enjoy working in art because young children are so uninhibited in their work and are receptive to art ideas. Teachers of older children are apt to consider this the age when teaching a subject becomes meaningful, where concepts can be grasped, and art is elective. The best thing that can be said about the in-between ages is that they are a challenge. Regardless of the organization of the school, for most children this will be the last public school art they receive. This fact is very important, because the attitudes and skills that are developed at this age will influence their reactions and feelings toward art in adult life.

This stage of development marks the end of art as a spontaneous activity and the beginning of a period of reasoning, when children become increasingly critical of their own products. For some this means a change from unconsciously drawing what is known to consciously relying upon what is seen. These attempts at naturalism indicate the shift to adult modes of expression.

Children have now become much more critical and aware of themselves. This developing self-awareness is expressed through a self-conscious approach to life. They are concerned about how they look, how they dress, what they say, and particularly about how they appear to others. Adolescents are reluctant to reveal their real thoughts or to openly discuss personal matters. A study of fourth to twelfth graders (Elkind and Bowen, 1979) used a questionnaire, including such items as "Would you get up in front of the class if you found a split in the seam of your jeans if it meant extra credit?" or "Do you worry if people like you?" A major finding was that young adolescents were significantly less willing than either younger or older students to reveal themselves to an audience. This is a period of heightened self-consciousness.

The significance of this stage might be better understood if it is considered a transition from a period when the adult world was all-powerful to a world in which young adolescents are beginning to assume an important role. After the Gang Age, they enter a stage when they develop intellectually to the point where they can tackle almost any problem, yet they remain childish in their reactions. The difference between children and adults can be seen in the diversity of their imaginative activity. Young children may play hide-and-seek with

FIGURE 197.
Although unlikely to talk about his concerns with adults, the young adolescent can put a lot of himself into his creative activities.

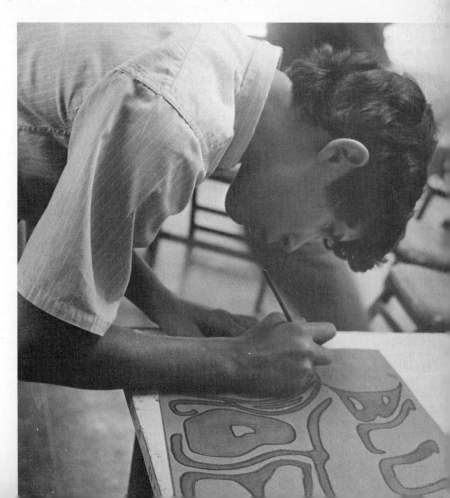

abandon; they will pick up a pencil and move it up and down while imitating the noises of an airplane; they will laugh or cry when amused or hurt, without inhibitions. Such unawareness is characteristic of children. If adults were to do the same things, they would be considered insane. For adults a pencil is a pencil, and a pencil is for writing. They have no time for games, and emotions must be kept under control. This change in the imaginative activity from unconscious to critical awareness can create conflicts in children and concern on the part of adults. This becomes especially apparent when we realize that at this age some girls are as tall as they will ever be, and therefore are considered big enough to behave as adults.

One parent recalled this stage of development with his own child in the following words:

> When Tommy, my son, was in this stage, of course he was a member of a gang, he had his fun, he had his group of children. He was always tall and a little bit out of proportion to the other children, but he didn't even recognize that, he didn't see it. He associated with younger children who were not as tall. He had his wooden gun, or his wooden stick—and enjoyed playing. But there came a time when I came home from my office—when I saw that when I approached the house he sort of tried to hide the gun, and I said, "Why don't you play with the children?" and he said, "Oh, I think—isn't it silly?" I said, "No, not silly at all, why don't you play with them? It is fun, isn't it?" And when I went into the house, of course he went on engaging in his pretend-to-be-games. He felt again as though he were no longer being watched, and since the smaller children accepted him in the group—in the gang—well, he continued the game. But these interruptions became more frequent as he grew older, and I could see him with his wooden gun, sitting there and watching them playing pretend-to-be-games, now and then participating or giving orders, but already standing outside. Until one day he put the wooden gun he had so carefully whittled into the basement, but still he could not part with it. Sometimes he went downstairs trying to improve it, but he no longer associated with the group, just watched them.

Just as youngsters have become more critically aware of their own actions, they have become more critically aware of their art products. During the gang age some children were quite reluctant to show their products to adults. Now they focus on the end product itself; a picture has value or is good, not because of the effort, interest, or involvement that went into it, but because of the visual appearance of the product. The recognition of the growing significance to the student of the final product must be accepted by educators. A questionnaire given to seventh and eighth graders asked on what basis these students liked what they had painted (Brittain, 1968a). Seventy percent indicated they liked

FIGURE 198.
This carved wooden figure from New Guinea is valued for its honesty of concept and directness of execution.

their art product when it turned out as they hoped it would or if they felt it was better than they had done before, whereas peer approval was important to only 18 percent, and teacher praise or professional appearance mattered to only a few. For youngsters, the emphasis has changed from the importance of the process, the effort involved and the intent, to the importance of the product. The child now asks: Does it look the way it should? Does it say what I want it to say? However, this concern with the product does not mean that these youngsters are eager to learn culturally determined art skills. Instead, they seem ready to explode with a creative force, akin to that in art from so-called primitive societies. The role of art in this stage of development is to support the youngster's individuality, to provide a socially acceptable release for emotions and tensions, and to ease the transition from the expression of a child to the type of expression typical of an adult. An untrained artist—untrained in the sense of Western traditions of line, color, form, and perspective—from a primitive society develops highly sophisticated images, but young adolescents have the same potential if they are motivated and their products are treated with respect. Untrained does not mean unartistic.

The Representation of the Human Figure

As expected, changes in the representation of the human figure follow the increased awareness and concern for changes that are beginning to take place in the bodies of preadolescents. Since girls tend to develop earlier than boys, there is usually a greater interest in drawing the human figure among girls. As bio-

FIGURE 199.
The representation of the human figure has changed dramatically from the earliest head-feet symbols. These sketches were made by a visually aware fourteen year old girl.

logical changes occur, there is more interest in drawing in notebooks, on scraps of paper, or on book covers. Usually the sexual characteristics of these drawings are greatly overexaggerated, reflecting the concern of these children over their physical development, for these sexual changes can no longer be experienced in a passive way. There is no reason to look upon these exaggerations as anything but normal. In fact, the very opposite may be true; that is, a child who is beginning to develop sexually and who does not include these changes within drawings may be showing a fear of these changes. Often these drawings are concealed from adults, and in some cases a sense of guilt or shame accompanies the drawings. These should not be censored.

Children will strive for greater naturalism and include joints in their drawings of the human figure. Before this age, youngsters usually employed clothes only for identification. Now, however, there is an increased awareness of changing appearances when clothes fold or wrinkle, when lights and shadows change with the sitting body, when color changes under different atmospheric conditions. The mere statement that a dress is red does not imply a visual analysis but merely factual recognition. A visual experience includes noticing that there are changes in red due to light and shade or to distance and reflected light, that pants change appearance while a person is running, or that folds and worn spots show. This increased visual awareness of the human figure is limited primarily to those who derive pleasure from the changing appearances of objects around them. For those not so visually aware, and at times for all youngsters, great pleasure is taken in cartooning and representing the human figure through satirical drawings. Boys seem particularly interested in developing this ability and sometimes will enjoy making cartoons of teachers, parents, and those of their classmates who hold enviable positions.

Probably one of the most difficult assignments youngsters can have at this pseudo-naturalistic stage is that of drawing themselves. The difficulty of coming to terms with one's own identity can clearly be recognized, not only in the drawings, but in the self-conscious and reluctant manner in which youngsters approach such a task. Although an examination of drawings done by preadolescent youngsters will look surprisingly like drawings done during earlier stages, there will be an increased awareness of detail with special attention to clothing, hair style, and facial features. The suggestion that individuals project their own personality into drawings has been given support in psychological literature. A youngster who is concerned about his nose may exaggerate this or leave it out entirely, although in drawing other people the nose may become a focal point for ridicule. The drawing of the self becomes, then, an indication of one's own ability to face oneself; the youngster who has developed or learned certain

FIGURE 200.

It is sometimes difficult for youngsters of this age to draw themselves. An honest appraisal is often forsaken in favor of an idealistic representation.

formulas for drawing a figure will produce a human figure drawing that is less expressive of the self and at the same time less artistically meaningful.

In a study of self-drawings by youngsters from twelve to fifteen years of age, it was found that they treated their drawings in derogatory terms (Brittain, 1968b). These students were asked to put comments on the back of their drawings, indicating the parts they liked best or the parts with which they had the most difficulty. The drawings themselves ranged from what might be more typical of a fifth grade youngster to a quite sophisticated sketch in fair proportion. However, the comments on the back of these drawings were invariably negative, such as "It's terrible," "What a lousy drawing," "It looks nutty," "The head is stupid," and "What a gooney-looking nut." The arms and legs particularly were described in negative terms. It is interesting to note that there seemed to be little relationship between the comments and an objective appraisal of the drawing itself. This raises the question of whether it is important at this age to develop skills in figure drawing or whether children will look at their drawings in negative terms, regardless of how the drawings look.

398

The Representation of Space

One of the important discoveries for the visually minded youngster is the apparent reduction in size of distant objects. The three-dimensional qualities of space are now understood by some youngsters, who discover the possibility of making drawings with this illusion of distance; consequently, many curriculum specialists, seize upon this as an indication that all children are ready to learn the mechanical rules of drawing in perspective. In fact, one can often find programs designed for seventh grade students that concentrate upon teaching perspective, starting with one-point perspective, then two-point perspective, then three-point perspective, with slanting roofs and stairs going off in a number of directions, with railroads disappearing into the distance and telephone lines marching across the page. Of course, for some youngsters at this age the rules to follow become merely mechanical and have no relationship to the world that they experience. Most children will be able to deal with the problems of representing space in depth, but the question remains whether time is best spent in trying to develop this competency.

FIGURE 201.

The rules of perspective are mechanically followed and vanishing points are used in this typical school exercise.

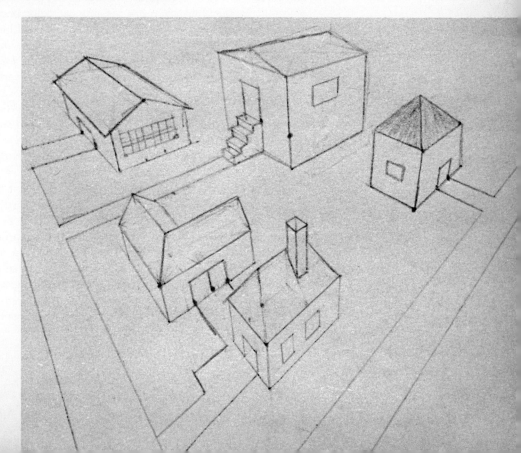

Some attempts have been made to teach perspective by other than the usual method of one- and two-point perspective, with vanishing points and horizon lines. Prentiss (1972) devised what he termed an "observational" method and compared it with the usual academic method and with a control group, which was not taught any formal method. For two weeks, 400 fifth, seventh, and ninth grade children were given a concentrated course. A drawing utilizing perspective was collected from these children before, after, and six weeks later. The judging of these drawings by experts and by other children indicated that neither method was supported; the control group with no formal instruction showed the greatest growth. Prentiss suggests that perspective as it was taught here may serve to confuse and even to deter growth, or that students reject or are apathetic toward teacher directed activities.

The means to represent distance must be discovered by students themselves. To take this discovery from them by "explaining" perspective deprives them of an important experience. The teacher must capitalize on the children's own findings and start on their level. "What makes the tree more distant in your drawing?" Let them become aware of their own discoveries: that they had drawn the tree smaller because distant objects appear to be smaller; that they had included less detail because one does not see as many details in distant objects; that they had given it a less intense color because the air in between makes the color appear less bright. All this should be used as a frame of reference for later experiences that may be less simple. One remark a teacher might hear is "I want the road going to the house in the background, but it looks funny." Using a previous experience for new discoveries, a good starting point would be "Let's see whether the road is doing the same as the tree." The child will soon discover that the road as it goes into the distance would grow smaller or narrower in a drawing just as the tree does and may also be less intense in color. Such discoveries originate with real experiences. Instead of depriving the child of the excitement of discovery, the teacher should provide stimulus and guidance whenever the need for it arises.

Trying to determine the developmental stages at which children can draw geometric solids, Mitchelmore (1978) had first, third, fifth, seventh, and ninth grade children copy a variety of forms. With these forms directly in front of them, children were asked to copy them with no time limit. It was found, as expected, that the youngest children merely drew a square to represent the cube. Some third and fifth graders carefully drew several sides, as if viewing each side separately, but it was not until seventh grade that most children attempted to draw several sides from one point of view. Even the ninth graders had difficulty with the task; only a third of them were able to draw a cube in

FIGURE 202.

This boy's drawing has not correctly followed the rules of perspective. But, as a work of art, it has a vitality that is missing in Figure 201.

perspective. Children who had difficulty with this task also had difficulty with some other spatial tasks. This indicates that drawing in perspective is not an isolated skill that can be easily understood, but is closely related to individual behavior and cognitive structures. Murphy and Bracewell (1983) noted three factors influencing children's strategies in drawing an object in perspective: how the object looks from the child's viewpoint, the child's mental representation of the object, and the graphic production process itself, as all lines are influenced by what has already been drawn on the page. The children in their study were able to copy a perspective *drawing* more easily than the object itself.

Drawing a cube is no easy matter. In the early attempts by young children a single side of the cube is drawn to represent the whole geometric solid. Even by fifth grade, fewer than a third of children studied by Lewis (1985) were able to successfully draw a cube in perspective. One study (Chen, Therkelsen, and Griffiths, 1984) had six year old and eight year old children draw a cube from life, from a photograph, and from a line drawing and had them repeat the task every twelve months. They also found that copying from a line drawing seemed easier for the children. After a few years, another group of children, eight and ten years old, also drew the cubes; the new groups did just as well or just as poorly as the first groups. Familiarity with the task did not give an advantage to the first group, which suggests that the ability to understand perspective is not dependent upon training. Chen and Cook (1984) provide some evidence that strategies used in copying drawings of geometric solids may be different from strategies used in drawing actual geometric solids; success on one task does not guarantee success on the other. It has been observed that some children who are taught shading or linear perspective can perform this skill to please adults but then revert to their own style of representation in drawings they make to please only themselves (Engel, 1981).

Children's concepts determine how they interpret their environment and treat space in their drawings. Liben (1981) devised a drawing task for children that required them to recall and draw how trees had been portrayed in pictures they had been shown; in some cases trees were shown perpendicular to the horizon, and in others the trees were shown perpendicular to a hill line. Children's success in remembering how the trees looked and drawing them was closely related to how children portrayed trees in their own drawings. Appar-

FIGURE 203.

Shame, shame! This youngster clearly does not understand the rules of perspective. Note the four wheels on the car, the tipped up puddles, and the lack of foreshortening in the sidewalk. Yet here we have a delightful haptic concept which could be ruined by insensitive instruction.

ently they remembered and drew according to their own concepts rather than to the way the trees were portrayed in the picture they were supposed to recall.

Certainly for the child who is more inclined toward haptic responses, the experience of being taught perspective can be a frustrating one. For such a child, and perhaps to a lesser extent for others, too, art may be more emotionally important. The illusion of distance as achieved through mechanical perspective is unique to our own culture. Possibly culture is not a good word to use here, for perspective seems to be more tied in with the teaching of art in public schools than with the field of professional art. Dubery and Willats (1972) note that by the fifth century B.C. painters were attempting foreshortening through oblique projection. Later systems of representing space include orthographic projection, axonometric projection, and isometric projection. At least some art today ignores perspective as it is usually taught; the professional artist may be much more concerned with representing a relationship to society than with attempting photographic likeness. And then there is Escher (1971), whose spoofs of perspective drawings seem to obey all the mechanical rules and yet confuse and confound the viewer. For some youngsters discovering methods of portraying three-dimensional space on paper, guided by a sensitive teacher, can be exciting; to other youngsters, possibly in the same class, perspective is irrelevant.

The Importance of Color and Design

It is easy to see that young teenagers have become very aware of design qualities within their sphere of influence. Although the teacher or worried parent may question their aesthetic taste, there is no doubt that youngsters have definite likes and dislikes in clothing, colors, and jewelry or other accessories. This increased awareness of design is sometimes used as an excuse to teach the formal elements of design, and one still hears of art classes spending time making plans for never-to-be-used wallpaper with half-drop repeats. The increasing awareness of color is sometimes used as an excuse to expend considerable effort in making color wheels or color charts. Both of these practices are gradually disappearing. Young teenagers have an intuitive sense of color and design, and the formal teaching of these factors seems unrelated to their interests.

Much has been written about the psychology of color and its emotional effects on individuals. Such emotional reactions to color are to a large extent determined by past experiences. To one person, horror might mean red, associated with blood; to another it might be green, associated with mold or decay.

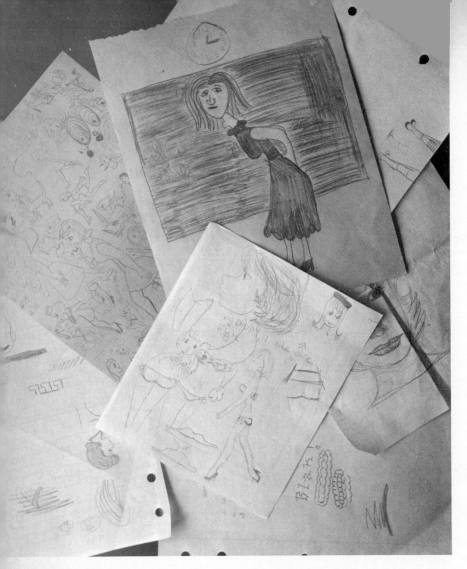

FIGURE 204.
These notebook pages and scraps of paper reveal a girl's interests and her concern about herself and things around her. This form of spontaneous art expression should not be repressed.

No generalizations should deny the individual's right to creative approaches to color. Emotional reactions to color are highly personal, and the nonvisually-minded child may use color in contradiction to nature. Color can be highly subjective.

   The notebooks of these youngsters may be filled with rather interesting and intricate designs. These are often related to lettering, such as designing one's name with fancy letters and seeing how these letters fit into other patterns, or they can become quite elaborate in a manner echoing the medieval manuscript calligraphy. Sometimes these doodles are of body parts that look quite grotesque or resemble preliminary sketches for a gargoyle, or they may look more like psychedelic forms that could impress adult artists.

These youngsters also develop a great sympathy and understanding for design in nature. The design on a turtle's back, the scales on a fish, or the pattern of moss as it is growing out of a crack in the pavement can be exciting discoveries. These elements of design are constantly around youngsters and make excellent raw materials from which a genuine understanding of the function of design can spring. In younger children there was an urge to collect many, sometimes unrelated, objects. This urge for collecting objects is not limited to the elementary school; young adolescents, too, can find a great deal of color and design in objects around them. These can be jars and bottles from the drugstore, which may be enjoyed because of their shape or tactile appeal; they can be parts of nature such as worn wood, pebbles, or feathers; or they may be something that has been discarded by society, in the form of a piece of junk mellowed by rust. Putting some of these objects into a setting designed for a work of fine art seems to transform them into things of beauty.

Because most youngsters of this age will not be exposed to further art experiences, attention can and should be paid to industrial products. Although the question of aesthetics is raised once we begin to consider the merits of a variety of designs for everyday objects, the tastes of the teacher should not be forced upon the students. Subtle discriminations in aesthetic judgments can be made by young adolescents (DePorter and Kavanaugh, 1978). A great deal more understanding can be achieved through discussion than by merely having the students guess which kitchen knife the art teacher likes best. The functional basis for good design can be understood. Discussions may have to start with the merits of the best-designed sports car, but the concern for and interest in design is much more important than indoctrinating students with an adult's concept of good taste.

The problems of color and design can take on new meaning when critically examined by young adolescents. These same art students will be paying taxes, voting, and starting families within the next ten years. Many selections of an artistic nature will be before them: the choice of a dining room set from the local furniture store, a television secured through a time payment plan, and a vote on the proposed new municipal building. It is not too early to raise questions about the visual quality of our environment. Much harm may be done in our society by citizens who are unaware of the possibility of action. Active participation in group discussions helps prepare them to assume responsibility for their environment as alert, perceptive adults.

FIGURE 205.
The radiating design quality, the arrangement of seeds, the moisture, and the surprising beauty to be found in small things may be seen in a slice of orange.

Growth As Reflected in the Art of the Young Adolescent

It is easy to see that the work of young children is closely related to their developmental level. Their feelings and emotions and understandings of the world around them are clearly reflected in their art products. In the same way the products of young adolescents reflect their reaction to the world, although maybe not as clearly. Just as there is great diversity in intellectual ability, physical development, and obvious differences in sex, there are also differences just as great in the art products of these youngsters. The range and variety of art work increases with each grade level. This can easily be seen in the middle or junior high school. The dainty drawing of a popular celebrity that is perfected by a timid girl is just as valid a means of expression as the elaborately decorated motor bike is for a boy.

Between the ages of twelve and fourteen we find many new problems arising for youngsters and many changes occurring, both in themselves and in their relationships to their peers and adults. Boys and girls alike are beginning to break numerous childhood ties to the family and are questioning adults' authority. In addition to their concern about personal appearance and their idealism and romantic feelings about becoming adult members of society, there is also fear and insecurity about the beginning stages of leaving childhood. Girls are no longer making war on boys, but may have a musical recording star for an idol. Boys are attracted to the opposite sex, but are not ready to admit this. Instead they are busy collecting baseball statistics, developing their muscular powers, and seeking out boys who have comparable interests in such things as video

FIGURE 206.
Fanciful doodles or cartoons, sometimes with names attached, seem a safe way to express hidden feelings.

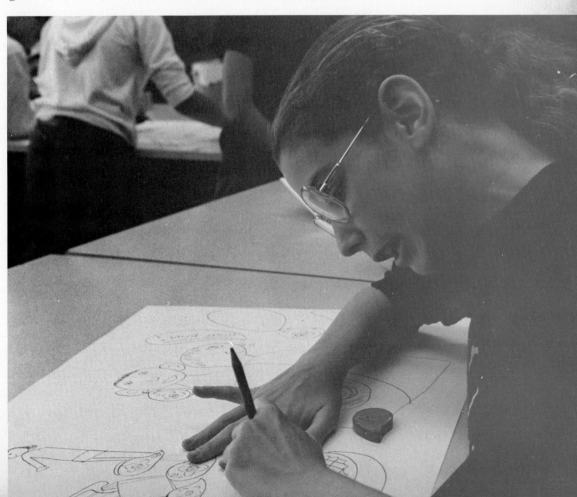

games, computer hacking, and three wheeled all-terrain vehicles. Experimentation with drugs sometimes begins at this age. When children were asked (Berndt, 1979) whether they would cheat, steal, or trespass if urged to do so by their friends, it was found that conformity to peers' antisocial behavior peaked at adolescence.

In some schools students are segregated by so-called ability levels. This may mean that some art classes consist of those who have achieved academic success while others may be composed primarily of those who are lowest on the academic ladder. A study by Madeja (1967), using secondary school students, found that academic achievement correlated highly with grades in art. At the same time he found that nonverbal tests of creativity of the same students showed no relationship to their grades in art. Apparently, art teachers are looking for some of the same attributes that teachers in math and science are seeking. The implications of this are somewhat frightening. Those students who have achieved respectability and are able to cope with the system are those who are rewarded in art too. At the same time, those who are not able to adapt to the school setting and are having problems achieving the type of success usually rewarded in schools are also failing in art expression. Perhaps the art program in the secondary schools needs a thorough overhaul, for it is essential that *somewhere* in the system students should be able to express feelings and emotions that are important to them without the fear of failure. The creative child may not be easily identified. In Japan, Inagaki (1979) found that teachers misidentified their creative children, being more influenced by verbal recall than by verbal originality. Creative students may not be well liked, and some teachers do not value creativity very highly (Torrance, 1962); this may be so even in the art room.

One college student was asked to write her recollections of her own experience in the junior high school she attended. This particular girl was not only a success in that she was able to go on to college; she was also considered well liked and well adjusted by her teachers. Included are only those parts that seem most pertinent to our discussion of the relationship of art to youngsters of this age.

Junior High/One Girl's View

Junior high is a period of my life I would definitely not want to live over again. It was sort of a changing point, the point where I stopped playing with dolls, started noticing boys, decided I want to be a writer, passed through puberty, first really became aware of such things as "popularity."

I wasn't too fond of life but it never occurred to me that life could be changed so it was any different; I accepted things as they came. Adulthood was a magic, privileged life, to be looked forward to, but for now I was stuck being an early adolescent, forced to accept life. I was usually optimistic about things getting better, but I didn't think anything I did could change them. Perhaps I would have been happier if I had felt at one with a crowd all of whom shared a common misery of being in junior high, but I couldn't verbalize my discontent. Discontent wasn't something you talked about. And if something was wrong, it was *me* that was wrong, not the environment. At the time, I did not think myself unhappy.

Social relations were a very important part of junior high. This did not mean boys so much as the other girls. Boys were something seen from afar, rarely contacted. Girls, however, were all around. Boys were extremely terrifying objects. I could scarcely stand up when I was in the presence of one I liked. When I was in eighth grade, a boy named George said "Hi" to me in the hall. I had never particularly noticed him before, but I was overcome. I instantly developed a deep binding crush on him. I don't think I could have stood it if he had started carrying on a conversation with me; I would have been completely overcome by it all, but much of my energy was spent in contemplating those "Hi"s.

Sex had very little to do with boys. It was a subject of its own, fascinating, secret, and frightening. I first heard dirty jokes at a slumber party in seventh grade. A slumber party was a Good Thing because being invited to one indicated being In. From dirty jokes, the way was open for bigger and better things. Any

FIGURE 207.

This drawing by a ninth grade girl becomes a social commentary on the junior high school population, reflecting her emotions and impressions about her peers.

passing reference to sex in a book was hugely shocking and hugely thrilling. I used to lie in bed at night and make up dirty stories of my own. At the same time, I was terrified at the whole thought. Starting to menstruate, feeling that I was suddenly a woman, was a very strange feeling. I was embarrassed by it.

School had very little relevance to anything. It was there and I had to go, and so I went. Homework was something to be avoided, done quickly, gotten out of the way as quickly as possible so I could do something more interesting. If I wasn't doing well, I didn't work harder. To be caught with homework undone was a stomach-tightening feeling, and so I did it. The only saving grace in most of my classes was that Mary sat next to me and we could pass notes. To have fun in school was an inconceivable concept.

If someone had sat down with me and said, "Talk to me about some of the things that are really important to you," I wouldn't have understood. It was one of the facts of life that nobody but yourself really cared about what you really thought, especially grown-ups. Parents might be nice to you, but if you told them your inner thoughts, they would either laugh or beat you up. If you had problems and worries, you didn't broadcast them, didn't even write them in a diary, because they couldn't be admitted, even to yourself. You knew what you were supposed to say and do, and you did it, and you tried to feel what you were supposed to.

I didn't draw as much as I had in grade school. I spent most of my spare time either reading (which I did a great deal) or writing. However, I doodled a tremendous amount, all over my notes, usually overdeveloped girls wearing short skirts. A lot of the time they carried knives; they were full of self-confidence and off to fight and win in the name of some unspecified desperate-but-worthy cause. Sometimes, in ninth grade, I would draw boys and girls walking together, but girls generally outnumbered boys in my doodles about 100 to 1. If I drew a regular picture, it generally had some sort of sexual overtones or else was drawn in some style of some subject which I thought would meet parental approval. Art class in school was sort of fun; it was the class period you could goof around and get A's without trying. Wallpaper design, three-point perspective, and lettering had no significance for me, but they helped break up the boredom of math and science.

I guess I was really pretty miserable in junior high. The school itself was pretty bad: fierce teachers who'd never try to understand a kid's thoughts; strictly enforced rules about needing a pass in the halls; stairway monitors who grabbed me; boys who called me "bitch" and hit me with their books; waiting in line for ages in the cafeteria for an unappetizing plate of food; looking at trees outside the window and wishing I could go out; having to stand up on the school bus; having to run up three flights of stairs from gym to science after a four-minute compulsory shower; having to stand in line for a toilet at lunchtime. I was trying to figure out who I was and where I was going and not having much luck, perhaps in part because I didn't realize that that was what I was doing. I certainly lacked self-confidence; I used to get all upset and cry if I was criticized and couldn't stand being laughed at. I haven't thought about junior high in a long time, this is the

THE AGE OF REASONING

first time I've brought out my memories in quite a while. I'd be just as happy to forget it.

Art Motivation

One of the central themes of adolescence is striving for an identity. Adolescents need to come to terms with themselves and be able to express intense feelings that need a constructive outlet. They are very aware of being alive and are developing an awareness that they can build, construct, and create objects. This is no time for prescribed busy work, when students are full of thoughts and directions. They resent having to perform art tasks set up by the teacher and denying their own expression. The prime role of the teacher during this period is to provide guidance and encouragement so that this expression can take on a meaningful form.

As previously mentioned, the art teacher is considered by students to be somewhat irrelevant to the production of art. It is important that the art teacher quickly establish a role different from that of the customary teacher. If the atmosphere is going to be such that mutual trust and exchange of ideas with youngsters is possible, then the usual classroom procedures may not be adequate. Youngsters of this age enjoy and need the opportunity to share and exchange thoughts with a few of their peers (Brittain, 1968a). Possibly the best physical arrangement for an art room would be to have tables arranged for several small groups of students so that activities could be discussed and evaluated by peers as well as by teachers. In addition, the opportunity for isolated work may be important for some students or for all students at some times. An occasional mural project that requires cooperative effort provides a chance for a group to solve artistic problems.

Often an ineffective art program is planned around the use of one material after another. The first three weeks may be devoted to pencil sketching, the following two weeks may be spent doing copper etchings, the next three weeks may be spent working in colored chalk, and so forth. The need for materials must grow out of the need for expression. The teacher who uses the materials approach may be afraid of facing the real expressive needs of adolescents. Such a program ignores the basic principle that it is more important to have something to say in art than to worry about the development of skills in case something might someday be expressed.

Any art motivation should stress the individual's own contribution. At this

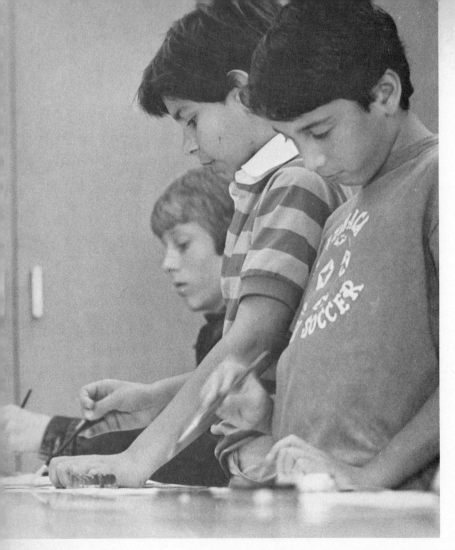

FIGURE 208.
At times, boys may feel that art is only for girls, that it is a sissy activity, but this need not happen. The project has to be meaningful and important enough to involve students.

stage of development it is important to reinforce individualistic thinking. An art program that is primarily concerned with productions may entirely miss one of the basic reasons for the existence of art in the school program, which is the personal involvement of the individual and the opportunity for developing a depth of meaningful self-expression. It is vital that all youngsters feel that their activities in art are their own. To a great extent the teacher's motivation is responsible not so much for the production of art but for the desire to produce. If the youngster is not involved, excited, and completely swept up in the art activity, then the drawing or painting becomes a mere exercise for the school system. Probably one of the most powerful features of any motivation is its relevance to the students. To some extent boys have less of an interest in the usual art program than girls have. A practical problem, such as making a three-dimensional working structure, can often challenge boys, particularly if there is some doubt implied that they can really do this. Sometimes such a project can become so engrossing that it serves as the basis for expanding into many of the more recognized art areas.

The development of a critical attitude toward the surrounding world has made the young adolescent much more concerned about naturalism. The schema seen earlier in drawings has now disappeared. However, the youngster may feel reluctant to become involved in art experiences. In part this may be because past performances in art have been ignored or even ridiculed. In part it is because of a developing critical awareness. In part it may be a reflection of the feeling that art is not an important activity.

At this age children have not yet developed full control over their emotions and a seemingly minor incident may be of extreme importance to a youngster. This intensity of feeling can be utilized within the art program, where the emotional attitudes can be expressed either directly or symbolically. Topics centering on religious themes, individual justice, or the expression of love or hate can involve a youngster quite completely. In such cases exaggeration or overemphasis of particular parts within a composition can be seen. Such distortions should be given support; the flexible use of color and the exaggeration of form can develop an emotional impact in the art product.

It is not diplomatic to say, "Put your innermost feelings down on paper about some adult whom you feel has treated you unjustly." Many children have been taught that it is not nice to have unpleasant thoughts about people, and in

FIGURE 209.
The young adolescent may criticize his immediate society. A fourteen year old boy's cartoon pokes fun at a friend.

some cases these feelings may very well be directed at parents and teachers. It is usually best to let such feelings of aggression, and in some cases love, be expressed more unconsciously. Such subjects as "The Ugliest Person in the World" provide the opportunity for the release of such feelings. "What would the ugliest person in the world look like? Would he have smooth or rough skin? Would he have a long or a short nose? How about his ears? Would his teeth stick out? And his hair? What color would go well with him? Could the ugliest person in the world be a woman?"

As already discussed, this stage of development is characterized, among other things, by a tendency toward two different types of expression. The extremely visually minded person and the extreme haptic are relatively rare; sometimes both tendencies can be seen in the same individual. Showing wrinkles and folds when clothes are in motion is usually an indication of visual awareness, whereas the use of distortion, the lack of visual depth in drawings, and the continued use of flat color may indicate a more haptic approach to one's environment. Any motivation should allow for all types of expression. Planning art activities best suited to the visually minded, as is the usual case, may restrict or definitely hamper the expression of those youngsters who are not capable, or are not ready, to portray their world in a method they do not understand.

Once again, it should be emphasized that the drawing or painting or other art product is not the objective or goal of any art motivation. Rather, the goal is to develop a more sensitive, aware youngster. An increased awareness of textural differences and tactile sensations cannot be achieved by telling a youngster to include more tactile properties in a painting. Time is needed in which to develop an awareness of a variety of textures and to experience these on an intimate basis. To merely "correct" the painting itself does not provide the experience of textures; it might be much more effective to allow the picture to be completed in the way that is important to the youngster. Once this is done, the broadening of the youngster's experience in tactile impressions can be undertaken.

Involving children in art experiences may take many different directions. The motivation itself should vary considerably, depending upon the conditions of the classroom, the interest of the students, and the objectives of the teachers, but it should also vary just for variation's sake. If the class is concerned with the expression of emotion, quite a different motivation would be necessary than if a problem in design or aesthetics were to be considered.

Youngsters of this age are becoming more aware of beauty, although this must be interpreted in their terms and not the teacher's. Time for thought and contemplation is required if children are to become more aware of and more

PLATE 30.

"My Barber," painted by a fourteen year old boy. This child has used flat areas of color and has not attempted to show light and shade. Notice the awareness of detail: the floor at an angle, the scissors and comb, the barber pole, and the Barber sign painted on the back of the window.

PLATE 31.

"Cityscape." The use of colored paper at this age provides an opportunity for overlapping, seeing forms abstracted, and experimenting with color variations, without the necessity to develop drawing skills. Art can take many forms, as in this impression of a city.

sensitive to the design qualities of various art forms. Turning a picture 180 degrees and looking at it as if it were an abstraction, relieved of its content, can call attention to the distribution of the various forms and colors. Obviously a painting of loneliness would be quite different in design quality from a painting portraying excitement. The design of an object as simple as a spoon can arouse critical discussion by means of searching questions. "Why isn't a spoon made out of cloth, or paper, or glass?" "Would the addition of holes in the handle of a spoon, or bumpy roses embossed upon the spoon bowl help or hinder its function?" "Would the spoon work better if its bowl were turned sideways?" The purpose of these questions would be to stimulate thinking about the relationship between material and expression and to sensitize youngsters to the design elements in their environment. This is not a time for listing or memorizing rules to follow; rather, it should be an opportunity for developing an awareness of art as an aspect of life.

A word needs to be said about motivating the youngster who has lost all self-confidence in art expression. This is the "I can't do it" child. It is relatively easy to motivate youngsters who are eager to draw and paint, but the child who refuses to budge may be the person who needs the experience the most. Often the problem can be easily solved by using a material that is not "sissy" or "arty." Clay, wood, or other three-dimensional materials are often a good way to start. A second approach is to start where the youngster himself is. This may be simply having Erik cut out racing cars and put these into a mobile or collage, or, if the problem is deeper than this, having him put some of his thoughts on a large cardboard, even cut out headlines from the newspaper so as to make his resentment an issue that can be dealt with openly. To try to coax a child, or to tell a youngster that he really can draw, or to make something for the teacher just this once, may do nothing but make Erik even more sure that art is not for him. The motivation, however it is given, or however it is developed, should provide the youngster with a desire to create and not be aimed at getting projects done, or putting grades in a book, or keeping youngsters busy.

Subject Matter

Youngsters have little opportunity in the usual classroom to have any voice in the subject matter covered. Mathematics follows a pattern that is difficult to break; history, science, and English are outlined in advance of the students' involvement in the class itself. In art, however, there is ample opportunity for the art teacher to make the content truly a matter over which students have some control. With the developing awareness of themselves as individuals with opinions, tastes, and voices of their own, it is important that students be involved in the planning in such a way that the projects become essentially theirs. In one study (Brittain, 1968a) the junior high school students clearly saw themselves as the source of ideas for art. In fact, the students involved in this particular study voiced amazement that adults would actually be interested in what junior high school students thought. One of the important roles that the teacher can play is that of an earnest listener who can make these youngsters feel that their thoughts and ideas are worthy of consideration and that they are not necessarily limited by having to look to the teacher for inspiration.

With the hope of broadening youngsters' horizons, more and more teachers take junior high school classes on museum trips. On one such expedition the children were supplied with sketch pads on which to draw whatever was most impressive there. One boy was most excited by an unfamiliar type of light switch, and so that is what he drew. Another child drew the fire extinguishers. As far as these children were concerned, the exhibit itself was of no great interest.

FIGURE 210.

A junior high school youngster's world provides excellent subject matter for art expression. A boy shows himself at home watching television; he has attempted to represent the room and furniture three-dimensionally.

Occasionally topics are pushed upon the person responsible for an art program, topics that may actually be detrimental to the development of a meaningful art education program. A poster for the local women's club bake sale, mass-p oducing table decorations for the annual teachers' meeting, or making a monogram for the gym team may all be worthwhile, so possibly the art teacher could handle a few of these tasks some Saturday morning; but the art program has a much greater role than to fill its time with busy work and service activities.

Ideally, no subject matter should be necessary. The purpose in any subject suggestions is to extend the frame of reference of students to enable them to see many possible avenues of expression, to encourage them to be self-motivated, and to use the arts for pleasurable, meaningful expression.

Feelings and Emotions

The expression of feelings and emotions should play an important part in the school art program. There is little opportunity for youngsters of this age to give vent to their feelings; sometimes they bubble to the surface and are expressed strongly outside school, and sometimes in school. The following suggestions should be used flexibly, and any motivation should open up many possible ways of expression rather than converging on a particular method.

Putting emotions and frustrations into art requires a great degree of sensitivity. A topic such as "Being Alone" would recall in every student walking home in the dark, or being left alone one Saturday, or the uncomfortable feeling of not knowing anyone in a crowd. Other topics could relate to feelings of joy or sadness, of love or hate, of contentment or anger, or to misgivings in a social situation. Sometimes the adolescent has special heroes or secret infatuations with a person far removed. Students might portray "My Favorite Person" or "The Sinister Thief." Sometimes these feelings will come out in abstract paintings, sometimes in three-dimensional constructions, and sometimes in direct representation.

The Self and Others

Youngsters now have an increased awareness of their own physical development and have a curiosity about the opposite sex. It is at this age that drawing from posed models may make an impact such as no other subject matter can. Munro (1956) even went so far as to suggest that the adolescent be given the opportunity to observe and draw from the nude model. Certainly hiding the body seems

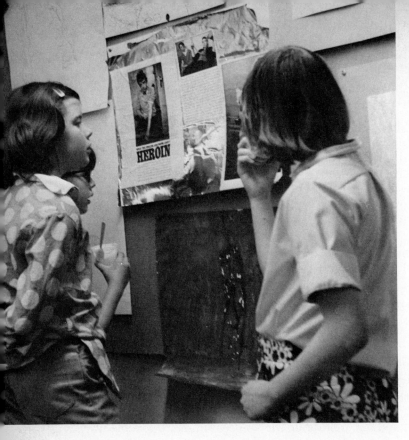

FIGURE 211.
Young adolescents are not isolated from the real world and its troubles. They are continuously exposed to all the elements of life within our society.

more the concern of adults than of youngsters; there is no doubt that pictures of nude females are readily available to most junior high school boys, although this is usually in the boys' lavatory and not the art room. However, the best time to introduce the drawing of the nude might be in the elementary school so that the junior high school youngster would treat the body in a matter-of-fact manner. Modeling in clay from the posed figure provides another means of expression. A plastic three-dimensional form can be readily altered and allows for showing action. The pose should be short for any type of presentation, and the model should be used only as a stimulus.

During drawing or modeling, care should be taken to provide ample opportunity for both haptic and visual representations, and the pose should be treated in such a way that the student can identify with the model through personal experience. That is, the drawing of the model should not be a lesson on proportion, balance, anatomy, or a study in light and shade. Rather, it should be an opportunity to see the model as someone involved in life, with problems, with faults, and with whom the student can feel some empathy.

With man as a subject, the number of suitable topics seems endless. Man (in the generic sense) has always been a fascinating subject for artists everywhere, and the twelve to fourteen year old is no exception. Large cutouts or silhouettes, or detailed drawings of a hand or eye, make a good start. Making self-portraits—without the use of a mirror, with a mirror; in small scale, in large; drawn, sculpted in clay, or carved full size out of styrofoam—is even somewhat frightening. Drawing others, sometimes lots of others, can be exciting if many of these are combined, with drawings by others, into groups or crowds. Rock festivals, crowded buses, or street scenes can be created. People are everywhere and may be used as models even though they may not know it. Youngsters themselves can be their own models, feeling the muscles stretch as they move, or noting the change in sensation as they put their heads down on their knees.

School Life

There are certain activities within school itself that provide ample stimulus for expression. These can range all the way from annoyance at some seemingly arbitrary rule to participation in a forthcoming fair or dance. In democratic society the opportunity should exist for constructive participation at all ages. This cannot be learned easily, but the opportunity to suggest changes in established

FIGURE 212.
Concern for themselves, resentment at rules, and awareness of the problems in society are all becoming important to junior high school students. Clarity, good lettering, and neatness in posters will come later.

procedures or to have a voice in meaningful decisions should always be encouraged. The prospect of making protest posters can be exciting in itself, and the concern for clarity of message and impact on the viewer can develop a real understanding of the problems that some of the artists in our society have to face. A serious school election, or events outside school such as a community action program can provide the impetus for expression; however, nothing will turn youngsters away from art so fast as the suggestion that everyone make a poster to help raise funds for the local civic club benefit. Dress regulations in the school, rules about passing in the hall, or reactions to shortening the lunch hour would all make excellent topics.

Since many students feel that school is something to put up with, art activities can play a dual role of helping students express their feelings and helping them become involved in school in a meaningful way. Any subject can be transformed into an art form: drawing or painting a dull, dull textbook or feelings in the stomach when you are unprepared for a test can be put into abstract form. Making your favorite teachers from boxes, sketching the band or the basketball team, or cartooning the cafeteria staff are all suitable. Of course there are "established" activities that should not be ignored if they lend themselves to the expression of this age group: the daily bulletin, the PTA newsletter, the memos to staff, and even the bulletin boards can be exciting if the students are responsible for layout, distribution, and keeping them current. Halls can be decorated or the basement repainted.

It must be mentioned that graffiti can also be an art form. Usually adults, particularly those adults in charge of cleaning and maintenance, view marks on walls, whether on buses or in public toilet areas, as willful destruction of property. Readily available spray cans make it easy to paint an area quickly. Graffiti are usually done by young adolescents who give vent to their emotions and communicate to others their sentiments without having to take the punishment of society. Possibly if these youngsters had an acceptable place where these feelings could be expressed, the drive to mark up public property would be reduced. Although those who mark their concerns and feelings on public property may not be considered artistically talented, they may be creative. One study (Schwartz and Dovidio, 1984) compared college students who admitted to having drawn on walls or desks in their younger days with students who never did that; the graffitists scored higher as a group on a creativity test. It is common to think that a young adolescent who marks up a wall with a personal message of some sort would be shunted aside in our educational system, but obviously the students in this study made it to college. The desire to express oneself in graffiti is not limited to those who are considered poor achievers.

FIGURE 213.

Sometimes expressing resentment at society, and sometimes just for fun, graffiti demonstrate the innate desire for expression beyond society's approved limits. This wall has become an outdoor art museum, recording the feelings of many individuals.

Design and Nature

The area of design is unlimited in its applications, and at this age an awareness of beauty and a concern for ornamentation are developing. Many shapes, patterns, and forms in shells, wood, moss, or other objects in nature can provide the stimulation for design experiences. Adapting forms from nature can be quite interesting. The discovery of a logical order in an orange or an apple core may come as a surprise. Leaves or bark of trees, dripping water or ripples on a puddle, a skeleton of a fish, or a frog's back can all be transformed. The camera makes an excellent means of studying such forms, but drawing them directly in greatly enlarged dimensions will provide insight into amazing dynamic design qualities of our natural environment.

Found objects, inventions made from industrial scraps, collections of discarded materials such as broken glass or bottles are all possible ingredients to include in collages, or to mount in frames for exhibit, or to surround with plaster. A personal insignia, such as a name on a jacket or a made-up coat of arms on a banner, not only provides some identification of the student in a tangible way but also is historically one means of identifying a region or a warring faction. Nature constantly provides a source for inspiration, either directly, as with tree branches to assemble, mount, or modify; or indirectly, as clouds making constantly changing patterns and moods. For the visually aware student, shade and shadow are worth investigating; for the more haptically inclined, there is the desire to convey impressions of movement and mood. For all, the discovery of positive and negative space can be the starting point for creative experimentation.

Art Materials

At any age art materials should play a secondary role in the art program. The material should be geared to the expressive needs of students. Now youngsters have become physically capable of dealing with almost any material, although plaster will still be spilled and paint will still drip, but the experience of working with these materials provides the best means of understanding them.

Care must be taken to insure that art is something special. The usual 12 by 18 inch size sheet of paper may no longer be the ideal size, and crayons may not be the best material to use for color. Both large materials and small materials can be intriguing at this age. The large materials provide the opportunity for real physical involvement, and the problem of doing a painting that is three feet wide and five feet high is a challenge in itself. At the same time, small muscle control makes it possible to do detailed ink drawings.

Because of the increased ability to work with complex materials, craft projects are often used now. These provide excellent opportunities for a variety of artistic experiences and expression of a utilitarian nature. However, the continued use of craftlike material may encourage a narrowing of interests and a concealment of true expression rather than an opening up of new avenues to explore. This is not to say that youngsters should not have the opportunity to concentrate on one art material. However, if a student constantly uses one material mechanically, producing without new discoveries, this may become a substitute for expression.

Depth of expression can be achieved in many ways. One way would be to concentrate on one material, using it for a variety of subject matter; another approach in depth would be to concentrate on a particular subject matter and utilize a great number of materials in its development. For example, the human figure can be sketched, painted, modeled in clay, abstracted, dismembered, drawn in detail, and so forth. At the same time, tempera or acrylic paint can be used to express emotions, study bold colors, compose abstract forms, communicate ideas, or illustrate a theme or mood.

New materials are now available for use in art classes, many of which were not readily available a few years ago. Although tempera paint is most commonly used, there is an increasing number of other paint materials that are suitable. Polymer, vinyl, and other water-soluble paints are available. Plastics of a great variety are usable, as are new drawing instruments and inks. Some of these new materials, and some old ones too, are potential hazards in the classroom; the possibility of strong odors, fire hazards, and danger to the skin are important considerations. A review of these problems and hazards of art materials was carefully documented by Siedlecki (1968, 1972). Mortality studies of artists and others (Franklin, 1981) show the risks of prolonged exposure to solvents and chemicals in paint. There is a Center for Occupational Hazards, which publishes a newsletter containing current information on hazardous materials and the legal as well as health implications of their use in the schools.

Probably the oldest three-dimensional material is clay. By now the potter's wheel can be mastered. As with many other projects, no preplanning is necessary. When working on a potter's wheel it is almost impossible for the beginning student to start with a preconceived notion of the finished product, for much depends upon the consistency of the clay, the speed of the wheel, and the positioning of the hands and the body. But clay can also be used as an excellent modeling material, and the casting of plaster molds can be exciting. Mixing cement with expanded mica, or plaster with sawdust, provides a material that can be both built up and carved down.

Many of the art materials that have been discussed in earlier stages are also appropriate at this level. However, it is important to make sure that any materials used are also used by professional artists. That is, the student should be able to identify with those people who consider art a vocation, rather than thinking of art as a childhood activity. Experimenting with the qualities of charcoal and india ink with brush can stimulate an interest in the potential use of these materials. Exploring other possibilities, such as making papier mâché moon men, paper-bag puppets, or plaster-and-wire space sculptures should involve the most reluctant youngster in art materials. When children are encouraged to invent or imagine unusual forms, such as strange machines, environments, and animals, their imagination can definitely be boosted (Kincaid, 1964). It should once more be emphasized that the main function of art materials is to provide a means for increased knowledge, understanding, and expression in the arts and not to be an end in themselves.

Computers and Art Education

By the time youngsters arrive in junior high school, they will have been exposed to computers in a number of different settings. For young children, the computer is just another part of school. For many children, the computer is part of the household, with its use ranging all the way from computer games to business purposes, letter writing, or balancing the family budget. Some serious

FIGURE 214.
Although the initial use of a computer to produce art may be exciting, the novelty soon wears off and youngsters find that the electronic image is removed from personal sensitivity.

questions have been raised about the uncritical acceptance of the computer into our daily lives. One review of the area claims that there are unavoidable dangers in the use of computers in education unless some serious, far-reaching critical questions can be answered (Sloan, 1985). There are also dangers in accepting the computer as part of an art program unless a clear purpose in using the computer is determined. That is, we must realize that the technology available in computer programs is comparable to other media, and we should utilize the best features of computer graphics programs for furthering and understanding the arts; the computer should not determine the content of art or how it should be taught.

With each new advance in technology there have been predictions of dramatic changes in the way children would be taught. Radio was supposed to bring the world into the classroom. Motion pictures were expected to revolutionize the way children learned. DiBlasio (1983) quotes Thomas Edison's 1919 remarks that the moving object on the screen would bring the subject before the children, and the cramming of indigestible knowledge into unwilling minds would be eliminated, with children scrambling for good seats in the classroom and begging for more films. Obviously, this has not been the case. The television screen and video tapes have gone through the same cycle, and computers will follow the same pattern. However, they do add to the art teacher's arsenal, and just as we have numerous films or tapes available for children to view, there is an increasing amount of software available for computer instruction.

Preschool children scribble. A three year old given a pencil will make a variety of marks on the page. If the same child is given a marking pen, the same general configuration will result. In using the computer with young children, there is no reason to believe that other images will suddenly appear or that youngsters will suddenly start drawing as if they were several years older. Many of the programs for computer graphics include a variety of line widths and textures and the ability to increase or decrease sizes or to straighten lines or make perfect circles. All of these attributes seem to be secondary to the ability to instantly erase what has been drawn. Preschool children seem to enjoy the experience of exploring the possibilities of the computer, but no more than any other material; in the process of printing, the images produced seem somewhat remote from the children's intentions.

An eight year old boy might make a drawing of a war scene. This is to be expected, considering the continual news and television views of conflicts throughout the world. On a computer screen, the boy does the same forms. However, now he has the opportunity to make the bullets fly through the air, to erase the planes that are shot down, or to rotate his cannons so as to give a three-dimensional appearance. If a color graphics program is available, a sense of realism can be incorporated into the image. It could be questioned whether this is an improvement and an artistic extension of the youngster's images. Producing a product does not necessarily mean an elevating experience, whether the product was produced by pen or by a computer.

Adolescents may be attracted to computers for producing a variety of art forms. Clements (1985) describes with enthusiasm the interest this age shows for utilizing the software available. He notes that schools may have expensive equipment for photography or ceramics, and most schools are already equipped with a variety of microcomputers for a variety of instructional purposes. Adolescents seem more interested in utilizing this technology than do younger children. Although it is clear that the software itself has limitations, and the image produced has a machinelike quality, devoid of personal drawing idiosyncrasies, it may be these characteristics that make it more appealing to the adolescent. It is relatively easy to blame the machine for errors, to have a distance between the product and the artist; it may be less personally threatening to manipulate forms produced at the touch of a button than it is to become involved in the creative product. For the intimidated adolescent or the insecure individual, utilizing a program on a microcomputer may provide the incentive for involvement in the arts. However, there is no evidence that using a computer will in itself have any positive effect on youngsters' attitude toward art or toward school. They may use the computer, but that doesn't mean they like it. A two year study (Griswold, 1984) of 288 children followed from the fourth to sixth grade found that participating in computer assisted instruction in reading and math did nothing to change the attitude of these children toward those subjects or toward school. Perhaps it is because, as Gottlieb (1986) has mentioned, teachers don't have a full understanding of how to use the computer, so programs are apt to be drill-oriented. Salomon and Gardner (1986) speculate that computers would be used differently in different school situations: to enhance acquisition of specified concepts in rigid schools and to explore newer possibilities in open schools. It is this latter type of exploratory usage that would best serve the art program.

The art room has been viewed in the past as a good center for the production of a variety of school related posters, notices, newspapers, and sundry matters involved with layout and lettering. Microcomputers can reduce these tasks to a manageable and sometimes interesting experience for junior high school students. The tedious lettering and amateurish quality of student-produced notices can disappear. Rather than focusing attention on the copying and construction of various letter forms, students can now look at the assortment of

FIGURE 215.

A computer can make many mundane tasks easier by providing a variety of visual images that can be altered, enlarged, or rotated; thus technical skill is of less concern than arrangement and message.

readily available formats and be concerned with the spacing, size, and importance of the message they are trying to convey. This is not to say that calligraphy is dead, but rather that the computer program has eliminated a good deal of the frustration that youngsters of this age feel when confronted with a mental image that their technical skills cannot produce.

A secondary school without access to computer facilities is strictly at a disadvantage. Classes in mechanical drawing have just about disappeared. This is partially because the need in industry has just about disappeared. Architects and interior designers rely heavily upon the capabilities of computer graphics and software packages to simplify their tasks. The ability to quickly produce a floor plan or a landscaped image by calling up trees, cars, or people without the necessity of long, tedious work makes the job of the designer much more appealing. The high school should not ignore this area.

The advancing field of artificial intelligence has made it possible to program computers to draw various lines and forms on a plotting table, thus generating "art" (Cohen, Cohen, and Nii, 1984). Of course, there are programs developed to teach a number of concepts in the art classroom. One program for teaching color theory (Meier, 1985) was developed at Brown University. This showed the changing appearance of color when modifying the primary colors and reduced the tedious paint mixing or paper pasting exercises that are usually required in teaching these concepts. Anderson (1985) feels that the laser video disk has great potential for the art room. The images can be produced on any television set, can be halted and examined in detail at will, and should never wear out in use. Microcomputers enable students to generate a large number of different solutions to a visual problem in a short time, allowing students to determine which solution they prefer (Ettinger and Roland, 1986). Students can also view computer images, discovering and exploiting their unique visual qualities, but the art teacher must consider whether a particular program will help teach something that is already taught in a better way.

As modern technology develops, the process of teaching art will also change. A number of years ago, it was considered important to teach block printing. These blocks were actually used in the production of books and needed to be the same thickness as the type, which was often set by hand. However, the need for people to produce block prints has long since disappeared. The copy machines can now produce an unlimited number of prints without the necessity of cutting away the nonprinting surfaces, such as on a block print. Lettering, mechanical drawing, and repetitive designs may soon be relegated to electronic machines, leaving students free to spend time in more creative activities.

Although the computer has the ability to free a person from some of the

FIGURE 216.
Education has to counteract the negative effects of the mass media. The expressive arts can provide the means to capture the imagination and stimulate the creativity of young adolescents.

mundane tasks, it also has the ability to arrest the imagination. With young children particularly, the process of drawing and painting provides an understanding and ordering of the environment; the computer images may thwart that development. A blank piece of paper and a drawing tool become an arena for the child's imagination. The push of the crayon, the running paints, the smearing chalk, all lend themselves to images and thoughts that are not possible with a computer screen. It probably is not until about the age of twelve that the mental operations in life can be transferred to a screen. Standard symbols can be varied in size and placement, but the results are predictable, may be repetitious, and lack vitality because the artist manipulates rather than originates.

The question must be asked: Why do we want to use a computer in the area of art anyway? We want to develop a thinking human being who cares about others, who perceives the world sensitively and can put together images and forms to create new configurations. Does the computer help in this process? For some things it may. But to expose a child to a rich environment of sensory experiences—the textures around us, the smell and sound that permeate our environment, the color and its variations, the movement of the wind and aliveness of nature—the computer will not help very much. The teacher in a classroom is responsible for the total development of the children in that room. This means more than just the ability to read intelligently, to manipulate numbers understandably; it also means developing creative, sensitive, aware adults who can think beyond the immediate tasks at hand.

Summary

This stage of development is one of very rapid changes. Girls discover that the mass media think they should be pretty and alluring. Boys' voices begin to change and most of them try to become very masculine; they are exposed to a diverse range of models to emulate, so that the outstanding athlete, or the numbers runner, or a television private eye seems more real than does the grocer down the street. Young adolescents not only want to be well liked by peers but also want and need the respect and attention of adults. The development of a critical attitude has made them aware of the surrounding world, sometimes painfully aware. Their growing concern for naturalism is reflected in drawings of objects and figures. Usually the schema, seen in earlier stages, disappears; for some children the discrepancy between feeling themselves to be adults and seeing their art products as childish brings a shock.

Creative growth must be an integral part of the art program. This is especially true between the ages of twelve and fourteen, when children become much more critical of their own work; the pressure to conform to adult standards of behavior or to the standards of the crowd may work to stifle the creative urge. The art teacher plays a vital role in developing individuality in expression, in providing the opportunity to delve deeply into an area of interest, and in showing that the thoughts and ideas of youngsters of this age are welcome. The art room should have an atmosphere that is free and flexible enough to support experimentation. It is important to stress that every project in which the child becomes involved should be accepted without any outside criterion or evaluation. That is, the child who produces pleasing looking products and the youngster who is not doing the type of work that suits the teacher's aesthetic taste should be treated with equal respect. This in no way means that a laissez-faire attitude should prevail. The very opposite is true. The half-hearted attempt, the stereotype, and the presence of copying should all be clear indications to the teacher that the program is not a meaningful one. To stimulate children's thinking, to have them come to grips with a problem, and to encourage a depth of expression are all much more important than making pretty end products. Art is not merely a subject matter area; it is the expression of the total individual. As children grow into adults the art program should constantly change to meet their needs.

It is unfortunate that school systems are arranged in such a way that at the onset of adolescence a program designed to provide an opportunity for the expression of feelings, emotions, and sensitivities should be dropped for the majority of the secondary school population. Attitudes that young adolescents develop from their art program in school will determine their future interest and participation in the arts. It is therefore vital that teachers of this age group show a high degree of involvement and enthusiasm in the art experience.

Related Activities

1. Compare a twelve year old girl's representation of females over several months. Are there any changes in drawings that reflect maturation? Compare these drawings with representations by girls a year younger.

2. Collect the drawings of a seventh grade. What proportion of the class is displaying visual tendencies by drawing distant objects smaller? What proportion apparently is showing a nonvisual type of space representation?

THE AGE OF REASONING

3. Observe the working process while students are using clay. Which youngsters give a subjective interpretation of the topic rather than a visual? How does this compare with their approach to painting?

4. Record examples of behavior that show the change from an unconscious approach to that of a critical awareness of the child's own actions. Are there any indications of the child's becoming critically aware of his own drawings?

5. Have children become aware of joints when drawing figures? Are differences in size and age indicated? Collect examples of such drawings. Are there differences in the age at which these changes occur?

6. Observe a class for several sessions. Can you pick out some students who seem to be less involved in their art activities? How does their work show this lack of involvement? Analyze some of the possible reasons for hesitancy or fear of expression. Plan definite steps to take to improve the meaningfulness of the art experience.

12

The Period
of Decision

Adolescent Art
in the High School
Fourteen–Seventeen Years

The Importance of High School Art

Art has by this stage of development become the product of conscious effort. For students in high school, art has become something they can do or leave alone. With young children art is primarily an expression of the self, done unconsciously. Eight year olds will draw like eight year olds even if they have not had much opportunity to use art materials. Sixteen year olds, on the other hand, will draw in the same way that they have been drawing for the past three or four years, unless they have had the opportunity and the desire to improve their artistic skills. This period is important, then, because it marks the beginning of purposeful learning in art. Art in the high school takes on a different atmosphere. It is now geared largely toward the teaching of skills and the development of positive attitudes toward art, yet students are now old enough to have established their own opinions and consequently may or may not accept

FIGURE 218.
In many respects the high school student is an adult: mentally, physically, and sometimes legally. The art program has to be relevant for a knowledgeable generation.

teacher values. For some, art is looked upon as something unrelated to the drive toward vocational goals; for others, art becomes that goal.

For most teenagers, art is no longer a part of their lives. At least on the conscious level, most sixteen and seventeen year old youngsters will not feel that art is essential to their needs. Art is constantly around them, it is dictating the clothes they wear, the buildings they live in, the packaging that induces them to buy, and the automobile they are saving for, but this is not part of what these youngsters consider art. For most high schoolers, art is something that was fun, but that belonged to the elementary school. Only about one out of seven high school students elects art when it is available, although half the schools do not offer art at all. The larger secondary schools are most likely to offer art courses, but even here students are often advised not to take art courses because of the fear that the more capable students will not be able to get into college unless their program is filled with the usual academic subjects. The fact that colleges do accept credits taken in high school in art is either not known or ignored. At any rate, art as an elective in high school is taken by a very small percentage of students.

The general public may not consider art an important part of learning; society seems to have accorded art courses a very minor place in the curriculum. There may be good reason for this. The program of art is often geared toward grooming students for an art career and giving some sort of recognition to those who are supposedly talented. For those teenagers who feel they do not have the talent (and this obviously includes most of them), the possibility of flunking or getting a poor mark in art is not appealing. Even so, not all art classes are filled with talented youngsters, because there are always a few students whom the guidance counselor feels must take a few "easy" courses so as to graduate. For the most part, however, art has not been in the mainstream of interests for students in the high school. This is really sad when we consider that, both for an individual's needs and for society's needs, art can fulfill a real purpose.

There is a great need to bring art closer to the conscious awareness of students in the high school. These are the people who will be making decisions in the future about our society, and it is vital to make art a part of their thinking. Many philosophers and artists have lamented the visible condition of our world, but efforts to change the elements that comprise it will have little success unless the need for this change is made apparent to the citizens of tomorrow. In today's society there is very little opportunity for self-identification, very little opportunity to feel responsible for what one is doing, very little opportunity to master a portion of one's life. Increasingly, demands are coming from sources outside the self: the hours one keeps are decided by the job requirement, the clothes one wears are decided by designers and fashion magazines or peer group pressure, the house one lives in has been built by someone else, the car that is driven was made miles away and is serviced by others, the food one eats is grown elsewhere and purchased in impersonal stores, and to build a fire outdoors or add on a room to one's house requires special permits from an unknown official. As yet society has not fettered art expression. There is a great need to provide a touch of saneness and a contact with one's own thinking, and the high school art program is a valid place for this to happen.

The High School Student

For the past ten, eleven, or twelve years of life, high school students have spent a considerable length of time in classrooms. Although there has been some experimentation in organization, students have typically spent six or more hours each day in classes with others of the same age and with a teacher in charge. For some, the age of compulsory education cannot be over soon enough. With others, the end of high school means that they now have a choice in deciding their own futures. However, graduation from high school does not necessarily mean the end of society's restrictions for adolescents. If they have a license to drive, they must pay an additional premium for car insurance; in most states they cannot legally drink or buy alcoholic beverages; their credit is no good; and generally teenagers receive the message that even after high school they are not fully trusted in adult society.

Conflicting pressures are brought to bear on adolescents by their three social groups: the family, the peer group, and the school. Like young adolescents, older adolescents are concerned about their crowd and with independence from adult domination; they are still seeking to establish an identity. But they have become a great deal more aware of the adult world of responsibility. They are also beginning to be aware of the fact that they must soon be on their own and must fit into society in order to make a living, although as many as a third of these students may already be working at part-time jobs. Love is no longer associated with fantasy and T.V. personalities, but begins to be more closely tied to the nearest members of the opposite sex and the prospects of marriage. Adult responsibilities may be only a year or two away, and it sometimes comes as a shock for girls to see a friend, just a year ahead of them, becoming a wife or mother. This is a time for many decisions. Art can play a special role with young people, if the art program is responsive to their needs.

Sex has begun to play an important role. There is no doubt that the awakening of sexual urges gives rise to some of the greatest concerns of this age. Girls

436

FIGURE 219.

This elaborate doodle is an art form in itself. Not all art is done by students in art class.

are bombarded with advertisements about how to make themselves more femininely alluring by the use of hair rinses, deodorants, cosmetics, by squeezing or padding the body, or by various dress styles. For boys, greater attention is often focused upon muscle building and attaining masculinity. This is a real problem for youngsters who develop later than their classmates. Added to all of this, of course, is the general feeling that somehow discussing sex with adults is taboo. The rise in venereal disease among the high school age population indicates increasing sexual activity. Half of the births to fifteen to nineteen year olds are illegitimate. It has been shown that in other cultures this uncomfortable period between puberty and marriage may be considerably shorter. Although some girls leave high school for marriage or childbirth, the marriage ceremony for others can sometimes be delayed well beyond college. High school students have not outgrown their concern about themselves. Adolescents are concerned about their hair, the pimples on their faces, and the proper clothes to wear. They practice before a mirror to perfect the image they hope to project. The older and closer to graduation the students become, the more they decide that they will have to live with themselves as they are. The crowd is still important, especially as a reinforcement of one's own feelings.

Modern adolescents are a new breed. They see more, know more, do more, avoid inactivity at all costs. They drive cars, trucks, dune buggies, and motor-

THE HIGH SCHOOL STUDENT

cycles; travel here and abroad; have considerable buying power for the artifacts of culture; initiate trends in food, music, dance, and lifestyles; at eighteen they can vote, and in some states they can marry and enter into binding contracts. They have more autonomy than any past generation of adolescents and yet are subjected to authoritarian control in school.

Everyone knows of the five year old who is anxious to be a fireman when he grows up, but rarely do we find a sixteen year old who is this definite about vocational goals. The possibility of making a real choice of a lifetime career is a frightening thought for the graduating senior. Often the choice is accidental. For the youngster whose family is less financially solvent, the part-time job may become a full-time occupation. For the more academically successful student, dear old Dad's college may be the easiest route into the insurance business. Few youngsters are able to maintain their idealism beyond eleventh grade, and earlier romantic interests in art are soon put aside. At twelve or fourteen, the possibility of becoming an artist may have sounded very nice, particularly for boys who imagined themselves painting delightful nudes in some attic. The idea of sending a high school student on to college as an art major may sound like the beginning of a fulfilling, interesting career, but this may not be at all true. In a survey comparing art, English, and psychology graduate students, Whitesel (1980) found that 82 percent of the art students lacked career counseling, and half of them were uncertain about their career goals. Education in art does not necessarily lead to an art career, but the values gained in pursuing the arts are important in themselves. Most college students who major in art never get an art-related position, but more often find employment as purchasing agents, insurance representatives, travel agents, and the like. The free-lance artist, painting in a private north-lighted studio and selling paintings to wealthy connoisseurs, is a myth. In following 31 former art students' careers, Getzels and Csikszentmihalyi (1976) found that, after five years, 15 former students had left the field of art or were unknown, 7 had stopped painting and were in art only peripherally, and 9 still continued in the field of art, with one outstanding achiever.

The Adolescent and Society

Puberty is generally recognized as being the end of childhood. Girls usually begin a period of rapid growth at about eleven years, and by menarche at about thirteen they will have developed the usual feminine bodily characteristics. Girls do not reach their full mature height until about seventeen. Boys start to shoot up about two years later than girls; they do not start slowing down until fifteen or sixteen, and they reach adult height at about nineteen. Their voices may begin to change, the Adam's apple grows, and a trace of fuzz appears on their faces at about fifteen. With both sexes there are skin changes, and it is not unusual for body parts to grow at different rates. All these changes are of concern to these youngsters and obviously have an effect upon how they view themselves in relation to the rest of society.

When adults say they do not know what the younger generation is coming to, they are speaking about the fifteen to seventeen year old. It is rather strange to consider the fact that these are the members of society who seem to be constantly getting into trouble. They are the ones who are caught speeding, the ones who experiment with drugs, the ones who put on the protest demonstration. Twenty-five percent of the reported crimes are committed by this age group (Carnegie Council, 1980). Adolescents are becoming more and more concerned with social problems and cannot accept the values of an older generation without testing them. Parents come in for their share of resentment, and the generation gap may be more a gap in understanding than in age. With changes in the family structure, there are more working mothers and more single-parent families. Sixteen year olds have little opportunity for rebelling in a socially acceptable manner, and too often parents are seen as rule makers. There are rather strict laws about child labor, which give older adolescents little

FIGURE 220.
One function of creative expression is an outlet for resentment against society at large or even the school environment. A seventeen year old boy clearly shows his opinion of food in the school cafeteria.

opportunity to find a place within the larger society. Society itself is responsible for some of this conflict, because it does not provide the means by which sixteen year olds can feel that they have a contribution to make or that this contribution will be accepted by the world of adults.

Some educators and psychologists now feel that high school is an affront to the adolescent—an insult. A few go so far as to suggest that it is no longer appropriate (or, possibly, legal) to require attendance, insisting that compulsory attendance violates individual rights (Weinstock, 1973). With earlier maturity, greater responsibility and accountability, and guaranteed rights as private citizens, the high school population is more truly composed of young adults, although most school administrations or criticizing parents are reluctant to admit it.

Yet the mechanics of education are changing. Some programs allow students credit for work in the community. In some places capable seniors move on to junior college for some of their credits or else omit the senior year entirely. The schools are participating in the life of the community, utilizing valuable resources of people and institutions. Schools can become part of a larger human resources center, serving a broader population—the entire community. In small towns the school has traditionally been a social center, anyway, along with the church.

The Secondary School Environment

Adults have the opportunity in our free society to make decisions about where they will work, the kind of people they want to be with, or if they want to be a part of society at all. The economically disadvantaged adult male has less opportunity for this freedom, but even he has a right to speak up, and this right is protected by law. For the youngster there is no comparable freedom. In fact, the law is usually quite definite in requiring certain courses in high school and school attendance for a specific number of years; even the number of days of attendance is usually clearly specified, and if the student is not there, everybody gets excited. Society looks upon the public schools as an extremely important part of the training of individuals to perpetuate society. Youngsters are admonished to graduate from high school, and if they reject the school system their chances for economic success are severely limited.

Although society may place a high value on an education, the youngster in the secondary school may view this in quite a different light. Often the high school is looked upon as something to survive rather than as something to enjoy. The successful student has learned to cope with the system but may not be getting the most out of the learning situation. It is fairly common for students not to study anything but what will appear on examinations; usually the main thing learned in a classroom is what the teacher expects rather than an understanding of the subject. It is a question of survival with the least amount of effort, and it is the rare teacher who is able to instill the classroom with an atmosphere of excitement for learning. Peer groups are typically defined by a shared philosophy: either that of "getting by" or of "getting ahead."

The typical high school program is made up of many isolated subjects that have a tradition from the past as solid academic requirements. Learning is fragmented, and the student has no choice but to attend one class after another according to the bell, which in itself may interrupt learning. Girls seem to get more satisfaction from school than boys, but for both, school tends to be a dull place where interest is found in the unexpected happening rather than in learning.

The art program must be one that involves students in hands-on, creative activities, not just lectures about art. For that matter, there is danger in assuming that adolescents will be receptive to lectures on any subject. In a recent experiment, designed to teach physics to humanities students in a prestigious university, Lancaster (1985) reports that a student complained that if she stopped to absorb a concept, she'd lose the next three points of the lecture. All students probably develop psychological buffers to insulate themselves from the wear and tear of the school. This detachment means that feelings of joy or distress are minimized, so the students' greatest complaint is boredom.

Rosenthal and Conway (1980) tested the theory that misbehavior in school may be typical of the more creative students. After administering both verbal and nonverbal tests of creativity to 57 Australian high school sophomores, they determined that nonconformity is not linked with higher levels of creativity. A study by Walker (1982) discovered that high school students who were judged as creative by their teachers tend to have positive attitudes toward their schools, whether these are traditional or progressive. Perhaps creative students are better able to cope with the school environment and are able to achieve satisfaction through socially acceptable means.

Students consider education primarily as the imposition of already established truths, with little or no concern paid to their personal needs or desires. Schools rarely have a course aimed at providing high school students with knowledge about themselves, their own struggle in society, or even about the dreams and wishes they may have for the future. The usual academic program for those who will attempt to go on to college has no real relationship to objects, people, or jobs. The alternate choice that students have is the vocational program, which is concerned primarily with providing job skills.

To some extent the secondary school system may be caught in its own web.

If the goal of education is not mastery of information—and many educators have come to this point of view—then the emphasis is on gaining knowledge about where information is to be found, utilizing this information, and developing positive attitudes toward learning. The usual routine of keeping track of the students as they come and go, worrying more about attendance than about ideas, and being concerned with grades rather than achievement may be a real stumbling block to change. There is no doubt that the high school student does build up a resentment to society through the public school experience. It may be that if change is going to be made it has to be made by the segment of the high school program that is most flexible and ready to change. Art seems well suited to lead in this respect.

FIGURE 221.
Personal involvement and satisfaction from an art task should be immediate. Hard work and the development of skills, such as in pottery, may at times be frustrating, but never boring.

The Basis for
Art in the High School

Art in the high school has tended to reflect society's opinions of the adolescent. Too often, controversial subjects are considered dangerous; a teacher who encourages students to think about politics, sex, or marriage, who raises questions about the process of law, or who gets a class involved in local issues may very well find himself looking for a new position the following year. Schools tend to isolate youngsters from the real world, at a time when their energies and idealism can best be incorporated into society. The art courses offered in the high school are apt to be planned well in advance by some committee in the state capitol, and courses have a step-by-arbitrary-step progression that is clearly stated in the syllabus. Sadly left out of the planning is the student, who differs in interests, concerns, and motivation from every other student and from last year to next.

The still life setup, the picture made with water colors, the linoleum blockprint, or the small clay sculpture may not be large enough in impact to involve today's youth. Educators should be able to develop an art program that is distinct in its nature and that helps to satisfy the needs of this age and to unfold possibilities for continued growth. Just because a course has a name implying the area of art does not mean that this course provides opportunities for high school students to become involved in a meaningful way with society, nor does it mean that they are now able to express their feelings and emotions about themselves or the world. The high school art program should be based upon young adults who are involved in and concerned about today's world, not a program that is oriented toward making artists. Living is a challenge, and art should reflect this challenge.

Clark and Zimmerman (1984) have discussed the continuing question concerning just which youngsters the art program should try to reach. There are those educators who hope to identify and measure artistic talent, wishing to channel youngsters with talent into the art program. But talent is on a continuum, from naïve to sophisticated, so it varies in degree. There remain a few unresolved questions. How early can superior talent be identified? Does it perhaps only emerge with maturity? Should high schools gear their programs for these few? Aren't programs that are good for the gifted also good for all students?

There is no correct art. Art has traditionally been a reflection of the culture in which it was found. There are no rules for artistic success, as the rules are made by people, and these are constantly changing. For art to be important it must be a reflection of the individual making it. This is as true at the high school level as it is for the professional artist. Those students who take art as an elective, as a relaxing activity, as a subject to use later as a hobby, as something to relieve the strain of daily living, and as a means of contact with oneself obviously have a variety of ways of utilizing art and a variety of ways of dealing with the world through artistic materials. But so do students who are considered "serious." Holtzman, et al. (1971) gave a great many perceptual, personality, and cognitive tests to eighty-five advanced college students who were judged by their professors to be successful and to have potential. These students had as their major field either abstract art, architecture, or engineering drawing. Highly significant differences were found between these three groups, which led to the conclusions that these three groups had contrasting modes of perception. It seems that there are as many different kinds of art expression as there are students; it would not seem wise to value one kind of expression above another.

Working directly with a material provides a tremendous satisfaction and a release from the pressures of intellectualizing. Most of the mental activity that goes on within the high school environment is limited to prescribed topics. Little opportunity is provided to think or act creatively, as that may be upsetting to the semitranquillity of the classroom. Constantly around us are problems concerned with art. The art program at the high school level should be an active one. The subject matter should be based upon more than the teacher's files, more than just the school environment; it should become a vital part of the community.

The basis for an art program in the senior high school should therefore be the same as that for individuals in society. Its purpose should be to involve students more fully in the culture in which they find themselves; it should provide a means of making tangible changes and the opportunity to face themselves and their own needs.

The Structure of an Art Program

The students who will be in the art program of a senior high school must be the first consideration in any planning. Very few of these students in an art course will actually do anything beyond school with art. Rather, they will become plumbers, clerks, scientists, used car dealers, homemakers, policemen,

FIGURE 222.

One of the purposes of an art program should be to provide the students with some of
the abilities and interests that will keep art important to them once they leave high
school. These young women are learning some of the procedures in weaving.

and so forth. A course of art should not be for the talented students, but for all
students, so that they discover that art is a valuable means of focusing energies
into creative problem solving, not only in school but also after graduation.

Probably the most important element is the attitude that prevails. If an art
course is looked upon as just another academic course with quizzes, examinations, lists of names of famous artists to be memorized, and projects to be
marked, art will lose its significance and impact upon students. Much time and
effort can be spent by the students and by the teacher in what is sincerely
considered a good art program. Such projects may include embossing metal
plaques, designing stained-glass windows, making safety posters, designing
monogrammed napkins, carving book ends, copying various lettering styles, or
carving a football player out of soap. The list of such school-type projects is
unlimited. These parallel the May baskets and sewing cards at the elementary

THE STRUCTURE OF AN ART PROGRAM

level. This approach to art education tends to make a sham out of what should be a vital and dynamic part of the school curriculum.

There is a serious question whether high school students actually learn or retain much from art classes as they are presently taught. A National Assessment of Art (1977) asked nine, thirteen, and seventeen year olds to do some drawing tasks, including drawing a table with four people sitting at it. The drawings were rated on such things as skill in foreshortening and overlapping. Needless to say, the seventeen year olds had more overlapping. However, with one year of art beyond elementary school, 50 percent of the seventeen year olds drew "acceptable" pictures. With four to six years of art beyond elementary school, only 56 percent of the seventeen year olds drew "acceptable" pictures, a minimal improvement at best. It seems that the artistic skills these students acquired with their additional years of classes did not show. The criteria for judging may be at fault; the representation of a table in perspective is not a drawing task that may be automatically equated with good art, and the more haptic student might be concerned with portraying relationships rather than a photographic likeness. But the fact that a national assessment can rule certain drawings as unacceptable puts pressure on teachers of art to conform and to teach specific formulas for success. Such standards, whether from a local administrator or from a national body, may set a direction exactly opposite to that of a meaningful art program.

It is possible to deal with art in such a way as to make a relevant and exciting program. Probably the first element would be to treat the adolescents as adults. The implications of this are great. Nowhere else in the school system can a youngster be looked upon as an important being, one who has a contribution to make, one who is the core of the program. Adults would not be interested in grades or other types of evaluation. Treating high school students as adults implies that we respect their opinions and realize they have had experiences that may go beyond ours in certain areas, and that they have turned to art as a free choice.

The Organization of the Art Class

Art in the high school should not be a program, which has connotations of a set curriculum; art in the high school should be a concept. Ideally there should be no end to what the students are doing. And ideally there should be no beginning either. In an active program students should be able to enter at any time and participate, to become immersed in an art activity, to explore in depth certain avenues of expression, without concern for previous credits earned in intro-

PLATES 32 AND 33.

Plate 32, "Monster," and Plate 33, "Mask,"
were constructed of papier mâché. Adolescents
are often very critical of their own art and can
become easily discouraged if it does not look
like their concept of professional art. However,
using uncommon materials such a papier
mâché can reduce comparison with slick products. As work progresses, this material requires
imaginative planning and flexibility; it also
lends itself well to expressing emotions through
strong form and color.

PLATE 34.

"Flowers," painted by a high school girl. The painting shows a sensitivity toward her subject that might not be shared by all students; for some students, a flower may be quickly rejected as inappropriate subject matter.

PLATE 35.

"Mallards," painted by a high school boy. Sometimes the interests of students are great enough to become a continuing theme in their art. Here a student's interest in birds has grown to such an extent that his work has developed a high degree of proficiency.

ductory art programs or without concern for proper prerequisites. There seems to be no evidence that segregating art students into ability levels has any particular value except to teachers who have a regimented curriculum to follow. Actually, students seeing a variety of activities, exploring many different media, and participating in large constructions can lend an excitement to an art program that cannot be achieved through a step-by-step sequence.

The usual time set aside for art in the curriculum at the high school level is not best suited to art experiences. Sometimes double periods are allowed, but the typical pattern is for the art class to fit in between an English lesson and a gym class. It is obvious that the type of program suggested here cannot fit nicely into a predetermined time schedule, because the involvement of youngsters cannot be automatically switched off after forty-five minutes. There may be reason to believe that art classes should not follow the usual academic class pattern. Possibly the usual pattern is not best for academic subjects either, but certainly art might better be offered on a Saturday morning when three hours at a time would be available for pursuing activities. Assuming that such restrictions as may be imposed by the high school administrators are inflexible, it is possible to live within the confines of daily scheduled periods, but even here other arrangements can often be worked out. The important thing is to remove the art program from the tightly scheduled list of activities and have it more in tune with the youngster's interests and drives than with the clock.

Sometimes it is difficult to even get some students to come to the art room. But it is possible to involve adolescents in art activities in non-school settings.

FIGURE 223.
This lively scene in a busy school cafeteria shows a girl's awareness of her surroundings, and is a successful drawing in spite of the inaccuracies of perspective.

FIGURE 224.
Art need not be limited to the classroom. Out of school programs can involve youngsters who have no time for art or who left school before graduation. Here are two young men involved in an outreach program in Philadelphia.

Out-of-school workshops, occasionally involving youths as apprentices, can be organized to tackle large art projects, painting huge murals, designing and constructing park areas out of neglected land areas, or offering art experiences for young children. Young (1984a) has described an effective outreach art program in Philadelphia, which has involved thousands of Afro-American youths in a community development program.

Although the classroom can be the center of a number of planning and discussion sessions, the real activity of the art class could take place elsewhere. As much as possible, the class should be centered in the community and in the youngster's own life. If some students are involved in architectural planning and building, it does not make sense to put together little models from toothpicks and styrofoam when actual building is going on continually outside school. If some students are involved in landscaping a park, building benches for the

448

area, and ordering trees or discussing planting with the community's building and grounds department, it does not make sense for them to be making sketches or layout designs to be filed in a drawer. If students are involved in painting, the subject matter for these paintings can rarely be found in the art room itself, and there is no reason why pictures or photographs need to substitute for the main street in town. Sketches can be made elsewhere and the final painting can be completed in the classroom itself, but the involvement in the subject matter should not be vicarious.

For those students who develop an interest in sculptural form, the industrial arts room may be a better place to do some planning; but the hammering together of parts and pieces or the welding of steel could probably best be done at those commercial establishments that the youngsters will be able to use once they leave school. Even the firing of clay should probably be in the hands of the youngsters themselves so that they develop an understanding of the firing process and the design and operation of the kiln. Essentially, then, the organization of the art activities should be centered in those parts of the community that can give support and facilities to students once they leave school. The art room should be primarily a central meeting and discussion location and not a closed, isolated studio.

Some questions will undoubtedly be raised about the possibility of students running wild with such a type of organization. This obviously will put a great deal of responsibility upon students. At the same time, it places additional responsibility upon the teacher, for it is no longer possible to control the thinking processes of those youngsters who become self-motivated. It is easier to play the role of prison guard, to have students lined up in neat rows in the classroom, to have all students doing the same project at the same time, to have goals set by the teacher, and to give tests to insure that students are developing those skills that the teacher has decided are important. But this is not art. Art is the quality of being human, a quality that is involved in experiences that provide the opportunity for growth and understanding of oneself and others. The production of some object in which one is not personally involved does not constitute art. The most important task of an art teacher is undoubtedly that of making art important and meaningful to high school students. Art activities are too often planned in a way that insures success. Art is not all sweetness and light, and many failures and frustrations are part of the learning process. The threat of grades or marks is poor motivation; threats are hardly the basis for developing a positive relationship with either art, the art teacher, or oneself. In one year or two, these high school students will no longer be in a position to be told what to do and when to do it. If students can be involved in art activities so that they

FIGURE 225.
What is ugly, what is beautiful? This furnace room is full of valves, pipes, and shut-offs that are often considered ugly, and hidden by fake ceilings or locked doors; but the plumber and perhaps the artist can see these as beautiful.

feel that these are truly theirs, they will be able to turn to the art teacher and others for guidance, but the drive essentially will originate in the youngsters themselves.

There are some procedures in art that need to be understood, such as making a plaster mold for a clay form. But these procedures should not be confused with artistic progress, since an activity such as that can be learned at the tenth grade level or twelfth grade level or not learned at all. Art cannot be preplanned in an arbitrary way. Stringing courses together on a continuum such as is necessary in certain areas of mathematics is not applicable to art. But some state instructional syllabuses view art as a sequence with Art I, followed by Art II, followed by Art III, like the beads that a nursery school child would string together.

Organizing the art room so that it is possible for many art activities to go on at the same time allows a great flexibility in the use of space. Unfortunately, when everyone is trying to do the same thing at the same time, there are bottles of ink all over the place, there are not enough pens, all the flat table space is being used; but the sink that was so crowded the week before when a project in tie and dying was underway is now left vacant. However, it does not have to be that way. Instead, the bored student from the study hall can find some excitement in the art room and get a taste of what goes on. The twelfth grader who is welding some junk together out in the yard can attract some tenth grade boys; the weaving goes on close to the potter; and, in the corner of the room, kitchen plans are being pored over to present to the local contractor next week. The art room can be exciting, confusing, sometimes organized, but never stagnant.

Youngsters of varying abilities and interests cannot be expected to show equal enthusiasm for all types of projects. The particular projects that these youngsters select are not important. The will to learn, with active involvement in a project, is of prime importance. The art teacher should be available for listening and for broadening the possible avenues of action that students take. It is not just his technical ability that becomes important, for he should be more a model of possible ways to explore and to investigate, not one who provides the answers when called upon. It is probably more useful to say "I don't know, but let's find out" than to always have a ready answer available. There must be opportunities for exchanging thoughts at intervals and opportunities for group discussion. Some basic problems may be encountered; an occasional lecture that provides specific information about artistic skill, the problems of architectural design, various methods that have been historically used in printing, or a survey of painting methods may be extremely valuable when the need arises.

FIGURE 226.
Developing new concepts and finding other means of expression for students is part of the teacher's responsibility. Here a lesson in contour drawing seems to have been exactly right for inspiring a drawing that conveys meaning and mood with an economy of line.

Art Activities

One of the most important activities in an art class is the opportunity to paint. Painting has long been considered the most expressive form of art. With painting, much can be expressed that is important to the high school student. There is no reason to plan exercises that lead up to painting, exercises that may be important to the teacher but not to the student. Painting from warm to cool, cutting paper shapes in order to visualize pictorial design, and exercises dealing with positive and negative space are all important at some point, but not necessarily for all students, and certainly not as an introduction to painting. Painting can be done with a range of materials, and there is no reason to expect that students should be in a lockstep procedure. Some students may enjoy polymers and oils, others tempera, and still others water color. To come face to face with an empty painting surface is a challenge, and the experience should be just as fundamental as that faced by the professional painter. Adolescents can easily become discouraged by the primitiveness and naïveté of their drawings and often seem afraid to project their thinking directly upon the paper. They are disturbed by the discrepancy between what they produce and what they feel is appropriate for an adult to draw or paint.

A very direct approach to this problem would be to enlarge the concept of adult art. Certainly the fresh and, in some cases, the blunt painting of some contemporary artists may awaken the adolescent to new possibilities. Even older masters such as Chagall and Dubuffet painted in a very unsophisticated manner. Teachers sometimes overestimate the sophistication of their students and may not understand what students are striving for. The aesthetic preferences of fifteen year olds were compared to what their teachers thought they would like (Rump and Southgate, 1978); secondary teachers had no significant recognition of the types of pictures liked by students. Another fruitful direction is to involve the student with materials and techniques in which the end product is not as readily comparable to professional products. The adolescent has developed the ability to work with more intricate procedures, and in some cases these can be a challenge.

The art program should involve students in their own school experiences. Although one sometimes hears of a program in which music, dance, and drama become thoroughly combined with art, these programs are very few. Frequently the art teacher feels that the rest of the school activities are irrelevant to the art program and for good reason. However, a real involvement of the student in school activities can work for the total benefit of the school itself. Most high schools have an abundance of empty halls. These provide excellent painting surfaces, and there is no reason why art students cannot take advantage of these large blank areas to paint murals. It should be pointed out that a mural is quite different from an easel painting; since the mural will be part of the architectural surface, the shape available presents a problem in which the architecture and the mural must be closely interwoven. Exhibits of paintings can also be displayed in the halls, but these must be ever-changing and carefully labeled. The exhibits become more than merely displaying a student's work for personal pleasure and self-esteem; they become also a means to make all students in the school aware of some of the excitement and variety available in the art area. Painting flats for the school play or designing the backdrops can

FIGURE 227.

The self provides an endless source of subject matter for art, drawing body parts in detail and noting changes in position. Here a boy humorously deals with his own fingers and mouth.

be important if students are involved in planning and take an active part in experimentation. Effects such as the use of film, smoke, flashing lights, and so forth can make this an exciting art experience.

Outside the immediate school is probably the most fruitful area for exploration. In the broad field of art, very few artists are actually painters. Many more people who are considered artists are involved in a wide range of occupations, including architecture, landscape design, interior decoration, industrial design, and so forth. It is not the intent to provide training in these areas to high school students, but rather to involve them in some of these areas and to provide them with some of these skills, so that art does not stop at the closing of the classroom door. There are many areas outside of the classroom in which the planning and designing functions of students can operate. Landscaping a part of the school grounds, making an abandoned piece of property into a small park or playground, developing a series of benches for a bus stop, all make appropriate art projects. It would be a blow to the high school student if these were left in the planning stage; there is no reason why bricks cannot be laid, trees planted, benches cast out of concrete, and playground equipment constructed. It is this type of involvement in a project that can capitalize upon the youngster's intense desire to make a meaningful impression upon society and provide personal satisfaction in the accomplishment.

There is little opportunity in our society for teenagers to become involved in

FIGURE 228.
Seeing the despoiling of the landscape by seemingly endless parking lots can challenge the imaginative thinking of a high school art class to seek more ecologically acceptable solutions.

apprenticeship training or to gain an understanding of the type of work that adults are involved in. Often a youngster will graduate from high school without having done any more manual labor than babysitting or shoveling snow from a sidewalk. Part of the art program can be incorporated into the community functions in a way that no other part of the high school can. Such involvement could include the planning and designing of a section of a house, such as the kitchen, garage, or bathroom. Most building today is done by a builder without the benefit of an architect. Builders often offer a variety of services, and sometimes the involvement of high school youngsters in such a program can be considered an advertising asset by the builders. This means that the art classes will actually be criticizing and evaluating different plans, checking the building codes, seeing the structure under way, and making recommendations as to the type of flooring or location and arrangement of storage space. Often the art program doodles in house plans, but rarely does the student become sufficiently committed to a project to see changes being made or to voice approval or criticism over an actual structure.

The area of art is almost unlimited in its possibilities. Photography can be important if some culmination, such as a publication, is the ultimate goal. Working with sculpture, if the sculptural forms become part of the community, can also be a powerful force. Printing can be worthwhile if it is related to actual printing and publication, such as a school paper and the high school yearbook, which are usually removed from the students' hands and put into those of a commercial printing house. Excellent journals and books, such as the Foxfire series (Wigginton, 1972–1984), contain material collected and articles written by high school students. Almost any art-oriented project can take on meaning if it is one that combines the needs of the adolescent youngster with opportunities to work on real problems.

The Importance of Design

The art program should also provide the basis for cultural directness and honesty. The negative implications and effects upon our thinking processes of accepting falsehoods and imitation as normal should certainly be decried. Pointing out dishonesty and sham when it occurs in architectural planning, in the purchasing of accessories, or in political life should make for a greater realization of such discrepancies.

The high school is an excellent place to begin to reeducate toward a feeling for design as an integral part of the function and use of an object or of a material. Functional design refers to three equally important relationships: the rela-

FIGURE 229.
Sensitivity to the patterns within natural objects provides a basis for understanding the relationship between design and function.

tionship between design and material, the relationship of design to tools or machinery used in its creation, and the relationship between design and purpose. For example, a piece of pottery made on a potter's wheel should look as if it were indeed made on the potter's wheel. If the effects of the working methods are hidden, the truth of functional design is lost. The purpose of a vase may be purely decorative, in which case it needs to be able to stand, or be hung, or be heavy enough so that it will not be easily knocked over. If the purpose of the pot is to hold flowers, however, its glaze must not compete with the flowers, nor should the pot be too wide or narrow for such a purpose. The natural qualities of the materials should always be utilized and preserved as much as possible. Wood, glass, textile, metal, each should be used honestly. Fine workmanship is an integral part of furniture design, and joints and braces need not be hidden under a decorative cover.

It is quite apparent that few people would purchase a toothbrush with a Victorian handle or one with an embossed design of flowers. The bristles of a toothbrush are not arranged in little scalloped designs, nor do they attempt to look like something other than bristles. However, we often find tableware with roses on the handle, lamps with scallops on the shade, and chairs with lion's paws for legs. Average Americans are fairly up to date when it comes to finding a better kind of transportation, range, or refrigerator. In the living room, however, they apparently want to retreat from today's world and are content with the furniture styled for our ancestors, electing flowers for the living room rug and a colonial weather vane for the garage. The question goes deeper than just introducing the best type of modern furniture or contemporary homes to the public. Students must be made aware of the discrepancy between the demand for truth and the quest for scientific knowledge on the one hand and the acceptance of imitations of eighteenth-century styles and wood-grained plastic foam ceiling beams on the other. Learning to recognize the honest use of materials develops through first-hand experience, for there is no formula of "right" answers.

Integrating Art

The study of art history is too often isolated from the practice of art. Sometimes at the college level, art history is taught with other histories in a College of Arts and Sciences or Social Sciences; the practice of art, the actual painting or sculpturing, is located in a different college entirely, such as in a College of Fine Arts or Performing Arts. And even the area of design may be located in a third college, along with weaving and pottery. There are some historical reasons for this. Art history has had a separate existence from art, often being more attached to museums, archaeology, and social history and considered an intellectual study. Art, as typified by painting, has been considered more intuitive, more the province of the talented, supported by patrons and free to reflect on society. Design has traditionally been associated with industry, with a vocation, and with the economics of producing and merchandising.

Although some high school programs still cling to these divisions, there is actually no reason why all of these areas cannot be pursued simultaneously, singly, or not at all. Just as there is a history of art, there is a history of music, a history of science, a history of philosophy, and a history of medicine. Possibly the history of medicine would be considered the most important by at least part of society, yet it is not offered in secondary schools. The only reason to include art history is to provide a background for understanding oneself and one's society. To deal with art history as a separate topic, to put this important and potentially exciting area into the framework of another isolated subject to be tested and studied-for-a-mark denies the personal human messages that art has for youth.

It is important that history, criticism, and the analysis of art begin with the tangible, a reference point that can actually be touched or that is a natural outgrowth of a problem of the student's own making. Many of these catalysts are already in the school or the community: the painting that the student is working on, the repainting of the school interior, or the designation of a building as a national landmark. The frame of reference for a painting can be expanded by seeing how artists from other cultures dealt with the same subject matter, how painters from a different time and place tried to communicate a similar theme, or how various artists conveyed a feeling for atmosphere or mood. The repainting of the school opens up many problems and solutions with color: reflectivity, warmth and coolness, preferences, durability, variability, and cost. And the possible designation of an historic building means research into county records, interviews with past and present owners, examination of the construction, drawing of floor plans, photographing various façades, writing up recommendations, and comparing with other buildings of the same era. Each of these examples involves the arts fully. An important issue that has life and meaning for a student may lead to a greater depth of involvement in the arts; it is also an important learning experience with a tangible personal meaning.

To some extent, all art might be considered metaphor. If a high school student selects a scene to paint, to capture on canvas or paper, the purpose behind the selection of the particular scene depends upon the reactions or subjective feelings of the student toward what is selected. Is the scene attractive? Are the relationships between the forms or colors pleasing? Does the scene recall past associations or stir the memory of a certain event? Does the scene stir up resentment, or is it symbolic of a disregard for nature? All of these and more may be at the heart of the selection; the painting itself needs to speak to these issues, so that painting now becomes a record of reaction, a record of interpretation. The high school student is no longer drawing and painting spontaneously; a deepened awareness of the environment, a more acute sense of self and purpose in creating become evident. The art teacher can help in this process, first by openly expressing feelings verbally—a feeling of joy with the sun shining or the sharing of a particularly smooth grained wood—and secondly by encouraging this openness in students—how does the painting make you feel, does it express what you want it to, how else might you do it?

Works of professional, recognized art seen in isolation, without any personal struggle of the student beforehand, lack the empathy, the personal message that can be read only by those who have also struggled to put thoughts and feelings into artistic form. The presentation of great art will fall on unsympathetic ears unless there are previous personal reference points to which to relate. The metaphor that is evident to the teacher may be meaningless to the student.

Lessons in art appreciation and criticism are frequently given to high school students, with the expectation that they will enjoy and understand the examples of art chosen for them to see. It is expected that they must learn to see beyond the obvious meaning, to see the metaphor. To illustrate that one thing can be interpreted in terms of another, Nisbet (1976) provides the example of "A mighty fortress is our God." Art may be explained in terms of symbolism, where the literal meaning is transformed into a different concept. Gombrich (1984) has said that our liking for bilateral symmetry is because we equate it with balance. Gombrich also provides some historical background of the use of metaphoric symbolism in designs, such as concentric circles, and in language, such as calling an airplane a silver bird. In our eagerness to have students see and comprehend all of these concepts, it is all too easy to move far from the understandings and interests of students.

In some instances, it could be difficult, if not disastrous, for the teacher to explain the meaning of a picture for a class. Barrett (1985) recounts an instance of a photograph that originally appeared in a magazine, was later used (with-

FIGURE 230.
Sensing the aesthetic appeal of objects in a museum exhibit, and seeing the way other cultures have dealt with artistic problems which the student himself has faced, can bring an appreciation of the history of art.

FIGURE 231.

Pen and ink illustrations such as this are not only fun to do but also develop skills useful in high school publications; however, their real value is in learning to put into graphic form ideas, concerns, humor, and social comment.

out permission) in a scandal sheet, and still later was hung in a museum show of serious artistic photography. The original interpretation of the photograph was innocuous, with an atmosphere of lighthearted innocence in a Paris café. Yet a drastically different interpretation was made by the museum's photography curator, who said that the picture appeared to be about a potential seduction. In such a circumstance, how is one to be sure of the artist's original intent? Naïve claims about the universality of meanings in photographs (or, for that matter, in paintings) can lead into deep waters. As Barrett puts it, "There seems to be an implicit assumption at work here which posits that the meaning of a word or an idea is the picture it produces in us and that if we can match the right pictures with words or expressions, we have meaning" (Barrett, p. 57).

It is the potter who is attracted to an exhibit of pots, the painter who is anxious to see the coming museum exhibit, and the photographer who appreciates the latest foreign films. It is personal involvement in the activity that stimulates the appreciation and the desire to see how others have dealt with problems similar to those faced by oneself. Art should not be separated into its various components; art history, design, criticism, crafts are all part of art. Each should be part of a learning framework to be utilized as needed to help the student understand the importance and meaning of art.

Art Materials

The material from which an art object is made does not have any artistic quality in its natural form. It is only through expression in art that the form assumes meaning and the material becomes an art material. The more opportunity there is for the high school student to manipulate, change, and build in diverse ways from a material, the better the material is. There are many materials that possess a high degree of structure that can stand in the way of expression. Such materials as colored tissue paper, leather scraps, copper foil, and enameling kits have limited variability and are usually not suited to high school art programs.

It would probably be best if no art materials at all were available for the high school student to use. This would mean that every material would have to be purchased or obtained through the student's own efforts. The clay would

FIGURE 232.
Learning how to use clay, getting to know its qualities, and feeling comfortable with the material so that it becomes a normal and natural means of expression were all necessary parts of modeling these heads.

have to be purchased locally or dug from a clay bank. Lumber would have to be obtained from the local building supply house, paper from a stationery store, and sculptural supplies from the local junkyard. The advantage in this type of arrangement is that the student will no longer feel that the art material is the prime responsibility of the art teacher. Also it means that the art student must put forth some effort in obtaining these materials and therefore will be able to continue using these sources after graduation. Interest in art may die because of the unavailability of materials. Knowing where to get them, how much they cost, and their care and proper handling are important elements in learning about the production of art. This is not to suggest that all students must purchase all their art materials, since this would obviously work to the disadvantage of the less affluent youngster. However, the budget for art supplies is customarily an exercise for the art teacher rather than a learning situation for the student. Rather than the art teacher requisitioning the materials and then passing them out when the time arrives, the student should be personally involved in knowing the sources, costs, and availability of the supplies used; this is an important part of art education.

Materials influence the design and final shape of an art form. It would be a mistake to consider a material only the means to an end, because thinking with the material itself and developing a feeling for the function and use of materials may well result in changes in design, revisions in original plans, and a greater flexibility. The high school student needs to know a good deal about a material before it can be utilized. Just how that material is to be used needs to be considered before an abstract lesson on materials can be presented. A material that is going to be used outside needs to be sturdy and may be quite different from a material used for an object that is going to be suspended and protected from the weather. A good deal of the student's knowledge can be acquired through experimentation. How permanent is a material? How heavy is it? Can it be colored? Does it burn? Can it be cast or carved? How much weight will it support? Is it waterproof? These are all questions that need to be answered about a material before it can be used appropriately. Of course, new materials are constantly available, or new ways of using old materials need investigation. This is one way of involving students in art procedures. Certain students can be quickly involved in some problems in art if they need to discover how to join aluminum sheets and have to decide if the best way is through stapling, riveting, using adhesives, soldering, or by clamping or screwing to a second material.

Students will develop the need for acquiring certain procedural skills, for these will be necessary to gain satisfaction and a sense of accomplishment and self-confidence. Procedures can be explained. These are the steps in preparing materials, in maintaining their working consistency, and in cleaning and preserving the results. Techniques, on the other hand, are highly individual and evolve, in part unconsciously, as a result of personal experiences. The working through a problem, the development of several possible solutions, the encouragement toward flexibility, and the final achievement of at least partial success will lead to a development of technique. Each individual will therefore evolve a working method that permits greater ease and depth of self-expression. Since art education in the secondary school does not prepare for a profession but rather serves to develop the mental, aesthetic, and creative growth of the individual, the teaching of skills must be focused upon the problem of finding adequate means of expression for the student.

The number of materials that could be considered appropriate for art expression seems infinite. For younger children it is sometimes important to restrict materials to ones that can be controlled, so that expression is not frustrated before it even takes form. However, for high school students, a new or difficult material can be an exciting challenge. Possibly because the elementary school uses drawing and painting extensively and high school students wish to display their active adulthood, there is a move away from easel painting as the prime means of art expression. Photography has a respectable place in the art repertoire; processing, making enlargements, or editing films are activities that embody much of the same decision making that goes into painting. Videotape presents a different set of problems, with the advantage of immediate playback. Computers are becoming increasingly common in the art room. But some of these activities can be expensive. Light itself can be used as a medium of expression; bright, dull, soft, fluctuating, colored, or moving lights can create interesting effects, but light combined with sound can be exciting. Plastics come in a variety of forms that can be poured, molded, glued, or carved.

A word should be said about the use of tools. The usual tools for an art class are brushes, pans for mixing paint, rollers, palette knives, scissors, and staplers. But there may also be need for a collection of hand tools such as screwdrivers, saws, chisels, hammers, pliers, and a few power tools, including a drill and a sander. These tools should be considered the property of the class, and their main purpose is to be used. Some tools are made for a special purpose, such as mixing plaster, troweling concrete, or mixing up certain adhesives. These are expendable. Durable and inexpensive cameras should also be considered part of the available tools, as should a tape recorder, record player, slide projector, and some equipment more often considered basic to the study of science, such as scales and a microscope. The materials and tools should be of good quality, because in no way should the expression of the high school student be valued less than the expression of the adult artist. It is probably

FIGURE 233.

When a student sets himself a problem, to see if he can really convey an idea artistically and interpret the subject through manipulation of the film and the printing process, then photography becomes an art medium.

better to limit the materials and tools available if budget problems are a consideration than to purchase those that cannot be fully used because they are not substantial enough to withstand the active use that teenagers will give them.

Summary

Fourteen to seventeen year olds are self-critical, introspective, idealistic, and have a growing concern about their relationship to society. No two teenagers are alike, but they have concerns that are common. For the most part, high school students do not have the opportunity or do not elect to take art courses; the art courses that are offered are often unrelated to the youngsters in these classes. Art should provide the opportunity for high school students to express feelings and emotions and to feel that their art is important to themselves and to others. The art program is in an enviable position to break away from the

FIGURE 234.
Elements within a high school student's life make good subject matter, to be dealt with in careful detail or interpreted freely with humor and significant exaggeration, but always with sensitivity.

academic pattern of giving grades and testing for the knowledge that the school thinks important. The students and the environment provide excellent sources for art projects that can be meaningful to students and can also have an impact on the school society.

Much of the art that is done by individuals after leaving the secondary schools is of practical value, such as furniture making, rug weaving, photography, pottery making, or furniture repair and refinishing. However, much misdirected time and effort are presently channeled into nonworthwhile activities by the "easy-to-make, just-follow-the-pattern" type of project. The structure of the art curriculum should give consideration to making art meaningful as a continuing activity. People need to have control over, and to identify with, a project of their own choosing. From the first conception of the idea, through the problem solving and technical mastery, to the final very personal result—this entire process must be grasped by the individual. Thus, any such creative activity should be an honest representation of its creator and of the material and should be designed for its true purpose or function. Art education is ideally suited to maintain this self-identification with the whole span of production, usually unattainable to any one person in our modern, technically oriented age.

Related Activities

1. Survey the art classes in a local high school to determine who actually takes elective art courses. What major sequence of courses are these students following? How do their academic abilities relate to the total high school population? What are the vocational interests of these youngsters?

2. List the materials presently being used by students in a senior high school. What type of use is made of these? Which of these art materials are used by adults who enjoy and actively engage in art, other than professional artists? On what basis can the use of the rest of the art materials be justified?

3. Observe an adolescent group outside school. Record the way in which these youngsters express themselves, both verbally and socially. Pay close attention to dress, hair styles, cars, verbal expressions. How much of this expression is controlled through pressure to conform to group standards? How do you see this expression relating to the high school art program?

4. Compile a list of occupations that could be considered as those of practicing artists. What are the specific differences between these occupations? What are some of the skills or training necessary for each of these occupations? What are some of the common backgrounds needed for all fields?

5. Interview several people who are recognized artists in business, in industry, or free-lance. What influenced their choice of career? At what age did they decide to enter the art field? To what extent was the public school art program helpful or influential in their vocational choice?

6. Examine several state syllabuses for art in the high school. To what extent are these programs designed as preparation for an art career? What activities are included that would be valuable for the usual high school student who does not intend to follow an art career?

13

Summary

Almost every child enjoys the opportunity for creative activity. The preschool youngster, the sixth grader, and the young adult in high school all look upon art as something that is enjoyable. It is rather sad that our educational system is organized in such a way that most students are gradually deprived of the opportunity to paint, draw, or construct, the farther they progress in the school system. The need for art is not outgrown.

Children's drawings are always a pleasure to observe. They contain a freshness of outlook that is the essence of childhood. Young children, particularly, express their ideas, thoughts, and emotions with an honesty that can almost be upsetting to adults. Sometimes professional artists are envious of the youngsters' spontaneous approach to painting, for their directness, frankness, and intuitive feeling for design may be what the artist is striving for.

Within itself, the act of drawing or painting is a learning experience. The problem of what to paint, how to paint it, the relationships of form and color, the use of heavy or fine line, the problems of light and dark are all part of the art experience. However, the organization of the elements in the picture or in the construction is only one segment of the experience, because the expression is a concrete configuration of the emotional and perceptual experiences that an individual has had in interacting with the environment. This is true at all levels of art. It is the expression of the self, the subjective reactions to the environment that make art expressive, not only to the producer but also to the viewer.

Within each work of art a youngster portrays feelings, intellectual abilities, physical development, perceptual sensitivities, creative involvement, social development, and aesthetic awareness. Although individual children vary considerably, there are general growth characteristics that are typical of any age, and the art products of these youngsters also change in predictable ways.

The very young child enjoys scribbling, but by the age of four, he is usually making scribbles that begin to look like the typical head–feet representation of a person. Most children when they reach kindergarten can draw a great number of objects, although these are only vaguely naturalistic. Soon a base line appears, and children place the objects they are drawing on this line across the bottom of the page. These early stages of children's development are marked by the direct and bold use of color, and it is at this age that children show a great deal of confidence in their own means of expression.

At about nine years of age or so, overlapping appears in drawings, and youngsters draw in much more detail and become more critical of their own products. Usually by the age of twelve, they are quite reluctant to show their drawings. For most children artistic development has come to a halt. Some youngsters may show an interest in portraying the environment naturalistically and be concerned with the problems of perspective and atmospheric effects; for others, these naturalistic aspects are difficult to understand, and they may get more enjoyment from painting nonobjectively.

The changes that take place in the art product are a direct reflection of the changing child; all of the variables that cause them to be different individuals with different personalities and different interests are also influencing their art products. It should be obvious that we cannot understand a work of art unless we understand the culture in which it was made, the artist's intentions, and the society and environmental conditions that surrounded its making. The same holds true for children's drawings. The school environment, the intent of the child, the intellectual and emotional factors involved, all must be understood if we are to appreciate the importance of art for children.

Teachers play an extremely important role in the development, not only of art, but of children themselves. Because art is essentially an expression of the self, because there are no answers in the teacher's stack of books, because art cannot be produced by the usual threat of failure or rewards, the teacher of art becomes a crucial person in art production. It is only through a strongly supportive teacher who encourages and interacts with youngsters that an increased sensitivity to the environment can grow. The development of positive attitudes toward the self and toward art is something that does not happen automatically. The creative spirit needs reinforcement, and the teacher is one who can provide the environmental conditions that will make the art experience an exciting and rewarding one. It is through identifying with the child's needs and interests that the teacher can best understand the desires of each child. This is particularly true for the child who may not turn naturally to art as a form of expression, for this may be the child who most needs the art experience.

Too often art programs are planned around materials, with emphasis being placed upon learning how to use each material, in the hope that a breadth of experience will somehow be valuable. It is not unusual to see an elementary classroom using crayons one week, finger paints the next, clay the following, and so forth. This constant changing of materials can be frustrating to children, who are more interested in expressing their thinking, feeling, and perceiving in a meaningful way than in doodling in different materials. It may only be the teacher who thinks that it is important to vary the activities for the mere sake of change. This overlooks the fact that becoming thoroughly familiar with a material so that it becomes a natural mode of expression, is an essential part of developing competence and confidence in one's own art.

Within the framework of the usual school system, there is little chance for youngsters to express feelings and emotions that are anti-school. By the time youngsters are in the junior high school, many have succeeded in developing methods of coping with this system, so that it is not unusual for youngsters to be more concerned with what will appear on a test than with the material to be learned. Art should not fall into the trap of competing with academic subjects, but should have the integrity to remain basically human. It should be the one area in the secondary school that youngsters can turn to without the concern for being evaluated and without the feeling that they must perform according to someone else's standards. Art can be a vital force in the lives of students if it is relevant to their thinking and becomes the avenue by which they can express the feelings about their society that they are not encouraged to express either in or outside school. For the secondary school student, the potential of art is tremendous, and the energies and enthusiasm of older children can make learning in art exciting and rewarding.

A major emphasis in this book has been that art is entwined with a child's creative and mental growth. There is no pretext that the function of art in the school is to make artists out of children. Rather, the emphasis has been that art can provide the opportunity for growth in ways that other subject matter areas cannot. Growth is not achieved by the development of intellectual capacities alone. The aim of an art program is a confident, creative child who is eager to express thoughts, who is sensitive to people and nature, who is a responsive, productive individual. We cannot do this developing for a child. Every individual has a potential that is greater than what is realized. Art should provide the impetus for constructive action and the opportunity for children to see themselves as acceptable beings searching for new and more harmonious organizations, developing confidence in their own means of expression. Children are the most essential ingredient in an art program, and art education has a vital role to play in their growth.

Summary Charts

This summary cannot do justice to the developmental stages and their significance as they influence the art products of children. This volume has attempted to show the interrelationship between children and their art and to emphasize the importance of an adult, aware of children's feelings and sensitive to the creative process. It is the teacher who is responsible for the learning environment, and a summary of developmental stages ignores the crucial interaction that is central to learning. However, the authors realize that for research purposes, it is sometimes important to have a brief explanation of the differences, changes, and similarities that exist, particularly in drawings, as children grow older. Some of our colleagues have attempted to make their own versions of a drawing scale, using the information presented in earlier editions. It was this fact that gave impetus to the following charts. No attempt has been made to deal with the variations and subtleties of motivation for each of the stages or the differences in materials that are suitable for each age. The way color is used and understood by children is a fascinating subject in itself, as is the formation of an intuitive sense of design; however, these topics are better understood by looking at the color plates than by reading a verbal description. The summary of each stage will be limited to a brief description and examples of drawings typical of each stage of development.

It should be emphasized that there is no one way that pictures will be drawn at any age. The stages melt into one another and children progress at different paces, depending upon numerous factors, so that one can even find a seventeen year old making scribbles around the edges of a calculus book, but it would be strange indeed to see a three year old making a detailed drawing of a person. The examples, then, should be considered as midpoints, and the stages themselves as convenient labels for a study of children's art and not as invariant categories.

The Scribbling Stage, Two-Four Years: Beginnings of Self-Expression

DRAWING CHARACTERISTICS	SPACE REPRESENTATION	HUMAN FIGURE REPRESENTATION
DISORDERED SCRIBBLING:		
Motor activity utilizing large muscles with movement from shoulder Kinesthethic pleasure Grasps tool with whole hand Swing of arm makes line Looks away while scribbling	Utilizes drawing surface Sometimes scribbles beyond paper Ignores previous marks placed on a page	No attempts made
CONTROLLED SCRIBBLING:		
Smaller marks Repeated motions Watches scribbles while drawing Uses wrist motion Can copy a circle	Stays within drawing area Draws around previous marks on the page May concentrate on certain parts of drawings	Circles, lines, loops and swirls made, which are prefigural
NAMED SCRIBBLING:		
Relates marks to things known Greater variety of line Holds tool between fingers Identification of subject may change in the process of drawing Longer attention span	Scribbles placed purposely Previous marks on the page are utilized Empty space may take on meaning Lines become edges of shapes	A scribble may be pointed out by the child as being a person Action may be named, such as running, jumping, swinging

The Preschematic Stage, Four-Seven Years: First Representational Attempts

DRAWING CHARACTERISTICS	SPACE REPRESENTATION	HUMAN FIGURE REPRESENTATION
Shapes for things are geometric and lose their meaning when removed from the whole	Objects seem to float around page	Head-feet symbol grows out of scribble
Placement and size of objects are determined subjectively	Paper sometimes turned or rotated while drawing	Flexible symbol, constantly changing
Objects drawn are not related to one another	Size of objects not in proportion to one another	People are looking at viewer, usually smiling
Art becomes communication with the self	Objects are distorted to fit space available	Gradual inclusion of arms (often from head), body, fingers, toes
Known objects seem to be catalogued or listed pictorially	Space seems to surround child	Distortion and omission of parts is to be expected
Can copy a square at four, a triangle at five		Clothes, hair and other details expected by end of this stage

The Schematic Stage, Seven-Nine Years:
The Achievement of a Form Concept

DRAWING CHARACTERISTICS	SPACE REPRESENTATION	HUMAN REPRESENTATION

Development of a form concept which is repeated again and again
Schema is altered only when special meaning is conveyed
Drawing shows concept, not percept
Bold, direct, flat representation
Drawings reflect a child's active knowledge of the environment
	Establishment of a base line on which objects are placed and often a sky line, with the space between representing the air
	Two dimensional organization of objects
	No or little overlapping
	Subjective space representation common
	  a. simultaneous representation of plan and elevation
	  b. X-ray drawings
	  c. fusion of time and space
	Multi-base lines
	Environment symbolized
		Repeated schema for person
		Body usually made up of geometric shapes
		Arms and legs show volume and are usually correctly placed
		Exaggeration, omission, or change of schema shows effect of experience
		Proportions depend on emotional values

The Gang Age, Nine-Twelve Years:
The Dawning Realism

DRAWING CHARACTERISTICS	SPACE REPRESENTATION	HUMAN FIGURE REPRESENTATION
Greater awareness of details	Disappearance of base line and emergence of the plane	Rigid schema no longer prevails
Self conscious of own drawings	Overlapping of objects	Greater awareness of clothing details
Greater awareness of physical environment	Beginning of interrelationships between objects	Less exaggeration, distortion, and omission of body parts to show emphasis
Events are characterized rather than drawn naturalistically	Sky now comes down to horizon	Body parts retain their meaning when separated
No understanding of shade and shadow	Attempts at showing depth through size of objects	Greater stiffness of figures

The Pseudo-Naturalistic Stage, Twelve-Fourteen Years: The Age of Reasoning

DRAWING CHARACTERISTICS	SPACE REPRESENTATION	HUMAN FIGURE REPRESENTATION
Critically aware of own shortcomings in art	Greater awareness of environment, but only important elements drawn in detail	Closer to correct proportions
Drawings can become shorthand notations	For visually minded, an awareness of depth; child draws as a spectator; attempt at perspective	Greater awareness of joints and body actions
Ability to focus upon selected parts of environment	For haptically minded, space determined subjectively; child draws as a participant	Facial expressions vary for meaning
End of spontaneous art activity	Action goes on within picture plane	Cartooning popular
Details such as wrinkles and folds become important for some		Person can be represented by less than total figure
Projection of non-literal, personal meaning into objects and events		Sexual characteristics over-emphasized

478

Adolescent Art, Fourteen-Seventeen Years:
The Period of Decision

DRAWING CHARACTERISTICS	SPACE REPRESENTATION	HUMAN FIGURE REPRESENTATION
Drawings tend to resemble 12 year level, without further instruction	Perspective can be learned and utilized by visually minded; awareness of atmosphere	Naturalistic attempts by some, awareness of proportions, actions, and visible details
Conscious development of artistic skills	Attention to non-naturalistic representation for haptically minded; portrayal of mood, shifting of space or distortion for purposeful emphasis	Exaggeration of detail for emphasis by some
Haptic drawings show subjective interpretation		Imaginative use of figure for satire
Visually minded students may get pleasure from visual details, light and shade		
Extended attention span		
Mastery of any material		
Control of purposeful expression		

Bibliography

Alschuler, R. H. & Hattwick, L. W. (1969, reprinted). *Painting and Personality*. Chicago: University of Chicago Press, 1947.

Amabile, T. M. (1979). The effects of external evaluation on artistic creativity. *Journal of Personality and Social Psychology, 37*(2), 221–233.

Amabile, T. M. & Gitomer, J. (1984). Children's Artistic Creativity: Effects of choice in task materials. *Personality and Social Psychology Bulletin, 10*(2), 209–215.

Anderson, C. M. & Stoffer, G. R. (1979). Creative thinking and juvenile delinquency. *Adolescence, 14*(53).

Anderson, F. (1985). Electronic media, videodisc technology, and the visual arts. *Studies in Art Education. 26*(4), 224–231.

Anooshian, L. J. & Young, D. (1981). Developmental changes in cognitive maps of a familiar neighborhood. *Child Development, 52,* 341–348.

Applegate, M. (1967). Relationships of characteristics of children's drawings to chronological and mental age. Unpublished doctoral dissertation, University of California at Berkeley.

Asch, S. E. (1952). *Social Psychology*. Englewood Cliffs, NJ: Prentice-Hall.

Ast, C. A. (1981). Two tests for haptic-visual aptitude: A discussion of their usefulness for elementary school children. *Studies in Art Education, 23*(1), 47–54.

Barrett, M. D. & Light, P. H. (1976). Symbolism and intellectual realism in children's drawings. *British Journal of Educational Psychology, 46,* 198–202.

Barrett, S. B. (1971). A study of the interrelationship and influences of scholastic aptitude and perception upon aesthetic sensitivity in college students. *Dissertation Abstracts International, 31*, 5835.

Barrett, T. (1985). Photographs and contexts. *Journal of Aesthetic Education, 19*(3), 51–64.

Barron, F. (1963). *Creativity and Psychological Health.* Princeton, NJ: Van Nostrand.

Barron, F. (1972). *Artists in the Making.* New York: Seminar Press.

Barron, F. & Harrington, D. M. (1981). Creativity, intelligence and personality. *Annual Review of Psychology, 32*, 439–476.

Bee, H. (1964). The relationship between parent–child interaction and distractibility in fourth grade children. Unpublished doctoral dissertation, Stanford University.

Beittel, K. R. (1966). Selected psychological concepts as applied to the teaching of drawing. Unpublished report, Cooperative Research Project No. 3149, Office of Education, U.S. Department of Health, Education, and Welfare.

Beittel, K. R. (1972). *Mind and Context in the Art of Drawing.* New York: Holt, Rinehart & Winston.

Beittel, K. R. & Burkhart, R. C. (1963). Strategies of spontaneous, divergent, and academic art students. *Studies in Art Education, 5*(1), 20–41.

Beittel, K. R., Mattil, E., et al. (1961). The effect of a "depth" vs. a "breadth" method of art instruction at the ninth grade level. *Studies in Art Education, 3*(1), 75–87.

Belcher, T. L. (1975). Effect of different test situations on creativity scores. *Psychological Reports, 36.*

Bell, C. (1914). *Art.* London: Chatto & Windus. (Republished: London; Arrow Books Ltd., 1961).

Berndt, T. J. (1979). Developmental changes in conformity to peers and parents. *Developmental Psychology, 15*(6), 608–616.

Biehler, R. F. (1953). An analysis of free painting procedures as used with preschool children. Unpublished doctoral dissertation, University of Minnesota.

Biel, A. (1982). Children's spatial representation of their neighborhood: A step towards a general spatial competence. *Journal of Environmental Psychology, 2*, 193–200.

Bilotta, J. & Lindauer, M. S. (1980) Artistic and nonartistic backgrounds as determinants of the cognitive response to the arts. *Bulletin of the Psychonomic Society, 15*(5), 453–356.

Birch, H. & Lefford, A. (1967). Visual differentation, intersensory integration, and voluntary motor control. *Monographs of the Society for Research in Child Development, 32*(2).

Bjorklund, G. & Krebs, M. (1985). Nation at risk or children at risk? *Education Week, 4*(24).

Blauner, R. (1964). *Alienation and Freedom.* Chicago: The University of Chicago Press.

Blaut, J. M. & Stea, D. (1974). Mapping at the age of three. *The Journal of Geography, 23*(7), 5–9.

Blum, K. S. (1979). A comparative analysis of normal and disturbed children's drawings. Unpublished master's thesis, Cornell University.

Blyth, D. A., Hill, J. P., & Thiel, K. S. (1982). Early adolescents' significant others: Grade and gender differences in perceived relationships with familial and nonfamilial adults and young people. *Journal of Youth and Adolescence, 11*(6), 425–450.

Boericke, A. & Shapiro, B. (1973). *Handmade Houses: A Guide to the Woodbutcher's Art.* San Francisco: Scrimshaw Press.

Boffoly, R. L. (1978). A factor analysis of visual, kinesthetic and cognitive modes of information handling. *Review of Research in Visual Arts Education, 8*, 17–27.

Boyer, E. L. (1983). *High School: A Report on Secondary Education in America.* New York: Harper & Row.

Bradley, M. & Bradbard, M. R. (1981). Effects of allowing four-year-olds to manipulate teaching materials on their learning of space and quantity concepts. *The Journal of General Psychology, 104*, 265–273.

Bradley, R. H., Caldwell, B. M., & Elardo, R. (1979). Home environment and cognitive development in the first 2 years. *Developmental Psychology, 15*(3), 246–250.

Bremner, J. & Moore, S. (1984). Prior visual inspection and object naming: Two factors that enhance hidden feature inclusion in young children's drawings. *British Journal of Developmental Psychology, 2*, 371–376.

Brissoni, A. (1975). Creative experiences of young children. *Art Education, 28*(1), 19–23.

Brittain, W. L. (1961). Creative art. In Fliegler, L. (Ed.), *Curriculum Planning for the Gifted* (Chap. 10). Englewood Cliffs, NJ: Prentice-Hall.

Brittain, W. L. (Ed.). (1964). *Creativity and Art Education.* Washington, D.C.: The National Art Education Association.

Brittain, W. L. (1968a). An investigation into the character and expressive qualities of early adolescent art. Unpublished report, Cooperative Research Project No. 6-8416, Office of Education, U.S. Department of Health, Education, and Welfare.

Brittain, W. L. (1968b). An exploratory investigation of early adolescent expression in art. *Studies in Art Education, 9*(2), 5–12.

Brittain, W. L. (1969). Some exploratory studies of the art of preschool children. *Studies in Art Education, 10*(3), 14–24.

Brittain, W. L. (1979). *Creativity, Art, and the Young Child.* New York: Macmillan Publishing Co., Inc.

Brittain, W. L. (1985). Children's drawings: A comparison of two cultures. *Journal of Multi-cultural and Cross-cultural Research in Art Education, 3*(1), 34–43.

Brittain, W. L. & Chien, Y-C. (1980). Effect of materials on preschool children's ability to represent a man. *Perceptual and Motor Skills, 51*, 995–1000.

Brittain, W. L. & Chien, Y-C. (1983). Relationship between preschool children's ability to name body parts and their ability to construct a man. *Perceptual and Motor Skills, 57*, 19–24.

Brog, M. (1985). Hemisphericity, locus of control, and grade point average among middle and high school boys and girls. *Perceptual and Motor Skills, 60*, 39–45.

Bronfenbrenner, U. (1968). Early deprivation in mammals and man. In Newton, G. (Ed.), *Early Experience and Behavior.* Springfield, IL: Charles C. Thomas.

Brookover, W. B., et al. (1967). Self concept of ability and school achievement. In Miller, H. L. (Ed.), *Education for the Disadvantaged* (pp. 64–68). New York: The Free Press.

Broudy, H. S. (1971). Enlightened preference and justification. In Smith, R. A. (Ed.), *Aesthetics and Problems of Education*. Urbana: University of Illinois Press.

Brown, E. V. (1979). Sexual self-identification as reflected in children's drawings when asked to "draw-a-person." *Child Development, 49,* 35–38.

Burgart, H. J. (1968). The development of a visual-verbal measure of general creativity: The symbol test of originality. Unpublished report, Cooperative Research Project No. 7–8168, Office of Education, U.S. Department of Health, Education, and Welfare.

Burkhart, R. C. (1962). *Spontaneous and Deliberate Ways of Learning*. Scranton, PA: International Textbook Co.

Burkhart, R. C. (1967). The relation of intelligence to art ability. In Mooney, R. and Razik, T. (Eds.), *Explorations in Creativity* (pp. 246–258). New York: Harper & Row.

Campbell, E. M. (1975). Do tests really motivate pupils? *The Australian Journal of Education, 19*(1), 15–25.

Carnegie Council on Policy Studies in Higher Education. (1980). *Giving Youth a Better Chance*. San Francisco: Jossey-Bass.

Carothers, T. & Gardner, H. (1979). When children's drawings become art: The emergence of aesthetic production and perception. *Developmental Psychology, 15*(5), 570–580.

Casey, M. B. (1979). Color versus form discrimination learning in 1-year-old infants. *Developmental Psychology, 15*(3), 341–343.

Castrup, J., Ain, E., & Scott, R. (1972). Art skills of preschool children. *Studies in Art Education, 13*(3), 62–69.

Cecere, J. G. (1966). The effect of verbal stimuli and artistic self-expression on children's motivation for writing. Unpublished doctoral dissertation, The Pennsylvania State University.

Chen, M. J. & Cook, M. (1984). Representational drawings of solid objects by young children. *Perception, 13,* 377–385.

Chen, M. J., Therkelsen, M., & Griffiths, K. (1984). Representational drawings of solid objects: a longitudinal study. *Visual Arts Research, 10*(1), 27–31.

Child, I. L. (1964). Development of sensitivity to esthetic values. Unpublished report, Cooperative Research Project No. 1748, Office of Education, U.S. Department of Health, Education, and Welfare.

Child, I. L. (1983). The psychological meaning of aesthetic judgments. *Visual Arts Research, 9*(2), 51–59.

Clare, S. & Suter, S. (1983). Drawing and the cerebral hemispheres: Bilateral EEG alpha. *Biological Psychology, 16,* 15–27.

Clark, G. A. & Zimmerman, E. D. (1984). *Educating Artistically Talented Students*. Syracuse, NY: Syracuse University.

Clements, R. D. (1964). Art student-teacher questioning. *Studies in Art Education, 6*(1), 14ff.

Clements, R. D. (1985). Adolescent computer art. *Art Education, 38*(2), 6–9.

Cohen, H., Cohen, B. & Nii, P. (1984). *The first artificial intelligence coloring book.* Los Altos, CA: Kaufmann.

Coie, J. D., Costanzo, P. R., & Farnill, D. Specific transitions in the development of spatial perspective-taking ability. *Developmental Psychology, 9*(2), 167–177.

Cole, N. R. (1940). *The Arts in the Classroom.* New York: The John Day Company.

Combs, A. W. (Ed.). (1962). *Perceiving, Behaving, Becoming: A New Focus for Education.* Washington, DC: Association for Supervision and Curriculum Development.

Concannon, J. (1970). A Review of research on haptic perception. *Journal of Educational Research, 63*(6), 250–252.

Condry, J. (1977). Enemies of exploration: Self-initiated versus other-initiated learning. *Journal of Personality and Social Psychology, 35*(7), 459–477.

Corcoran, A. L. (1954). Color usage in nursery school painting. *Child Development, 25*(2), 107 ff.

Covington, M., Crutchfield, R., Davies, L., & Olton, R. (1972). *The Productive Learning Program.* Columbus, OH: Charles E. Merrill.

Cox, M. V. (1978). Spatial depth relationships in young children's drawings. *Journal of Experimental Child Psychology, 26*, 551–554.

Cratty, B. J. (1970). *Perceptual and Motor Development in Infants and Children.* New York: Macmillan.

Crutchfield, R. S. (1963). Independent thought in a conformist world. In Farber, S. M. & Wilson, R. H. L. (Eds.), *Conflict and Creativity: Part Two of Control of the Mind* (pp. 208–228). New York: McGraw-Hill.

Csikszentmihalyi, M. G. & Getzels, J. W. (1971). Discovery-oriented behavior and the originality of creative products. *Journal of Personality and Social Psychology, 19*(1), 47–52.

Daniel, R. A. (1958). The effect of frequency of coloring book usage upon the creative drawings of third grade children. Unpublished doctoral dissertation, The Pennsylvania State University.

Darlington, R. B., Royce, J. M., Snipper, A. S., Murray, H. W., & Lazar, I. (1980). Preschool programs and later school competence of children from low-income families. *Science, 208*, 202–204.

Davis, A. M. (1983). Contextual sensitivity in young children's drawings. *Journal of Experimental Child Psychology, 35*, 478–486.

Davis, D. J. (1969). *Teaching Methodologies in Art: An Experiment in Depth and Breadth Approaches to Instruction.* Lubbock: The Texas Tech Press.

Davis, D. J. & Torrance, E. P. (1965). How favorable are the values of art educators to the creative person? *Studies in Art Education, 6*(2), 42.

Davis, G. A. (1971). Instruments useful in studying creative behavior and creative talent, Part 2. *The Journal of Creative Behavior, 5*(3), 162–165.

Day, M. D. (1985). Evaluating student achievement in discipline-based art programs. *Studies in Art Education, 26*(4), 232–240.

Day, M. D. (1969). The compatibility of art history and studio art activity in the junior high school art program. *Studies in Art Education, 10*(2), 57–65.

Dempsey, A., Jr. (1971). A descriptive study of ideational patterns and the evaluation of graphic form in drawings by preschool children. Unpublished doctoral dissertation, The Pennsylvania State University.

Dennis, W. (1966). *Group Values through Children's Drawings.* New York: Wiley.

DePorter, D. A. & Kavanaugh, R. D. (1978). Parameters of children's sensitivity to painting styles. *Studies in Art Education, 20*(1), 43–48.

DiBlasio, M. K. (1983). If and where to plug in the computer: A conceptual framework for computer assisted art instruction. *Studies in Art Education, 25*(1), 39–47.

Dissanayake, E. (1980). Art as a human behavior: Toward an ethological view of art. *The Journal of Aesthetics and Art Criticism, 38*(4).

DiVesta, F. J. (1974). *Language, Learning, and Cognitive Processes.* Monterey, CA: Brooks/Cole Publishing Company.

Dodge, N. M. (1984). The perceptual-motor and spatial processes underlying the relationship between young children's drawing and handwriting. Unpublished master's thesis, Cornell University.

Doerr, S. L. (1980). Conjugate lateral eye movement, cerebral dominance, and the figural creativity factors of fluency, flexibility, originality, and elaboration. *Studies in Art Education, 21*(3), 5–11.

Dorethy, R. & Reeves, D. (1979). Mental functioning, perceptual differentiation, personality, and achievement among art and non-art majors. *Studies in Art Education, 20*(2), 52–63.

Dubery, F. & Willats, J. (1972). *Drawing Systems.* New York: Van Nostrand Reinhold.

Duke, D. L. (1984). *Teaching—the Imperiled Profession.* Albany: State University of New York Press.

Duke, L. L. (1983). The Getty Center for Education in the Arts. *Art Education, 36*(5), 4–8.

Duncum, P. (1985). The fantasy embeddedness of girls' horse drawings. *Art Education, 36*(6), 42–46.

Dyson, A. H. (1982). The emergence of visible language: Interrelationships between drawing and early writing. *Visible Language, 16*(4).

Eisner, E. W. (1966). The development of information and attitude toward art at the secondary and college levels. *Studies in Art Education, 8*(1), 43–58.

Elkind, D. & Bowen, R. (1979). Imaginary audience behavior in children and adolescents. *Developmental Psychology, 15*(1), 38–44.

Emery, M. S. (1898). *How to Enjoy Pictures.* Boston: Prang.

Engel, M. (1981). The mind, art and history. *Review of Research in Visual Arts Education, 14.*

Escher, M. C. (1971). *The Graphic Work of M. C. Escher.* New York: Ballantine Books.

Ettinger, L. & Roland, C. (1986). Using microcomputers in the art curriculum. *Art Education, 39*(1), 48–51.

Evans, R. G. & Forbach, G. B. (1983). Facilitation of performance on a divergent measure of creativity: A closer look at instructions to "be creative". *Applied Psychological Measurement, 7*(2), 181–187.

Eysenck, H. J. (1971). Factors determining aesthetic preferences for geometrical designs and devices. *British Journal of Aesthetics, 11* (154–166).

Farrell, E. & Rogers, P. (1982). Is aesthetic response independent of age, sex, and I.Q.? *Journal of Aesthetic Education, 16*(4), 96–98.

Flavell, J. H. (1985). *Cognitive Development.* Englewood Cliffs, NJ: Prentice-Hall, Inc.

Foster, S. (1977). Hemisphere dominance and the art process. *Art Education, 30*(2), 28–29.

Francis, A. S. (1973). Creativity as an outlet for frustration and an aid to learning. Unpublished master's thesis, Cornell University.

Franken, R. E. & Diamond, D. C. (1983). Picture recognition memory in children: Effects of homogeneous versus heterogeneous classes of pictures. *Perceptual and Motor Skills, 57,* 749–750.

Franklin, B. A. (1981, May 17). Paint use is linked to artists' cancer. *The New York Times,* 17.

Frankston, L. (1963). Some explorations of the effect of creative visual art experiences upon the poetry writing quality of eighth grade students. *Studies in Art Education, 5*(1), 42–59.

Frankston, L. (1966). Effects of two programs and two methods of teaching upon the quality of art products of adolescents. *Studies in Art Education, 7*(2), 23.

Freedman, D. G. (1976). Infancy, biology, and culture. Chapter 2 in Lipsitt, L. P. (Ed.), *Developmental Psychobiology.* New York: Wiley.

Freeman, N. H. (1980). *Strategies of Representation in Young Children.* New York: Academic Press.

Freeman, N. H. & Janikoun, R. (1972). Intellectual realism in children's drawings of a familiar object with distinctive features. *Child Development, 43,* 1116–1121.

Furze, C. T., Tyler, J. G., & McReynolds, P. (1984). Training creativity of children assessed by the obscure figures test. *Perceptual and Motor Skills, 58,* 231–234.

Gardner, H. (1970). Children's sensitivity to painting styles. *Child Development, 41,* 813–821.

Gardner, H. & Gardner, J. (1973). Developmental trends in sensitivity to form and subject matter in paintings. *Studies in Art Education, 14*(2), 52–56.

Gazzaniga, M. S. (1973). The split brain in man. In Ornstein, R. E. (Ed.), *The Nature of Human Consciousness.* San Francisco: W. H. Freeman and Company.

Gerber, R. V. (1979). Development of competence and performance in cartographic language by children at the cognitive level of map-reasoning. Unpublished doctoral dissertation, University of Queensland.

Geschwind, N. (1979). Specializations of the human brain. *Scientific American, 241*(3), 180–199.

Getzels, J. W. & Csikszentmihalyi, M. (1976). *The Creative Vision.* New York: Wiley.

Getzels, J. W. & Jackson, P. W. (1962). *Creativity and Intelligence.* New York: Wiley.

Gibbens, T. C. N. (1968). Drugs and the young law breaker. *Mental Health, 25*(3), 36–37.

Gibson, J. J. (1966). *The Senses Considered as Perceptual Systems.* Boston: Houghton Mifflin.

Ginsburg, H. & Opper, S. (1969). *Piaget's Theory of Intellectual Development.* Englewood Cliffs, NJ: Prentice Hall.

Gliner, C. R., Pick, A. D., Pick, H. L., & Hales, J. A. (1969). A developmental investigation of visual and haptic preferences for shape and texture. *Monographs of the Society for Research in Child Development, 34*(6).

Goertz, E. C. (1966). Graphomotor development in preschool children. Unpublished master's thesis, Cornell University.

Goleman, D. (1977, October). Split-brain psychology: Fad of the year. *Psychology Today.*

Golomb, C. (1977). Representational development of the human figure. *The Journal of Genetic Psychology, 131,* 207–222.

Gombrich, E. H. (1984). *The Sense of Order.* Ithaca, NY: Cornell University.

Goodnow, J. J. (1978). Visible thinking: Cognitive aspects of change in drawings. *Child Development, 49,* 637–641.

Goor, A. & Rapoport, T. (1977). Enhancing creativity in an informal educational framework. *The Journal of Educational Psychology, 69*(5), 636–643.

Gordon, W. J. J. (1961). *Synectics: The Development of Creative Capacity.* New York: Harper & Row.

Gottlieb, A. M. (1986, January 5). Computer-Literacy Race: A global printout. *New York Times, 135*(46, 645), Sec. 12, 67–68.

Gowan, J. C. (1981). Art and Music as stimulants to right hemisphere imagery and creativity. In Gowan, J. C., Khatena, J., & Torrance, E. P., *Creativity: Its Educational Implications.* Dubuque, IA: Kendall/Hunt.

Gowler, D. & Legge, K. (1978). "Locked-in" employees and organizational design. In Legge, K. & Mumford, E. (Eds), Designing Organisations for Satisfaction and Efficiency. Westmead, England: *Gower Press, Teakfield Limited.*

Greenfield, P. M. (1966). On culture and conservation. In Bruner, J. S., Olver, R. R., & Greenfield, P. M. (Eds.), *Studies in Cognitive Growth* (pp. 225–256). New York: Wiley.

Greer, W. D. (1984). Discipline-based art education: Approaching art as a subject of study. *Studies in Art Education, 25*(4), 212–218.

Griswold, P. (1984). Elementary students' attitudes during 2 years of computer-assisted instruction. *American Educational Research Journal, 21*(4), 737–754.

Groff, P. (1978, May). Art and reading: Is there a relationship? *Reading World,* pp. 345–351.

Guilford, J. P. (1964). Progress in the discovery of intellectual factors. In Taylor, C. W. (Ed.), *Widening Horizons in Creativity.* New York: Wiley.

Guilford, J. P. (1968). *Intelligence, Creativity and their Educational Implications*. San Diego, CA: Robert R. Knapp.

Gutteter, L. J. (1976). The psychological functioning of early adolescents who have failed to develop a precise drawing style. *Studies in Art Education, 18*(1), 50–60.

Hamblen, K. A. (1985). The issue of technocratic rationality in discipline-based art education. *Studies in Art Education, 27*(1), 43–46.

Hamblen, K. A. (1983). Tissue paper economics and other hidden dimensions of the studio model of art instruction. *Studies in Art Education, 25*(1), 32–38.

Hammill, L. C. & Larsen, S. C. (1974). The effectiveness of psycho-linguistic training. *Exceptional Children, 41*, 5–14.

Hardiman, G. W. & Zernich, T. (1977). Influence of style and subject matter on the development of children's art preferences. *Studies in Art Education, 19*(1), 29–35.

Hardiman, G. W. & Zernich, T. (1982). The relative influence of parts and wholes in shaping preference responses to painting. *Studies in Art Education, 23*(3), 31–38.

Hardiman, G. W. & Zernich, T. (1984). Subjective responses to paintings as originals, colored slides, and colored prints. *Studies in Art Education, 25*(2), 104–108.

Hardwick, D. A., Woolridge, S. C., & Rinalducci, E. J. (1983). Selection of landmarks as a correlate of cognitive map organization. *Psychological Reports, 53*, 807–813.

Harlow, H. F. (1965). Mice, monkeys, men and motives. In Fowler, H. (Ed.), *Curiosity and Exploratory Behavior*. New York: MacMillan.

Harlow, H. F., McGaugh, J. L., & Thompson, R. F. (1971). *Psychology*. San Francisco: Albion.

Harrington, D., Block, J., & Block, J. H. (1983). Predicting creativity in preadolescence from divergent thinking in early childhood. *Journal of Personality and Social Psychology, 45*(3), 609–623.

Harris, D. B. (1963). *Children's Drawings as Measures of Intellectual Maturity*. New York: Harcourt Brace Jovanovich.

Harris, M. (1980). *Culture, people, nature* (3rd Ed.). New York: Harper & Row.

Harris, P. (1977). The child's representation of space. In Butterworth, G. (Ed.), *The Child's Representation of the World*. New York: Plenum Press.

Hartley, J. C., Somerville, S. C., Jensen, D. C., & Eliefja, C. C. (1982). Abstraction of individual styles from the drawings of five-year-old children. *Child Development, 53*, 1193–1214.

Hattie, J. A. (1977). Conditions for administering creativity tests. *Psychological Bulletin, 84*(6), 1249–1260.

Hazen, N. L. (1982). Spatial exploration and spatial knowledge: Individual and developmental differences in very young children. *Child Development, 53*, 826–833.

Heilman, H. (1954). An experimental study of the effects of workbooks on the creative drawing of second grade children. Unpublished doctoral dissertation, The Pennsylvania State University.

Heisler, W. J. (1977). Worker alienation: 1900–1975. In Heisler, W. J. & Houck, J. W. (Eds.), *A Matter of Dignity*. Notre Dame, IN: University of Notre Dame Press.

Heller, M. (1980). Reproduction of tactually perceived forms. *Perceptual and Motor Skills, 50,* 943–946.

Herman, J. F., Kolker, R. G., & Shaw, M. L. (1982). Effects of motor activity on children's intentional and incidental memory for spatial locations. *Child Development, 53,* 239–244.

Herman, J. F. & Roth, S. F. (1984). Children's incidental memory for spatial locations in a large-scale environment: Taking a tour down memory lane. *Merrill-Palmer Quarterly, 30*(1), 87–102.

Herman, J. F., Roth, S. F., Miranda, C., & Getz, M. (1982). Children's memory for spatial locations: The influence of recall perspective and type of environment. *Journal of Experimental Child Psychology, 34,* 257–273.

Hoege, H. (1984). The emotional impact on aesthetic judgments: An experimental investigation of a time-honored hypothesis. *Visual Arts Research, 10*(2), 37–48.

Hoepfner, R. (1984). Measuring student achievement in art. *Studies in Art Education, 25*(4), 251–258.

Holladay, H. H. (1966). An experimental and descriptive study of children's pre-representational drawings. Unpublished doctoral dissertation, Cornell University.

Holland, J. D. (1955). Children's responses to objects in daily living, a developmental analysis. Unpublished doctoral dissertation, The Pennsylvania State University.

Holtzman, W. H., Swartz, J. P., & Thorpe, J. S. (1971). Artists, architects and engineers—Three contrasting modes of visual experience and their psychological correlates. *Journal of Personality, 39,* 432–449.

Hooper, J. (1977). Children's drawings of a table and an adaptation of Piagetian coordination of perspectives task. Unpublished master's thesis, Cornell University.

Houssiadas, L. & Brown, L. B. (1980). Egocentrism in language and space perception. *Genetic Psychology Monographs, 101,* 183–214.

Huber, J., Treffinger, D., Tracy, D., & Rand, D. (1979). Self-instructional use of programmed creativity-training materials with gifted and regular students. *Journal of Educational Psychology, 71*(3), 303–309.

Huston-Stein, A., Friedrich-Cofer, L., & Susman, E. J. (1977). The relation of classroom structure to social behavior, imaginative play, and self-regulation of economically disadvantaged children. *Child Development, 48,* 908–916.

Hyman, R. (1964). Creativity and the prepared mind: The role of information and induced attitudes. In Taylor, C. (Ed.), *Widening Horizons in Creativity.* New York: Wiley.

Inagaki, K. (1979). Relationships of curiosity to perceptual and verbal fluency in young children. *Perceptual and Motor Skills, 48,* 789–790.

Ives, S. W. (1984). The development of expressivity in drawing. *British Journal of Educational Psychology, 54,* 152–159.

Ives, W. & Houseworth, M. (1980). The role of standard orientations in children's drawing of interpersonal relationships: Aspects of graphic feature marking. *Child Development, 51,* 591–593.

Ives, W. & Rovet, J. (1982). Elementary school children's use of construction rules in drawings of familiar and novel objects: A cross-cultural replication. *Journal of Genetic Psychology, 140*, 315–316.

Johnson, L. J. (1963). The effect of interpolated writing on paired-associate learning. Unpublished master's thesis, Cornell University.

Jones, L. H. (1964). Student and teacher interaction during evaluative dialogues in art. Cooperative Research Project No. S-050, Office of Education, U.S. Department of Health, Education, and Welfare.

Juhasz, J. B. & Paxson, L. (1978). Personality and preference for painting style. *Perceptual and Motor Skills, 46*, 347–349.

Kagan, J., Moss, H. A., & Sigel, I. E. (1963). Psychological significance of styles of conceptualization. In Wright, J. & Kagan, J. (Eds.), Basic cognitive processes in children. *Child Development Monographs, 28*(2).

Kaltsounis, B. (1971). Instruments useful in studying creative behavior and creative talent, Part 1. *Journal of Creative Behavior, 5*(2), 117–126.

Kaltsounis, B. (1972). Additional instruments useful in studying creative behavior and creative talent. *Journal of Creative Behavior, 6*(4), 268–274.

Kalyan-Masih, V. (1976). Graphic representation: From intellectual realism to visual realism in draw-a-house-tree task. *Child Development, 47*, 1026–1031.

Kennedy, J. M. (1982). Haptic pictures. In Schiff, W. & Foulke, E., (Eds.), *Tactual Perception*. New York: Cambridge University Press.

Kennedy, J. M. & Fox, N. (1977). Pictures to see and pictures to touch. In Perkins, D. & Leondar, B. (Eds.), *The Arts and Cognition*. Baltimore: Johns Hopkins University Press.

Kern, E. J. (1978). The study of art. *Studies in Art Education, 19*(3), 50–53.

Kincaid, C. (1964). The determination and description of various creative attributes of children. In Brittain, W. L. (Ed.), *Creativity and Art Education*, pp. 108–115. Washington, DC: National Art Education Association.

Kirst, W. & Diekmeyer, V. (1973). *Creativity Training*. New York: Peter H. Wyden.

Kloss, M. G. & Dreger, R. M. (1971). Abstract art preferences and tempermental traits. *Journal of Personality Assessment, 35*, 375–378.

Knapp, R. H. & Green, S. (1960). Preferences for styles of abstract art and their personality correlates. *Journal of Projective Techniques, 24*, 396–402.

Kogan, N. & Pankove, E. (1972). Creativity ability over a five year span. *Child Development, 43*, 427–442.

Korzenic, D. (1975). Changes in representation between the ages of five and seven. *Psychiatry and Art, 4*, 95–104.

Kuo, Y. Y. (1967). A comparative study of creative thinking between delinquent boys and non-delinquent boys. Unpublished doctoral dissertation, University of Maryland.

Kutnick, P. (1978). Children's drawings of their classrooms: Development and social maturity. *Child Study Journal, 8*(3), 175–186.

Lancaster, H. (1985). Now it's only fair that physicists sit through 2 days of Beowulf. *Wall Street Journal, 205*(55), 33.

Lansing, K. M. (1956). The effect of class size and room size upon the creative drawings of fifth grade children. Unpublished doctoral dissertation, The Pennsylvania State University.

Lansing, K. M. (1983). A response to research papers by Kiefer and Taunton. *Arts and Learning SIG*, Proceedings Journal, *1*, 39–42.

Lansing, K. M. & Richards, A. E. (1981). *The Elementary Teacher's Art Handbook*. New York: Holt, Rinehart and Winston.

Lark-Horovitz, B. & Norton, J. (1959). Children's art abilities: Developmental trends of art characteristics. *Child Development, 30*(4), 433–450.

Larsen, S. C. & Hammill, D. D. (1975). The relationship of selected visual perceptual abilities to school learning. *Journal of Special Education, 9*, 281–291.

Laurendeau, M. & Pinard, A. (1970). *The Development of the Concept of Space in the Child*. New York: International Universities Press.

Lawler, C. O. & Lawler, E. E., III. (1965). Color-mood associations in young children. *Journal of Genetic Psychology, 107*, 29–33.

Lee, L. C. (1968). The concomitant development of cognitive and moral modes of thought: A test of selected deductions from Piaget's theory. Unpublished doctoral dissertation, The Ohio State University.

Leeds, A., Dirlam, D., & Brannigan, G. (1983). The development of spatial representation in children from five to thirteen years of age. *Genetic Psychology Monographs, 108*(1), 137–165.

Leeds, J. A. (1984). Copying and invention as sources of form in art. *Art Education, 37*(2), 41–46.

Levin, H., Hilton, T., & Leiderman, G. (1957). Studies of teacher behavior. *Journal of Experimental Education, 26*, 81–91.

Lewis, H. P. (1985). Children's drawings of cubes with iterative and non-iterative sides. *Studies in Art Education, 26*(3), 141–146.

Lewis, H. P. (1963). Spatial representation in drawing as a correlate of development and a basis for picture preference. *The Journal of Genetic Psychology, 102*, 95–107.

Lewis, H. P. & Livson, N. (1980). Cognitive development, personality, and drawing: Their interrelationships in a longitudinal study. *Studies in Art Education, 22*(1), 8–11.

Liben, L. S. (1981). Copying and reproducing pictures in relation to subjects' operative levels. *Developmental Psychology, 17*(3), 357–365.

Liebermann, A. L. (1979). Exploratory studies of children's pre-representational drawings. Unpublished master's thesis, Cornell University.

Liedes, L. A. (1975). Disclosures of beauty and ugliness by selected six-year-old children. Unpublished doctoral dissertation, The Pennsylvania State University.

Light, P. H. & MacIntosh, E. (1980). Depth relationships in young children's drawings. *Journal of Experimental Child Psychology, 30*, 79–87.

Liikanen, P. (1975). Increasing creativity through art education among preschool children. *Jyvaskyla Studies in Education, Psychology and Social Research, 29.* (Finland).

Lippitt, R. & White, R. K. (1960). An experimental study of leadership and group life. In Haimowitz, M. L. & Haimowitz, N. R. [Eds.], *Human Development* (pp. 312–326). New York: Thomas Y. Crowell.

Livingston, J. F. (1972). What the reading test doesn't test—reading. *Journal of Reading, 15*, 402–410.

Lloyd, J. & Barenblatt, L. (1984). Intrinsic intellectuality: Its relations to social class, intelligence, and achievement. *Journal of Personality and Social Psychology, 46*(3), 646–654.

Lowenfeld, V. (1939). *The Nature of Creative Activity*. London: Kegan, Paul, Trench, Trubner and Co.

Lowenfeld, V. (1945). Tests for visual and haptical aptitudes. *American Journal of Psychology, 58*(1), 100–111. Reprinted: In Eisner, E. & Ecker, D. (Eds.), *Readings in Art Education* (pp. 97–104). Waltham, MA: Blaisdell, 1966.

Lowenfeld, V. (1952). *The Nature of Creative Activity*, (Rev. ed.). New York: Harcourt Brace Jovanovich.

Lowery, J. (1982). Developing creativity in gifted children. *Gifted Child Quarterly, 26*(3), 133–139.

Lublin, J. S. (1984, December 31). Running a firm from home gives women more flexibility. *The Wall Street Journal, 204*(127), 11.

MacDonald, S. (1985, January 6). The desk set: Well-designed offices are harder to achieve in age of technology. *The Wall Street Journal, 205*(6), 1.

MacGregor, R. N. (1967). Imposed controls in subject matter and art media choice. *Alberta Journal of Educational Research, 13*,(2), 103.

Machotka, P. (1966). Aesthetic criteria in childhood: Justifications of preference. *Child Development, 37*(4), 877.

Madeja, S. S. (1967). The effects of divergent and convergent emphasis in art instruction on students of high and low ability. *Studies in Art Education, 8*(2), 10.

Maeroff, G. I. (1985). Training parents helps toddlers, experiment finds. *New York Times, CXXXV*, (46,550), C1 & C14.

Majewski, S. M. (1978). The relationship between the drawing characteristics of children and their sex. Unpublished doctoral dissertation, Illinois State University.

Malone, C. (1967). Safety first: Comments on the influence of external danger in the lives of children of disorganized families. In Miller, H. L. (Ed.), *Education for the Disadvantaged* (pp. 53–64). New York: The Free Press.

Marantz, K. (1981). Response to Golomb. *Review of Research in Visual Arts Education, 14*, 52–53.

Marschalek, D. (1983). A review of basic cognitive processes and their relevance to understanding responses to works of art. *Visual Arts Research, 9*(1), 23–33.

Marshall, M. L. (1954). A comparison of schizophrenics, children, and normal adults on their use of color. Unpublished doctoral dissertation, Vanderbilt University.

Marx, J. L. (1983). The two sides of the brain. *Science, 220*, 488–490.

Maslow, A. H. (1962). *Toward a Psychology of Being*. New York: Van Nostrand.

Matoba, K. (1985). Little league and child art. *Art Education, 38*(4), 30–31.

Maxwell, J. W., Croake, J. W., & Biddle, A. P. (1975). Sex differences in the comprehension of spatial orientation. *The Journal of Psychology, 91*, 127–131.

McCallum, R. S. & Glynn, S. M. (1979). The hemispheric specialization construct: Developmental and instructional considerations for creative behavior. Proceedings, National Association of School Psychologists, San Diego.

McKinney, J. D. & Forman, S. G. (1977). Factor structure of the Wallach-Kogan tests of creativity and measures of intelligence and achievement. *Psychology in the Schools, 14*(1).

McPherson, M. W., Popplestone, J. A. & Evans, K. A. (1966). Perceptual carelessness, drawing precision, and oral activity among normal six year olds. *Perceptual and Motor Skills, 22*, 327–330.

McVitty, L. F. (1954). An experimental study on various methods in art motivations at the fifth grade level. Unpublished doctoral dissertation, The Pennsylvania State University.

Mednick, S. A. (1973). The associative basis of the creative process. In Bloomberg, M. (Ed.), *Creativity* (pp. 160–177). New Haven: College & University Press.

Meier, B. (1985). Bucolic: A program for teaching color theory to art students. *Computer Graphics and Applications, 5*(7), 57–65.

Melkman, R., Koriat, A., & Pardo, K. (1976). Preference for color and form in preschoolers as related to color and form differentiation. *Child Development, 47*, 1045–1050.

Michael, J. A. (1959). The effect of award, adult standard, and peer standard upon creativeness in art of high school pupils. *Research in Art Education*, Ninth Yearbook, National Art Education Association, 98–104.

Michael, J. A. (1970). *A Handbook for Art Instructors and Students Based upon Concepts and Behaviors.* New York: Vantage Press.

Millar, S. (1975). Visual experience or translation rules? Drawing the human figure by blind and sighted children. *Perception, 4*, 363–371.

Miller, S. R., Sabatino, D. A., & Miller, T. L. (1977). Influence of training in visual perceptual discrimination on drawings by children. *Perceptual and Motor Skills, 44*, 479–487.

Mills, E. A. & Thomson, D. R. (1981). State of the arts in the states. *Art Education, 34*(1), 40–44.

Mills, J. C. (1973). The effect of art instruction upon a reading developmental test: An experimental study with rural Appalachian children. *Studies in Art Education, 14*(3), 4–8.

Mitchell, J. (1982). Reflections of a Black social scientist. *Harvard Educational Review, 52*(1), 27–44.

Mitchelmore, M. C. (1978). Developmental stages in children's representation of regular solid figures. *Journal of Genetic Psychology, 133*, 229–239.

Mitton, S. (Ed.). (1977). *The Cambridge Encyclopaedia of Astronomy.* New York: Crown Publishers, Inc.

Moholy-Nagy, S. (1976). *Native Genius in Anonymous Architecture.* New York: Schocken Books.

Morgan, A. B. (1928). *Elements of Art and Decoration.* Milwaukee: Bruce Publishing Co.

Morris, D. (1969). *The Human Zoo.* New York: McGraw-Hill.

Munro, T. (1956). *Art Education.* New York: The Liberal Arts Press.

Murphy, J. A. & Bracewell, R. J. (1983). The development of perspective drawing skill. *Arts and Learning SIG*, Proceedings Journal, *1*, 43–54.

National Assessment of Art. (1977). *Design and Drawing Skills.* Washington, DC: U.S. Government Printing Office.

Necka, E. (1984). The effectiveness of synectics and brainstorming as conditioned by socio-emotional climate and type of task. *Polish Psychological Bulletin, 15*(1), 41–50.

Neperud, R. W. (1966). An experimental study of visual elements, selected art instruction methods, and drawing development at the fifth grade level. *Studies in Art Education, 7*(2), 3.

Newman, F. M. (1981, November) Reducing student alienation in high schools: Implications of theory. *Harvard Educational Review, 51*(4), 546–564.

Nichols, G. W. (1877). *Art Education Applied to Industry.* New York: Harper & Row.

Nisbet, R. (1976). *Sociology as an Art Form.* New York: Oxford University Press.

Novlianskaia, Z. N. & Melik-Pashaev, A. A. (1979–1980). Psychological principles in the esthetic development of children and the problem of esthetic education. *Soviet Education, 22*, 74–88.

O'Hare, D. & Westwood, H. (1984). Features of style classification: A multivariate experimental analysis of children's responses to drawings. *Developmental Psychology, 20*(1), 150–158.

Palermo, D. S. & Molfese, D. L. (1973). Language acquisition from age five onward. In Rebelsky and Dorman (Eds.), *Child Development and Behavior* (pp. 401–424). New York: Alfred A. Knopf.

Parnes, S. J. (1967). *Creative Behavior Workbook.* New York: Scribners.

Parsons, M. J. (1971). Herbert Read on education. In Smith, R. A. (Ed.), *Aesthetics and Problems of Education* (pp. 42–63). Urbana: University of Illinois Press.

Pearlman, C. (1984). The effects of level of effectance motivation, IQ, and a penalty/reward contingency on the choice of problem difficulty. *Child Development, 55*, 537–542.

Pentz, M. R. (1965). A study of kindergarten children's concept of five. Unpublished master's thesis, Cornell University.

Phillips, V. K. (1973). Creativity: Performance, profiles, and perceptions. *The Journal of Psychology, 83*, 25–30.

Piaget, J. (1955). *The Language and Thought of the Child.* New York: Meridian.

Piaget, J. (1959). *Judgment and Reasoning in the Child.* Paterson, NJ: Littlefield, Adams.

Piaget, J. (1960). *The Child's Conception of the World.* (Trans. by Tomlinson, J. & Tomlinson, A.). Paterson, NJ: Littlefield, Adams.

Piaget, J. (1976). *The Grasp of Consciousness.* (Trans. by Wedgewood, S.). Cambridge, MA: Harvard University Press.

Piaget, J. & Inhelder, B. (1967). *The Child's Conception of Space.* New York: Norton.

Piaget, J. & Inhelder, B. (1971). *Mental Imagery in the Child.* New York: Basic Books.

Pittman, T. S., Emery, J., & Boggiano, A. K. (1982). Intrinsic and extrinsic motivational orientations: Reward-induced changes in preference for complexity. *Journal of Personality and Social Psychology, 42*(5), 789–797.

Platt, P. (1971). *Big Boy* (also teachers manual, *Early Reading Program*). Menlo Park, CA: Addison-Wesley.

Prentiss, B. V. (1972). A study of the effect of the teaching of perspective on the drawing quality of children in the 5th, 7th and 9th grades. Unpublished master's thesis, Cornell University.

Prince, G. M. (1970). *The Practice of Creativity.* New York: Harper & Row.

Quackenbos, G. P. (1871). *Composition and Rhetoric.* New York: D. Appleton and Co.

Ramsey, I. L. (1982). Effect of art style on children's picture preferences. *Journal of Educational Research, 75*(4), 237–240.

Rand, C. W. (1973). Copying in drawing: The importance of adequate visual analysis versus the ability to utilize drawing rules. *Child Development, 44,* 47–53.

Read, H. (1958). *Education through Art.* New York: Pantheon Books.

Read, H. (1966). *The Redemption of the Robot; My Encounter With Education Through Art.* New York: Simon and Schuster.

Reichenberg-Hackett, W. (1964). Influence of nursery group experience on children's drawings. *Psychological Reports, 14,* 433–434.

Richardson, A. G. (1985). Sex differences in creativity among a sample of Jamaican adolescents. *Perceptual and Motor Skills, 60,* 424–426.

Rosario, J. & Collazo, E. (1981). Aesthetic codes in context: An exploration in two preschool classrooms. *Journal of Aesthetic Education, 15*(1), 71–82.

Rosenberg, J. (1980). *Rembrandt: Life and Work*, Ithaca, NY: Cornell University Press.

Rosenthal, D. A. & Conway, M. (1980). Adolescents' creativity and non-conformity in school. *Psychological Reports, 47,* 668.

Rosenthal, R. & Jacobson, L. (1968). *Pygmalion in the Classroom.* New York: Holt, Rinehart & Winston.

Roubertoux, P., Carlier, M., & Chaguiboff, J. (1971). Preference for non-objective art: Personal and psychosocial determiners. *British Journal of Psychology, 62*(1), 105–110.

Rousseau, D. M. (1977). Technological differences in job characteristics, employee satisfaction, and motivation: A synthesis of job design research and sociotechnical systems theory. *Organizational Behavior and Human Performance, 19,* 18–42.

Rump, E. E. & Southgate, V. S. (1966–1967). Variables affecting aesthetic appreciation, in relation to age. *British Journal of Education Psychology, 36–37,* 58–71.

Rump, E. E. & Southgate, V. S. (1978). Teachers' understanding of pupils' aesthetic preferences. *Review of Research in Visual Arts Education, 8,* 37–42.

Rush, J. C. & Lovano-Kerr, J. (1982). Aesthetic education research, teaching art, and Harvard Project Zero: Some observations. *Journal of Aesthetic Education, 16*(4), 81–91.

Russell, I. & Waugaman, B. (1952). A study of the effect of workbook copy experiences on the creative concepts of children. *Research Bulletin*, The Eastern Arts Association, *3*(1).

Rutter, M. (1983). School effects on pupil progress, Chapter 1 in Shulman, L. (Ed.), *Handbook of Teaching and Policy*. New York: Longman.

Salome, R. A. (1965). The effects of perceptual training upon the two-dimensional drawings of children. *Studies in Art Education*, *7*(1), 18.

Salome, R. A. (1967). A comparative analysis of kindergarten children's drawings in crayon and colored pencil. *Studies in Art Education*, *8*(2), 21–36.

Salome, R. A. & Reeves, D. (1972). Two pilot investigations of perceptual training of four-and five-year-old kindergarten children. *Studies in Art Education*, *13*(2), 2–10.

Salomon, G. & Gardner, H. (1986). The computer as educator: Lessons from television research. *Educational Researcher*, *15*(1), 13–19.

Scardino, A. & Roberts, K. (1985, November 24, 6E). Ideas and trends. *New York Times*, *135*, (46, 603.).

Scher, A. & Unruh, W. R. (1982). Position and orientation features and the development of spatial concepts. *Canadian Journal of Psychology*, *36*(3), 515–519.

Schwartz, F. R. (1970). *Structure and Potential in Art Education*. Waltham, MA: Ginn-Blaisdell.

Schwartz, M. & Dovidio, J. (1984). Reading between the lines: Personality correlates of graffiti writing. *Perceptual and Motor Skills*, *59*, 395–398.

Sedlak, R. A. & Sedlak, D. M. (1985). *Teaching the Educable Mentally Retarded*. Albany: State University of New York Press.

Seltzer, V. C. (1980). Social comparison behaviors of adolescents. In Pepitone, E. A. (Ed.), *Children in Cooperation and Competition* (pp. 253–291). Lexington, MA: Lexington Books.

Sharer, J. W. (1980). Distinguishing justifications and explanations in judgments of art. *Studies in Art Education*, *21*(2), 38–42.

Sibley, A. G. (1957). Drawings of kindergarten children as a measure of reading readiness. Unpublished master's thesis, Cornell University.

Siedlecki, J. T. (1968). Potential health hazards of materials used by artists and sculptors. *Art Education*, *21*(9), 3–6.

Siedlecki, J. T. (1972). Potential hazards of plastics used in sculpture. *Art Education*, *25*(2), 21–26.

Siegel, A. W., Herman, J. F., Allen, G. L., & Kirasic, K. C. (1979). The development of cognitive maps of large and small scale spaces. *Child Development*, *50*, 582–585.

Silberman, C. E. (1971). *Crisis in the Classroom*. New York: Vintage Books.

Simmons, R. & Locher, P. (1979). Haptic perception of nonrepresentational shapes. *Perceptual and Motor Skills*, *48*, 987.

Sloan, D., (Ed.). (1985). *The Computer in Education: A Critical Perspective*. New York: Teachers College.

Smith, N. R. (1985). Copying and artistic behaviors: Children and comic strips. *Studies in Art Education, 26*(3), 147–156.

Smith, W. (1872). *Art Education, Scholastic and Industrial.* Boston: James R. Osgood.

Snow, C. P. (1961). *The Two Cultures and the Scientific Revolution.* New York: Cambridge University Press.

Speller, K. G. & Schumacher, G. M. (1975). Age and set in creative test performance. *Psychological Reports, 36,* 447–450.

Spitz, H., & Borland, M. (1971). Redundancy in line drawings of familiar objects: Effects of age and intelligence. *Cognitive Psychology, 2,* 196–205.

Springer, S. P. & Deutsch, G. (1985). *Left Brain, Right Brain.* New York: W. H. Freeman and Company.

Stacey, J. T. & Ross, B. M. (1975). Scheme and schema in children's memory of their own drawings. *Developmental Psychology, 11*(1), 37–41.

Stein, H. B. (1972). A comparison of the effects of two kindergarten training programs on reading readiness and creativity. Unpublished master's thesis, Cornell University.

Stenhouse, L. (1967). *Culture and Education.* New York: Weybright & Talley.

Stewart, G. R. (1954). *American Ways of Life.* Garden City, NY: Doubleday.

Stipp, D. (1986). Who says the idea of child inventors is patently absurd? *Wall Street Journal, CCVII*(6), 1, 12.

Stone, B. G. (1980). Relationship between creativity and classroom behavior. *Psychology in the Schools, 17*(1), 106–108.

Streb, J. H. (1984). Thoughts on phenomenology, education, and art. *Studies in Art Education, 25*(3), 159–166.

Strommen, E. (1983). *The representation of spatial relations in children's drawings.* Unpublished honors thesis, Cornell University.

Swerdlow, J. A. (1981). A question of impact. *Wilson Quarterly, 5*(1), 86–99.

Taunton, M. (1980). The influence of age on preferences for subject matter, realism, and spatial depth in painting reproductions. *Studies in Art Education, 21*(3), 40–52.

Tegano, D. W., Fu, V. R., & Moran, J. D., III. (1983). Divergent thinking and hemispheric dominance for language function among preschool children. *Perceptual and Motor Skills, 56,* 691–698.

Templeman, K. D. (1962). A study of the relationship between the haptic and visual creative types and reading achievement in first and sixth grade children. Unpublished master's thesis, Cornell University.

Thompson, L. S. (1895). *Manual of Drawing for Regents' Schools.* Boston: D. C. Heath.

Torrance, E. P. (1962). *Guiding Creative Talent.* Englewood Cliffs, NJ: Prentice-Hall.

Torrance, E. P. (1967). Non-test ways of identifying the creative child. In Gowan, J. C., Demos, G. D., & Torrance, E. P. (Eds.), *Creativity: Its Educational Implication.* New York: Wiley.

Torrance, E. P. (1972). Career patterns and peak creative achievements of creative high school students twelve years later. *The Gifted Child Quarterly, 16*(2), 75–88.

Torrance, E. P. (1983). Role of mentors in creative achievement. *The Creative Child and Adult Quarterly, 8*(1).

Trisdorfer, A. (1972). A study of the ability of pre-school children to copy triangles. Unpublished master's thesis, Cornell University.

Trist, E. (1978). Adapting to a changing world. In *Readings on the Quality of Working Life*. Ottawa: The Labour Gazette, Labour Canada.

Trost, C. (1984, November 27). Labor letter: A special news report on people and their jobs in offices, fields and factories. *The Wall Street Journal, CCIV*(104), 1.

Van Sommers, P. (1984). *Drawing and Cognition*. Cambridge: Cambridge University Press.

Vernon, M. D. (1965). The development of perception in children. In Gordon, I. J., *Human Development* (pp. 177–184). Chicago: Scott, Foresman.

Walker, W. J. (1982). Potentially creative adolescents view their school experiences. *Psychological Reports, 51*, 1271–1274.

Wall, J. (1959). The base line in children's drawings of self and its relationship to aspects of overt behavior. Unpublished doctoral dissertation, The Florida State University.

Wallach, M. A. & Kogan, N. (1965). *Modes of Thinking in Young Children*. New York: Holt, Rinehart & Winston.

Wallach, M. A. & Wing, C. W. (1969). *The Talented Student*. New York: Holt, Rinehart & Winston.

Walter, W. G. (1963). *The Living Brain*. New York: Norton.

Wampler, J. (1977). *All Their Own*. New York: Schenckman Publishing Company, John Wiley and Sons.

Ward, W. (1969). Creativity and environmental cues in nursery school children. *Developmental Psychology, 1*(5), 543–547.

Washburne, C. & Heil, L. M. (1971). What characteristics of teachers affect children's growth? In Glock, M. D. (Ed.), *Guiding Learning*. New York: Wiley.

Watson, A. J. (1979). Multiple seriation and learning to read. *The Australian Journal of Education, 23*(2), 171–180.

Weinstock, R. (1973). *The Greening of the High School*. New York: Educational Facilities Laboratories.

Weston, C. R. (1984). An investigation into three approaches to teaching art and their effectiveness in motivating creativity in first year pupils identified as haptic, indefinite and visual. Unpublished Supervised Special Study, Westhill College, University of Birmingham, UK.

White, B. L. & Castle, P. (1964). Visual exploratory behavior following postnatal handling of human infants. *Perceptual and Motor Skills, 18*, 497–502.

White, K. & Allen, R. (1971). Art counseling in an educational setting: Self-concept change among pre-adolescent boys. *Journal of School Psychology, 9*(2), 218–225.

Whitesel, L. S. (1980). Career attitudes of art students. *Studies in Art Education, 22*(1), 36–41.

Wieder, C. G. (1984). The left-brain/right-brain model of mind: Ancient myth in modern garb. *Visual Arts Research, 10*(2), 66–72.

Wigginton, E. (1972–1984). *Foxfire 1–8.* Garden City, NY: Anchor Press/Doubleday.

Wilde, G. J. & Murdoch, P. A. (1982). Incentive systems for accident-free and violation-free driving in the general population. *Ergonomics, 25*(10), 879–890.

Willats, J. (1977). How children learn to draw realistic pictures. *Journal of Experimental Psychology, 29*, 367–382.

Williams, A. J., Poole, M. E., & Lett, W. R. (1977). The creativity/self-concept relationship reviewed: an Australian longitudinal perspective. *Australian Psychologist, 12*(3), 313–317.

Williams, F. E. (1972). *A Total Creativity Program for Individualizing and Humanizing the Learning Process.* Englewood Cliffs, NJ: Educational Technology Publications.

Wilson, E. O. (1978). *On Human Nature,* Cambridge, MA: Harvard University Press.

Wilson, H. B. (1978). Toward industrial democracy. In *Readings on the Quality of Working Life.* Ottawa: The Labour Gazette, Labour Canada.

Wilson, L. L. (1899). *Picture Study in Elementary Schools.* New York: Macmillan.

Wilson, M. & Wilson, B. (1982). *Teaching Children to Draw.* Englewood Cliffs: Prentice-Hall.

Witkin, H. A., et al. (1962). *Psychological Differentiation.* New York: Wiley.

Wodtke, K. H. & Wallen, N. E. (1965). The effects of teacher control in the classroom on pupils' creativity-test gains. *American Educational Research Journal, 2*(2), 75–82.

Workman, E. A. & Stillion, J. M. (1974). The relationship between creativity and ego development. *The Journal of Psychology, 88*, 191–195.

Worthington, R. K. & Typpo, M. (1980). Spatial concept learning in preschool children: Motoric experiences and verbal repetition as adjuncts to passive listening. *Perceptual and Motor Skills, 50*, 183–186.

Yates, M. E. & Fisher, V. L. (1980). Effects of models on children's spontaneous drawings. *Journal of Creative Behavior, 14*(3), 220–222.

Young, B. (1984a). Afro-American artists and the Brandywine workshop. *Art Education, 37*(2), 6–8.

Young, B. (1984b). The coordination of perspectives and drawing ability in minority children from low socioeconomic environments. *Visual Arts Research, 10*(2), 22–29.

Young, A. W. & Bion, P. J. (1981). Identification and storage of line drawings presented to the left and right cerebral hemispheres of adults and children. *Cortex, 17*, 459–464.

Index

Dyson, A., 283

Education, 2, 69, 74, 77, 81
Egocentrism, 222, 229, 316
Eisner, E., 105
Elardo, R., 199
Electroencephalogram, 362
Elementary-school child, 121, 281
Elementary-school program, 132, 143ff
Eliefja, C., 30
Elkind, D., 393
Emery, J., 175
Emery, M., 55
Emotional growth, 59, 179, 204, 216, 253,
    288, 326
Emotions, 249, 295, 308, 322, 395, 408,
    413, 417
Emphasis, 309, 322
Engel, M., 260, 402
Enrichment programs, 199
Environment, 198, 262, 267, 277, 318, 405,
    422
Escher, M., 403
Ettinger, L., 428
Evaluation of creative work, 25, 174ff
Evans, R., 91
Exaggeration, 275, 322, 350, 365, 413
Exhibits, 180, 453
Expressive ability, 132
Eye–hand coordination, 202
Eysenck, H., 117

Farrell, E., 355
Fiber-tipped pen, 211, 253, 301
Field-dependence and field-independence,
    363
Finger paint, 214, 336, 339
Fisher, V., 177
Flavell, J., 43
Flexibility, 59, 81ff, 97, 158, 234, 288
Fluency, 82, 84
Folding over, 267
Forbach, G., 91
Form
    concept, 246, 257ff
    discrimination, 196
Formal operations, 44

Forman, S., 77
Foster, S., 369
Fox, N., 357
Frame of reference, 137, 165, 294, 334,
    459
Francis, A., 288
Franken, R., 126
Franklin, B., 423
Frankston, L., 127
Freedman, D., 333
Freeman, N., 223, 289, 303
Friedrich-Cofer, L., 81
Front view, 260, 295
Fu, V., 374
Furze, C., 90

Gang age, 39, 305ff
Gardner, H., 122, 426
Gardner, J., 122
Gazzaniga, M., 371
Geometric shapes, 47, 120, 191, 205ff, 241,
    260, 283
Gerber, R., 314
Geschwind, N., 371ff
Getz, M., 314
Getzels, J., 80, 95, 379, 438
Gibbens, T., 382
Gibson, J., 362
Ginsburg, H., 145, 203
Gitomer, J., 214
Gliner, C., 363
Glynn, S., 371ff
Goertz, E., 200
Goleman, D., 369
Golomb, C., 223
Gombrich, E., 460
Goodnow, J., 276
Goor, A., 81
Gordon, W., 87
Gottlieb, A., 426
Gowan, J., 98, 373
Gowler, D., 15
Grading, 174ff, 382, 449
Graffiti, 420
Green, S., 117
Greenfield, P., 45
Greer, W., 57